Between States

BETWEEN STATES

*The Transylvanian Question
and the European Idea during World War II*

Holly Case

STANFORD UNIVERSITY PRESS

STANFORD, CALIFORNIA

Published with the assistance of the Hull Fund, Cornell University

Stanford University Press,
Stanford, California

Library of Congress Cataloging-in-Publication Data

Case, Holly.
    Between states : The Transylvanian question and the European idea during
World War II / Holly Case.
        p. cm.
    Includes bibliographical references and index.
    ISBN 978-0-8047-5986-1 (cloth : alk. paper)—
    ISBN 978-0-8047-9204-2 (pbk. : alk. paper)

        1. Transylvania (Romania)—History—1940–1947. 2. World War, 1939–1945—
Territorial questions—Romania—Transylvania. 3. Romania—Foreign relations—
Hungary. 4. Hungary—Foreign relations—Romania. 5. Romania—Foreign
relations—1914–1944. 6. Hungary—Foreign relations—1918–1945. I. Title.

DR280.7.C37   2009
940.53'1—dc22   2008022445

Printed in the United States of America on
acid-free, archival-quality paper

Typeset at Stanford University Press in 11/13 Garamond

For my parents

Contents

Maps, Tables, and Figures

MAPS

TABLES

FIGURES

Acknowledgments

I owe an enormous debt of gratitude to many people for their good nature, support, and critical readings of this work at various stages. Although this book bears only the faintest resemblance to my doctoral dissertation, without that critical first step I most certainly would not have been able to write this book. I am therefore very thankful to my mentors at Stanford University, including dissertation committee members Amir Weiner and Paul Robinson, as well as James Sheehan, Aaron Rodrigue, Katherine Jolluck, the late Wayne Vucinich, the "kruzhok," and Stanford's Center for Russian, East European and Eurasian Studies. My other Stanford debts are to my dear friends Brett Whalen, Caitlin Murdock, and Randall Harp, first-rate study and conversation partners. But the one person who was there with me every step of the way, and continues to be my intellectual lifeline and mentor is Norman Naimark. No amount of thanks or praise could do justice to all he has done for me. When I first met him in person, he told me he would read the thesis only once. So far he has overshot that estimate by a factor of four, not to mention all the bits and pieces he has read at various stages, the countless recommendations he has written, the greater and lesser professional cares he has addressed, opportunities he has provided, and successes he has facilitated. There is, I think, no rarer combination of historical acumen and intellectual generosity than he.

I also had the good fortune of having a second mentor in the field in the person of István Deák, who has nudged me along since the first nervous letter I sent him before applying to graduate school, and who has demonstrated to me what being a historian looks like. I also owe a great deal to Jeremy King, who has provided distance mentorship at so many critical moments in my career and whose work I admire immensely. Special thanks are similarly due to Omer Bartov and Rogers Brubaker for their advice and support, as well as to Mark Mazower for his careful reading and insightful comments on drafts of this project.

To my colleagues and the staff of the Department of History at Cornell University who gave me the time and the space to write this book to my satisfaction I am extremely thankful. This applies especially to my colleagues Vicki Caron, Barry Strauss, Mary-Beth Norton, Valerie Bunce, Peter Katzenstein, and my faculty mentor, Mary Roldan, as well as to members of Cornell's "Write Club," particularly Ed Baptist, John Parmenter, Jason Smith, and beloved friend Suman Seth. Above all, however, I want to thank Isabel Hull and Peter Holquist, brilliant historians, great friends and mentors, constant advocates.

My institutional debt to Cornell is also considerable. Over the past four years I have received research funding from the President's Council of Cornell Women Affinito-Stewart Faculty Grant, Junior Faculty Research Grant from the Institute of European Studies, Cornell University's Institute for the Social Sciences Small Grant, Cornell University Dean's Grant, and Cornell University Einaudi Summer Research Travel grants. Furthermore, the publication of this book was aided by the Hull Memorial Publication Fund of Cornell University. In addition to support I received from Cornell and Stanford, I also received grants and fellowships from the American Council of Learned Societies, the National Security Education Project, and the International Research and Exchanges Board.

There are a number of other individuals who have helped me along at various stages, including Katherine Verdery, who provided me with contacts in Romania, and Vladimir Tismaneanu, Peter Black, and Irina Livezeanu, who offered insightful comments on some of the material found in Chapter 5. Additionally, Deborah Coen, Paul Hanebrink, Robert Nemes, Charles King, Chris Davis, Keith Hitchins, and Andrea Orzoff made helpful suggestions on parts of the book or pointed me in directions which proved very fruitful.

I had many occasions to present parts of the material to be found herein to audiences that offered excellent feedback and advice. Among these venues were the American Association for the Advancement of Slavic Studies' annual convention, four conferences/workshops/seminars organized in connection with Brown University's "Borderlands" project, talks delivered at Princeton, Cornell, and Stanford, and conferences, symposia, or scholarly workshops at Berkeley, the School of Slavonic and East European Studies in London, the Maxwell School of Syracuse University, the United States Holocaust Memorial Museum, the Woodrow Wilson International Center for Scholars, the University of North Carolina Chapel Hill, Harvard University, Brown University, and in Budapest. Parts of Chapters 5 and 6 were previously published as "The Holocaust and the Transylvanian Question in the 20th

Century," in *The Holocaust in Hungary: Sixty Years Later* (New York: Columbia University Press, 2006); "The Holocaust and the Transylvanian Question in the Aftermath of World War II," in *The Holocaust in Hungary: A European Perspective*, ed. Judit Molnár (Budapest: Balassi Kiadó, 2005); "A holokauszt es az erdélyi kérdés a második világ háború után," in *A holokauszt Magyarországon európai perspektívában* (Budapest: Balassi Kiadó, 2005).

Among my greatest debts is that to the three anonymous reviewers at Stanford University Press, whose careful readings and constructive criticisms inspired me to rethink much of what I had originally written. Two of these reviewers later revealed themselves to me—namely Jeremy King and Mark Mazower—so I now have the opportunity to thank them directly. All three reviewers demonstrated the value of peer review with their incisive, detailed, and categorically constructive comments. I am also extremely grateful to editors Norris Pope and John Feneron at the press, whose kindness and consummate professionalism are unmatched and very much appreciated. Finally, special thanks go to copyeditor Mary Ray Worley, and to Bill Nelson for the lovely maps.

Gone are the days when Western scholars could benefit from claiming to be the sole "objective" commentators on East-Central European history (not that this was ever an accurate description of their role, as this narrative also demonstrates). Critical approaches drawing on recent historiographical trends are now being produced at a faster rate *within* the countries of East-Central Europe than beyond them. It is an exciting time to be studying the twentieth-century history of East-Central Europe, and to be part of an emerging international scholarly community that is at once so fruitfully collaborative and so new. This study of World War II in Transylvania rides a wave of historical inquiry into a previously understudied and misunderstood time and place, part of a new historiography built on intense exchange among scholars from within and beyond the region, exchange of the sort that was simply not possible in the Cold War, pre-Internet days.

Among the countless scholars abroad who have helped me along the way are Sorin Mitu, Zoltán Szász, Viorel Achim, Ferencz Horváth, Mark Pittaway, László Karsai, Virgiliu Ţârău, Gábor Egry, Sebastian Balta, Stefano Bottoni, Francois Bocholier, and Krisztián Ungváry. Especially sincere thanks go to Vladimir Solonari and Ottmar Traşcă for sharing with me some of the material they found in the Romanian National Archives in Bucharest and for engaging in protracted scholarly symbiosis with me, which I hope has had mutually positive effects on our work.

A number of archivists and librarians abroad have been very helpful, as well, including Béla György of the National Széchényi Library in Budapest,

Szilveszter Dekány and Mrs. Lajos Klippel of the Hungarian State Archives, and Florica Muntean and Livia Ardelean of the State Achives of Romania's Cluj County branch. I am also grateful for the kindness, encouragement and practical support of Dániel Lőwy and his charming parents, Maja Néni and Dodi Bácsi. They and others, including friends Andrea Székely, Roxana Crişan, and Călin Morar-Vulcu, very much embody the Transylvania I love.

Dan Grecu, Lajos Asztalos, and András Fodor deserve acknowledgment for graciously providing me with period maps and images, as do Gheorghe Bodea for sharing his books and an afternoon with me, and Ioan-Aurel Pop and the Center for Transylvanian Studies for making a gift of their periodical series to me, as well as the countless others in Hungary and Romania who offered their time, resources, and goodwill.

Many and sincerest thanks to the numerous individuals who allowed me to interview them on their experiences during the war, some of whom have—to my great sorrow—since died. Although their words are not quoted here, I learned a great deal from these people, among them Egon Balas, Ede Laczkó, György Neufeld, Teréz Kosahuba, Valeria Şerdean, Pál Vajna, István Rácz, János Istvánffy, Endre Weiss, Izrael Benjamin, Martin Preisler, Martin Berger, Elena Berkovits, Albert Gaston, Martha Gotthard, George Gotthard, Adrienne Krausz, Armand Lakner, Andrei Rozenberger, and Otto Smilovits. My host families in Cluj and Budapest also deserve special mention and thanks, among them Dan and Rodica Văţulescu, Rozália Sántha, and Bori Czakó and Máté Gallai.

In addition to some of the individuals already named, there are a few other people who have read this entire book or its draft predecessors and offered extensive comments and ideas. To them I am forever grateful. These include Zoltán Tibori-Szabó, Róbert Pölcz, Gábor Egry and Vladimir Solonari. All of them deserve more praise and thanks than I can offer here, especially the latter two, who went far beyond what I could have asked of them to make this a better book. Their expertise as historians, keen noses for sources, and unmatched conscientiousness make me very proud to be working in this field among them.

Institutionally I have benefited enormously from the staff and resources of the United States Holocaust Memorial Museum. The "footprint" of my research forays there is clear from my footnotes, but I have also received from the USHMM the luxury of time and space to dedicate to this project at various stages, first as a Jacob and Yetta Gelman Fellow, and later as a Pearl Resnick Postdoctoral Fellow. I also managed to extend my stay at the Museum thanks to the J. and O. Winter Fund for Holocaust-related research. During my several visits there, I was aided most by staff members Ferenc

Katona, Vincent Slatt, and Radu Ioanid. I also found a great friend in David Reynolds. I would like to thank Marianne Szegedy-Maszák for allowing me to view her father's journals from the 1930s and 1940s, which are now housed at the Museum.

I owe another institutional debt to the staff and fellows of the Woodrow Wilson International Center for Scholars, where I spent three months as a fellow in the East European Studies program doing final revisions. There I was assigned a research assistant, John Liszewski, who showed boundless energy and willingness to take on yet another hunt for an obscure source. Heidi Fancher, the Wilson Center's photographer, helped me with two of the images found in this book. And long before I was a fellow at the Center, I benefited greatly from attending the Junior Scholars' Training Seminar organized and funded through the East European Studies program.

My mum and dad, Linda and Tom, my brother Tom (Gene), and sister Christianne also deserve my most heartfelt thanks. All have shown great patience and goodwill toward my sometimes rather incomprehensible academic enterprises. I furthermore owe a great deal to one other individual who has not read a word of this book, but has nevertheless born witness to various stages of its development with good humor and healthy sarcasm, namely my friend Ágnes Matuska. Most of all, however, I thank my husband, Vladimir Mičić, who opened the door of the archive in Cluj for me the first time I went there, learned Hungarian "for fun," and endured being treed by shepherd dogs during an ill-conceived hike from Cluj to Feleac in the pouring rain (later hail) and gale-force winds. If anyone has paid the price for my research, it is most certainly he.

If this book has redeeming features, they are due to the great help I have received. If it has shortcomings, these are my own.

Note on Nomenclature

I have used place names in this book either in their English form—if such exists—or in the form officially adopted by the states in control during the time period in question. Thus I refer to the capital of Transylvania as "Cluj" between the two world wars up to the Second Vienna Arbitration (August 30, 1940) and after 1944, and as "Kolozsvár" from 1940 to 1944 when the city was under Hungarian state control and prior to Trianon. For the first reference to each place, a footnote will contain alternative versions of the place name for that location (i.e. Cluj [R], Klausenburg [G]). It will be helpful for the reader to note the following abbreviations

G = German	H = Hungarian	R = Romanian
SL = Slovak	SR = Serbian	

The only exception to the above is when the name of a place is mentioned in a source I quote directly, in which case I use the author's version of the name.

Here are the most frequently mentioned city and other place names in their various forms, for quick reference.

German	Hungarian	Romanian
Klausenburg	Kolozsvár	Cluj (Cluj-Napoca since 1974)
Kronstadt	Brassó	Brașov
Torda	Torda	Turda
Großwardein	Nagyvárad (or Várad)	Oradea (or Oradea Mare)
Hermannstadt	Nagyszeben	Sibiu
Temeschwar	Temesvár	Timișoara
Arad (or Altarad)	Arad	Arad
Weißenburg (or Karlsburg)	Gyulafehérvár	Alba Iulia

Names and Labels

People's names—and here I mean both the first and last names of individuals, as well as the categories used to assign individuals to national-ethnic groups ("Hungarians," "Romanians," etc.)—are famously deceptive in this region. In the case of individuals' names, there is frequently considerable variation even within a given document, as orthographies were one of the primary windsocks of state hegemony, and could also prove a valuable means of defense or advantage for individuals who wielded them skillfully and at the right moment. For example, someone who bore the name János Jankó when presenting himself to Hungarian state officials, might use the romanianized version of the same name, Ion Iancu, with Romanian state officials. Similarly, state officials could "decide" someone's nationality for them by arbitrarily assigning them a Hungarian- or Romanian-sounding name. For the most part, I have opted to avoid the use of individuals' full real names found in archival sources altogether, in accordance with Hungarian law (1995.LXVI.32.§). The real names I do use are those of public figures for whom I settle on a single, representative orthography, or of persons whose names appear in published sources. For other individuals, in lieu of real names I have chosen pseudonyms that reflect ambiguity when it is present (the name "Maria," for example, could be Hungarian, German, or Romanian), and national-ethnic preference when such is explicitly stated by the individual (for someone who gives their nationality as Hungarian, for example, I might render their pseudonym as "János" rather than "Ion"). This is an imperfect solution, as not all individuals who declare they are of Hungarian nationality on one occasion would do the same on any other, but it has the advantage of reflecting some agency and perhaps even *utility* to the process of national identification.

East-Central Europe

East-Central Europe is the term I use to describe the region at the center of my analysis, and although I am unwilling to define its precise limits or assign to it the status of an enduring geopolitical entity, I will say that in my mind it includes both Hungary and Romania in all their historical and present state forms.

Transylvania

Historically, Transylvania (Ardeal (or Transilvania) [R], Erdély [H], Siebenbürgen [G]) meant the principality of Transylvania, a rather small triangular piece of land tucked into the easternmost curve of the Carpathian Mountains. After the Treaty of Trianon (1920), Transylvania came to be understood as all the territory annexed by Romania from Hungary, which included the historical province of Transylvania, part of the Banat, and the so-called Partium. For the purposes of this work, I will use the term Transylvania in this latter sense, unless otherwise indicated.

Felvidék and Délvidék

These are the territories that Hungary lost to Czechoslovakia and Yugoslavia respectively with the Treaty of Trianon. The Felvidék (literally "upper region") includes all of present-day Slovakia and Carpatho-Ukraine, while the Délvidék (literally "southern region") I use in reference to the territories reannexed to Hungary from the Kingdom of Yugoslavia (including parts of Bačka/Bácska, Baranja/Baranya, Prekomurje/Muravidék and Medjumurje/Muraköz) in April 1941.

Regat

This term refers to the Romanian Kingdom or the "Old Kingdom" as it was prior to 1918, including the Danubian Principalities of Moldavia and Wallachia (the latter encompassing Muntenia and Oltenia), and Northern Dobruja. The *Regat* does *not* include Bessarabia, Bucovina, or Transylvania, which were added only after World War I. It also does not generally include Southern Dobruja, though that territory was annexed in 1913. The term *Regățeni* refers to individuals from the Regat.

Second Vienna Arbitration

The name of the Axis-arbitrated agreement that gave Northern Transylvania to Hungary on August 30, 1940, is highly politicized. Indeed the very words used for the agreement clearly reflected the two countries' differences of opinion on its nature. While the Hungarians called it a *döntés* (decision), Romanians referred to it as a *dictat* (dictate). (It is interesting to note, as well, that the Treaty of Trianon, which gave Transylvania to Romania in 1920, is often called a *békediktátum* (peace dictate) by Hungarians.) The term is often translated into English as the "Second Vienna Award," but I have chosen here to translate it as "Second Vienna Arbitration," which I believe best reflects the nature of the agreement and is an exact translation of the German *Schiedsspruch*.

Between States

And now, today, yet again on the verge of a new era, Europe must see its own conscience in the reflection of the two [states'] history.

—From the introduction to *Hungary and Romania: Two Countries on the European Stage*, published in Budapest during the summer of 1940

If Europe did not exist today, it would have to be invented.

—Romanian Deputy Prime Minister and Foreign Minister Mihai Antonescu in a speech on "Why we fight" from March 19, 1942

Introduction: Between States

The Transylvanian Question—or the struggle between Hungary and Romania for control of Transylvania—seems at first sight a sideshow in the story of the Nazi New Order and the Second World War. These two allies of the Third Reich spent much of the war arguing bitterly between themselves *but they* over Transylvania's future, and Europe's leaders, Germany and Italy, were *also had* drawn into their dispute to prevent it from spiraling into a regional war. *their own* But precisely as a result of this interaction, the story of the Transylvanian *ambitious* Question offers a new way into a rather larger question—the history of the *in each.* European idea—or how state leaders and national elites have interpreted what "Europe" means and what it does. For tucked into the folds of the Transylvanian Question's bizarre genealogy is a secret that no one ever tried to keep, but that has somehow remained a secret nonetheless. The secret is this: small states matter. The perspective of small states places the struggle for mastery among Europe's Great Powers in a new and perhaps chastening perspective. In short, when we look closely at what people in small states think and how they behave, the history of twentieth-century Europe itself looks suddenly very different.

TRANSYLVANIA

Transylvania figures in the international imaginary as a shadowy, mountainous land with looming castles populated by bloodthirsty supernaturals. But in the Hungarian and Romanian *national* imaginaries, Transylvania is another place entirely. Like the center line of a Rorschach test, the region is located at the nexus of two mirror images, similar yet opposite. For both, it exists at the core of the nation yet on the periphery of the state, as the easternmost territory of the nineteenth-century Kingdom of Hungary and the westernmost territory of post–World War I Greater Romania.

In the mid-1800s, a traveler to Transylvania would have heard Hungarian, Romanian, German, Yiddish, Romani and occasionally other languages spoken on the streets of its towns and villages—Hungarian and German more in towns and cities, Romanian more in villages. The territory was also marked by breathtaking religious diversity, home to Roman and Greek Catholics, Orthodox, Lutherans, Calvinists, Unitarians, and Jews. Ruled by Habsburgs and governed by Hungarian magnates, in 1868 the Principality of Transylvania was formally united with the Kingdom of Hungary as part of the Austro-Hungarian Monarchy.

What is now called Transylvania encompasses the historic Principality of Transylvania along with the rest of the territories Romania annexed from the Kingdom of Hungary with the post – World War I Treaty of Trianon. Never reconciled to the loss of Transylvania, the interwar governments of Hungary lobbied for its return. Meanwhile the interwar governments of Romania sought to prevent a revision of Trianon. Yet on August 30, 1940, following Axis arbitration, Northern Transylvania was given back to Hungary, while Southern Transylvania remained under Romanian state control. The region was divided between the two states for four years across which unfolded a battle over its ultimate fate and the fate of Europe. Transylvania, once merely a place, was now both a question and a European problem.

Starting in the mid-nineteenth century, Transylvania began its slow but steady transformation from a place into a question. Chapter 1 outlines the various stages and components of that transformation, emphasizing how state leaders in Hungary and Romania came to see the region's ethnic, religious, and linguistic diversity as both challenge and opportunity. It charts the emergence of new notions of statehood, showing how leaders in the two states—eager to flex their national independence—derived a national politics that was inherently transnational, fashioning foreign policy to achieve domestic political goals and vice versa. To advance national politics and achieve those goals, geographers, ethnographers, demographers, and politicians developed entire systems of thought that doubled as state propaganda. Overall, the analysis reveals how the interstate dynamic between Hungary and Romania ran much deeper than high diplomacy, saturating domestic politics, social science, cultural institutions, and ideas of statehood. More significantly, this dynamic also gave rise to a set of ideas about Europe, ideas that entailed intensive Great Power involvement in small-state affairs. The various international treaties of the mid- to late nineteenth century, and later the interwar League of Nations system, fixed the terms of that involvement such that even Hitler and Mussolini were forced to take them seriously in the quest to reinvent Europe.

EUROPE

"Europe" is a loaded term: loaded with history, loaded with politics, loaded with ideas. But for many of us, it is still loaded with Germany, perhaps France, Russia, Great Britain, and occasionally Italy.[1] These countries seem to form the main content, the primary frame of reference for our understanding of what Europe is and what it does. We have focused our gaze on the Great Powers because they made the big decisions, changed the geopolitical landscape, set and altered the terms of debates. The greatness of their power made them the object of our fascination and we are right to look to power for answers to some of the big questions.

When we look to small powers, we look to them in isolation and focus on the smallness of their power. This is especially true for treatments of the Second World War. Poland: crushed. Czechoslovakia: maimed. Yugoslavia: dismantled. The steamroller of Nazi Germany, and the Red Army that by sheer force of numbers countered the might of Germany, left the lands and peoples in between flattened, ruined, humiliated, imprisoned for decades to come. We speculate: could Poland, Czechoslovakia, Romania, or Hungary have taken on the Nazis or the Soviets? When we look to small powers, we tend to see victims taking in a last breath before disappearing under the ravaging waves of history.

Recent historiography has sought to correct for some of the gross oversimplifications that inhere in the above perspective by returning some agency to the East-Central Europeans of the last century.[2] The overall thrust of this new historiography has been to point to how leaders and groups within these states share some of the guilt for the great disasters of twentieth-century European history—namely, the Holocaust and Stalinism. There is more to come in this vein, and indeed it forms a crucial part of the memory work being undertaken in both "halves" of Europe since the fog of Cold War mythmaking cleared.[3]

This book deviates somewhat from the course set by this new generation of historians. It is not meant as a corrective, but rather merely a shift in perspective. We need to look again at small powers, not because they could or could not have stood up to the Nazis or the Soviets, and not because they make imperfect victims, but because they do not fit the story we like to tell about the war, what preceded and what followed it. Looking more closely at them causes the story itself to change. The Great Powers were crushed and fragmented after the Great War, and when their boundaries unraveled, newly independent smaller states entered the scene, particularly in Europe's East.

Their history is often told as a subset of German history, as a time-lagged ap-
ing of the rise of Fascism and the failure of liberal democracy. Yet the closer
one approaches the historical actors of mid-century in this region, the more
their sharp edges and stark ideological distinctions start to fade and often
disappear. Chapter 2 takes the reader to the Eastern Front, where Hungarian
and Romanian soldiers fought together—if not side by side—against the
Soviets. What did soldiers and statesmen feel they were fighting for there?
The answer is an odd one that explodes the image of wartime Europe as a
continent locked in an ideological battle between Fascists and Communists,
genocidal maniacs and well-meaning liberal democrats.

Instead, what Europe has been and done since the second half of the
nineteenth century has in no small part hinged on how "marginal" states
have interpreted its role and function in international relations. It is certainly
true that the United States, Great Britain, Russia, and France could afford to
set standards for sovereignty, self-determination, human rights, and minority
protection only to ignore them at home.[4] If the states of East-Central Europe sought to do the same, they had to explain why, at least to a European,
sometimes even to a global network of Great Power arbiters. Yet the necessity of elucidation meant that East-Central Europeans quite often played a
significant role in interpreting what those terms meant and how they should
be applied in practice.

In the twentieth century especially, as old-style Great Power diplomacy
faded, small-state actions and interactions gained in importance. The people who ran or aspired to run smaller states could thus influence how and
whether the rules applied, what compliance looked like, and the forms enforcement could take. If we are to talk of Europe, then, we need to talk
about how people in this region have understood what Europe is and does
and have projected that understanding onto political projects of the past
and present. The phenomenon this book sets out to explain—through the
unlikely back door of the Transylvanian Question—is how "Europe" came
to be understood as a "substantial entit[y] to which interests and agency can
be attributed."[5]

Yet such projections were not merely matters of high politics and diplomacy. They affected domestic policy as well and were coupled with an ex-
pectation of broad popular participation and interest in territorial concerns.
Chapter 3 thus moves to the Transylvanian home front during the war, where
states were engaged in a different set of battles over property, institutions,
and people. In those battles, state interests often clashed with the desires and
aspirations of citizens, creating complicated scenarios requiring the mediation of mid- and low-level officialdom. Just as the proliferation of newly

independent small states in the twentieth century altered European diplomatic culture, forcing Great Powers to take small-state interests seriously, so did the imbrication of states with their presumed national-ethnic population base force states to take small-group and individual matters seriously, even when states did not settle them to individuals' satisfaction. The chapter thus forms part of a larger methodological claim regarding approaches to history, emphasizing the importance of examining how state policy functions at *all* levels, and how it affects and is itself affected by the macro and micro forces that inform it and that it seeks to inform.

THE WAR

World War II, the heavy center of this study, was long considered a rupturous event, a deviation from Europe's "true" path. Recent historiography has chipped away at this assumption, highlighting continuities across the interwar/war and the war/postwar periods, challenging the Library-of-Congress periodization of the war.[6] The work of Mark Mazower has shown how "National Socialism, in particular, fits into the mainstream not only of German but also of European history far more comfortably than most people like to admit. . . . Its revolutionary rhetoric masked greater continuities of ideas and institutions with the past."[7] By showing up illiberal tendencies in even the most expressly liberal interwar governments, Mazower depicts a Janus-faced Europe that could have gone either way and was satisfied going the way of the Nazis and Fascists for a time.

This analysis takes a slightly different tack by probing how it was that illiberal aspirations yielded liberal rhetoric and practices—and vice versa—in two East-Central European states from the interwar period throughout World War II and beyond: how minority rights never died; how the demographic principle of national self-determination remained influential; how the idea of Europe as the dispenser of justice, security, and legitimacy remained constant preoccupations spanning democratic liberalism to extremism; how forces that wanted to kill, expel, deport, and disenfranchise minorities held back, or were held back by the Allies, by one another, even by Nazi Germany.

Chapters 4 and 5 highlight these continuities. In the former, we see how Hungarian and Romanian statesmen clung to minority rights rhetoric through the darkest days of the war, forcing Nazi Germany and Fascist Italy to defend a set of values previously touted by the League of Nations in order to prevent a regional war they could ill afford. Chapter 5 addresses the events of the Holocaust, which ordinarily serves as a signpost for the radical political shifts precipitated by the war, feeding the tendency to view wartime policies as radically different from what came before and after. Popular anti-Semitism is the oft-cited driving force behind policy toward the Jews in Hungary and Romania during the war, and certainly virulent anti-Semitism was a persistent, key element of the interwar and wartime political landscape. Yet neither the specific content of anti-Semitism in Hungary and Romania, nor the events of the Holocaust can be divorced from the long-standing interstate dynamic between the two states, whose inconsistent policies vis-à-vis the Jews charted a course that was frequently out of phase with the ebb and surge of popular anti-Semitism. Tracing policy vis-à-vis the Jews in the region since the second half of the nineteenth century up to the present day, the analysis shows how such policy has long been in lockstep with territorial considerations, a consistent preoccupation of Hungarian and Romanian leaders.

The Rebirths of Europe

If Western, or "Core," Europe, as some would now call it, is the place where most ideas about Europe are born, East-Central Europe is where they have been tested, and where many of them have gone to die.[8] Hitler's New European Order is a prime example. Chapter 6 probes not why it failed—a question historians have already done an excellent job of answering—but what made it attractive to two states in East-Central Europe, and whether it could be considered either new or dead, given that Hungarian and Romanian leaders' understanding of Hitler's New European Order did not differ substantially from their understanding of the post–World War I Allied vision, or for that matter from the post-1989 vision, except in one crucial matter: the so-called Jewish Question. A further objective of the chapter is thus to analyze the politicking around the identity and status of the Jews in these two states *after* the war in an attempt to fathom how regional preoccupations like the Transylvanian Question are related to conceptions of Europe, and again how real people have figured into those conceptions.

There is also a telos in part of this book's premise, namely, to track down the origins of current understandings of Europe from the East-Central European perspective. How do East-Central European states and peoples see Europe now, and where do their ideas about Europe come from? Since 1989, a number of historians, politicians, and others in the region have tried to (re)assert their nations' historic roles as integral parts of Europe.[9] Like nationalist and Communist historiography, these works are often very selective and tendentious, inclined to interpret "Europe" as a fixed entity with a uniform culture, frequently locked in conflicts with an "Eastern" enemy, variously defined as Mongols, Ottomans, Russians, or Soviets.[10] The resulting notion of the "buffer state" or "last bastion" is shared from Bosnia to Ukraine to Estonia.[11] These interpretations frequently demonize immediate neighbors to the east and south as "backward," "Balkan," "Asiatic," "uncivilized," in short, "un-European."[12]

Works of this sort have a long pedigree, one branch of which I will trace back to the second half of the nineteenth century to reveal how they are symptomatic of an image of Europe that was shaped by localized preoccupations with territorial sovereignty. Since that time, the meaning of "European-ness" has been less about what ties Spain to Estonia than about resolving tensions between neighboring states, most of which have revolved around the problem of sovereignty as manifest in anxiety about minorities and boundaries. Understandings of Europe in this region have thus long been filtered through preoccupations with territory lost, and territory gained, meaning that the shape and content of Europe for these states and peoples was and continues to be tied to the shape and content of state boundaries, both real and imagined. In the case of Hungary and Romania, the events of the war represent not a diversion from those preoccupations, but a confirmation of their primacy and their implication in the struggle to mold Europe's future.

The title of this work, *Between States*, thus has a threefold significance. First to highlight *the European idea as emerging from relations between neighboring states*, whose interactions flavor the ideologies and experiences that are presumed to define European-ness. A second is to describe the situation in which the region under consideration found itself during the major upheavals of the twentieth century, one of *perceived transition* to something different, better, more just. Europe itself was "between states," existing in an expectant limbo, the outcome of which was uncertain. This uncertainty gave rise to the third and final significance of being "between states," namely *the condition of Transylvania*, divided between Hungary and Romania, both with claims on its entirety, its future dependent on who could win the peace as much as on who could win the war. Just as Transylvania was "between states," so, too, were its inhabitants. This is their story, and the story of where one set of ideas about Europe went to be reborn many times over.

CHAPTER ONE

The "Transylvanian Question" and European Statehood

The Transylvanian question appears to affect only
Hungary and Romania. But insofar as both states have
conflictual interests with other states in the region, the
Transylvanian question can readily become a first-order
European question, and if it is badly resolved, it can upset
chances for peace in the neighboring states and in the
whole of Europe.

> —Count Albert Apponyi, head of the Hungarian
> delegation to the peace conference at Versailles, 1920[1]

Throughout history, the problem of Transylvania was
not merely of domestic Transylvanian significance, but
extended beyond those boundaries, possessing even international importance.

> —From an article in the Romanian Communist
> newspaper Scînteia [The Spark], September 25, 1944[2]

THE TRANSYLVANIAN QUESTION

Transylvania is what one Hungarian anthropologist has described as "the epicenter of the frontier land," playing a leading role in the formation of two national imaginaries.[3] Its centrality to those imaginaries emerged mostly during the nineteenth century and became more entrenched over the first half of the twentieth. The result, Romanian historian Lucian Boia argues, is that "Hungarians have come to dream of a remote historical period when the Romanians were not there" and the "Romanians . . . are tempted to separate [Transylvania] retrospectively from the Hungarian crown and from any Hungarian historical and political project . . . integrating it into a general Romanian history."[4]

Transylvania enjoys a position at once unique and essential to the national metanarratives into which the territory has been woven. In a conversation with Hitler during the Second World War, Romanian leader Ion Antonescu referred to Transylvania as the "cradle of Romania."[5] And in 1942, Romanian diplomat Vasile Stoica wrote that Transylvania "constitutes a fortress, as if intentionally created to be the center of a nation . . . and today it is the heart of our ethnic space, the center of the Romania of yesterday and tomorrow."[6]

In the Hungarian national imaginary, Transylvania occupies the center of true *Hungarianness,* "a little Hungarian microcosm."[7] The only region to have been ruled by powerful Hungarian princes, even when the rest of the Hungarian Kingdom was under Ottoman or Habsburg rule, Transylvania possessed what one wartime Hungarian diplomat called "a strange mystique. . . . The Transylvanian principality stood as the stunning achievement of Hungarian political talent [and] an integral and carefully guarded part of a person's Hungarian national consciousness."[8] At the post–World War I peace conference, Hungarian delegates argued that Transylvania had been "the stage for the most remarkable events in Hungarian history. Here Hungarian blood flowed in streams for the freedom and independence of the nation."[9] The Hungarian leftist poet Endre Ady would later opine: "Transylvania you are Hungary, and if the world needs Hungary, you will remain with us."[10]

Since the late nineteenth century, both Hungary and Romania have made claims on Transylvania. Nevertheless, solutions to the Transylvanian Question were not consistently cast in winner-takes-all terms. A variety of solutions were proposed and considered at various points, including during World War II. Among the options put forward were autonomy or independence for Transylvania, a reorganization of the Dual Monarchy into a federation in which Transylvania would be given separate status, partial revision of the Treaty of Trianon to give the border regions back to Hungary, the creation of a "Danube Federation" to effect a kind of shared sovereignty over regions like Transylvania, or the delineation of an autonomous region in the majority-Hungarian eastern core of Transylvania, the Szekler Land.[11]

It is also the case that many of the most seemingly single-minded individuals who make appearances in this story pondered a variety of solutions to the Transylvanian Question. Iuliu Maniu, whose voice comes through during the war as among the most adamant and uncompromising lobbyists for the complete return of Transylvania to Romania, had once proposed autonomy, even independence for the region. Hungarian prime minister Pál Teleki, who oversaw the return of Northern Transylvania to Hungary in 1940, did not consistently favor the reannexation of the whole of Transylvania to Hungary.

Furthermore, within the region many cultural and intellectual groups and figures tried to circumvent the politicking of the two would-be nation-states around the Transylvanian Question by asserting a regional identity distinct from and superior to both the "Regat" Romanian and "core" Hungarian varieties.

During the Second World War, frustrations with state leaders' efforts to manhandle their own national constituencies domestically and across the border found frequent expression through an array of venues. Hungarians in Transylvania often openly resented the "parachutists" from Trianon Hungary who had come to take administrative posts in Northern Transylvania without adequate knowledge of local conditions and minority languages.[12] This resentment mirrored the one many Transylvanian Romanians had expressed when Transylvania was annexed to Romania after World War I, who felt patronized, bullied, and misunderstood by the imported "Regăţeni" officials who, like the "parachutists," possessed limited or no knowledge of the region and its diverse population.[13]

In short, there has been much disagreement over how the Transylvanian Question should be resolved—on the level of high diplomacy, on the front lines of battlefields, in local administration, and in interactions between individuals in "everyday" settings. Indeed, since the Transylvanian Question emerged simultaneously with modern nation-states in this region, it has involved not just territorial aspirations, but the myriad dilemmas of nation- and state-building. Far from being a modern manifestation of long-standing antagonisms between Hungarians and Romanians, the Transylvanian Question is thus a product of changes in the European geopolitical landscape that began in the mid to late nineteenth century with the decline of the Ottoman Empire. These changes raised questions about the rights of the nation and the individual within it; about the terms of citizenship and national belonging; about the nation's role in "Europe" and the international order; about the structure of society; about overlaps and fractures between class, religious, race, linguistic, and gender categories; about challenges to state sovereignty over territories and populations; and about relations with neighboring states and Great Powers. These dilemmas often clustered around particular people and places, taking on lives of their own. Hence the proliferation of "questions" in the nineteenth century: the Polish Question, the Eastern Question, the Jewish Question, the Macedonian Question, and the Transylvanian Question. And as these questions moved into the twentieth century, it became apparent that resolving them would require reconciling boundaries with ideas—ideas not only about nations, but about Europe.

The stakes in these questions were thus very high from the outset. The fate of Transylvania was so important to leaders of Hungary and Romania that attempts to obtain or retain the territory more than once determined the success or failure of governments, shaped wartime alliances, and radically changed the demographic constitution and ideological bearing of both states. On the micro level, attempts to resolve the Transylvanian Question also affected how soldiers understood what they fought and died for; caused people to change their address, citizenship, religion, marital status, mother tongue, or nationality; pushed them up or down the social hierarchy; gave or took away property, jobs, privileges, and even lives. And being fully aware that the Transylvanian Question would be resolved one way or another only with the blessing of one or more Great Powers—among them the United States, Great Britain, France, Germany, and the Soviet Union—statesmen and other elites in Hungary and Romania lobbied incessantly to raise the Transylvanian Question to the status of a European problem. Determining who should have Transylvania, they contended, was a decision affecting the political stability, economic health, and prospects for peaceful coexistence of the entire continent and furthermore should serve as a litmus test for the justness and efficacy of the European balance of power, international law, and agreements between states.

Such attempts to raise the profile of the Transylvanian Question did not always produce the desired results, nor was the fate of Transylvania the only issue that influenced decision making among political elites and the attitudes of their constituencies in these countries. Both states and their inhabitants had other concerns before and during World War II: widespread and sometimes debilitating social inequality, intensifying ideological extremism, and two expansionist Great Powers—Germany and the Soviet Union—on their respective borders, not to mention other territories *besides* Transylvania they had gained, lost, or feared losing to neighboring states. Yet the extent to which governments and citizens understood even these issues in terms of their relation to the Transylvanian Question is remarkable. Part of the goal of this book is thus to reveal the extent to which the Transylvanian Question saturated everything from politics to diplomacy, from social relations to legal structures in Hungary and Romania before and during World War II, and what the legacy of that saturation has been since.

Yet by now emphasizing the centrality of the Transylvanian Question to ideas of Europe in these two states may seem overdetermined. There are, after all, plenty of people in both Hungary and Romania who are "over" or "past" the Transylvanian Question as a contest for territory, including most Hungarian and Romanian politicians and state leaders. Furthermore, today Hungarians' historical preoccupation with territorial revision is certainly fertile ground for satire even within Hungary, and the freakishly ultra-Romanian Gheorghe Funar era in Transylvania's capital of Cluj has been the butt of many a good joke as well.[14] Hence suggesting that the Transylvanian Question accounts for the way ideas of "Europe" developed in these states certainly *would be* overdetermined if the question were understood merely in terms of states' aspirations to control a particular swath of territory.

But historically speaking, the Transylvanian Question has not always or only been about gaining control of a place called Transylvania. It has been about sovereignty, about the viability and vitality of peoples and states, and about the legitimacy of governments and European orders. The Transylvanian Question has also been about who belongs to the state, and to whom the state belongs, and as such about the transformation from "old-style" diplomacy to population politics with its accompanying emphasis on international propaganda, geopolitics, and demography.[15] In short, the balls that were tossed into the air during nineteenth-century processes of nation- and state-building are still in the air, are still being juggled by the states and peoples of East-Central Europe, and are not likely to come down anytime soon. This chapter therefore probes the origins of Transylvania's transformation from a place into a question and how an idea of Europe emerged out of the process.

State, Nation, Individual

The *Oxford English Dictionary* provides insight into the evolution of the notion of statehood in the European context. The definition of the word *state* as it was used at different periods in history reveals a concept undergoing a significant transformation from the early modern to the modern periods. During the fifteenth, sixteenth, and seventeenth centuries, for example, most definitions of *state* referred to individuals: "person of standing, importance or high rank," or "the rulers, nobles, or great men of a realm."[16] Many of these definitions later became obsolete. Among those that did *not* fall out of usage were the meanings of *state* as "the body politic as organized for supreme civil rule and government" and "a body of people occupying a defined territory and organized under a sovereign government."[17]

These definitions show how the territory, government, and person of the ruler earlier constituted a single identity. In the modern era, however, the person of the ruler has ceased to define the state, which is instead defined by people and territory. Perhaps the first move in this direction was an emphasis on the "state-running" or "state-making" power of peoples. In 1846, during the so-called Reform Era, a critical moment in the history of Hungarian state-building, Hungarian statistician/ethnographer Elek Fényes outlined three essential features of the Hungarian consciousness: outstanding political talents, "state-making" abilities, and love of freedom, courage, gentleman's honor, and chivalry.[18] Fényes's autostereotype presents the Hungarian as embodying all the characteristics of a good leader, ascribing the qualities of rulers to the nation as a whole.

The conflation of states with peoples and territory was evident shortly thereafter, under the influence of the French Revolution and the ideas of individuals like Johann Gottfried Herder and Johann Gottlieb Fichte. Thus, by the 1860s, in a German encyclopedia, the definition of *state* is given as "the collectivity of sedentary people that is united into a moral-organic personality under the superior force driven by their common interest."[19] The "people" here assume the role of the "personality" of the state, subsuming the role once played by the ruler. An 1890s definition of *state* from a Hungarian encyclopedia lists the first two constituent elements of the state as "the population" and "the territory," respectively.[20] The same is true in the case of the first Romanian encyclopedia published in 1904.[21]

The transformation of the state's essence from sovereign to territory and population was helped along by ever more frequent and detailed censuses, which made it possible to situate national and linguistic proclivities within a bounded geographical space.[22] Similarly, the gradual transfer of sovereign status from rulers to people can be traced through the evolving legal systems of states, including the legal framework for prosecuting "slander against the nation" (or insulting the nation's honor) in Hungarian law. The law had its origins in the mid-nineteenth-century Habsburg Monarchy. In its earliest incarnation, this sort of crime took the form of insults or slights to the *person* of the monarch or emperor.[23] There was a constitutional ban on verbal attacks on the monarch, and a Hungarian law from 1848 establishes the "person of the king" as "sacrosanct [*szent és sérthetetlen*]."[24] In 1878, a law was introduced which formally criminalized slights to the king, rendering them punishable by up to five years in prison. Going a step further, the law also criminalized affronts to the constitutional state formation, its institutions, the polity comprising nations within the Hungarian state, the parliament, and the state's lawmaking institutions.[25] In 1913, on the eve of the First World War, three new articles were added to the 1878 law, further delineating punishments for various slights to the person of the king, but also criminalizing the act of calling for an end to the monarchy.[26] The explanation of the motivations for altering the law—which were published along with the law itself—also foreshadowed its transformation from a law protecting the honor of the king to one protecting the honor of the nation. Lawmakers opined that "it is undeniable that ... the preservation of the king's reputation is a condition for the unity and survival of the Hungarian state ... against which any assault must be beaten back and prevented."[27] The justification thus forged a link between the reputation of the king and the survival of the Hungarian state.

A further step toward a law protecting the "nation" from slander came after World War I, when all laws protecting the honor of the king were transferred onto the person of the regent, Miklós Horthy.[28] The criminalization of slights to the *nation*'s honor happened less than a year later, with a law making slander against the nation punishable by up to five years in prison and the confiscation of all personal property.[29] In this way the person of the sovereign was replaced by the nation as the legal object of slander. In a precedent-setting case from 1932, a court ruled that representatives of state authority were not the only viable targets for slander against the nation.[30] This opened the way for *individual* members of the state-forming [*államalkotó*] nationality to become targets of slander against the nation, a phenomenon that was common in the slander trials that took place during World War II.[31]

CULTURE AND THE IMAGINED STATE

Despite the similarities between the basic definitions of statehood from the Hungarian and Romanian perspective, early encyclopedias also reveal a critical difference in the way the state was viewed. In the 1904 *Enciclopedia Română*, the definition of *stat* makes a clear distinction between *state* and *people* [*popor*], which is absent from the Hungarian definition. A "people," we learn from the definition of *popor*, is synonymous with a "nation" [*naţiune*] and "has both an ethnic and political character," but should by no means be confused with a "state."[32] This difference is significant, as it recognizes "Romania" as a state, but as a state that did not encompass the Romanian "people" or "nation," since so many Romanians were living *outside* Romania's state boundaries at the time.

Like Hungarian lawmakers, then, Romanian national elites were preoccupied with the imbrication of state, nation, and individual, but their emphasis was on how the nation could survive in the absence of the state. This emphasis remained even after World War I, when Romanian elites felt national unification had finally been achieved with the acquisition of Transylvania and other territories in the east. "The nation manifests itself as individual, society, and state," wrote a Romanian professor of sociology and member of the Romanian Academy, Dimitrie Gusti, during the debates surrounding the drafting of the 1923 constitution.[33] In the final draft of the constitution itself, Article 33 proclaimed that "all powers of the state emanate from the nation."[34] But what was meant by the *nation*? Gusti opined:

> The nation [*națiunea*] exists and does not exist. The nation exists only when there is created a consciousness and sentiment of mutual defense, of a moral, intellectual, social and economic community of the members of which it is composed. Other- wise we cannot speak of a nation, but rather of a vegetative and biological essence which under [the right] circumstances, can become many times less important, creating that which we call a people [*popor*]. With every increase in the culture of a people that rests in its members it will be richer, and the nation will become more real. Culture creates the nation.[35]

This tantalizing opportunity to "create" a nation that would integrate through culture "our brothers" who were "raised at the source of foreign cultures: Hungarians, Russians, and Germans" was an active interest of Romanian political and cultural elites throughout the interwar period. It resulted in am- bitious cultural projects ranging from the "nationalization" of architectural style to the "romanianization" of names, places, and people.[36] These projects were grafted on to interpretations of the region's history that drew out the continuity of the Romanian presence and the presumed cultural superiority of the Romanian people.[37]

The emphasis on culture in nation-building in Transylvania goes back fur- ther still, to the mid-nineteenth century. As early as 1847, one young advocate of Romanian unification living in Paris commented that "our goal should be nothing less than the national unification of all Romanians. First we must create a unity of minds and hearts; over time, this will unify us politically."[38] A poem by the revolutionary Transylvanian Romanian Andrei Mureșanu from the summer of 1848—which later became the Romanian national an- them—called on Romanians to "unite in your minds; unite in your souls!"[39] Spiritual unity was thus placed at the center of the Romanian nationalist project, whose advocates sought to achieve it through enhancing awareness of a common culture. Hence it was Romanian cultural organizations, like Astra, founded in 1861, and the Liga Culturală [Cultural League] in 1891, that formed the basis for first the cultural, and later the political unification of Transylvania with Romania.[40]

It was cultural figures, like the poet Mihai Eminescu, who placed culture at the center of the Transylvanian Question. "We are more afraid of Hungarian schools than we are of their Diet, their ministers, and their soldiers," he wrote in 1870.[41] After World War I, works such as Liviu Rebreanu's popular novel

Ion portrayed the cultural oppression suffered by Romanians in Hungarian
Transylvania before unification, and the idealism and challenges accompanying the cultural unification of the Romanians of Transylvania with those of
the Regat.[42]

Later, Hungarian elites inherited the problem of preserving the nation in
the absence of the state when they lost Transylvania to Romania after World
War I. In response, they chose similar tactics to address the conundrum,
stressing the importance of maintaining and developing cultural unity. In
the words of historian Zsuzsanna Török, for many elites of the interwar
Transylvanian Hungarian diaspora, "a shared national culture rejoined what
politics had separated. Culture became politics." This conflation was embodied in the interwar organization known as the Folk Literary Society [Népies
Irodalmi Társaság] subordinated to the Hungarian prime minister's office,
which was charged with supporting the Hungarian minority in Transylvania
and tracking minority policy in Romania.[43]

Culture thus provided the link between the individual, the nation, and
the state. It offered an explanation for nationness that did not rely on the
existence of a state, while at the same time opening up the possibility of the
cultural nation becoming a political one. As one member told the Romanian
chamber of deputies in 1915:

> Our educational Leagues, our concern for the Roumanians on the other side of
> the Carpathians—all this movement implied, fundamentally, a mental reservation.
> It all resolved itself into a provisional attitude, destined to last just so long as the
> European situation which prevented us from realising our national ideal. (*Applause*)
> For our ultimate object, which was cherished in the minds of us all and made all
> our hearts beat, has always been the same—a union of the nation not merely intel-
> lectual but also political.[44]

Nationness, then, was a state of mind, because if it were not, there was no
way to explain why the national state had not emerged together with the nation, or how the nation could exist in the absence of the state. When people
were able to overcome their "mental reservation," the nation immediately
became what Gusti called "more real." This process demanded the *internaliza-
tion* of both nation and state by the individual. In 1937, a Hungarian minority
leader pointed to the "profound conviction" held by many Hungarians that
"the Hungarian nation, despite any superficial evidence to the contrary, has
preserved its unity unshaken *on the inside, in the soul and in the spirit*."[45] A comparable understanding of the role of the "soul" in preserving in the nation
is also evident in Ion Antonescu's assessment of why Romania lost so much
territory during the summer of 1940.

> The Romanian nation has lost its borders before; it has received the thundering of invasion before. But its soul and the consciousness could not be conquered by anyone, for from one century to the next for countless centuries the Romanian mind has been built up over generations who, on the territory of Transylvania and everywhere, were subject to every kind of oppression and abasement, but they knew that they carry the eternal light of Romanian culture and conviction.[46]

Antonescu also often said that Romania had lost its borders "inside" before it lost them for real, and that it needed to win them back "inside" before they could be returned.[47] As the nation's political boundaries became dependent on a consciousness of nationness, it was incumbent upon each member of the "nation" to believe in the nation in order for it to maintain a geopolitical presence. In fact, the 1938 Romanian constitution made precisely this demand on its citizens by adding the following provision: "All Romanians, regardless of their ethnic origin or religious beliefs, are obligated to see the fatherland as the most basic fundament of their purpose in life, to sacrifice themselves for the defense of its integrity, independence and dignity . . . without which the existence of the State cannot be perpetuated."[48]

Beyond the constitutionally mandated belief in and defense of the nation, during the 1930s and 1940s, Romanian scientists were also seeking to eliminate the nation's dependence on national consciousness by lending a biological reality to the state's boundaries. Historian Marius Turda has noted that, in the context of hyperconsciousness of "the physical contours of the nation" that typified this period, "anthropological and serological research provided scientific legitimacy to the assumption that there was a racial nucleus within the Romanian nation that the natural and social environment could not obliterate."[49]

THE STATE IN THE INTERNATIONAL COMMUNITY

The process of defining the relationship between state, nation, and individual found an uncanny parallel in discussions about the legal relationship between the international community and the state or nation. The contradictions inherent in liberal conceptions of national and individual rights came starkly to the fore during the 1830s and 1840s, as Hungarian politicians emphasized the need to create a strong nation-state and "turn everyone into a free Hungarian."[50] With the Hungarian revolution of 1848–49, the revolutionary leadership moved toward a complete break with the Habsburg Crown, which took place in April 1849. Yet the Hungarian revolutionaries met with increasing resistance from the non-magyar elites, especially those claiming to represent

1848

Romanian speakers, who in all amounted to roughly 57 percent of the population of Transylvania at the time.[51]

Revolutionary leader Lajos Kossuth initially believed that the revolutionary reforms—including the abolition of serfdom and the promise to secure *individual* civil liberties—would make the nationalities loyal to the newly independent Hungarian state and give them an incentive to become Hungarians. Promising them specific *collective* rights to use their own language, create their own institutions, and organize politically struck him as anathema.[52] But for the magyar revolutionaries as much as for representatives of the non-magyar nationalities, the "nation" demanded the same rights as the individual. Transylvanian Romanian activist Timotei Cipariu thus declared in the spring of 1848 that "Europe" represents "liberty, equality, fraternity, for all [individuals] and for all peoples alike,"[53] and the Romanian poet Mihai Eminescu would later charge that the individual rights extended to members of the nationalities in Hungary were not rights at all. "I prefer a fight to unjust rights; I would rather die than become Hungarian."[54]

Attempts to resolve or ignore the tension between collective and individual rights and the state's role in securing one or both affected the evolution of interstate relations and diplomacy in the region, limiting the range of possible answers to period "questions," like the Transylvanian Question. In 1849, exiles from the principality of Wallachia's failed revolution and revolutionaries in Hungary made a brief attempt to form a common revolutionary front. "The key struggle in Europe today is the one between liberty and tyranny, between the people and the throne," not between the national movements, wrote the Romanian revolutionary poet Cezar Bolliac.[55] László Teleki, a Transylvanian who was serving as Hungary's unofficial ambassador to Paris, agreed, advising Kossuth to be as "liberal in the distribution of rights to the various nationalities as possible" and create "a system which would compensate for the absence of a homogeneous nation by reconciling the rights of individuals and nationalities."[56] But the agreement signed between the Romanian émigré revolutionaries and the Hungarian revolutionary leadership in the early summer of 1849 remained a dead letter; the revolution was definitively crushed with the help of tsarist Russian troops shortly thereafter.

Kossuth was aware that the European Great Powers would ultimately decide the fate of the revolution. Thus, in his speeches of the time, he argued that the strivings of the freedom-loving Hungarians would decide the fate of Europe, Hungary's problems were Europe's problems, Hungary's glory would be Europe's glory, and Hungary's defeat would be Europe's defeat.[57] Transylvanian Romanian delegates to Vienna made a comparable argument in the spring of 1849, emphasizing "the necessity of the unification of the

Romanians in the interest of humanity; Romanians are in the avant-garde of Western civilization in the East."[58] These efforts to raise the profile of Hungarian and Romanian aspirations to the level of a "European" interest initiated a pattern in Hungarian-Romanian relations, one punctuated by the two states' attempts to mitigate their vulnerability vis-à-vis the Great Powers while consolidating their own power in the region.

One early attribute of these efforts was revolutionary vanguardism. László Teleki, for example, boasted in 1849 that "France's role in [17]89, the emancipation of Europe, has fallen to us, and in my opinion, we have no choice: we must either accept that role or we fail. . . . Our fate is to have the greatest glory of the world or death. Our task is more difficult than that of the French in '89. *Liberté, égalité, fraternité* is not enough. In lieu of the national unity of peoples, we must offer the reconciliation of individual and national rights and a respect for others."[59] Similarly, C. A. Rosetti, a Romanian émigré revolutionary in Paris, lamented: "If only we had been a truly Romanian government, the glory of liberating the world from slavery would have been ours."[60] These revolutionaries thus cast national independence and consolidation—processes that began "at home"—as capable of setting important, Europe-wide precedents.

Once Hungary gained practical autonomy in all but military, diplomatic, and customs affairs through the Ausgleich [Compromise] with Austria in 1867, and the principalities of Moldavia and Wallachia unified into the new, and increasingly independent, state of Romania in 1859, the two states' attempts to fashion more or less independent foreign policies were greatly influenced by their relationship to cohabiting nationalities and rising would-be nation-states in the region.[61] The latter included the Hungarian Kingdom, the Kingdom of Romania, and the Kingdom of Serbia. Leaders in both Hungary and Romania—ever conscious of the fact that Great Powers would play a role in defining the significance of the region on both the geopolitical and cultural map of Europe—alternated between uneasy cooperation and open competition with one another, a pattern of behavior that has carried through to the present day. Over the course of the second half of the nineteenth century, attempts at cooperation repeatedly faltered on the question of nationality policy, specifically as it related to Romanians in Hungary.

The formal unification of Transylvania with Hungary in 1867 was one flashpoint around which tensions arose between the Romanian elites and the Hungarian leadership. The Hungarian revolutionaries of 1848 had already declared union with Transylvania, but the act was rolled back with the defeat of the revolution and the advent of neoabsolutism in the Habsburg Monarchy. Nevertheless, Hungarian leaders made it clear that unification was the sine qua non for Hungary's cooperation with the Habsburg dynasty, and it was ultimately realized as a result of the Ausgleich. Although the merger did not take place from one day to the next, the full absorption of Transylvania into the Hungarian political and legal structures frustrated many leaders of Hungary's nationalities living there as the mediating influence of the Austrian crown practically disappeared.

On the heels of unification and the Ausgleich came Hungary's nationalities law of 1868, in which the newly autonomous Hungarian Kingdom sought to codify its relationship with the nationalities in legal terms. The law presupposed the existence of a "single, indivisible Hungarian nation," but one that "consisted of different nationalities."[62] It was liberal in its conception, stressing individual liberty, yet providing no substantial collective rights to the non-magyar nationalities.[63] The heated parliamentary debates surrounding its adoption, and the opposition of the nationalities' leaders showed that the law was hardly a piece of consensus legislation. In the end, it was incompletely implemented and imperfectly enforced, such that the nationalities policy of post-Ausgleich Hungary became one of active, oftentimes aggressive "magyarization."[64] This included forced name and religion changes, limited access to schooling in non-magyar languages, and the linking of social opportunity and mobility to magyar self-identification.[65]

Hungarian statesmen who advocated magyarization hoped it would transform the country into a viable nation-state that would not be vulnerable to internal agitation or the intervention of other rising nation-states in the region acting in the interests of their minorities living in Hungary. A preoccupation with sovereignty permeated Hungarian politics throughout this period as Hungarian politicians and statesmen—even those who saw advantages for Hungary in the Dual Monarchy framework—sought greater influence over foreign policy issues, as well as more control over the Hungarian military.[66]

At the same time, arguments for full Hungarian independence foreshadowed those that would later be used to assert Hungary's claim to Transylvania. Indeed both independence and specific territorial claims represented systematic attempts to pin down a set of rules about statehood and sovereignty more generally, rules behind which "Europe" stood as the legitimating force. In the preface to the English translation of his memoirs, published in New York in 1880, Kossuth wrote:

> My nation cannot sink under the suffering which has been dealt out to it. The Hungarian question has a historical, legal, geographical, national, political, and arithmetical basis; it is closely connected with the interests of European freedom and the equilibrium of power. Such questions appeal to the logic of universal history. The cry may be silenced for a time, but cannot be effaced from the record of facts upon

which it has been inscribed by history. This question will demand a place amongst the open questions of Europe until it is solved according to right and justice, or until the nation renounces it.[67]

Here the bases for Hungarian claims to independence—historical, legal, geographical, national, political, and arithmetical—are *not* the same as those Kossuth employed in 1848–49, which tended to be more vague and idealistic references to "freedom." Their evolution reflected the rising importance of territory and population as foundations for legitimate European statehood.

Meanwhile, Romania gained its independence from Ottoman suzerainty following the Congress of Berlin in 1878. In 1883, it joined the Triple Alliance (Austria-Hungary, Germany, Italy), a move that seemed paradoxical to some Romanian statesmen at the time, given the antagonism between the Kingdom of Romania and the Kingdom of Hungary on the subject of the Romanian element in Transylvania.[68] During that same year, the Csángó-Magyar Society oversaw the resettlement of several thousand Szeklers from Bukovina to the Hungarian Kingdom, ostensibly to prevent them from being harassed and assimilated by the Romanian majority there. A further objective underlying the transfer was to bolster the number of magyars in areas where non-magyars constituted a majority, specifically the Banat. The society's actions thus point to the emerging interest in ethnoterritorial consolidation, affirming the link between people and territory.[69]

In the early 1890s the Memorandum movement, initiated by leaders of the Romanian nationality in Hungary, called for equal status of Romanians with other nationalities in Transylvania and demanded that certain legal, political, and economic policies and measures be altered. During this time, the Romanian legation in Berlin reported on the activities of Transylvanian Romanian students and the Romanian legations in Vienna, Paris, and other cities, who worked to lend the idea of a unified Romanian state "a more lasting efficacy."[70]

The so-called Memorandum was handed over to the court in Vienna in the summer of 1892. An epilogue declared that the memorandum was "intended to inform European public opinion."[71] When it was rejected, Romanian politicians and statesmen began to speak more openly of the role Romanians living in Hungary could play in the Romanian Kingdom's own national development and security. In 1893, Romanian foreign minister Dimitrie Sturdza declared before the Romanian assembly:

> The strength of the Romanian Kingdom rests on two foundations. The first is that our country is inhabited by a compact Romanian population. The second [is] that beyond the boundaries of the kingdom, we are surrounded by Romanians. The greater the power of resistance of the Romanians living outside the Kingdom is,

[handwritten margin note:] Romania under Ottoman not Hapsburgs

the more secure the position of the Kingdom itself becomes. The danger for the Kingdom comes when the national existence of the Romanians living outside the Kingdom is threatened. It is a matter of utmost importance for the survival of the Kingdom that the Romanians of Hungary not become magyarized. . . . But also the European Great Powers have an eminent interest in the continued existence of the Romanian Kingdom, as well as in that of the entire Romanian people.[72]

In linking the situation of the Romanians in Hungary to the interest of the "European Great Powers," Sturdza employed a rhetorical strategy that was already a trope in discussions of the emerging Transylvanian Question.[73]

In 1895, Eugen Brote, vice president of the executive council of the Romanian National Party in Transylvania, went one step further by putting these same assertions before a Great-Power audience. Brote published a "political exposé" in German on the "Romanian question in Transylvania and Hungary." He prefaced the piece with the observation that the issue was one that "absorbs the interest of all political circles far beyond the country's borders" and "encroaches on international politics."[74] After outlining the oppressive nature of Hungary's magyarization policies and describing the Transylvanian Romanians' resistance to those policies, Brote went on to explain how treatment of nationalities, interstate relations, and the European interest converged in Transylvania. With its nationality policy, Hungary was upsetting Romania's security by turning Romanians into Hungarians, knowing full well that Romanian leaders could not stand by and allow this to happen. Furthermore, by undermining the shared institutions of diplomacy and the military within the Dual Monarchy, Hungary was "attacking the Great Power status of the Habsburg Monarchy" at the expense of European peace and counter to the interests of the European Great Powers.[75] In short, Hungary's policy in Transylvania was a hazard to the delicate balance of power in Europe.

Over the coming two decades, the Romanian state distributed a number of controversial subventions to support Romanian cultural and educational institutions in Hungary.[76] When the First World War broke out, the tensions regarding the nationality situation in Transylvania, which had gone through another series of attempted compromises, also came to a head. Already in 1914, the Romanian administration was actively lobbying for a territorial revision that would either give Transylvania to Romania or make it autonomous.[77] Although at the beginning of the war Romania was an ally of the Central Powers, it secretly negotiated an alliance with the Entente on August 17, 1916. The Entente then called upon Romania to attack the Habsburg Monarchy, promising, in return, parts of Bukovina, all of the Banat, historical Transylvania, and Eastern Hungary up to the Tisza River if the Entente should win the war.[78]

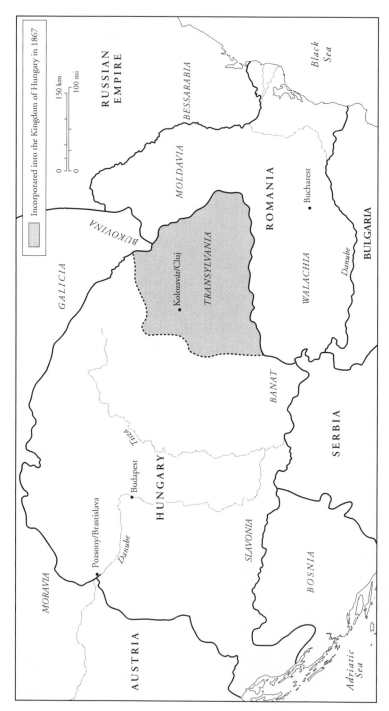

MAP 1. Hungary and Romania in 1910.

Within the map:

Incorporated into the Kingdom of Hungary in 1867

150 km
100 mi
0
0

RUSSIAN EMPIRE

BESSARABIA

MOLDAVIA

Black Sea

BUKOVINA

GALICIA

TRANSYLVANIA

Kolozsvár/Cluj

ROMANIA

Bucharest

WALACHIA

Danube

BULGARIA

BANAT

Tisza

Budapest

HUNGARY

Pozsony/Brastislava

Danube

MORAVIA

SLAVONIA

SERBIA

BOSNIA

AUSTRIA

Adriatic Sea

Romania declared war on Austria-Hungary ten days later and traversed the Carpathians the same night. The Habsburg and German troops managed to fight off the Romanian offensive, but nevertheless lost the war. The Entente did not keep its promise to give Romania territory up to the Tisza, but historical Transylvania and the surrounding territory on its southern and western borders were given in the end.[79] The Treaty of Trianon, which was the Entente's peace with Hungary, resulted in massive territorial losses for Hungary to the new neighboring states of Czechoslovakia and Yugoslavia, as well as to a much-diminished Austria, and a much-enlarged Romania. Romania acquired therewith a territory of 102,000 square kilometers and 3.5 million inhabitants, just under half of whom had declared Hungarian as their mother tongue on the 1910 Hungarian census.[80]

On December 22, 1918, an estimated fifty thousand Hungarians demonstrated in Kolozsvár (soon to be Cluj) against the annexation of Transylvania by Romania. Two days later, on Christmas Eve, Romanian troops entered the Transylvanian capital.[81] The Treaty of Trianon was not signed by the Hungarian delegation until June 4, 1920. In the meantime, a Communist regime came to power in Hungary in 1919. Short-lived though it was, lasting less than five months, the so-called Hungarian Republic of Soviets had profound repercussions for Hungary and Romania for decades to come. The Hungarian Communist leader Béla Kun was intent on protecting revolutionary Hungary from the territorial losses incurred at the Paris-area peace conferences. He sent armies against "reactionary" Czechoslovak and Romanian troops advancing to claim territory. The French intervened and, along with the Romanian army, occupied Hungary, reaching as far west as Budapest.[82] Later Iuliu Maniu would write to Mussolini that by this act "Hungary was saved from the claws of Bolshevism by Romanians."[83] The Romanian military presence in Budapest thus not only spelled the end of the Communist revolution, but also aggravated the sense of injustice and humiliation that the loss of Transylvania had stirred up in many Hungarians.

The situation of Hungarian military weakness and political instability at the end of the war that had made the Romanian occupation possible was a looming precedent in the minds of state and military leaders in both Hungary and Romania. Hungarian leaders wanted to avoid a repeat of 1919 at all costs, while Romanian statesmen could boast that they had played a part in defeating Bolshevism in its Hungarian incarnation, a useful card to play in the competition for the Allies' and later Hitler's favor.[84]

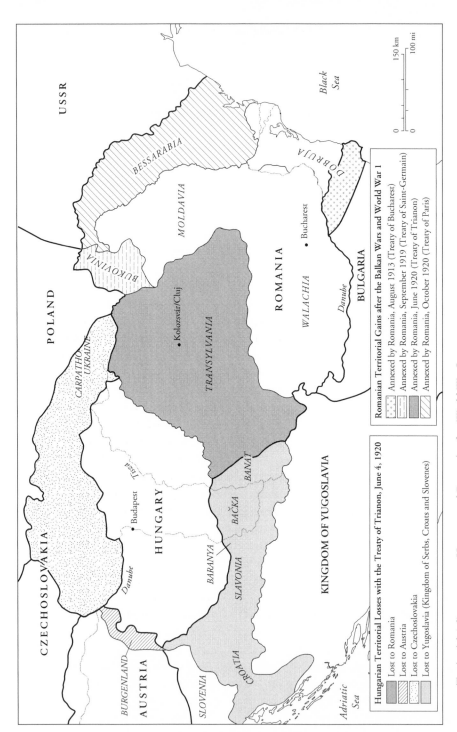

Romanian Territorial Gains after the Balkan Wars and World War 1

Annexed by Romania, August 1913 (Treaty of Bucharest)

Annexed by Romania, September 1919 (Treaty of Saint-Germain)

Annexed by Romania, June 1920 (Treaty of Trianon)

Annexed by Romania, October 1920 (Treaty of Paris)

Hungarian Territorial Losses with the Treaty of Trianon, June 4, 1920

Lost to Romania

Lost to Austria

Lost to Czechoslovakia

Lost to Yugoslavia (Kingdom of Serbs, Croats and Slovenes)

USSR

*Black
Sea*

150 km

100 mi

0

0

BESSARABIA

MOLDAVIA

DOBRUJA

• Bucharest

BUKOVINA

ROMANIA

• Kolozsvár/Cluj

TRANSYLVANIA

WALACHIA

Danube

BULGARIA

POLAND

*CARPATHO
UKRAINE*

CZECHOSLOVAKIA

Tisza

BANAT

BAČKA

Budapest •

HUNGARY

BARANYA

SLAVONIA

KINGDOM OF YUGOSLAVIA

Danube

BURGENLAND

AUSTRIA

SLOVENIA

CROATIA

*Adriatic
Sea*

MAP 2. Territorial Adjustments to Hungary and Romania after World War I.

INTERWAR INTERVENTIONS

After World War I, anxieties, agitation, and preoccupations were reversed around the Transylvanian Question. Despite the Romanian government's assurances that minorities of the new Greater Romania would be protected, skepticism on this point was widespread.[85] Nearly two hundred thousand refugees fled to Trianon Hungary, among them many intellectuals and state officials whose livelihoods became difficult or impossible with the advent of Romanian state control over the region.[86] These refugees from Transylvania and the other territories Hungary lost to Yugoslavia and Czechoslovakia in particular had difficulty finding work in the crowded, war-damaged rump Hungary. Whereas in 1914, Hungary had one state official for every 377 inhabitants, by 1921 that number had risen to one for every 134.[87] Together the refugees formed an unsatisfied and extremely vocal lobby for the reversal of Trianon and the restoration of Transylvania and the other lost territories to Hungary.[88] Though they were not the only ones in Hungary calling for revision of the treaties, their presence and activism served as a constant reminder of what was lost.

The next blow to Hungarian domination in Transylvania came in the form of the Romanian land reform of 1921. The reform was implemented differently in each province, and since in Transylvania "landholding and national differences could not be separated," the province's reform mandate was especially unpopular with the landholding Hungarian population.[89] Large landowners, most of whom were Hungarian noblemen, lost much of their holdings, which were then parceled out to landless or small-holding peasants, most of whom were Romanian villagers.[90] The reform also affected church-owned properties, which had previously supported religious schools. Furthermore, although the urban population did not feel the effects of the reform directly, individuals who opted to leave for Hungary were often forced to sell their property for a fraction of its former value.

In general, the new shape of the international system highlighted conflicts between Hungarian and Romanian domestic and foreign policy. On the diplomatic level, the French-sponsored "Little Entente" mutual defense agreement between Romania, Czechoslovakia, and Yugoslavia was codified in a series of treaties in 1920–21 in an effort to thwart Hungarian revisionist tendencies. At the same time, the League of Nations was established to address interstate conflicts and minority grievances. During the course of the treaty negotiations, minorities were concluded to "constitute obligations of international concern." In making this claim, British historian C. A. Macartney wrote in 1934, "It is laid down, and admitted, that minority questions are not, as they would appear to be, matters which concern exclusively the states of which the minorities form part, but that international intervention is, in their case, justified."[91]

In fact, with the application of the principle of (national) self-determination and the creation of the League, the legal personality of a state resembled that of an individual, and the grievances of an individual or a minority group could become politicized as interstate conflicts. [92] Members of a minority could petition the League with grievances. Furthermore, nations could, and did, appeal to the League for legal mediation in disputes with other nations, as according to international law, the state was "entitled to protect its subjects in another state from gross injustice at the hands of such other state."[93]

This provision was much debated following the 1920 Treaty of Trianon, when the state of Hungary initiated a series of cases against the state of Romania on behalf of individuals with property in Transylvania who had retained or acquired Hungarian citizenship. Such cases frequently aimed at the recovery of property that was redistributed during the Romanian Agrarian Reform Law of 1921.[94] Legally, these cases implied that the minority could be backed up by a state and the state was represented in the minority. Yet one Hungarian legal specialist complained during World War II that "The Council, like the minority committees, were not legal, but political organs," and that the minorities themselves were little more than "objects of the League of Nations proceedings," rather than real "litigants [*perben álló fél*]."[95] The political and diplomatic implications of these disputes were cause for unease on both sides, as Romanian state leaders felt they represented an assault on Romania's sovereignty, despite Hungarian claims to the contrary.[96] Above all the grievance of a minority became a means of bringing interstate tensions over transferred territory to the attention of the international community during the interwar period.

The minority treaties also made room for states to petition the League of Nations on behalf of their *noncitizen* minorities in other states, which Germany—as a member of the League Council from 1926 to 1933—did quite frequently on behalf of the German minorities living outside Germany's borders, mostly in East-Central Europe.[97] Hungary was never given a seat on the council, but in the years immediately after the signing of the Treaty of Trianon, did submit several complaints to the council on behalf of the Hungarian minority living in Transylvania.[98] Furthermore, petitions of Hungarians from Transylvania were especially numerous; the only more prolific minority in this regard were the Germans of Upper Silesia.[99]

Compliance with the treaties proved very difficult to assess and enforce, not least of all because the minority treaties were crafted with the under-standing that minority concerns should ideally be addressed in the domestic arena and only reached the League of Nations Council if domestic resolution proved impossible. Romania had signed the Minority Treaty on December 9, 1919, but at the peace negotiations, the Romanian delegate I. C. Brătianu had voiced harsh criticism of the treaty, casting it as a threat to Romania's sovereignty.[100] Romanian governmental resistance was such that the treaty was never codified, either in Romanian law or in the constitution of 1923. Just after the new constitution appeared, the Bulgarian legation in Bucharest complained that its lack of provisions for minority protection constituted a coordinated effort to throw "dust in the face of Europe."[101] In 1925, Hungar-ian prime minister István Bethlen similarly lamented that the minority treaties had "practically no value at all" given that "the League of Nations had yet to pour life and meaning into them."[102]

Beyond ignoring the provisions of the Minority Treaty, the Romanian constitution also partially obscured the presence of minorities in its open-ing article, which asserted that "the Kingdom of Romania is a unitary and indivisible national state," and in subsequent articles that made mention of "Romanians" as a category including all state citizens, regardless of "eth-nic origin."[103] In this way, Romanian statesmen did what their Hungarian counterparts had done before them since 1848, implying that all a person could want was to have his or her individual rights secured by the state.[104] Accordingly, during a parliamentary debate in 1923, the Romanian minister of justice declared that "the minorities do not comprise a unified entity separate from the Romanian nation. In a healthy nation-state there is but one nation: the Romanian."[105] Romanian statesmen and officials were nevertheless quite conscious of the challenge minorities posed to Romanian state sovereignty, which is perhaps why the first four articles of the constitution dealt with the territory of the state and its inviolability.[106] A commission sent to Romania by the American Committee on the Rights of Religious Minorities in 1927 to report on the condition of minorities there concluded that "practically every question . . . involving the minorities, has to do with Roumania's conception of the problem of self preservation."[107]

With the growing emphasis on "national rights" as status-equal with "indi-vidual rights," "justice" as applied to states took on the character in common parlance and understanding of "justice" as applied to the individual.[108] As with debates over the desirability of individual versus national rights during the mid- to late nineteenth century, in the wake of the First World War, this tension yielded a preoccupation with "justice" for the nation. Commonly, representations of "injustice" used individuals to personify the state or the

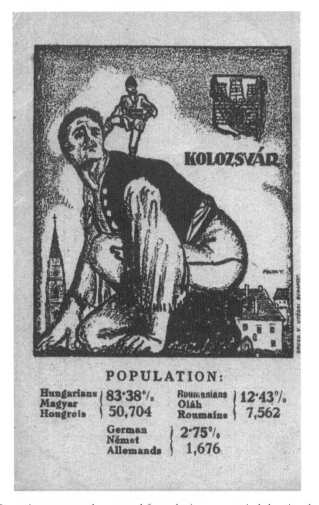

POPULATION:

Hungarians Magyar Hongrois	83·38% 50,704	Roumanians Oláh Roumains	12·43% 7,562
	German Német Allemands	2·75% 1,676	

FIG. I. Hungarian propaganda postcard from the interwar period showing the pre–World War I population statistics of Cluj. The illustration depicts the injustice of having Romanians (represented by the small man dressed in Romanian peasant attire) rule over the city's Hungarian majority (represented by the large man). The majority Hungarian population of the city thus served as an argument for the revision of Trianon. From the collection of András Fodor; reprinted with permission.

nation.[109] Post-Trianon Hungary was "fallen, mutilated, lying in anguish as a bleeding trunk" of her former self.[110] "Which of the principles and interests [of international justice and the liberty of peoples] required this special severity towards Hungary?" Hungarian delegates to the postwar peace conference wondered.[111] Furthermore, it was no longer only for the state to provide "justice" for the individual (as Kossuth believed in 1848),[112] but also for the individual member of a minority to secure "justice" for the kin-state. For if Hungarians were severed from the national body, the Hungarian nation could be neither "healthy" nor "viable" nor "its true self," wrote a Hungarian Calvinist priest in a 1937 article aptly entitled "It's Impossible."[113]

The actual shift in the Hungarian state leaders' emphasis from minority rights to territorial claims in diplomatic engagement can be traced through the country's diplomatic maneuverings leading up to the Second Vienna Arbitration. Interwar Hungarian statesmen were very careful not to push for revision unless the chances of achieving it were good. A Hungarian diplomat serving in Switzerland thus wrote in 1928 that "we should never show, even with a single word or gesture, that we continue to want and seek full [territorial] integrity."[114] So it was that up until early 1940, the Hungarian leadership generally focused its diplomacy on the situation of the Hungarian minority in neighboring states. Only thereafter did Hungarians abandon the focus on minority rights in the interest of pursuing territorial claims, or rather *linking* the problem of minority rights to claims on territory.[115]

The first notable trend in this direction was increasing disenchantment with the League of Nations "security system."[116] Intimations that Hungary would withdraw from the League on the grounds that it had failed to protect the Hungarian minority in the successor states from oppression soon followed.[117] As Germany sought first to secure the rights of the German minority in neighboring states, and then territorial gains in Czechoslovakia, the revisionist aspirations of Hungary became complementary to those of Germany.[118] After long hesitation, Hungary finally withdrew from the League in April 1939, a decision which brought it still closer to the Axis.[119]

Meanwhile, statesmen representing Czechoslovakia, Yugoslavia, and Romania (the Little Entente) tried to keep the focus of their interactions with Hungary on the issue of minority rights.[120] When that became impossible for Romania's leadership following the annexation of Bessarabia and Northern Bukovina by the Soviet Union on June 26, they pushed for a population exchange with Hungary, hoping thus to prevent the minority issue from becoming a territorial one.[121] Nevertheless, the shift was already manifest by February 1940, when the Hungarian ambassador to Great Britain, in a conversation with Lord Halifax, explicitly stated that "the core of the question has moved from the minority to the territorial question."[122] The "territorial question" was addressed a few months later, on August 30, 1940, when the Axis-mediated Second Vienna Arbitration gave Northern Transylvania back to Hungary.

After Vienna, it was Romania's leaders and advocates who emphasized

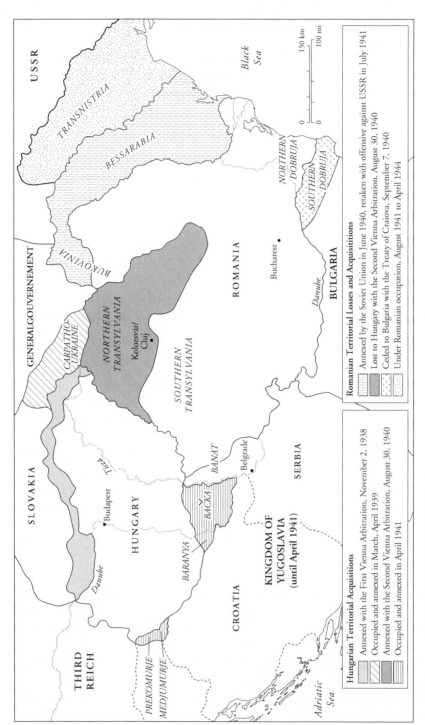

Black
Sea

USSR

TRANSNISTRIA

BESSARABIA

BUKOVINA

NORTHERN
DOBRUJA

SOUTHERN
DOBRUJA

GENERALGOUVERNEMENT

CARPATHO-
UKRAINE

NORTHERN
TRANSYLVANIA

Kolozsvár/
Cluj

SOUTHERN
TRANSYLVANIA

ROMANIA

Bucharest

Danube

BULGARIA

SLOVAKIA

Budapest

Tisza

HUNGARY

BARANYA

Danube

PREKOMURJE

MEDJUMURJE

BANAT

BÁČKA

Belgrade

SERBIA

KINGDOM OF
YUGOSLAVIA
(until April 1941)

CROATIA

THIRD
REICH

Adriatic
Sea

150 km
100 mi

0
0

Romanian Territorial Losses and Acquisitions

Annexed by the Soviet Union in June 1940, retaken with offensive against USSR in July 1941

Lost to Hungary with the Second Vienna Arbitration, August 30, 1940

Ceded to Bulgaria with the Treaty of Craiova, September 7, 1940

Under Romanian occupation, August 1941 to April 1944

Hungarian Territorial Acquisitions

Annexed with the First Vienna Arbitration, November 2, 1938

Occupied and annexed in March, April 1939

Annexed with the Second Vienna Arbitration, August 30, 1940

Occupied and annexed in April 1941

MAP 3. Hungary and Romania During World War II.

"justice" and "rights," both at home and in diplomatic negotiations. And how was this "justice" to be achieved? In large part by cataloging slights against the Romanian minority in Northern Transylvania in preparation for the coming peace settlement.[123] Just as in the Hungarian case during the interwar period, the suffering minority was to serve as the ambassador of state interest to the international community. Nor was it a coincidence that the man who orchestrated this propaganda action, Mihai Antonescu, had written several books during the interwar period on the League of Nations.[124]

MINORITIES AND "INTERNAL AFFAIRS"

To understand how calls for "justice" and "rights" came to be cast in terms of a European mandate, it is important to emphasize how the Hungarian/ Romanian minority issue evolved from concerns about the presence of *other* minorities within the two states and the role played by Great Power actors in attempting to secure those minorities' right to exist as such. As of the middle of the nineteenth century, few statesmen in either Hungary or Romania saw Romanian or Hungarian elements on their respective territory as the threat to state sovereignty they would later come to represent. Instead, the groups that most sharpened state leaders' sensitivity to issues of sovereignty and the potential of minorities to undermine national independence were, in Hungary, the Germans, and in Romania the Jews.

In both countries, brushes with European Great Powers and minority rights came simultaneously with national consolidation and increasing independence. When Russia, having lost the Crimean War, evacuated the (Romanian) Danubian Principalities of Moldavia and Wallachia in 1856, the French ambassador to the Congress of Paris tried to make the peace contingent on the Principalities' effective emancipation of its approximately 270,000 Jews.[125] At the time, the Jews of Romania were considered "foreigners" and as such enjoyed none of the benefits of citizenship. The proposal of the French ambassador met with vehement opposition from the ruling princes of the Principalities, who argued that emancipation on such a scale would "bring the country to certain ruin."[126] These objections were recognized and the emancipation clause did not make it into the final draft of the peace treaty.

The legacy of this early successful resistance to Great Power intervention on behalf of minorities has proved extremely tenacious in Romania. The pattern of international pressure and Romanian resistance was to repeat itself a number of times throughout the nineteenth and twentieth centuries, arguably up to the present day.[127] Variations on 1856 occurred in 1859, following the de facto unification of the Principalities; in 1867 after government-initiated mass expulsions of Jews from Romania; in 1878 at the Congress of Berlin, where Romanian independence was officially recognized by the Great Powers; and in 1919 with the creation of Greater Romania and the attempted Great Power imposition of the minority treaties. Romanian leader Ion Antonescu even evoked this legacy of resistance in 1943, as part of a caustic rebuke addressed to Hitler. In it, he railed against Axis efforts to mediate between Hungary and Romania in minority matters, linking his own defiance to Axis mediation activities to 1856 and the post–World War I Romanian resistance to the minority treaties.[128]

Yet Romanian statesmen saw in efforts of Western European Jews on behalf of their coreligionists in Romania a force both to be vehemently opposed, as well as to be emulated. The Alliance Israélite Universelle [Universal Jewish Alliance], established in 1860, developed a strategy for putting pressure on Western states to intervene on behalf of the Jews in the East.[129] The strategy involved cataloging slights and atrocities against Jews for presentation to foreign diplomats and statesmen. In making efforts to counter the strategy, Romanian statesmen became adept at casting their objections to the resultant pressure in terms of resistance to Great Power meddling in Romania's "internal affairs" and as means of securing and preserving the sovereignty, independence, and territorial integrity of Romania.[130] But they also utilized the methods pioneered by the Alliance in making the case against Hungary on behalf of the Romanian minority there, especially from the 1880s up to the First World War.

How both the friction with the Great Powers as well as the habit of seeking a Great Power audience for Romanian minority grievances came to be bound to ideas of Europe in Romania is also explicable in terms of the pressure brought to bear on Romania to be kinder to its Jews. At the 1878 Congress of Berlin, French plenipotentiary William Henry Waddington insisted that Romania could join the "great European family" only if it recognized "the grand rule of equality of rights and freedom of religion." Article 44 of the Treaty of Berlin represented an explicit, if toothless, codification of freedom of religion in Romania and became "the focus of public outrage" in Romania, for which the Jews were blamed. In 1879, the Romanian Chamber Commission declared that "there are no Roumanian Jews and never were, but only such as were born in the country, but are assimilated neither in language nor customs and do not aspire to be."[131] Over the next several years, Article 44 became an increasingly dead letter.[132] But what spilled over from the Congress of Berlin was the sense that "Europe" took an explicit interest—however hypocritical—in the fate of minorities in the would-be nation-states of the East.

A State within the State

In line with the emerging imbrication of states and peoples, the German minority and German/Austrian states took on special significance first in Hungary, and later in Romania as well. Germans and their kin-states came to be perceived on the one hand as a threat to state sovereignty, but on the other as a model for the mobilization or manipulation of minorities as arms of kin-state interests. It was from encounters with Austrian politics that Hungarian statesmen of the nineteenth century first sought advantage reversal to favor Hungarians over Austro-Germans in political life and statecraft. This they achieved in 1867 with the Ausgleich. And it was the nationalist Germans in Hungary who caused state leaders to fear for the would-be nation-state's newly won sovereignty thereafter. As such, in the rhetoric of the time, although Austrian neoabsolutists and German nationalists were operating on two different political levels, their combined impact on Hungarian politics sped along the process by which nationalities became ever more closely associated with their kin-states.

In 1861, Hungarian revolutionary veteran and legal expert Károly Csemegi wrote a six-part article series entitled "The Nationalities in Hungary." He dedicated some of the series to a discussion of ties between minorities (Serbs, Slovaks, Romanians, Ruthenians) in Hungary and their brethren in other states, raising the possibility of the further collapse of the Ottoman Empire and what effect the emerging "new formations" would have on the minority question in Hungary. "Is it not natural for isolated races to long to unite with the rest of their nationality with the force of their instincts?" he wondered. Still, that such a development could result in "the dismemberment of Hungary" was "pure fantasy [*puszta rémkép*]" in his view. Instead, "only one real danger threatens Hungary and all its nationalities without exception, and that danger can be sought up the Danube [River], rather than down it." By the time Csemegi's text was republished in 1902, the situation had so changed that this reference required a footnote clarifying what Csemegi meant by this statement. Csemegi saw the *real* danger to Hungary, the note explained, as emanating from Vienna, which wanted "the nationalities to merge into one and become German by means of centralization." Thus the nationalities living in Hungary would do well to stand by the Hungarian leadership in the interest of securing their "rightful claims."[133]

In 1902, this argument would have been a hard sell in light of rising anxiety about the Romanian, Serbian, and Slovak national movements, but concerns about the threat of germanization hardly disappeared from Hungarian political rhetoric after Csemegi's appeal. During a session of the Hungarian parliament in 1882, assemblyman Otto Hermann observed that members of a certain minority nationality living in Hungary had indeed forged ties with a foreign country, taken the citizenship of that country, and within Hungary sought "to create thereby a state within the state."[134] What was worse, he continued, these people, "who eat Hungarian bread use every moment to denounce the Hungarian nation abroad." "As a result," Hermann concluded, "I summon the attention of the honorable house and expect that the government will do its duty and not keep its hands in its lap in the face of this movement."[135] The minority in question was not the Romanians, Serbs, Slovaks, or Ruthenians, but the Germans.

As was the case with the Alliance Israélite Universelle and Romania, just as the Germans were perceived a potential threat to Hungarian state sovereignty starting already in the mid-nineteenth century, their methods of nationalization, state centralization, and, after World War I, initiatives on behalf of their minority abroad, and the relationship those initiatives had to Germany's revisionist aspirations, served as a model for the Hungarian state's own policies and initiatives. During the 1882 parliamentary debate, for example—which was centered around the Transylvanian Saxons' criticisms of Hungary's magyarization policies in the German press—these ironies were eminently manifest. Just as Csemegi had slammed Vienna for its "centralizing" and "germanizing" tendencies vis-à-vis the nationalities in 1861, representatives in the Hungarian parliament in 1882 countered Transylvanian Saxons' claims that they were the victims of harsh magyarization policies with counterclaims that it was the Saxon minority that had forced its language and administration on many Hungarians and Romanians living in Transylvania.[136] At the same time, these representatives alternately denied and defended the existence of state-driven magyarization in Hungary, arguing that Hungary had the right to defend its own nationality and propagate the "language of state" with all the means at its disposal, much as neoabsolutist Austria had done.[137]

Following the First World War, from which Germany, Austria, and Hungary emerged as the biggest losers in terms of both territory and prestige, Hungarian leaders both mimicked and criticized Germany's interventions on behalf of the German minority in the postwar successor states. Just as the German foreign ministry linked "the revision of minority obligations . . . inextricably with the question of borders," Hungary's leaders adopted much the same strategy during the interwar period.[138] And just as the Germans "supplemented these efforts . . . by diplomatic conversations in the Western capitals and in Geneva, in which they argued that as long as the borders remained unrevised, there would be no peace in Eastern Europe," Hungar-

ians did the same.[139] And when Nazi Germany began aggressively demand-
ing better treatment of the German minority in Czechoslovakia, Hungarian
statesmen argued that the Hungarian minority should have the same rights
as the German minority there.[140] Thus when, in June 1940, Germany planted
a swastika flag atop the castle at Trianon, the revisionist solidarity between
Germany and Hungary seemed triumphantly confirmed.[141]

Nevertheless, throughout the interwar period the German minority in
Hungary was often perceived as disloyal—or loyal only to Germany—and
potentially threatening to Hungarian state sovereignty due to the support it
enjoyed from Weimar, and later Nazi Germany.[142] Germans' resistance to
magyarization and outspoken critiques of Hungarian policies made them
frequent targets of the law adapted to punish slander against the Hungarian
nation after World War I.[143] And German efforts to bend Hungary's western
frontier during World War II were cause for distress in governing circles as
well.[144]

By raising concerns about state sovereignty, Germany, Austro-Germans,
and the German minority in Hungary played both subtle and unsubtle roles
in the emergence and various approaches to the Transylvanian Question. On
April 19, 1939, Hitler told the Romanian foreign minister, Grigore Gafencu,
that the Hungarians "have no regard or sympathy for the German minorities.
As for me, I am only interested in my Germans . . . and what the German
minorities do not want, the Reich does not want either."[145] In May 1939, even
as Hungary was regaining territories from dismantled Czechoslovakia with
Nazi German help, its leaders also feared the German state might make
claims on Hungarian territory inhabited by ethnic Germans.[146]

Just prior to World War II, there were about 479,000 speakers of German
living in Trianon Hungary, and 550,000 in Transylvania.[147] The 1941 Hungarian census registered 740,000 German speakers.[148] In 1942, Hitler's rov-
ing ambassador, Hermann Göring, was reported to have said to Romanian
dictator Ion Antonescu: "After all, why do you quarrel with Hungary about
Transylvania, which is actually more German than Roumanian or Hungarian?"[149] Furthermore, as an added condition to the Second Vienna Arbitration, Hungary was required to sign an agreement with Germany which
included special provisions for the protection and support of the German
minority in Hungary.[150] Hitler even went so far as to suggest that if Hungary
could develop a positive relationship with its German minority, its chances of
obtaining further territorial compensation would significantly improve.[151]

Honoring this agreement proved challenging for the Hungarian administration, including the new government officials in Northern Transylvania.
The Germans (Saxons and Swabians) of Transylvania had, in many respects,

been tied to political and cultural trends in Germany for much of the mid- to late interwar period.[152] They had formed their own *Volksgruppen*, and many Saxon men volunteered for or were otherwise funneled into the SS. There were *Volksbund* organizations active in all major Transylvanian cities, and their increasing isolation from the Hungarian polity was cause for considerable anxiety on the part of the lord lieutenant of two Transylvanian counties, Béla Bethlen, who feared—as Otto Hermann had in his speech before the Hungarian parliament in 1882—that the Germans were creating a "state within a state."[153]

Romanian statesmen inherited components of this ambivalent relationship with Germany and the German minority, most significantly with the troubled last years of the Triple Alliance and the German occupation of Romania in 1916 following Romania's defection to the Entente. With the post–World War I annexation of Transylvania and Bukovina, Romania's own German-speaking population went from near zero to 745,421 practically overnight.[154] The Saxons of the old Principality of Transylvania, the Danube Swabians of the Banat, and the Austro-Germans of Cernăuți [Czernowitz] became objects of rigorous romanianization policies directed from Bucharest.[155] There were also sizable German populations in recently acquired Bessarabia and Dobruja. Although the Deutsche Volkspartei [German People's Party], representing the interests of Romania's new German population generally voted along with the governing party until 1927, during the 1930s, the National Socialists gained strength among the Saxons and Danube Swabians of Transylvania, a process which accelerated following Hitler's rise to power in Germany in 1933.[156] As in Hungary prior to World War I, Romanian leaders feared the German minority was creating a "state within a state," a concern that was fed by the assertions of the German minority leadership itself, which declared "our relationship with the [Romanian] state is [the same as] the relationship of Germany to Romania. . . . For us no sacrifice is too great for the achievement of the goals of German foreign policy and the German Reich."[157]

Yet even as the Germans seemed a thorn in the side of both states, there were also strains of quiet competition for their favor; which state would the Transylvanian Saxons and Banat Swabians rather inhabit? Their preference was perceived as legitimation for each state's claim to Transylvania.[158] Thus, when Saxons and Swabians threw down their lot with the "other side" by forming a coalition with a minority or governing party, it was a tense and emotional affair.[159]

This genealogy reveals that minority-protection rhetoric and strategies evolved in part around Germans and their kin-states, Austria and Germany.

Historian Eric Weitz has noted how German leaders, in brokering the Berlin Congress of 1878 and the Berlin Conference of 1884–85, precipitated the shift away from old-style Great Power diplomacy toward population politics.[160] Following in this tradition, interwar German governments played a significant role in framing minority protection strategies through their own efforts on behalf of the German minority living in other states. Thus it was that leaders in Hungary and Romania had come to associate minority rights not only with the rhetoric, international agreements, and diplomatic maneuvering of Britain, France, and the League of Nations, but also—perhaps even primarily—with Germans and Germany's resistance to the League. This association would later affect the nature of interactions between the three states during World War II, as will become evident in Chapter 4.

Connecting the Dots and Filling in the Blanks

Talk of minority rights was nevertheless just one of the ways Germany and other interwar states sought to justify claims to territory. Like Germany after Versailles, in making the case for their right to Transylvania, Hungarian and Romanian statesmen, intellectuals, and politicians employed a number of strategies beyond protection of minority rights. Complementary to the ethnodemographic focus were a series of historical, economic, and qualitative arguments for why the region should belong to them. Politicians and lobbyists in both Hungary and Romania had been awed by the success of the Czech government in exile—headed by Tomáš Masaryk and Edvard Beneš—in convincing the victorious powers to create a Czechoslovak state out of what had been Austro-Hungarian territory.[161] Thus, in addition to employing prewar strategies for raising the Transylvanian Question to the level of a European concern, they also took pains to learn the lessons of the Czechoslovak success, mimicking or countering many of the strategies that had apparently worked so well for Czech leaders.[162] Hungarian efforts in this direction were especially intense, given that Hungary had revisionist claims on the new state of Czechoslovakia.

For Hungarian and Romanian leaders, finding and reaching an audience for their arguments was a matter of intense consideration. Initially this audience was the Allies after World War I; both states' activists sought and found powerful friends and spokespeople for their causes in Great Britain, France, and the United States. For the Romanians, this included British historian R. W. Seton-Watson and much of the circle around the London-based *New*

Europe journal.[163] The former, appropriately carrying the title of Masaryk Professor of Central European History in the University of London, published works opposing Hungarian revisionism.[164] Seton-Watson also received regular generous stipends from the Romanian government for his efforts, not only during the interwar period, but also during the war, despite the fact that he was working for British intelligence at the time.[165] For Hungary it was British historian C. A. Macartney, who ran a radio program under the auspices of the BBC in Hungary during World War II, the British MP Sir Robert Gower, publicist/politicians Sir Robert Donald and Lord Rothermere, and others.[166]

During the interwar period, the Transylvanian Question was addressed in scores of books, pamphlets, maps, newspaper and journal articles in French and English, and later in Italian and German.[167] After the Second World War broke out, the production and distribution of English and French publications on the Transylvanian Question diminished but did not disappear, and propaganda efforts were supplemented by a marked increase in the number of German and Italian publications.[168] These publications tended to be highly polemical, and many of them were state-sponsored or distributed by organizations—diplomatic and cultural—connected to the state.[169]

Advocates of both states' interests maintained the importance of the "powers of evocation" embodied by maps in particular, expressing the belief that "such demonstrable visual propaganda has a much more smashing effect than text."[170] In fact, just a few weeks after seizing power in Romania, Ion Antonescu discussed plans to distribute "propaganda maps" that would help to "direct" the foreign press.[171] One major challenge was thus to illustrate ethnographic predominance on maps of Transylvania. In an ethnographic atlas of Romania published during World War II, we read the following: "The mountain valleys of Transilvania, within their neighboring hills, and with the rivers Theiss and the Danube, the Black Sea and the river Dniester, in all enclosing some 300,000 sq. km., have always had a Roumanian population. . . . The Roumanians, within their natural boundaries, thus form a solid union."[172] This brief introduction, printed in parallel French and English (as *La Roumanie: atlas ethnographique/Roumania: Ethnographic Atlas*), is followed by a historical description of how the "natural ethnical territory of the Roumanians has suffered much in the course of the centuries," and a series of maps showing the ethnographical contours of the region over the period from 1856 to 1930. Each of the maps shows the territory of Romania (as of spring 1940, that is, before the Second Vienna Arbitration and the loss of Bessarabia and Northern Bukovina to the Soviet Union) with a practically homogeneous ethnic mass of Romanians, the only exception being central

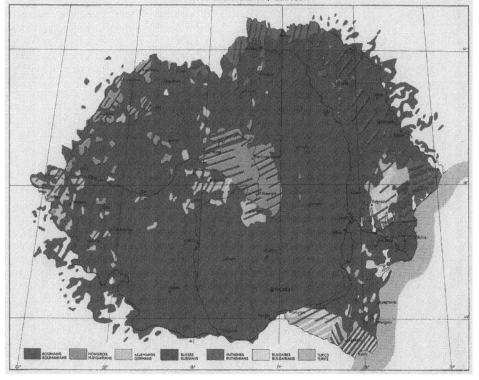

CARTE ETHNOGRAPHIQUE DE LA ROUMANIE, D'APRÈS LES DATES STATISTIQUES DU RÉCENSEMENT 1930. PAR PROF. EMANOIL TR. SIMTION

ETHNOGRAPHICAL MAP OF ROUMANIA, ACCORDING TO THE RESULTS OF THE CENSUS OF 1930. BY PROF. EMANOIL TR. SIMTION

FIG. 2. Romanian ethnographic map published in an English- and French-language atlas. *La Roumanie: atlas ethnographique/ Roumania: Ethnographic Atlas* (Bucharest: Institutul de arte grafice, 194[?]). The map is based on data from the 1930 Romanian census. The atlas was likely published at the behest of Ion Antonescu in late 1940 or early 1941 to refute Hungarian maps representing Transylvania's ethnographic distribution published just before the negotiations for the Second Vienna Arbitration.

Romania (or Eastern Transylvania) with its undeniably large and compact population of Szeklers. These maps, which the authors claim were based on the work of French, German, and even Hungarian cartographers, "illustrate the numerical superiority of the Roumanian element within the Bounds of Roumania" as well as the "scattered nature of the minorities within Roumania."[173] The final map, the atlas explains, is based on the figures of the 1930 Romanian census. It highlights "the natural evolution which has taken place

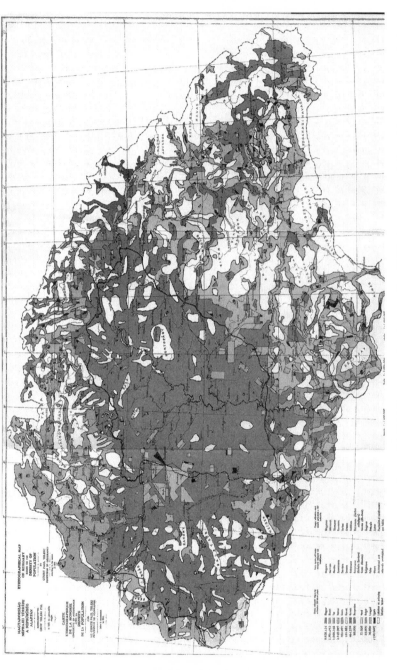

FIG. 3. Geographer and statesman Count Pál Teleki's map used at the post–World War I peace negotiations. The map was crafted to address the "essential problems" Teleki saw with colored-in maps by combining ethnographic and population-density data. This approach made the Romanian presence in Transylvania appear much less pervasive. Count Pál Teleki, *Ethnographic Map of Hungary based on the Density of Population According to the Census of 1910* (The Hague: W. P. van Stockum & son, 1920).

since the Treaty of Trianon," with Romanians making advances—indicated by red stripes—into even the most ethnically homogeneous minority settlements of the Szeklers.

In the penultimate paragraph of the atlas, the author(s) discuss how these maps "differ considerably from the map of Count Teleki Pal, which was presented by Hungary at the Peace Conference." Teleki, the Hungarian statesman and geographer who would serve as prime minister of Hungary from 1939 until his suicide in 1941, had indeed created a very different ethnographic map of Transylvania for presentation at the 1920 peace conference. In a memo on the Transylvanian Question delivered at Neuilly on January 14, 1920, the head of the Hungarian delegation, Count Albert Apponyi, outlined "two essential problems" with the way nationality statistics had been represented on maps up to that point. One was that they tended to color in entire territories without consideration for the fact that some areas were "completely uninhabited." The other was that the colored-in areas on such maps revealed nothing about the actual number of people living there, only their nationality.[174]

Teleki came up with alternative means of representing nationalities statistics to address both of these "essential problems." The result was a map that, instead of "coloring in" sparsely populated areas, left them blank. Furthermore, the size of color blocks on Teleki's map corresponded to a fixed number of inhabitants (one hundred per millimeter of "colored-in" space on the map in Figure 2). The result was a picture of Transylvania that was much less obviously "Romanian" than the ones using the "old" method. Instead of a contiguous mass, the map showed Romanians living in isolated strips, mingled with members of other nationalities in a kaleidoscope of color, the boldest of which (red) represented Hungarians, while the faintest (lavender) the Romanians.[175] The conclusions to be drawn from such a map, Apponyi argued, were as follows: that the Carpathian Mountains formed a natural, for the most part uninhabited barrier between the boundaries of Hungary and Romania such that there were no large contiguous masses of Romanians extending from the Carpathian Basin into Romania, and that the Hungarians were in the absolute majority on the eastern boundaries of Hungary.[176]

Over the course of the interwar period, Teleki explored other ways to complicate the "colored-in" picture of Transylvania which the Romanian state had relied on at the conference. In a memorandum presented in Paris in 1937, he cited an example of "primitive and superficial" cartographic representations from a 1930 atlas, where "10 million Magyars are represented by a coloured surface of 730 mm², 12 million Rumanians by an almost double surface—1340 mm²."[177] Shading in the gaps between settlements, he argued,

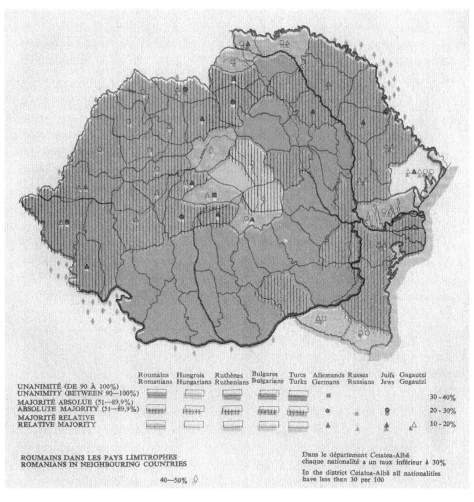

	Roumains Romanians	Hongrois Hungarians	Ruthènes Ruthenians	Bulgares Bulgarians	Turcs Turks	Allemands Germans	Russes Russians	Juifs Jews	Gagautzi Gagautzi
UNANIMITÉ (DE 90 À 100%) UNANIMITY (BETWEEN 90—100%)									
MAJORITÉ ABSOLUE (51—89,9%) ABSOLUTE MAJORITY (51—89,9%)						■			30 - 40%
MAJORITÉ RELATIVE RELATIVE MAJORITY						●	●	●	20 - 30%
						▲	▲	▲	◢ 10 - 20%

ROUMAINS DANS LES PAYS LIMITROPHES
ROMANIANS IN NEIGHBOURING COUNTRIES

40—50% ◇

Dans le département Cetatea-Albă
chaque nationalité a un taux inférieur à 30%

In the district Cetatea-Albă all nationalities
have less than 30 per 100

FIG. 4. A "colored-in" map by Romanian demographer Sabin Manuilă showing areas of "unanimous," "absolute," and "relative" ethnic Romanian majority. The map deemphasizes the presence of Hungarians near the border with Hungary as part of an effort to undermine Hungarian revisionist claims. Sabin Manuilă, *Étude ethnographique sur la population de la Roumanie/Ethnographical Survey of the Population of Romania* (Bucharest: Imprimeriile Statului, Imprimeriile Națională, 1938), xxxvii.

thus gave the illusion of ethnic and linguistic contiguity. A 1938 atlas created by Sabin Manuilă illustrates this phenomenon. The map is based on the 1930 Romanian census figures, showing areas of "unanimous," "absolute," and "relative" ethnic majority (where "unanimous" is counted as 90 percent or above, "absolute" as 50 to 90 percent, and "relative" as any number larger than the next-largest minority group).[178] The description concludes that "in all the districts on the western frontier that separate Romania from Hungary, the Romanians have without exception an absolute majority."[179]

Teleki and Rónai argued that a more accurate way to show the ethnic composition of each individual settlement was with colored dots of different sizes, representing both the size of the community and the proportion of a given nationality living in that community. Their approach was used for a map that appeared in a German-language publication of the Hungarian Historical Society published just prior to the arbitration at Vienna, and timed to make Hungary's claims compelling to German readers.[180] The map shows Transylvania, already joined with Hungary (even though it illustrates the period from 1930 to 1939, that is, *before* the Second Vienna Arbitration), and Romania does not appear on the map at all. It features red, yellow-orange, and lavender circles of different sizes representing settlements of Hungarians, Germans, and Romanians respectively. Not surprisingly, the red dots are the most prominent and visible, while the lavender ones fade into the background. As with Teleki's 1920 map, much of the area is blank, indicating unsettled areas.

About a month after the transfer of Northern Transylvania to Hungary, Ion Antonescu opened a cabinet meeting with a discussion of this map. He showed it to his ministers, saying, "look how they reveal the eloquent injustice that was done to Romania." He noted the shifty use of colors and vowed to make similar maps showing Romanians in red and Hungarians in a "faded color."[181] This is presumably how the *La Roumanie: atlas ethnographique/Roumania: Ethnographic Atlas* came to be.

But as the featured Manuilă map reveals, the Romanian ethnographic atlas was not only a reversal of the Hungarian version. Its author(s), commenting on Teleki's map, complained that "no one uses his method of including geographical 'blanks,' which is really devoid of scruples," and estimated that seven hundred thousand people were blanked out in this way.[182] So it was that the "colored-in" map remained a mainstay of Romanian cartographic representations of ethnographic data in the *atlas ethnographique/Ethnographic Atlas*.

In a telling hybridization, some Hungarian maps from the post-Trianon period combined the "colored-in" and "dotted" cartographic strategies, including a map from a book entitled *The Treaty of Trianon and European Peace* from 1934 by István Bethlen, a longtime Hungarian statesman and former prime minister.[183] It shows the border region with Romania "colored-in" with Hungarians, visually belying the claim of the Romanians' "absolute majority" status in the border region. Nevertheless, Bethlen could not maintain that

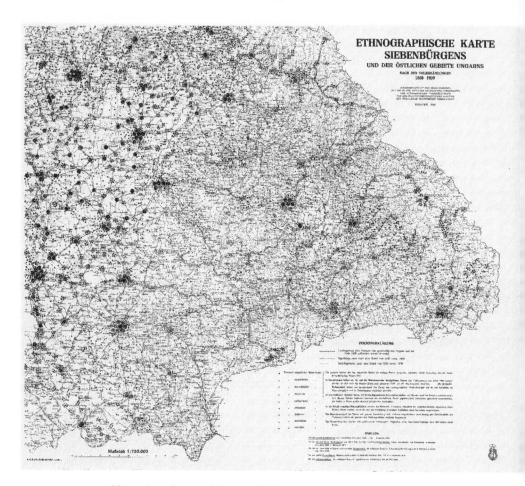

FIG. 5. Hungarian ethnographic map of Transylvania published just prior to the arbitration at Vienna, with population clusters represented by dots of different sizes and colors. *Ethnographische Karte Siebenbürgens und der östlichen Gebiete Ungarns nach den Volkszählungen* 1930–1939 (Budapest: Der Staatswissenschaftlichen Institut der Ungarischen Statistischen Gesellschaft, 1940). The map was included in a German-language publication of the Hungarian Historical Society around the same time. *Siebenbürgen* (Budapest: Ungarische Historische Gesellschaft, 1940), map inset 277. A variation on Teleki's population-density ethnographic map from 1920, the map downplays the presence of the Romanian ethnic element in Transylvania. Upon seeing it, Ion Antonescu was incensed and vowed to his cabinet members that he would retaliate with better Romanian cartographic propaganda. *Stenogramele*, vol. 1, doc. 7, 134–35.

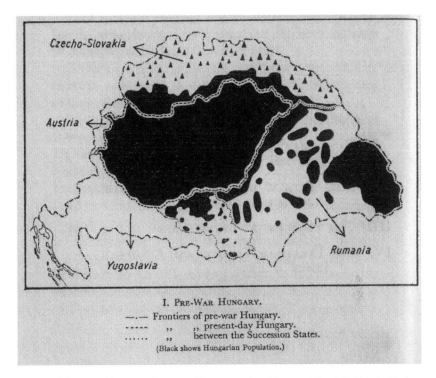

I. Pre-War Hungary.

—.— Frontiers of pre-war Hungary.
-----   ,,   ,, present-day Hungary.
......   ,,   between the Succession States.
(Black shows Hungarian Population.)

FIG. 6. Ethnographic map of prewar Hungary printed in a 1934 book by István Bethlen, who was among those representing Hungary at the post–World War I treaty negotiations. The map combines colored-in and population-density approaches, emphasizing the presence of Hungarians along the border with Hungary. István Bethlen, *The Treaty of Trianon and European Peace* (New York: Longmans, Green and Co., 1934), xix.

the entire territory of Transylvania was homogeneously Hungarian, so, like Apponyi, he emphasized the mass of Hungarians constituting an "absolute majority" on the eastern frontier.

Still, Bethlen had yet to exhaust the repertoire of arguments put forward by members of the Hungarian delegation to the peace conference in support of their claim on Transylvania.[184] Like them, he emphasized the "vitality" of the "Magyar race," and that it was thus not the *quantity* of a people alone that should matter in finding a suitable territorial settlement, but their relative *quality*.[185]

> The question [is] whether it is right and useful, or even compatible with the interests of civilization, to take the government of territories with an ethnically mixed population from the hands of the race showing a marked superiority over the oth-

ers both in cultural and in economic life and which, in possession of governmental skill and knowledge as well as of traditions, has been rightfully holding the power in that territory for centuries, and to hand over this power to the inferior race, from the moment when by a process of continuous immigration the race of these inferior newcomers happens to outnumber the aborigines?[186]

Hungarians were thus cast as having a particular capacity to govern which other neighborhood nationalities lacked. Teleki made a comparable argument in 1937, namely, that the "numerical proportion" of a population should not be the sole basis for territorial adjustment. Rather, "the vitality of the different elements or nationalities, their culture, religion and other factors must be taken into account."[187] When these were factored in, the clean "language boundaries" shown on maps like the Romanian ones based on the 1930 census could not be said to reveal the whole picture. During a meeting with Transylvanian elites in October 1940, Teleki declared: "My whole life I have struggled against the false conception that there exist territories that can be characterized by the presence of a single nationality."[188]

The various strategies used by Hungarian and Romanian cartographers, demographers, ethnographers, and politicians to represent Transylvania's ethnic composition and to use these representations to legitimate their claims on the region confirm the perceived link between territorial entitlement and population politics. Furthermore, the existence of these works published in French, English, and German, and often distributed by diplomatic means, reveals much about how these states understood the Transylvanian Question as one that could attract the interest—and ultimately precipitate the intervention—of "Europe."

Making a Case to the "New Europe"

The self-consciousness with which authors and statesmen undertook the publication and distribution of material on different aspects of the Transylvanian Question is clear from official reflections on their content and distribution. In September 1941, Romania's subdirector to the interior ministry's delegation in charge of relations with Hungary proposed the production of "informative brochures destined for foreign offices, political personages and the broader public" outlining the "idea of a unified Transylvania, its economic ties to Romania, the permanence of the Romanian element there . . . the incapacity of Hungary to rule over the territory," and so forth.[189] Just two months later, Croat diplomats in Sofia were already receiving such brochures from their Romanian counterparts and noting how the Hungarian ambassador was lecturing the Bulgarian press on how to best represent Hungary's interests.[190]

In November 1942, a Hungarian diplomat in Bucharest wrote to Pál Balla, council to the foreign minister, that "the Romanian scholarly propaganda is much more prolific and, unfortunately, at first glance of much higher quality than ours" and was "capable of leading Western European public opinion astray."[191] He proposed stepping up the publication of visual propaganda in particular. In October 1943, József Balogh, editor of periodicals published in French and English on Hungarian affairs, complained that "Trianon introduced us to a terrifying new enemy: the propaganda aimed against us. . . . [It has] already once defeated us. And what happened yesterday could be repeated again tomorrow."[192]

The idea that propaganda had a demonstrated power to move boundaries was shared by politicians and diplomats in Romania. In July 1940, the Slovak ambassador to Bucharest observed that the Romanian foreign ministry was engaged in intensive study of Hungarian propaganda—especially maps—from 1919 as a model for their own anti-revisionist propaganda campaign.[193] Ion and Mihai Antonescu were quick to continue along this course following their rise to power. In a cabinet council meeting on October 4, 1940, the discussion turned to the Hungarian propaganda success and Romanian propaganda's relative lack of "organization." Ion Antonescu declared propaganda to be "a new army" upon which "the future of the state depended." He told his minister of foreign affairs, Mihail Sturdza, to "put [his] diplomats to work" in the interest of reversing the "injustice" done to Romania with the Vienna Arbitration.[194] Nor would this be the last attempt to organize and coordinate Romanian propaganda around the Transylvanian Question.

In his capacity as Romanian propaganda minister, Mihai Antonescu initiated a much more systematized effort to gather information in preparation for the upcoming peace conference. On June 16, 1942, he called together specialists from the administration and academic intelligentsia and formed a commission consisting of seven sections, each with between six to thirty members. The sections were as follows: 1. Historical (thirteen members); 2. Press and propaganda (twenty-three); 3. Ethnic, biological, and statistical (eleven); 4. Political (thirty); 5. Juridical (fifteen); 6. Economic (sixteen); 7. Financial (six). In his address to those gathered, the propaganda minister emphasized that Hungary's success in achieving territorial revision was not a result of the war, but of effective "international propaganda," and that the fate of all states in the future would depend not only on their success in battle, but also on their "power of persuasion, force of conviction, and presentation of the truth." The problem of Transylvania, he stressed, was of particular importance, one that required the compilation of "documentary material" so that "we have it ready at the moment of the peace."[195]

Members of the Hungarian administration noted such initiatives with mounting outrage and horror. Thus, a status report on the situation in Kolozsvár sent to Hungarian council to the foreign minister Pál Balla and interim foreign minister László Bárdossy on October 20, 1941, reads as follows:

> The whispering campaign still circulates the news of liberated Transylvania's upcoming reannexation [and] the "victorious" Romanian army's arrival. But the main emphasis of the propaganda is . . . on preparations for the permanent settlement of Europe's borders, information gathering, secret censuses, and generally on securing such intellectual weapons which will in some way serve to support or prove—by means of crude falsification of history and statistics—Romania's supposed historical right to Transylvania to those arbitrating the decision.[196]

Shortly thereafter, the political division of the Hungarian foreign ministry launched its own effort to systematically prepare for the future peace conference. The person put in charge of the initiative, István Kertész, was an official at the Hungarian embassy in Bucharest. In November 1942, the head of the political division, Aladár Szegedy-Maszák, drafted a memorandum outlining the desiderata for the peace conference dossier. Thereafter Kertész, much as Mihai Antonescu had done, sought out experts to fulfill the division's mandate. Unlike in the Romanian case, however, these individuals were contacted individually or in small groups, oftentimes in cafés or private homes, where they "received assignments without being informed of the scope and ultimate purpose of their endeavors."[197]

Like its Romanian counterpart, the Hungarian group was a combination of top-down directives and think-tank-like foment. It was charged with completing specific assignments initiated by the prime minister's office and the foreign ministry, but also with "gathering and processing basic documentary material" on its own initiative and "providing information on Hungarians and the nationalities, on Hungary and its neighbors which will aid in the scientific preparation for the postwar settlement." Among the first ministry-mandated assignments for the group was a comprehensive inventory of "atrocities and brutalities perpetrated against Hungarians in Romania" from 1918 to 1940, which was completed in March 1944. With its 143 pages, the document was the most extensive of all the completed assignments as of October 19, 1944. Meanwhile, the first study undertaken on the group's own initiative was a critical analysis—in German, Italian, French and English—of 29 Romanian ethnographic maps, showing their "falsifications and distortions." [198]

In neither case were the Axis powers the only target of such propaganda.

At the same time the Romanian foreign ministry was sending propaganda brochures to its fellow Axis ally Bulgaria, it was also instructing the Romanian legation in Washington, D.C., on strategies for countering Hungarian propaganda in the U.S.[199] In 1942 Romanian sociologist Anton Golopenția complained—somewhat disingenuously given that he was involved in similar activities for the Romanian state at the time—that "Hungarian experts" were engaged in the production of political propaganda regarding the "historical rights [and] European mission of the Hungarian state, . . . Hungary's contribution to the civilizing of peoples with whom it finds itself in conflict." That propaganda could be found in multiple versions abroad, "published in numerous periodicals, among which were many in the most widely used languages in the world."[200]

Two diplomats in particular, the Hungarian György Barcza and the Romanian Raoul Bossy, practically tripped over each other as they sought to win over British, American, and even Soviet agents and statesmen to their respective states' causes.[201] The peace, when it came, and whoever brought it, would be based on a predictable set of principles—a combination of national and historical rights, minority issues, the demographic principle, and the desire to fashion a "new Europe" after the war, one that would amend injustices and relieve tensions, one that would need both leaders and supporters.

Just as Hitler spoke often of the "New European Order," so too did the Allies struggle to conceptualize an alternative vision, one that would ultimately claim to solve the same problems. In 1941, a journal called *New Europe* appeared, published in New York with an editorial staff made up predominantly of exiles from France, Poland, and other areas of occupied Europe. The editors explained the purpose of *New Europe* to its readers: "Europe is shaken in her deepest moral and material foundations. The changes wrought in her will be lasting. The European body-politic has been permanently altered. Its reshaping is a responsibility and a duty we owe to those who have died so that the world could be freed from spiritual serfdom. However, we must beware of losing the second world peace in the manner of the post-Versailles experience."[202]

Yet the shape an Allied "new Europe" was to take remained unclear. In October 1941, John Wheeler-Bennett wrote an article in *New Europe*'s pages openly wondering: "What have we to offer as an alternative" to the Nazi "'New Order'? [F]rankly we cannot offer any blueprint. . . . Through the gloom of battle and suffering—we grope towards the dawn."[203] In a 1941 book Louis Adamic lamented: "Since Hitler there haven't been any new ideas in Europe worth mentioning. . . . There is as yet no idea beyond hatred of Hitler with which to challenge his 'New Order.'"[204]

The Atlantic Charter of 1941 was crafted to address this embarrassing void, but its main novelty was an express interest in the "equality of states," which was infinitely more appealing from the perspective of the exiled governments of a nonexistent Poland or an occupied Czech Protectorate than to Hungary and Romania, both of which already enjoyed a kind of de facto equality within the Axis system. In fact, in a conversation with the Slovak ambassador to Romania in mid-May of 1942, Romanian diplomat Vasile Stoica commented that the "difference between the Atlantic Charter and the position of Berlin and Rome is not great and is likely to grow even smaller as the war continues."[205]

Part of the lack of clarity on the Allied side regarding the content of an Allied "new Europe" can be explained in terms of the ambiguity inherent in the Axis vision, an ambiguity fostered by the German leadership. In April 1940, Goebbels told the German press: "If anyone asks how do you conceive the new Europe, we have to reply that we don't know. . . . Anybody can interpret it as they wish."[206] By the autumn of 1942, leaders in the Axis camp—from the Antonescus to Ribbentrop—had begun to lament the lack of content in the German vision for a New European Order.[207]

Because the goals and rhetoric associated with both Allied and Axis "new Europes" were indistinct, propaganda efforts of states like Hungary and Romania did not require much tailoring to German or Allied tastes, as these were effectively the same as far as the factors that would determine the fate of Hungary, Romania, and Transylvania were concerned. According to an article entitled "Hungary in the 'New Europe,'" published in August 1941,

> Everybody knows that all of those plans going into the engineering of the newly constructed Europe are merely theories, since for the time being we cannot know which forces will be the ones to bring this new organism into being. There is nevertheless something comforting about those theoretical conceptions. For example, that the reordering powers of today do not want to sit at the [peace] conference table so that they can act under the influence of malicious propaganda without being familiar with the situation, as they did after the last war.[208]

Both the Axis and the Allies pinned their hopes on a "new Europe" that would emerge after the war and out of the war, so the idea of a "new Europe" stood like a vessel waiting to be filled with content and meaning depending on who could reach it first.[209]

Hungarian and Romanian statesmen, minorities, and state-enfranchised nationalities all had plans for what the "new Europe" should look like, and it is not surprising that those plans addressed particular regional concerns. The content of Hungarian and Romanian propaganda since World War I thus changed little from the interwar period to the Second World War, always gravitating toward a series of themes and preoccupations that the two states understood to be decisive in determining who had the right to claim Transylvania and the bases for that claim.

TRANSYLVANIA AS A "EUROPEAN PROBLEM"

On August 11, 1942, the lord lieutenant of Szolnok-Doboka County in Hungary wrote a letter to the head of the German-Italian Officers' Commission, which was undertaking a fact-finding mission on the situation of minorities in Northern and Southern Transylvania at the time. The letter began by suggesting that the "nature of the problems" of the minorities was such that they "have a partially diplomatic character." The report continued with a brief history lesson for the commissioner. In centuries past, he wrote,

> Magyardom took an understanding and tolerant position vis-à-vis Romanians; perhaps much too tolerant, such that it was possible, over the course of centuries, for many hundreds of thousands of Hungarians living here to become Romanians. This is in conjunction with the fact that magyardom bled and was weakened in centuries-long battles for Western culture. Hence the Romanians—who immigrated or lived in the safety of the mountains—could influence and romanize the national consciousness of a plundered and weakened magyardom.[210]

At the same time the letter was drafted, the Romanian press and radio were reporting on the Romanian state's "exaggerated kindness" toward the Hungarian minority and the "limitless freedom" Hungarians and other minorities enjoyed during the interwar period.[211] "Between the Danube and the Tisza we have been the granite protective barrier of civilization and Christendom against eastern threats."[212] These and other articles and broadcasts of the Romanian press and radio were gathered by the Hungarian foreign ministry, translated into German, and compiled as evidence of anti-Hungarian propaganda in Romania, again to make the case that the territory should belong to Hungary.[213]

The marked similarities between the arguments of the two sides, coupled with attempts to discredit the position of the other state in the eyes of the Great Powers—in this case Germany—were characteristic features of propaganda around the Transylvanian Question. Ever frustrated by the likelihood that the Transylvanian Question would be relegated to the status of a regional, as opposed to a continental issue, the two states' leaders lobbied hard to cast Transylvania's fate as a matter of pan-European importance.[214]

As demonstrated earlier in this chapter, such efforts had precedents in the mid- to late nineteenth century. Hence it could not have come as a sur-

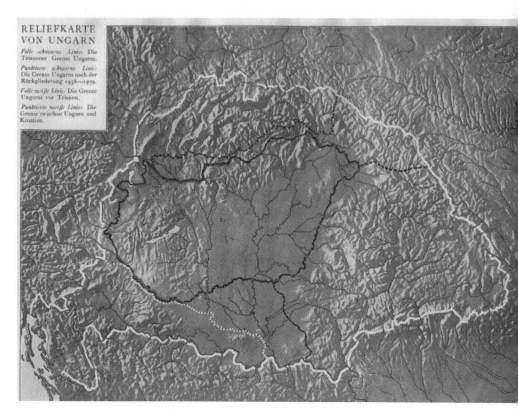

RELIEFKARTE
VON UNGARN

Volle schwarze Linie: Die
Trianoner Grenze Ungarns.

Punktierte schwarze Linie:
Die Grenze Ungarns nach der
Rückgliederung 1938—1939.

Volle weiße Linie: Die Grenze
Ungarns vor Trianon.

Punktierte weiße Linie: Die
Grenze zwischen Ungarn und
Kroatien.

FIG. 7. Hungarian relief map from 1940, showing how the old borders of the Hungarian Kingdom are natural boundaries defined by the Carpathian Basin. "Reliefkarte von Ungarn," in *Siebenbürgen* (Budapest: Ungarische Historische Gesellschaft, 1940), *8.

prise to those present at the peace conference in 1920, when the head of the Hungarian delegation sought to position the Transylvanian Question within a broader European context. "At first glance, the Transylvanian Question concerns only Hungary and Romania, but since both states also have contested interests with other states, the Transylvanian Question can easily become a first-order European question, and if it is resolved unfairly, the peace of the neighboring states and with it the peace of all Europe can be turned upside-down."[215] In 1931, Hungarian geographer-statesman Pál Teleki went further with this claim, arguing that "[territorial] revision is not just a demand of the defeated [of World War I], but a European physiological necessity [*élettani követelmény*]."[216] The assertion was in harmony with the attitudes of European diplomats and statesmen of the time, who maintained that "the preservation of peace is vastly more vital than is the grievance of any one nation."[217]

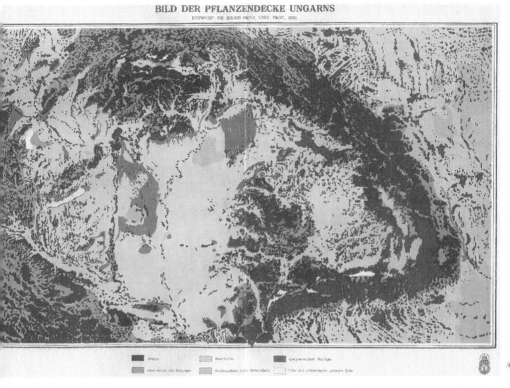

BILD DER PFLANZENDECKE UNGARNS

FIG. 8. Hungarian vegetation map from 1940, showing how the Hungarian plain is bracketed by forests serving as natural boundaries. Like the relief map, the vegetation map was used to legitimate revisionist claims. "Bild der Pflanzendecke Ungarns," in *Siebenbürgen* (Budapest: Ungarische Historische Gesellschaft, 1940), *10.

Beyond the "Europeanization" of the conflict over Transylvania, other common themes included topographic and historical justifications for state and regional boundaries, territorial primacy (who settled Transylvania first), treatment of minorities (our side treats them too well, their side treats them badly), the European interest (who has served it better throughout history) and civilization (who represents it better), and finally, demographic injustice and the imperfect realization of "national self-determination" (generally coupled with representations of census data or a critique of the "Versailles system").

Both bodies of state propaganda backed up claims to territory with arguments about the "naturalness" of state boundaries, where "natural" was understood in terms of geographical, climatological, and other physical features of the landscape, including the drainage of river systems, the shape of mountain ranges, and the types of vegetation. "It is an undeniable truth that nature created Transylvania to be in symbiosis with Hungary," we read in an article entitled "Transylvania" from a 1940 Hungarian public affairs journal. "This is determined above all by the Carpathians which bind the two lands together, as a castle wall binds together multiple ramparts. Furthermore, beyond the Carpathians are territories with no natural boundaries, . . . within the Carpathians is a unified, geographically framed country."[218] Hungarian propaganda starting with the peace treaty negotiations after World War I thus emphasized "the self-contained unity of the Carpathian Basin," using relief and vegetation maps to show that Hungary's prewar borders followed the natural contours of the landscape.[219]

Romanian propaganda countered this logic in numerous venues, including several German-language publications from 1939 to 1940, one of which called Transylvania "a nature-given supplement to Romanian living space."[220] A similar publication from 1943 draws on the historical etymology of the Hungarian word for Transylvania, Erdély, coming from "*erdő elé*," or "beyond the forest." "The fact that the Hungarians called Transylvania 'the country beyond the forests' proves that in wishing to establish themselves in this land which stretched eastwards of them, they had to penetrate the natural obstacles on the western frontier of the former province of Dacia, that is, the enormous forests which rolled eastwards to the crest of the Carpathians."[221] Instead of focusing on the forest and mountains around the Carpathian Basin, Romanian commentators thus focused on the stretch of forest between Hungary proper and the former Principality of Transylvania. This representation provided geographical substantiation for the assertion that "from the Remotest times, Transylvania had no real, homogeneous ties with the Hungarian state. It formed a principality apart; at a certain period it was attached to the realm of Wallachia and Moldavia, as it was later to that of Hungary."[222]

Romanian propaganda was further centered around historical maps of the Principality of Transylvania and the political boundaries that historically separated it from the Kingdom of Hungary.[223] In 1940, a series of seventeenth- and eighteenth-century maps was reprinted in a Romanian propaganda booklet published in English. They showed the Principality of Transylvania together with the principalities of Moldavia and Wallachia, with Hungary off the edge of the map to the left or not pictured at all. By their chosen center, these maps suggested the principalities were part of a regional nexus, if not a geopolitical unit.

In drawing out historical precedents for the inclusion of Transylvania within their boundaries, Hungarian and Romanian sources emphasized different episodes in the region's history. For Romania, the initial precedent was the province of Dacia within the Roman Empire. This province encompassed much of the territory of present-day Romania and was initially inhabited by the Dacians, who were later romanized. Romanian historians claimed the Romanians were direct descendants of these romanized Dacians, a version of events that is generally called the theory of Daco-Roman continuity. Hungarian historiography, on the other hand, argued that, around the year 270, Dacians ceased to be mentioned in the sources. Their absence from the historical record after that date, coupled with the Hungarian roots of many Transylvanian place names, implied that the ancestors of modern-day Romanians were not present in the region when the Magyar tribes arrived some six centuries later.[224] During World War II, Hungarian and Romanian ethnographers, archaeologists, and historians fought a pitched academic battle over the reliability of the evidence supporting their respective claims.[225]

Yet, as in the case of demographic data, the question of who settled in Transylvania first was often overshadowed in international propaganda efforts by the question of who settled it better. Arguments regarding the qualitative historical attributes of the Hungarians and Romanians abounded, manifestations of the influence of Darwinism on the discipline of geography.[226] Significantly, these qualitative assessments regularly reflected on the two nations' levels of "civilization" and "European-ness." The portrayal of the Hungarian or Romanian nation as the protective buffer for Western civilization through centuries of assaults by non-Christian—mostly Mongol and Ottoman—invaders from the South and East was a recurring theme in these assessments. Their nations' historical sacrifices, the propaganda suggested, allowed the West to develop as it did and meant that the West owed something to its self-sacrificing buffer peoples: it owed them "justice."[227]

Among the positive traits ascribed to Hungarians and Romanians in the propaganda literature were civility, loyalty, and generosity. Both claimed to represent a higher, more "European" form of civilization than the other and regularly described one another as culturally "Asiatic" or "un-European," stereotypes that paralleled those ascribed to Jews and Soviets in both countries, and a common trope in German anti-Semitic and anti-Soviet propaganda. In a history of Romania prepared by a Hungarian historian in 1938, the author commented on how Europeans would find all but the most educated Romanians "foreign" to European culture and civilization.[228] The fact that Hungary had obtained Northern Transylvania from Romania, a Hungarian commentator noted in a newspaper article in August 1941, meant that "Western Europe" now reached into the Carpathians. "Western Europe can thank Hungary for this" as Europe's "eternal eastern border guard" and defender of "civilization, order [and] the rule of law."[229] The article went on to describe the "Asian" threats of "bloody tyranny" and "eternal war" that lay in wait just beyond Hungary's eastern borders, implying that Romanians were incapable of running a stable state.[230]

In a similar move, Romanian sociologist Anton Golopenția questioned Hungary's "biopolitical preoccupation" with Transylvania in the journal *Geopolitica și Geoistoria* [Geopolitics and Geohistory] in 1942. "Does Europe need to guarantee its civilization vis-à-vis Eastern forces through the strengthening of its 'eastern boundaries' with semi-asiatic, non-Aryan elements? . . . The leaders of Europe—who have no regard for peoples that conceal their own decline and fill their hollowness with colonists and exotics—will hardly allow it."[231] A Romanian radio commentator in 1942 was more explicit: "The Hungarians came from Asia . . . and have stayed Asian for a thousand years, spreading an Asiatic air without absorbing the Latinate culture" as the Romanians had.[232]

As was the case with German propaganda of the time, such designations were crafted to bear on the fate of Europe as well. According to one Romanian newspaper in 1942, "The New European Order must be understood as a concrete expression of the new world which will be born from the combined values of the truly European nations. We are speaking of nations with European spirits, and not of the latifundia that sprang from . . . Asia's discharged magnates."[233] The article explained that the New European Order will only be achieved when a "new Europe" includes Romania "in its full and complete size," as it was prior to 1940, including the territories that it lost to Hungary with the Second Vienna Arbitration.

The newspaper's allusion to the "New European Order" was echoed many times over in the Hungarian and Romanian press and propaganda. The only goal of the war, wrote Hungarian right-wing politician and publicist György Oláh in the spring of 1941, was to see to it that, when the war ended, "Europe's future is rebuilt on firm foundations."[234] During the period of their alliance with the Axis, both states' leaders were conscious of being part of Hitler's *neue europäische Ordnung* in the making, one that was built on the ruins of the post–World War I "Versailles system" and promised to make up for that system's failures.

In July 1941, the Hungarian foreign ministry drafted a statement on the nationalities question in Transylvania in which the author reminded readers that the Hungarian minority had "suffered every imaginable political humiliation, economic exploitation, and cultural oppression in Romania for twenty-one years in line with the spirit of the Versailles Europe."[235] At about the same time, a leader of the Hungarian minority in Romanian Southern Transylvania complained that "Europe was only once 'organized' in accordance to the principle—or better, the pretext—of national self-determination and ethnography at the peace conferences around Paris. It is unfortunate for Europe . . . that this principle soon . . . became a political tool in the hands of the victorious Great Powers."[236] Meanwhile, a view repeatedly voiced by the Romanian press, politicians, and leadership was that the postwar peace had given Romanians a state but had stunted their ability to consolidate and defend it. In a speech delivered during a parliamentary assembly meeting on April 4, 1934, Romania's National Peasant Party leader and former prime minister, Iuliu Maniu, lamented the lack of security the peace settlement had given to Greater Romania in the face of revisionist neighbors' claims on the newly acquired territories.

> We expect this peace settlement to give the Romanian people the assurance of fixed boundaries and the peace of mind necessary for productive work and the pacification of souls led seriously astray during the course of nearly two thousand years by the immigration of so many peoples so eager in their aspirations to exploit Romanian lands and to denationalize the native population. Nevertheless, it is with great sadness that we must ascertain that these hopes have not been realized to the extent we wished.[237]

Some years later, in a wartime speech, Mihai Antonescu declared that the outcome of World War I represented a "military" and "spiritual" victory for Romania but could not form the basis for a lasting order.[238]

Just as both countries felt slighted by the "Versailles system," both also sought to represent the vanguard of the forces charged with bringing a new order into being. A 1940 Hungarian propaganda document translated into English for Allied consumption and seeking to justify Hungary's territorial demands on Romanian territory complained that Romania "slipped through the solving of the Transylvanian Question 'smoothly,' and in contrast to the fate-like end of the other Versailles creations, . . . retained more than half of their Trianon booty."[239] A Transylvanian member of parliament later declared that the "historical, political, and moral value-judgments" upon which the post–World War I peace was built "cannot be the foundation for the new Europe."[240]

Hungarian vanguardism was often accompanied by accusations that the Romanian state was still clinging to the old, defunct Versailles system. Thus in response to a 1941 Romanian memorandum, the Hungarian government responded: "The Romanian government still lives in the mistaken belief that it is a member of the . . . Little Entente and the eastern guard of the Paris-area peace dictates and can thus . . . subordinate Hungary and freely continue the oppression of the Hungarian minority [in Transylvania]."[241] The new Europe, in the Hungarian interpretation, was founded on the destruction and elimination of the old. Romania's attack on the rectitude of the Second Vienna Arbitration was thus "an attack on one of the first decisions of the New European Order."[242]

Romanian interest in Hitler's "New European Order" was linked less to the destruction of the old than to the creation of a new, better system that would iron out the inconsistencies and enforce the ideals of the old one. In his letter to Mussolini dated December 28, 1940, Iuliu Maniu opined that "whatever this [new] order should be, it cannot be a return to the pre-1914 Europe or that of the Middle Ages, which recognized a feudal Hungarian state. Hungarians, it seems, interpret the New European Order thus."[243] Some propaganda efforts made even more explicit links between the "old" interwar order and the "new" European order. In June 1942, the following could be heard over the airwaves from the "Greater Romania" radio station: "The new Europe is coming together. Whether it is called the 'Little Entente' or something else is not of the least importance. In any case it destroys all those who seek to realize their imperialist dreams in Central Europe."[244] The station made frequent allusions to Hungary's efforts to prevent the creation of a better Europe. "On the one hand there is the sacred conviction that justice is a condition and element of the New European Order; on the other side is the attempt to overturn all the borders of Europe. It is clear who is fighting for the just Europe and who is fighting against it."[245] Transcripts of these and other broadcasts and clippings from the Romanian press were translated into German by Hungarian authorities as a means to discredit Romania for waging a propaganda war against Axis-allied Hungary and, by extension, against the New European Order itself.

One intriguing aspect of "New European Order" propaganda crafted to mimic German rhetoric and aspirations is how disconnected it was from the war with the Allies. Critiques were of the Versailles *system*, not of France, England, or the United States, and mention of the Soviet Union or Bolshevism was rare. Presumably this was in part because the revision of Versailles through the Munich Agreement received the blessing of Great Britain, and many British, French, and American statesmen favored a "just" revision of the treaties. Furthermore, Hungarian and Romanian commentators rarely condemned the *principles* on which the post–World War I "new Europe" was based, merely their incomplete or ill-conceived application. Both states continued propaganda efforts targeting the Western Allies during World War II, and as is apparent from the above examples, the critique of the Versailles system was generally a thinly veiled means of casting Hungarian-Romanian tensions in terms the Great Powers could understand and accept. The underlying assumption was that the war would "save" Europe by making it more cohesive and just. A Romanian newspaper from July 1942 thus asserted that "the Romanian nation fights and works honorably and loyally on the side of the Führer for the salvation of Europe and in the interest of the European community."[246]

Indeed, "justice" was generally understood in national—often explicitly ethnodemographic—terms, adapted from the post–World War I emphasis on national self-determination. In the Romanian literature, it meant the creation of a Romania that was "powerful, unified, in possession of its historical lands, supported by the integrity of its full national range and therefore by all of its material resources and biological powers." Such a Romania, it was argued in a newspaper article in 1942, was "a European necessity."[247] Restoring Romania's pre–World War II borders meant undoing the Second Vienna Arbitration, which had given Northern Transylvania to Hungary.[248] The injustice of the revision made Hungary "the only barrier to the peaceful harmony of the peoples of Europe," and thus "not yet mature enough for the New European Order."[249]

In the Hungarian definition of the new Europe's essence, we can discern many similar themes. The main difference was in the perception of which were the "truest" of Europe's historical boundaries. In Hungary's case, they were the boundaries of the old Hungarian Kingdom, the restoration of which was "not just a German and Hungarian imperative, but an imperative and condition of Europe's future," according to a 1931 speech delivered by Pál Teleki.[250]

In a definition of national self-determination offered in a 1940 Romanian propaganda pamphlet on the injustice of the Second Vienna Arbitration, the author used the definition to justify Romania's right to "unite all Romanians under a single nation-state."[251] Just as a "powerful, unified" Romania grounded in the "biological powers of the nation" was a "European necessity" in Romanian eyes, so did Hungarian diplomats and statesmen argue for the strengthening of Hungarians and the Hungarian state in the interest of the new Europe. In December 1941, Hungarian prime minister László Bárdossy delivered a speech in which he declared that, in order to become part of the New European Order, Hungarians had to "emphasize their national uniqueness."[252]

A member of the Hungarian Transylvanian Party, Gyula Zathureczky, was even more explicit in a piece published in the fall of 1942 entitled "Hungary's Position in Europe." After citing Hitler as having said that "everyone must make the ideas and demands of the time their own," he went on to conclude that "this means that we have to keep, nurture, and develop our Hungarianness, because . . . only in this way can we live in Europe with the calling and duty that we have lived with until now, and without which we cannot live at all."[253] Zathureczky had argued a few months earlier that "Hungary will have a special role and particular task in the newly ordered Europe. It can only fulfill this role and task if it has free control over all the material and spiritual powers that are its attributes and its possessions."[254]

So it was that statesmen in both Hungary and Romania posited the need for strong nation-states in which "national particularities" could be emphasized to the benefit of Europe.[255] According to a 1942 Hungarian propaganda bulletin, "from the standpoint of the whole of Europe it is of foremost importance who has possession of Transylvania, who stands as a reliable guard on that bastion: the Hungarian or the Romanian."[256]

Casting the Transylvanian Question as one that affected "European peace" and touched on "European interests" was a self-conscious propaganda strategy on the part of Hungarian and Romanian statesmen. In his 1942 consultations with Romanian intellectuals, Mihai Antonescu stressed the need to link Romania's territorial aspirations to European interests. In the dossier the state would compile for the coming settlement—be it Axis or Allied—Romania needed to show that Hungary's historical interests were incompatible with those of the New European Order, and also to "present the problems of Transylvania through a European lens, viewed within the framework of European experience and the need for European reconstruction, not only Romanian [reconstruction]."[257]

The "European lens" was nevertheless a shifty optic, for it was trained on these states, their pasts and futures, just as state leaders in Hungary and Romania strove to attract its focus to particular issues. There is a palpable paranoia in much of the political writing of the time—and indeed since the last decades of the nineteenth century—that "Europe" might be getting the wrong impression or focusing on the wrong things. A 1942 article in the official organ of the German-Hungarian Society addressed the issue of the "Image of Hungary in Europe," closing with the fear that "Europe" had come to see Hungary as a "tyrannical" nation, especially as it stood up to the interests of its neighbors.[258] In a memorandum from spring 1940, former Hungarian prime minister István Bethlen argued for the need to present Hungarian interests as crucial for determining the outcome of the peace:

> There can be no doubt that at the end of the current war, the victor will redraw the map of Europe and create a New European Order. For that reason Hungary must do all that it can so that when that time comes, the victor honors the interests of the Hungarian nation. . . . It is essential for us to get to know the intentions of the two opposite sides as they relate to the coming reordering of Europe; and if those intentions do not sufficiently take into consideration Hungarian interests, we must

act now, by both official and unofficial channels, to convince the side in question to change its conception if it wants a lasting peace, and to win it over to our conception.[259]

Bethlen thus emphasized the importance of convincing *both* sides, rather than simply choosing the one that took Hungarian interests more seriously. Hungarian member of parliament János Makkai clearly agreed:

> Today Hungary is an independent and sovereign state whose foreign policy is determined by its ethnic interests, its national and human ideals, and its place in Europe. . . . Now every great European nation is clear on the fact that Hungary has to be considered in the coming organization of Europe. The lessons of the past and the tasks of the present demand that we realistically view our own calling and that we appreciate the strength of Europe's chief ideas and ideals.[260]

Hungary's prime minister from 1942 to 1944, Miklós Kállay, showed an especially explicit indifference to the matter of who won the war when he said that "Hungary would cease to have any reason for continuing to be a belligerent the moment her national, 'popular,' territorial, and spiritual integrity was guaranteed. She would adhere to any side which guaranteed these things, but them she could not betray."[261] In fact, already in December of 1941, Hungarian censors were instructed not to allow the publication of any assertion that the victory of one or the other side in the war was certain.[262] "Let us wait to see how the war ends [and] who is the victor," said Hungary's interior minister, Ferenc Keresztes-Fischer, in a speech before the Hungarian parliament on November 16, 1942.[263]

In March 1942 Romania's prime minister, Mihai Antonescu, made no bones about what the Romanian leadership's primary goals were. Even when speaking to German officials, he maintained that "the only goal of his [Antonescu's] policies and his life is the winning back of Northern Transylvania. All of his thoughts and deeds are directed toward this goal."[264] As for Ion Antonescu himself, in a cabinet meeting on September 21, 1940, when his own and his government's enthusiasm for the alliance with Germany was especially high, he told his ministers that "we will go one hundred percent unto death alongside the Axis. Either we will triumph with the Axis, or we will fall with the Axis. . . . However, it goes without saying that I want to reverse the Vienna Arbitration, and I am preparing a campaign for world public opinion."[265]

Ion Antonescu's political nemesis, Iuliu Maniu, shared the view that influencing "world public opinion" in the matter of Romania's "rights" was of particular importance. He constantly pushed the Antonescus to think ahead to the coming peace, regardless of who should preside at the table. On April 1, 1941, Maniu told Romanian demographer Sabin Manuilă:

However long and horrible the war is, some day it has to end, and it is certain that the final outcome will be fixed at a peace conference composed of important personalities, who will represent especially the Great Powers. It is thus of supreme importance that informative material regarding the Romanian people should on the one hand be compiled and systematized, but also gathered successively up until the peace conference. Above all, the decisive factors should be presented at the conference in a convincing manner.[266]

Manuilă would later serve on the "Statistical and Ethno-Biological Section" of Mihai Antonescu's effort to gather documentation for the peace.

Conclusion

The Romanian delegation to the Paris Peace Conference in 1946 came prepared with a massive arsenal of documentation. Some of that documentation had been compiled under the direction of Mihai Antonescu, who, after being sentenced to death for war crimes by a people's tribunal in May 1946, was executed by firing squad on June 1, together with Ion Antonescu. One of the items in the Romanian delegation's dossier at the peace conference was the colored-in "Ethnographic map of Roumania" based on the 1930 census, the very same one found in Sabin Manuilă's 1938 *Ethnographical Survey of the Population of Romania*.[267]

Yet the continuities do not end there. In the case of Mihai Antonescu, it is worth noting that among his interwar published works were several works on international law, a book about the Romanian land reform and the Hungarian optants question, and a two-volume study of the League of Nations system, in which he criticized the League for being insufficiently vigorous and assertive.[268] A copy of that work was given to the Library of Congress in 1934 as a gift of the Carnegie Endowment for International Peace.[269] This is the same man who was to become a key political leader during the period of Romania's alliance to the Axis and would later try to spring Romania from that alliance to join the Allies.

Even Ion Antonescu, destined to become "Hitler's favorite ally," earned his stripes leading Romanian forces against the Central Powers in World War I, planned the Romanian invasion of Hungary in 1919 that brought Romanian soldiers into the city of Budapest, and participated as a delegate to the peace conference in Paris after World War I.[270] He served as military attaché to France and Great Britain between 1922 and 1926, and as of 1936, he was known for his outspokenly "pro-French" orientation. In fact, he spoke French with Hitler.[271] Furthermore, when in the late fall of 1940 his Legionnaire foreign minister

Mihai Sturdza suggested British historian R. W. Seton-Watson's Romanian government stipend be discontinued on the grounds that Seton-Watson was a "democrat" and working for British intelligence, Ion Antonescu intervened to perpetuate the stipend. In his December resolution to that end, he wrote, "Seton-Watson has been a good friend of Romania. He always supported us in the matter of Transylvania. His democratic activities don't interest me."[272]

The biography of one backstage figure whose career spanned this time period reaffirms the constancy of preoccupation with the competition for territory irrespective of the means by which it was institutionalized or the venues through which it was expressed. The sociologist Anton Golopenția was among the intellectuals invited to join the propaganda effort initiated by Mihai Antonescu in the summer of 1942. In that capacity he was assigned to work in the "Ethnic" section—Section 3, for "Biology and Statistics"—along with the demographer Sabin Manuilă and nine others.[273] Golopenția had studied in Geneva on a League of Nations fellowship in 1930, and his adviser during his university studies was none other than Dimitrie Gusti—the man heavily involved in the drafting of the 1923 Romanian constitution, specifically in defining the relationship between the "state" and "nation."[274]

During the negotiations preceding the Second Vienna Arbitration, Manuilă and Golopenția were charged with presenting the original material of the 1930 Romanian census to the arbitrators. Thereafter Golopenția participated in the preparation and analysis of the 1941 Romanian census and published a variety of works decrying the deceptions of Hungarian demographers as they related to Transylvania. From 1941 to 1944, he also served on the editorial committee of the new journal *Geopolitica și Geoistoria* [Geopolitics and Geo-history], which played up the nexus between "history, geography, sociology, demographics, and statistics" that had come to be considered so crucial as a means of justifying Romania's claims to the territories it had lost.[275] (Incidentally, this was also a field in which Golopenția's and Manuilă's Hungarian counterpart, Pál Teleki, played a similarly innovatory role[276]). Golopenția later served as statistical expert at the peace conference in Paris in 1946, where he made the case for Romania's demographic claim to Transylvania.[277]

Nor was Golopenția the only individual whose career highlights continuities across the war and postwar divide. Ion Christu was a member of the "Economic Section" of Mihai Antonescu's wartime information-gathering initiative and later became a Romanian minister and served in an advisory capacity to the delegates to the Paris Peace Conference.[278] The Transylvanian-born Romanian diplomat Vasile Stoica, who was active in propaganda production asserting Romania's right to Transylvania during World War I and who claimed in 1942 that he saw little difference between the Atlantic Charter and Hitler's New European Order, served as the general secretary in the Ministry of National Propaganda in the summer of 1940 (in which capacity he lobbied the U.S. and Great Britain to help preserve Romania's territorial integrity), and assisted in the preparation of documentation on Romania's minority rights record for the Paris Peace Conference.[279]

The case of Hungary is quite similar, for although historian István Deák has argued convincingly that "a basic trait of the Horthy era was political inconsistency," in one matter at least Hungarian politicians and statesmen were remarkably consistent, namely, in seeking means to recover part or all of the lost territories, foremost among which was Transylvania.[280] From the Moscow-trained Jewish Bolshevik Béla Kun to the pro-German right-wing extremist Béla Imrédy, the goal of recovering Transylvania was a central and unchanging feature of the political landscape in Hungary.[281] As one Hungarian diplomat said to the former Hungarian justice minister, on the matter of territorial revision, "the difference between us can only be in the means we find most appropriate at a given time for the achievement of our shared goal."[282]

It is hardly a coincidence that geographers, demographers, anthropologists, and historians were themselves statesmen—or that their services were enlisted by statesmen—seeking to influence the way the Transylvanian Question was ultimately resolved. The young fields of geopolitics and racial anthropology provided them with a critical forum for hammering out the relationship between individual, nation, and state to make more convincing arguments for national (re)unification. It is little wonder that individuals like Sabin Manuilă and Pál Teleki had their hands in both pursuits.[283] These individuals were less concerned with documenting the past and the present and more preoccupied with creating a blueprint for the future.

Reflecting on the legacy of Teleki shortly after his suicide, geographer Ferenc Fodor stressed Teleki's interest in geography and geopolitics. He wrote: "If political geography is the science of the past and only in part of the present, then geopolitics is only in part a science of the present, but mainly concerns itself with the future. [Teleki] considered geopolitics, as an independent science, to be more politics than geography."[284] In light of Teleki's forward-looking orientation, it seems appropriate that his life and work were memorialized with the creation of a research institute named after him. Beginning in 1943, the institute oversaw the gathering and synthesis of documentation for the postwar settlement. So it was that the material for the territorial and nationality questions used by the Hungarian delegation to the Paris Peace Conference in 1946 was prepared by experts at the Pál Teleki Institute for Political Science.[285]

CHAPTER TWO

"Why We Fight"

"You have demands, I suppose?"
"Yes."
"With regard to the U.S.?"
"No."
"Great Britain?"
"No."
"Russia?"
"No."
"So whom are you making demands of?"
"Romania."
"So you'll declare war on Romania?"
"No, Sir, we are allied with Romania!"
>   —U.S. official receiving Hungary's declaration of
>   war on the United States, December 13, 1941[1]

"Jawohl, Herr General! For Transylvania!"
>   —Romanian soldier's answer to German general Richard
>   Ruoff, who asked during a front inspection whether the
>   soldier knew what he was fighting for on the Eastern Front.[2]

On March 19, 1942, Romanian deputy prime minister Mihai Antonescu delivered a speech entitled "Why We Fight." In a German translation of the speech published that same year, just after the title page, a quote drawn from Antonescu's words hovers alone on an otherwise blank page. It reads, "We are not playing on all international arenas. We are banking on the honor and justice of the future Europe." In the speech, the prime minister emphasized that "we must win not only the war, but also the peace," concluding with a summary of Romania's historic and ongoing mission: "Never—*never!*—will our territory belong to anyone else besides our people or those born of our seed!"[3]

That same day, the new Hungarian prime minister and foreign minister, Miklós Kállay, delivered a speech before the Hungarian chamber of deputies in which he outlined the program of his war cabinet. In it he emphasized that

Hungary, far from serving foreign interests by committing itself fully to the Axis, "is above all fighting for Hungarian interests. . . . [W]e fight for a more just world order, a new Europe." Hungary, Kállay went on, "is no accidental state formation, but a historical, geographical, and cultural necessity," proven by the fact that Hungary had been called upon to take part in the creation of "the new Europe."[4]

On that day in March, Hungarian and Romanian leaders were intent on explaining why they had joined the Axis war effort. Both mentioned the creation of a new Europe wherein "justice" would prevail, evoking the viability of their states and the territory they encompassed. Yet the generalized assertions of these two men settle like a dense fog over the movement of troops and the machinations of governments, allowing only shadows and outlines through. The historian straying into this fog stumbles upon a strange war, and an even stranger answer to the question of "why we fight."

AUTUMN 1942

Although the big offensive had barely begun, already in early fall of 1942 morale among Germany's fighting partners on the Eastern Front was low. It was bitterly cold, and bombs and shells of the enemy mixed with those of their allies in an almost constant barrage. "Oh God, stop this terrible war," wrote a Hungarian corporal in his diary that September.[5] The situation nevertheless continued to deteriorate, and the war dragged on. Ad hoc cemeteries filled with mass graves of fallen soldiers dotted the landscape, and tens of thousands of Hungarian and Romanian soldiers were captured by the Soviets, such that by April 1943, both armies had sustained overall losses in excess of half their mobilized fighting forces on the Eastern Front.[6] A German situation report made on Christmas Day 1942 says that the Romanian soldiers had completely lost the will to fight.[7]

Complaints about the way the Germans treated their allied forces surfaced ever more frequently: empty German personnel vehicles refusing to pick up retreating Hungarian and Romanian troops; condescension and corruption among German officers; arbitrary confiscation of weapons, vehicles, and other equipment; failure to communicate critical information; disparity in rations and equipment distribution; harsh criticism in the face of devastating losses, and so forth.[8] Nor were the Germans pleased with what Field Marshal Gerd von Rundstedt called their "League of Nations army." The Hungarians "only wanted to get home again quickly and had no proper enthusiasm, even before the winter began," and the Romanian officers were "beyond description," utterly devoid of what another German field marshal called "'Prussian' breeding."[9]

But the Germans were starting to lose the war, and their allies felt it as much as their enemies did. In late December 1942, Romanian soldiers and officers wondered why they were fighting in Russia for Germany and Hitler when the Allies were clearly going to win.[10] And what did Romania want from the Soviet Union in the autumn of 1942? All the territory it had lost to the USSR in 1940 had already been recovered, and Romanian troops were now fighting a thousand kilometers away from Romania.[11] Already in January, the Slovak ambassador to Romania observed that Romanian public opinion was no longer convinced of the necessity to fight Bolshevism, especially as soldiers returning from the front and the formerly Soviet-occupied territories began telling their families back home that conditions in the USSR were in some respects better than in Romania.[12] Likewise, the Hungarian army chief of staff, Gyula Kovács, wrote in August 1942: "Neither the mobilized army nor probably the nation itself sees clearly what the goal or point of this war or our involvement in it is . . . ; we hate neither Bolshevism nor the Russians."[13]

After the Don offensive in winter 1942–43, with an Allied victory starting to loom on the horizon, the governments of Hungary and Romania tried to reach an agreement regarding the need to make common cause to fight the USSR. If the Allies win, they reasoned, the British and other Western allies would not be able to prevent the Soviets from entering East-Central Europe. A united front against the Soviets, in the interest of self-preservation, was one of the few options that remained. But as became clear from the negotiations, from the beginning the primary preoccupation of the two states' representatives was not with fighting Bolshevism, but with fighting each other. When the Hungarian delegate, Miklós Bánffy, showed up in the Romanian capital to discuss the matter on June 19, 1943—following a series of more indirect contacts starting in February—the Romanian delegate, Gheorghe Mironescu, immediately turned the discussion to the matter of Transylvania. Bánffy replied indignantly that he had not come to Bucharest to discuss territorial matters, and within two weeks the negotiations broke down definitively.[14]

What the negotiating parties were trying to prevent that June was a situation in which the Soviets succeeded in penetrating the Danubian Basin because "Romania and Hungary are only concerned with waiting for the right moment to begin the fight for Transylvania."[15] Indeed, for many that fight had already begun, and it was the impending German defeat that threatened to end it in a way neither state's leadership had anticipated.

THE BATTLE BEGINS

In late September 1938, Czechoslovakia was carved up by Nazi Germany with the blessing of Britain, France, and Italy. At that point the Romanian king, government, and opposition leaders agreed that forging closer ties with Germany was imperative for securing Romania's frontiers.[16] Following the Munich Agreement, Hitler agreed to give part of southern Slovakia back to Hungary with the Vienna Arbitration on November 2. Hungary had lost this territory to the new state of Czechoslovakia following the First World War. With the Vienna Arbitration, Hungarian revisionist aspirations were partially. These aspirations further encompassed a sizable piece of northeastern Yugoslavia and the vast territory of Transylvania to the east, which had been part of Romania since the end of the First World War.

The Munich Agreement and the Vienna Arbitration thus set an important precedent for a series of border changes that were to take place in East-Central Europe during the course of the war. Through them Hitler showed himself to be the one force in Europe willing and able to effect border shifts. It was not long before military action—as opposed to diplomatic negotiation—became the primary means of achieving those shifts, for Germany at least. In the spring of 1939 the Germans seized the western (mostly Czech) part of Czechoslovakia, allowing the remainder of what is now Slovakia to declare its independence from Czechoslovakia on March 14, 1939. Hungary acquired still more territory when Hungarian army forces entered Carpatho-Ukraine and other parts of eastern Slovakia.[17] The Hungarian leadership advocated the army's forceful entry into Carpatho-Ukraine partly to prevent Romania from occupying some of the region for itself. If Hungarian and Romanian troops were to meet in Carpatho-Ukraine, the result would be war between the two states.[18] Nevertheless, these acquisitions meant that Hungary was increasingly indebted to the Axis.[19] In December Hungarian prime minister Pál Teleki told the Hungarian ambassador to Britain, "Should Transylvania be returned, we shall bind ourselves in perpetuity to the Germans, who will then demand we pay the price. And that price will be fighting alongside them; the country itself will be the price paid for revision."[20]

In May 1940, the successful German offensive in the West reinforced the belief that Germany would win the war. When France surrendered on June 17, Teleki told the Hungarian parliament that "today . . . the Europe of Versailles and Trianon and the Paris-area peace conferences is no more. I believe the national assembly of the Hungarian nation . . . cannot let this moment pass without celebrating."[21] Hungary's leadership was thus emboldened to pursue further territorial revision with Axis assistance.[22] At a meeting with Hitler in Munich on July 11, Teleki told the Führer that of all the territories Hungary had lost after World War I, Transylvania was the one Hungarians valued the most.[23]

Fearing Transylvania would be Hungarian revisionists' next target, Romanian prime minister Armand Călinescu noted the "aggressive attitude of the Hungarian press and the radio stations of Budapest, [and] the concentration of masses of troops on the Romanian border." His response was to call in more men from the reserves; Romania, he said, would defend its borders at all costs.[24] At the beginning of April, the Romanian government engaged a Transylvanian Romanian, Vasile Stoica, as state subsecretary to the Propaganda Ministry, whose primary obligation was to lobby the United States and Great Britain in the interest of retaining Transylvania.[25] But the next blow came from the other direction. In the summer of 1940, the Soviet Union, with the consent of Hitler, annexed Bessarabia and Northern Bukovina from Romania. Romania's King Carol II came under fire from his former chief of staff, Ion Antonescu, who quoted the king's ministers as saying, "We are armed to the teeth" and "we won't cede a single furrow," meanwhile letting Bessarabia and Northern Bukovina go without firing a shot.[26]

By the second half of August, Hungary had twenty-three divisions parked near the border with Romania.[27] Direct negotiations between representatives of the two states to reach a settlement had ended in failure; the Romanians proposed a population transfer, and the Hungarians demanded territory.[28] Hitler decided, in the interest of avoiding a crisis in the Balkans, to invite Hungary and Romania to Vienna to resolve their dispute with the help of Axis arbitration. "All this is naturally to be accompanied by a threat," wrote Count Galeazzo Ciano, the Italian minister of foreign affairs, in his diary on August 26. "Whoever does not accept the advice will take upon himself all responsibility for future consequences."[29]

After meetings with the Hungarian and Romanian delegations, and after both sides had agreed to accept the terms of the arbitrated proposal unconditionally, the Axis delegates offered what they called "a synthesis between the ethnic and territorial principals."[30] A map and document outlining the terms of the Second Vienna Arbitration were presented on August 30. The arbitration gave the northern part of Transylvania—amounting to around forty-three thousand square kilometers, or about 40 percent of Transylvania—to Hungary. In terms of population, there were approximately 2.5 million people living in the territory to be annexed by Hungary; just over a million would declare themselves Romanian by nationality on the 1941 Hungarian census.[31] When the map was presented, Ciano reported, the Hungarians could not contain their joy. "Then we hear a loud thud. It was [the Romanian foreign minister Mihail] Manoilescu, who fainted on the table. Doctors, massage, camphorated oil. Finally he comes to, but shows the shock very much."[32]

In Romania there was widespread popular outrage at the territorial losses inflicted by the Second Vienna Arbitration.[33] Shortly after the decision was announced, a Romanian landowner in Northern Transylvania reportedly declaimed at a newspaper kiosk: "What do those thieving Hungarians want this time? . . . With what do they plan to make war? They've got nothing. . . . The Hungarian army is shit—worthless. It's got no benzene. In two days the Romanians could get to Budapest against such a horde."[34] Throughout late August and early September, demonstrators converged on Bucharest and the Transylvanian capital of Cluj. In Bucharest, a speaker demanded that "the entire country should be mobilized. Transylvania will not be surrendered."[35] And in Cluj—soon to be called by its Hungarian name, Kolozsvár—demonstrators declared that it was the "immutable will" of the Romanian people "to refute with utmost determination the dictate of Vienna which wants to give Transylvania to the Hungarians," insisting they would "defend Transylvania to the last."[36]

The demonstrators' message was conveyed to Carol II in a telegram, and it was largely due to the unpopularity of his government's decision to accept the terms of the Second Vienna Arbitration that the king was forced to abdicate on September 6. In the words of a Romanian delegate to the negotiations in Vienna, Valer Pop, "The sovereign lost a third of the country's territory without a fight. He was completely isolated and could not in the least measure count on the loyalty of the army."[37] Although Carol's young son, Mihai I, ascended to the throne, the new head of the country was really Ion Antonescu, a longtime military leader and statesman whom Carol II had called upon to form a government on September 4.[38]

By September 11, 1940, the Hungarian army had reached the Transylvanian capital, where soldiers discovered at the railway station that the sign bearing the name of the city had already been changed to its Hungarian form: Kolozsvár.[39] Four days later, on September 15, there was a parade of Hungarian and Italian military personnel and equipment, featuring the regent of Hungary, Miklós Horthy, on a white horse. The *New York Times* quoted Horthy's festive speech, in which he declared that he had never doubted this day would come. "It was not the force of arms that deprived us of this region, but Trianon. That sad period of Hungarian history is now ended."[40]

By now both countries' leadership had become convinced that allying themselves with Nazi Germany—the force that could move European borders—was the only thing to do.[41] For the longtime Francophile Teleki, the

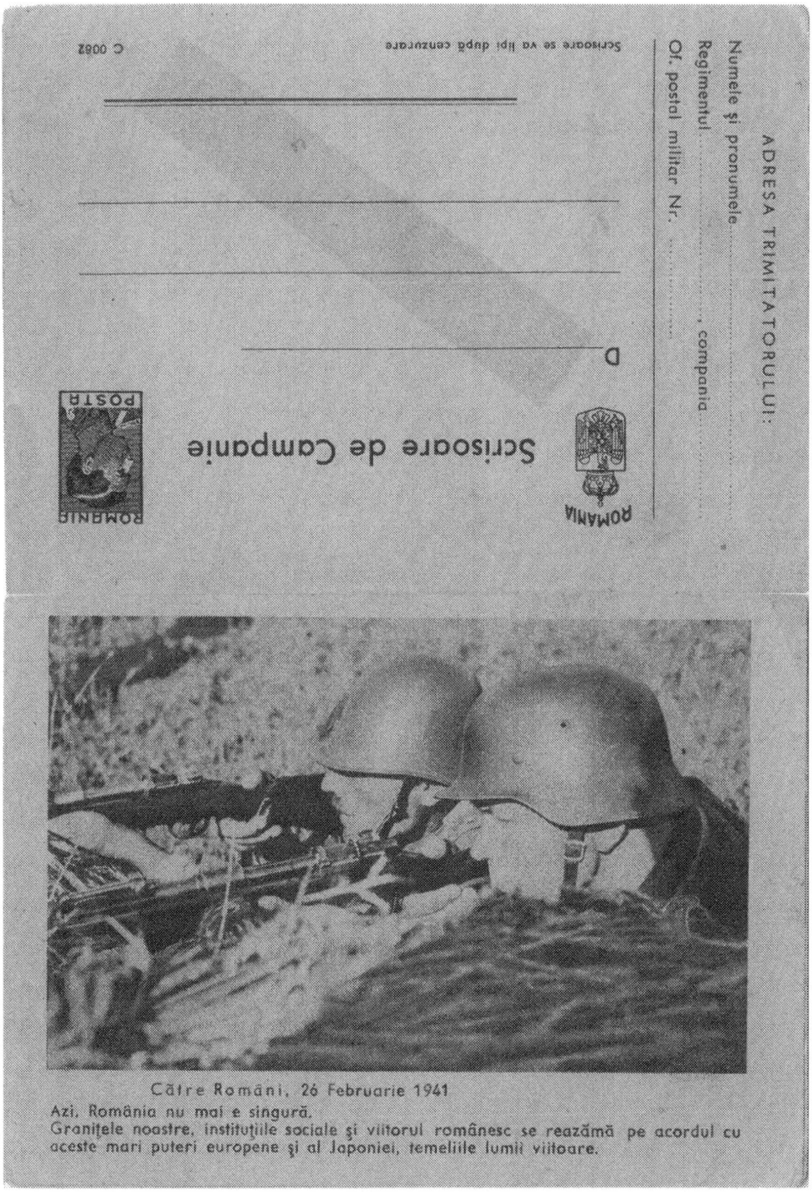
ADRESA TRIMITATORULUI:
Numele și pronumele
Regimentul ... compania
Of. poștal militar Nr.
ROMANIA
Scrisoare de Campanie
D
ROMANIA
POSTA
Scrisoare se va lipi după cenzurare
C 0082
Către Români, 26 Februarie 1941
Azi, România nu mai e singură.
Granițele noastre, instituțiile sociale și viitorul românesc se reazămă pe acordul cu aceste mari puteri europene și al Japoniei, temeliile lumii viitoare.

FIG. 9. Romanian military postcard of a Romanian and German soldier fighting side by side, citing Ion Antonescu's speech to the nation on February 26, 1941, in which he links the alliance with Germany to the security of Romania's borders. "Today, Romania is no longer alone. Our borders, social institutions, and the Romanian future are backed by our agreement with these great European powers and Japan, the foundations of the future world." From the collection of Dan Grecu; reprinted with permission.

Ostaşi! Pe umerii voştri apasă răspunderea asigurării prin luptă a drepturilor acestui neam.
Mareşalul Antonescu, Decemvrie 1940

FIG. 10. Romanian military postcard showing Romanian artillerymen and featuring an excerpt from a speech delivered by Ion Antonescu in December 1940. Antonescu called on soldiers to fight for the "rights of the nation." "Soldiers! Upon your shoulders rests the responsibility of securing the rights of this nation through battle." From the collection of Dan Grecu; reprinted with permission.

territorial gains made with the help of the Germans meant that Hungary's leaders owed Germany support. Antonescu—formerly himself an outspoken Francophile—saw two options: one was to wait for a future peace settlement to undo the Second Vienna Arbitration, and the other was to undo it through the force of arms.[42] Antonescu chose both. Romania would take up arms for the German war effort to achieve the status of favored ally so Hitler would give Transylvania back to Romania in a future peace settlement.

Hungary and Romania joined the Tripartite Pact within days of each other, with Hungary the first to join on November 20, 1940. Hungary's leadership at the time believed that being first would put the country in the position of "primus inter pares" vis-à-vis the other "small" allies, which within a few days included Romania and Slovakia, and later Bulgaria, Yugoslavia (briefly), and then Croatia.[43] Teleki and Hungarian foreign minister István Csáky even tried—albeit unsuccessfully—to make Hungary's joining the pact contingent

on a German promise to support the Hungarians' further revisionist aspirations.[44]

Romania joined three days after Hungary on November 23. During an
audience with Hitler, Antonescu did not hide the fact that the reannexation
of Northern Transylvania was his ultimate goal. Paul Schmidt, Hitler's interpreter, recalled: "Before he saw Hitler, it was drummed into him that he must
not say a word against the [Second Vienna] Arbitration. He spoke for two
hours about nothing else . . . He made long speeches just like Hitler, usually
starting off at the creation of Rumania, and somehow relating everything he
said to the hated Hungarians, and the recovery of Transylvania."[45] On returning to Bucharest on November 25, Antonescu announced that he had won
the trust of the German people and that, thanks to the alliance, "Romania
will have her rights."[46]

Hungarian and Romanian leaders thus sought to take advantage of German interests in the region to achieve their own foreign policy goals.[47] The
German leadership, meanwhile, sought to avert conflict between the two
states and use its mediating position to gain their support—military, economic, and moral—in the German war effort. Already in November 1938,
Germany's foreign minister Joachim von Ribbentrop had explained: "The
fundamental principle of our policy with respect to Hungary and Romania
must, for the time being, be to keep both irons in the fire and to shape things
in the German interest depending on how the situation develops."[48] Fully
aware of what Ribbentrop later called the "completely abnormal Hungarian-
Romanian attitude when it comes to Transylvania," the German leadership
alternately praised and scorned the two states' policies, often to their leaders'
faces, but mostly to the other state's leadership.[49] At Vienna, Ribbentrop
accused the Hungarians of running an anti-German policy and repeatedly
threatened them (as Ciano said, "Courtesy is not his forte"), while later settling the arbitration much to their satisfaction. Meanwhile, he recommended
himself to the Romanian delegation in Vienna as a "friend of Romania,"
later to devastate the Romanians with the scope of the territorial adjustment
they had been forced to accept in advance of the arbitration.[50] As for Hitler
himself, Ciano opined that "the only thing he has at heart is that peace be preserved there, and that Rumanian oil continue to flow into his reservoirs."[51]

WAR WITH THE SOVIET UNION

It was not until the German offensive against the Soviet Union in June 1941
that the question of the level of troop commitment to the Axis war effort

was seriously considered in Hungary and Romania. Leaders in both states believed that the "Axis powers would reward their allies to the extent that they take part in the war."[52] Having lost territory to three revisionist states (Hungary, the Soviet Union, and Bulgaria) already, Antonescu felt Romania had nothing to lose and everything to gain by contributing troops and resources to the Axis front against the Soviet Union in late June 1941. The result was the reannexation of Bessarabia and Northern Bukovina by Romania in September 1941. Romanian troops also occupied a large territory between the Dniester and the Bug rivers known as Transnistria. Throughout the war, however, the Romanian administration refused to annex Transnistria, making it quite clear to both the Germans and the Allies that territorial gains in the East would not be accepted in exchange for Transylvania.[53]

As for Hungary, the call to make sacrifices for Axis interests (and territorial compensation) came earlier, with the invasion of Yugoslavia in April 1941. At the behest of Hitler, Hungarian leaders had made a pact of nonaggression with Yugoslavia in December 1940. The pact assured Yugoslav neutrality in the event of a conflict with Romania, and when, in April 1941, Hitler talked Horthy into breaking the pact and participating in the Axis invasion of Yugoslavia, Prime Minister Teleki committed suicide. His replacement was László Bárdossy, formerly Hungarian ambassador to Romania. In the words of one Hungarian historian, the choice of Bárdossy betrayed "what fundamental importance was assigned to the expected Romanian developments by the oligarchy that determined Hungary's fate."[54]

Hungary was promised territorial compensation for participation in the attack on Yugoslavia in the form of the Délvidék (Bácska and a small piece of Baranya).[55] Nevertheless, as Ulrich von Hassell, a member of the board of the Central European Economic Council, commented on the occasion of Teleki's suicide, "At that time a fight with Romania would have been popular," far preferable to the invasion of Yugoslavia.[56] In mid-June 1941, on the eve of the Axis invasion of the Soviet Union, the Hungarian ambassador in Berlin, Döme Sztójay, advised Horthy as follows:

> From every sign we have gotten up till now it seems certain that the Reichschancellor will give the western part of the Banat to Hungary once Romania is pacified—or rather compensated—with the recovery of Bessarabia. Recently I have heard comments to the effect that in the event of the possible liquidation of the Soviet Union the Reichschancellor wants to give Romania the entire territory of the principality of Moldavia. Yet in spite of whether Romania earns "subsequent merits," it is conceivable and does not seem impossible that the Führer will, in turn, want to settle the Transylvanian Question in Hungary's favor, either [by giving us] all of Transylvania, or making some more favorable adjustments to the border [laid down in] Vienna. Naturally Antonescu will fight with every means at his disposal

against this eventuality. Nevertheless, if Hungary also earns subsequent "merits," there is greater hope that the Transylvanian Question will be resolved in our favor than without [those merits].[57]

Hungary's later prime minister, Miklós Kállay, was very explicit about the role Transylvania played in the government's decision to join the offensive against the Soviet Union in his a posteriori evaluation of the situation: "If we do not take part in the war against the Soviet Union like Romania, then Hitler will be forced . . . to change his position regarding the Transylvanian Question to the Romanians' advantage."[58] The Hungarian leadership was acutely aware of Romanian attempts to reach "Kolozsvár . . . by way of Odessa and Sebastopol."[59]

Nor were Romanian authorities ignorant of Hungary's troop commitment strategy. In early September 1941, the Romanian Secret Intelligence Service reported on claims made by the secretary of the Hungarian Legation in Bucharest that "the sacrifices being made by the Hungarian army in the war against the Bolsheviks will be repaid by Germany at a future peace conference when the territorial aspirations of Hungary will be realized radically and immediately."[60] Romanian officials also feared that, being so heavily invested in the east, Romania could not fend off a potential attack from Hungary in the west.[61] Commenting on a report dated September 5, 1941, that Hungarian prime minister Bárdossy was withholding troops from involvement on the Soviet front, the Romanian Ministry of Internal Affairs concluded: "Probably the Bárdossy government does not want to mobilize, but rather to keep its forces intact [for] entrance . . . into [Southern] Transylvania."[62] The Secret Intelligence Service also heard that the Hungarians of Southern Transylvania were talking about the "intensive preparations" Hungary was making for "a military action against Romania for the conquest of Southern Transylvania."[63]

On December 19, two established and respected Romanian politicians and harsh critics of the Axis alliance, Iuliu Maniu and Constantin I. C. Brătianu, wrote to Ion Antonescu to decry the "great and deeply unpopular" sacrifices being made in the interest of the Axis war on the Soviet Union. "The continuation of the war under existing conditions cannot lead to a reintegration of the country, but only to the complete sapping of the country, exposed to the magyar danger. . . . First we must provide the defense of our own frontiers and the recognition of lost Transylvania which cannot be achieved except with a powerful and well-equipped army."[64] Maniu and Brătianu also warned that in the meantime Hungary was likely arming itself for a battle with Romania for Transylvania.

The reports and suspicions that Hungary was preparing for a fight were not unfounded. Hungarian military and civilian leaders—fearing a rerun of the 1919 catastrophe, when weakened Hungarian forces were pushed back as far as Budapest by Romanian troops[65]—did keep troops and supplies in reserve for an eventual fight with Romania. Hungarian leaders initially hesitated to contribute to the offensive against the Soviets in June 1941, arguing that doing so would weaken Hungary's border defenses facing hostile Romania and Slovakia.[66] This reluctance grew rather than diminished over time, especially following a series of border incidents in Transylvania in September 1942.[67] In fact, the massacre of over three thousand Serbs and Jews in Hungarian-controlled Bácska in January 1942, and the subsequent quiet removal/resignation of Prime Minister Bárdossy were arguably linked to Hungary's efforts to keep Hungarian forces within the state's boundaries.[68]

Even following the buildup of troops in anticipation of the assault on Stalingrad in the spring and summer of 1942, Hungary had half as many divisions as Romania on the Eastern Front.[69] As late as April 1943, Hungarian leaders had still refused to mobilize troops and resources from the reannexed territories—most notably Transylvania—for frontline service, arguing that these areas were "not yet in a position to contribute to the military expenditures of the country."[70] Furthermore, both the regent and the successive prime ministers of Hungary, like Antonescu, took every opportunity to broach the subject of Transylvania with Hitler, as they were by no means satisfied with the compromise of winning back only part of the region.[71] In a meeting between Hitler and Prime Minister Kállay in June 1942, Kállay made two "little requests" on behalf of Regent Horthy, the first of which was "that firstly the Lord God and secondly [Hitler] should turn a benevolent eye if the Hungarians started a fight with the Rumanians."[72]

In the fall and early winter of 1941, Antonescu made a series of statements suggesting that a showdown with Hungary was imminent. "With strong faith I repeat," he wrote in a statement to the Romanian refugees from Northern Transylvania in September 1941, "We will not forget a single piece of Romanian land. No humiliation will remain irreversible." As he was lying ill in a Bucharest hospital, he wrote in the hospital's guest book: "I do not wish to, nor will I, die until every last Romanian furrow is reannexed."[73]

Antonescu's pronouncements resonated with Romanian public opinion. In a report on southeastern Europe from 1942, Berlin economist Karl Janovsky observed that "no nationally conscious Romanian would ever let go of Transylvania. An 'either-or' is mentioned as the only possible solution for the Transylvanian Question."[74] In mid-March of the same year, a German visitor to Bucharest observed "great fear of Russia" among the population, "but everything is overshadowed by their hatred of Hungary and the quest

[*Streben*] for Transylvania."[75] A month later Mihai Antonescu told the Croat ambassador to Romania, Branko Benzon, that it was an "open secret" in Romania that the war in the east was "practice for the war against Hungary."[76]

OPERATION BLUE

The 1942 summer offensive was to be one of the most ambitious the Germans had undertaken since the beginning of the war. The plan was to occupy Soviet territory up to the Don River, secure a position on the Volga, and ultimately proceed to the oil fields of the Caucasus.[77] Operation Blue was to include the forces of Germany's allies in increased numbers, and negotiations between Germany and Hungary and Romania began already in the winter and early spring of 1942. On January 8, Ribbentrop gave a speech in Budapest crafted to encourage the Hungarians to commit troops for the upcoming offensive. In the speech he criticized "anti-revisionist states" like Romania that had, during the interwar period, resisted "every reasonable and peaceful revision" of the postwar peace treaties.[78] There followed another visit to Budapest by German Field Marshal Wilhelm Keitel on January 20, also to settle the matter of Hungary's military contribution to the summer offensive. Keitel told the Hungarian leadership that the Transylvanian Question would be solved in favor of Romania if Hungary did not contribute to the extent expected by Reich officials.[79]

Ribbentrop's speech fueled the political forces in Romania opposed to Antonescu's policies, as Romanians now appeared to be fighting the "Axis" fight for the wrong kind of territorial revision. Antonescu found himself under increasing pressure to take action on Transylvania. In February 1942, a flyer reportedly circulated and pasted on buildings and walls throughout the Southern Transylvanian city of Turda "by the thousands," read as follows:

Mareșale, Mareșale	Marshal, Marshal
Îndreaptă oștile tale	Direct your armies
De voinici și de viteji	Of strong and brave men
Peste Sighet, peste Dej	Over Sighet, over Dej
Și să te vedem acuș[i]	So that we might see you soon
Intrând victorios în Cluj	Entering victorious into Cluj[80]

Romanian troops, especially those mobilized from Transylvania, expressed their dissatisfaction at being sent to the Eastern Front. One transport of soldiers fired shots at Antonescu's villa in Predeal while their train stopped at the station there.[81] A German report on the attitude of the Romanian population in March indicated that "all the way down to the poorest Romanian everyone counts on a showdown [*Abrechnung*] with Hungary sooner or later. All the sacrifices that were made for the extended campaign in the east should have been saved for the showdown with Hungary, which is simply inevitable."[82] Furthermore, Romanian soldiers hesitated in their battle in the east, "with the enemy at their back."[83] General Ion Gheorghe, a member of the Romanian legation to Berlin, noted in his recollections that, both among the Romanian civilian population and in the army, people spoke of war not with the USSR, but with Hungary.[84]

To counter his slipping credibility, Antonescu told Hitler on February 17 that Romania would mobilize even more troops, a million, if need be, but needed to be assured that Hungary "neither during nor after the war would have any kind of advantaged position."[85] Antonescu also insisted that Hungary be expected to contribute significantly to the offensive so that it could not hold troops back for an invasion of Romania.[86] A witness to conversations between Hitler and Antonescu from February 1942 reported: "On each visit he [Antonescu] indicated pretty plainly his firm intention of one day recovering the whole of Transylvania by force of arms."[87] And in May 1942, the U.S. secretary of state noted that "a large part of the army within Rumania was near the Hungarian frontier."[88]

The Romanian leader's efforts yielded no tangible results, however, and concerns about the direction of the war intensified following the disastrous fall 1942 offensive. The government's credibility problem was communicated in a conversation between Mihai Antonescu and German ambassador Manfred Freiherr von Killinger in late October 1942. "We cannot afford to act like heroes in the east and like cowards in the west, tolerating Hungary's offences, because this will offend our population and provoke a problematic internal situation," Mihai Antonescu told the ambassador.[89] In fact, a Romanian security services report on the attitude of Romanian refugees from Northern Transylvania dated December 28, 1942, registered refugees' "dissatisfaction and concern" that "our soldiers are sent to the front to fight for a territory that was never part of Romania without having so much as a guarantee on the part of Germany in the matter of ceding Transylvania."[90] Another report, dated January 25, 1943, said that "if it was a matter of the conquest of Transylvania, [Romanians] would go [to the front] with their wives and everything without so much as a sigh."[91]

The flip side of this sentiment was the belief among members of the Romanian leadership, soldiers, and citizens that making common cause with the Germans was really about getting back Transylvania. In Turda and elsewhere in Romania during February 1942, crumpled balls of paper were passed secretly from hand to hand. On them were printed what were said to be the words of Romanian leader Marshal Antonescu: "When I come back from Odessa I won't be going through Cernăuți, but through the princely Sighetu Marmației on towards Cluj."[92] In March 1942, as preparations for the major offensive were under way, Romanian deputy prime minister Mihai Antonescu undertook a major propaganda campaign to convince the public and the troops of the necessity of the offensive. In a speech he delivered to that end, he criticized Hungary for its treatment of Romanians in Northern Transylvania. The speech sounded over loudspeakers in the Romanian capital of Bucharest, where it was heard by "a huge crowd" that shouted "salutes" every time Transylvania was mentioned. A witness reported that the listeners in the ballroom of the Law Faculty cried "Get Transylvania back!" at regular intervals throughout the speech.[93] Thereafter the Romanian deputy prime minister was called upon to explain to Ambassador von Killinger why his speech had veered so far from the Axis platform. Killinger warned Antonescu to keep propaganda as much to the Bolshevik menace as possible and away from the Transylvanian Question, but Antonescu claimed that talking about Transylvania was the only way to inspire the troops.[94]

Despite Killinger's warning to Mihai Antonescu, the belief that military engagement would result in territorial payoffs was nevertheless encouraged by the Axis. On June 20, Killinger himself wrote that Romania knew "what thanks it could expect" for its loyalty and commitment to the Axis war effort.[95] And indeed, a few days earlier, Mihai Antonescu had met with dozens of Romanian historians, demographers, diplomats, and other specialists to document, among other things, the extent and substance of Romania's contribution to the Axis war effort.[96] A barrage of radio and newspaper propaganda during the spring of 1942 was crafted to reinforce the conviction that "the Romanian soldier dies not only for the civilized order of Europe, but also for the integral and Greater Romanian national ideals."[97]

According to a broadcast of the Romanian government's clandestine radio station, "Greater Romania," from April 1, Berlin knew well what Romania's rights were; "the sacrifice of the Romanian soldier will secure the realization of justice."[98] As preparations for the offensive were being finalized, "Greater Romania" radio was more explicit: "Berlin has already on several occasions stressed that in the New European Order it will consider which nation [*Volk*] made what sacrifices in the war. Hungary is taking part in the fight only formally, and so it is possible that it will lose the other half of Transylvania."[99] Soon even a Romanian insurance broker living in Budapest was declaring that "when the war is over and the Germans win, the Romanians will get Cluj, the capital of Transylvania."[100]

That these sentiments were shared by the Romanian rank and file is evi-

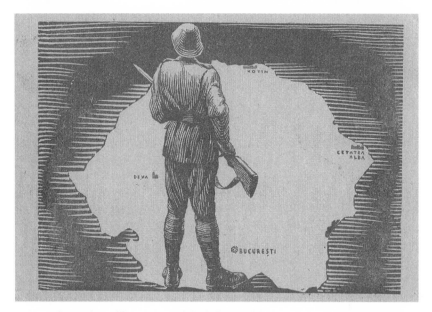

FIG. 11. Romanian military postcard depicting a soldier standing guard over Greater Romania, with borders as they were during the interwar period (i.e., before the loss of Bessarabia, Northern Bukovina, Southern Dobruja, and Northern Transylvania). This card was postmarked February 1944. From the collection of Dan Grecu; reprinted with permission.

dent from a report of the Romanian security service of the Regional Police Inspectorate of Cluj from January 19, 1943, which noted: "Romanian soldiers, when asked why they are fighting, say that they are fighting only for the recovery of Transylvania."[101] Such a response should have come as no surprise, given that in speeches to their troops, the military command stressed the connection between the activities of the Romanian army and the restoration of Greater Romania's borders. On April 19, 1942, General Petre, commander of the Romanian Third Army, spoke to new Romanian recruits in Turda: "We can spare no sacrifice in the interest of restoring the country's boundaries to the way we carry the image of the country in our souls and in our thoughts."[102]

Similar speeches were delivered by the Hungarian military command and state leadership, who spoke of the Hungarian soldier's mission on the Eastern Front and in the war more generally: to recover Hungary's thousand-year borders. In November 1941, a battalion commander of soldiers returning home from service at the front told his troops, "We have come home not to rest, but to prepare for every possible turn of events in order to reconquer our old Hungarian homeland."[103] Just two weeks later, a Transylvanian representative gave a speech in parliament in which he declared, "We are not afraid so long as there is yet one Hungarian soldier, for that soldier will not only defend what we have recovered, but will also reconquer what we have not yet recovered."[104] In several speeches in May and June 1942, as new recruits were being readied for the summer offensive, officers reminded troops that "everywhere and in whatever direction you are fighting, . . . you are fighting for the old borders of our thousand-year homeland of Hungary."[105] A brigadier general told his recruits that "the Hungarian soldier does not yet stand guard everywhere on the borders of his ancestors. Dirty hands still rule the land of our ancestors. It is your duty to reclaim our place here and to reconquer the territory of our ancestors in its entirety."[106] And during a speech delivered by a military pastor at an event in Kolozsvár celebrating the sacrifices of Hungarian troops, the speaker told his audience that every drop of blood spilled by Hungarian soldiers "is a holy seed from which Greater Hungary must emerge and be resurrected."[107]

Many Hungarian soldiers thus understood their presence on the Don steppe as a way of defending the territories they had acquired with Axis assistance, and potentially making still further gains. The impromptu heroes' cemeteries erected along their path reflected this conviction, marked as they were with the words "For Greater Hungary." The fact that over 50 percent of the Hungarian military elite during World War II were from territories Hungary had lost after World War I—with nearly one in four high-ranking officers born in Transylvania—served to intensify the emphasis on recovering the lost territories in military circles.[108]

"What were we doing at the Don, more than a thousand kilometers from the borders of our homeland?" wondered Antal Radnóczy, who served with the Hungarian Third Army as a quartermaster. "They sent us into battle to preserve and defend the territories we had won back. Along the Don River we knowingly defended—with great sacrifice—the Hungarian-inhabited Northern Transylvania, Felvidék, and Délvidék."[109] This view was echoed by Imre Gróf, who was mobilized to the front on July 1 from Kaposvár. "We had to help the Germans," he wrote; "that was the only way we could keep the territories we had gotten back."[110] Even after the staggering defeats and heavy losses of the 1942–43 winter offensive, Hungarian chief of staff János Vörös declared that only with an Axis victory could the Hungarians achieve their "national objective," the reestablishment of Hungary's thousand-year borders.[111]

Back home in Hungary, the links between the state's involvement in the war against the Soviet Union and the fate of Transylvania were also well known. In mid-July 1942, as many as five hundred members of the extreme-right Arrow Cross movement converged on the Northern Transylvanian cities of Nagyvárad and Kolozsvár to celebrate the Hungarian army's efforts and to push for still more territorial gains.[112] In a 1942 report on attitudes in Budapest at the time, Berlin economist Karl Janovsky wrote that "one has been forced to take part in the war, as it was high time to make some recompense for the massive, multiple reannexations the country has enjoyed since 1939."[113]

The fact that Hungarians and Romanians were fighting on the same side, while effectively engaged with one another in what Ion Gheorghe called an "ill-fated and exhausting bidding war," made for some awkward scenes at the front.[114] By their own request the two countries' armies had to be kept separate at all times.[115] For the Don offensive, this meant using the Eighth Italian Army as a buffer between the Hungarian Second and the Romanian Third armies.[116] Nevertheless, in the heat of battle it was not always easy to prevent contact between the two. On August 12, 1941, for example, part of the Romanian Third Army advanced near the rear of the Hungarian Mobile Corps. The Hungarian captain in charge of the corps demanded that the Romanians retreat or the Hungarians would turn around and fight them.[117]

Events at the front provided alternative ways for the two countries to fight each other. One such method was by censoring reports on the successes of the other country's armed forces out of the daily press.[118] Another was through manipulation or oppression of minority soldiers. Both armies had members of the other nationality serving in them, and the treatment of these minority soldiers was a matter of constant friction between the two states.[119] Reports that minority draftees were beaten, harassed, or assigned to do hard labor with insufficient rations were common.[120] In the face of Soviet propaganda, one Hungarian captain wondered, "How can we possibly trust those who are not Hungarians?"[121] The possibility of desertion was particularly appealing to members of minorities fighting with the Hungarian and Romanian armies.[122] Between 1941 and 1944, 70 percent of deserters from the Ninth Division stationed in Northern Transylvania were of self-declared Romanian nationality.[123] A Hungarian soldier remembered a scene in which four ethnic Romanians were shot in front of his division for attempting to desert.[124]

In Romania, draft notices were issued to members of the Hungarian minority as a means to get them to leave the country and never return.[125] The method was so effective that an entire guard battalion had to be created within the Hungarian army to accommodate Southern Transylvanian Hungarians fleeing military service in Romania.[126] Using the draft to get rid of people who represented the interests of minorities was another strategy employed by both states.[127] Also, to keep from having to issue weapons to unreliable minorities, both states sent many minority draftees into labor service battalions where they served along with Jews, rather than having them fight alongside the regular forces.[128]

Sometimes sending minority soldiers directly to the front seemed an even more expedient means of getting rid of them.[129] A report on the attitude of Northern Transylvania's Hungarian population from late October 1941 describes how the Hungarians there were incensed that Romanians were not drafted into the Hungarian army, and as a result, only Hungarians were sent to fight and die on the Eastern Front.[130] Over time, the number of non-magyar soldiers serving at or near the front or doing occupation duty increased considerably, such that they constituted as much as 50 percent of some occupation units stationed in Ukraine.[131]

But it was not only minority soldiers whose loyalty was a matter of concern. By the end of January 1943, both the Hungarian and Romanian armies had sustained considerable losses, particularly in soldiers captured by the Soviets.[132] Hungarian and Romanian Communists working for the Soviet government sought to win over the prisoners of war—especially officers—by pointing to the senselessness of the battle against the Soviet Union when the real problem was Transylvania. In a speech to Hungarian prisoners of war on September 7, 1943, Hungarian Communist Mátyás Rákosi—who would later serve as party chief during the Stalinist period in Hungary—raised the "important question" of whether, following an Allied victory, Hungary "would have to give up the territories it received with Hitler's help."[133]

The Communist propaganda campaign was particularly effective among Romanian officers and soldiers, who were eager to fight *against* rather than *alongside* the Hungarians for Transylvania. Following the German invasion of the Soviet Union in late June 1941, the illegal Communist Party in Romania called upon "every true patriot of the country" to overthrow the Antonescu regime and run the Germans out. The goals of the nation, it asserted in pamphlets and manifestos, should be Romania's independence and the liberation of Northern Transylvania from the Hungarians.[134]

With the advent of the Red Army victories at the Don and the arrival of tens of thousands of Romanian soldiers in prisoner-of-war camps, the Romanian Communists in the Soviet Union set to work convincing them to fight for the Soviets. The one presumed sticking point was the matter of Bessarabia and Northern Bukovina, which the USSR had annexed from Romania in the summer of 1940 and which Romania had won back in the wake of the Axis attack on the USSR in the summer of 1941. But the Communists had an answer: "Bessarabia? You must think realistically! The Soviet Union, our friend, will be our neighbor. Borders will have no meaning after the war anyhow. For us the most important thing should be the benevolence of our big neighbor in the east so that we can get Northern Transylvania back. And you, don't you all have the desire to have all of Transylvania, this ancestral land of ours, belong to Romania again?" The answer; a resounding "Yes."[135]

Between January and April 1943, over two thousand Romanian prisoners of war petitioned Soviet military authorities to join the fight for the "liberation of Romania." At the end of October, members of the division "Tudor Vladimirescu," reportedly made up of nearly ten thousand Romanian—and even some minority—soldiers and officers, participated in an inaugural celebration around an open fire. Song, dance, and inspirational speeches were followed by a soldier's recitation of a poem about Transylvania. Colonel Malenkov of the Soviet military was reportedly present and offered those gathered words of encouragement. "Rest assured: Transylvania will again belong to Romania!"[136] On November 15, 1943, "Tudor Vladimirescu" received its first orders. By March 1944, it was declared ready for frontline action and assigned to the army group of the Second Ukrainian Front, and in early September 1944, it fought under Soviet command in the battle for Transylvania.[137]

Hungarian Communists' attempts to win over Hungarian officers and rank-and-file to the cause were less successful. Historian Péter Gosztonyi has noted that "the 'territorial question' played a major role in the attitude of the [Hungarian] prisoners of war." Endre Sik, a Hungarian Communist activist who made a number of speeches to captured Hungarians, observed with distress how his audiences were willing to accept the ideology, but feared for the loss of Hungarian territory. So it was that attempts to establish a Kossuth Legion (comparable to the "Tudor Vladimirescu") failed.[138]

Opportunities for the two states to do battle with each other also offered themselves in the arena of diplomacy. One strategy employed by Hungarian and Romanian leaders and diplomats was to insult or question the loyalty of the other state in conversations with German statesmen and officials. In a letter drafted to Hitler in June 1941, on the eve of Operation Barbarossa, Horthy wrote that "the Romanian is the only race that I despise. There everyone steals, lies, and cheats, everyone can be bought, and in the course of their short history they have deceived and betrayed every one of their friends and allies."[139] In January 1942, Horthy reminded Hitler that Romania had started World War I on the side of Germany and Austria-Hungary and had switched sides to gain territory, and that there were many in Romania who wanted to do the same thing now.[140]

In a letter to Mussolini from December 1940, Iuliu Maniu criticized Hungary's long-standing "politics of opportunism and duplicity," stretching back to World War I and throughout the interwar period. Hungary's claims of loyalty to the Axis would thus "fool no one, least of all the Führer."[141] In the fall and early winter of 1942, Mihai Antonescu began criticizing Hungarian prime minister Miklós Kállay to the German leadership for his unreliability.[142] And in a June 1942 meeting to discuss strategies for winning the peace, Mihai Antonescu also stressed the importance of portraying Hungary as an equivocating two-timer, pretending to be "democratic" and "liberal" for the Allies, while playing the opposite role with the Axis.[143] Kállay reciprocated, calling Marshal Antonescu "the greatest diplomat in Europe, considered the most beloved friend of the Führer, while having his agents everywhere on the other side."[144]

Already in the summer of 1942, reciprocal accusations of disloyalty had been integrated into broader propaganda efforts. The clandestine radio station "Greater Romania," broadcasting on June 7, charged that "the Hungarians are using all their energy to maintain their friendship with England." The Hungarian government translated this and other anti-Hungarian and Romanian revisionist statements into German for presentation to the German government with this commentary: "In response to numerous Romanian attacks [of this sort, we] could reply: There's the pot calling the kettle black."[145]

JUMPING OUT

As they were criticizing one another for their disloyalty to the Axis and their opportunistic politics, as early as the summer of 1942, representatives of both Hungary and Romania were putting out feelers to the Allies. By early spring of 1943, these efforts had greatly intensified and enjoyed much more substantive support from both governments.[146] Hitler was informed of these attempts and accused Hungarian prime minister Miklós Kállay and his Romanian counterpart, Mihai Antonescu, of increasing disdain for the Axis and the war. His suspicions were largely correct.[147]

As the behind-the-scenes machinations of the Hungarian leadership became ever more apparent domestically, the extreme right in Hungary also criticized Kállay for endangering the country's territorial acquisitions through attempts to make a deal with the Allies. On March 31, 1943, representatives of the extreme-right Arrow Cross Party wrote a letter to Horthy warning him that the Western European powers had given Hungary Trianon, while the Axis had given them the Second Vienna Arbitration. If Hungary should break away from the Axis, they argued, "a Trianon fate will await us once again!"[148] Joining the Allies would mean "another Trianon-type dismemberment" for Hungary, wrote Béla Imrédy, head of the Hungarian Renewal Party [Magyar Megújulás Pártja] on May 5, 1943, in a letter to Horthy.[149]

These concerns seemed more credible the closer the Soviet forces drew to the Hungarian border. By mid-March 1944, as Horthy was preparing a radio speech for March 15—the day the Germans decided to force Kállay's resignation and occupy the country—the appeal of joining the Allies was not nearly as strong. The Soviet Union would be the force to determine Hungary's postwar fate in the event of an Allied victory, so it was in Hungary's interest to stay with the Axis, at least militarily.[150] Nevertheless, as the Soviets approached Hungary's eastern border, Horthy did try to withdraw some troops from the front. In a letter to Hitler dated February 12, he argued that the country needed to defend itself against invasion. "It would be difficult to say whether there will ever be an invasion from the west, but I see an attack on Northern Transylvania as certain."[151]

Pressure was also mounting in Romania, and the Antonescu government was the target of sharp criticism for its increasingly unpopular alliance with the Axis, which had failed to produce a definitive promise from Hitler regarding the return of Northern Transylvania.[152] Former prime minister Iuliu Maniu, an Anglophile politician from Transylvania, was especially critical of Antonescu's failure to come up with a viable plan for the recovery of Transylvania.[153] Throughout the war since the Second Vienna Arbitration, Maniu had been in regular contact with the British and American governments. In January 1943, following the disastrous defeat at Stalingrad, Maniu sought to make it clear to the Allies that the Romanians were against continuing the war in the east and that the "supreme national goal" was the recovery of Northern Transylvania. That territory, he argued, had been given to Hungary by the Axis as "punishment" for Romania's dedication to Britain and France during the interwar period.[154] But the diplomatic landscape was shifting, as evidenced by the declaration of the British foreign secretary, Anthony Eden, that spring stating that Britain did not recognize the validity of the Second Vienna Arbitration. In April, Mihai Antonescu was openly incensed that "the government and people of Romania, together with the army, now find themselves fighting against those who recognize their rights and alongside those who negate them."[155]

Meanwhile, the Communist Party of Romania [Partidul Comunist din România] tried to make common cause with Maniu's National Peasant Party and two other parties. Already on September 6, 1941, the Communists proposed the creation of the United National Front [Frontul Unic Național] of the Romanian people and drafted the front's platform, calling for the overthrow of the Antonescu government, annulment of the Second Vienna Arbitration, and the military reoccupation of Northern Transylvania. This platform was then forwarded to the Front's potential allies from among the liberal parties on January 26, 1942.[156]

In the spring of 1944, after repeated warnings to the Hungarian leadership regarding its attempts to play both sides, Hitler decided to occupy Hungary.[157] On March 18, Horthy was called to Kleßheim, where Hitler expressed his fury at the "betrayal" of the Italians (who had ousted Mussolini and switched sides in the war in early September 1943) and voiced his determination not to allow Hungary to do the same. He then announced his plan to occupy the country. When Horthy suggested Hungary could resist occupation, Hitler replied that "the Romanians, Slovaks, and Croats were all enemies of Hungary," eager and willing to attack to recover lost territory at the first opportunity.[158] To further justify the need for Germany to occupy Hungary, Hitler said that Romania would not commit more troops to the fight against the Soviet Union "because the Hungarians would pounce on them from behind." Occupying Hungary would free up Romanian troops for the fight in the east, to the benefit of all.[159] In exchange for "independence," Horthy should agree to German occupation, the dismissal of Kállay, and the formation of a new pro-German government.

The German occupation of Hungary was hardly a joyful occasion for the Romanian leadership. Already in November 1943, former Romanian ambassador to Berlin Raoul Bossy wrote that such a turn of events might serve only to transform Hungary into a victim of German aggression, causing the Western Allies to "definitively recognize [Hungary's] territorial acquisitions."[160] Yet shortly after the occupation had begun, Hitler invited Antonescu to Kleßheim to discuss the recent events and their implications for the alliance. He told the Romanian leader that, "in light of the disloyal behavior of the Hungarian government, and considering that neither Hungary nor Romania ever took to the Vienna Arbitration, and given that Italy is now out of the picture, Germany no longer considers it appropriate to act as signatory of the Vienna Arbitration."[161] He also hinted that, should the situation with Hungary "become aggravated," the Romanian leadership would be informed.[162]

In expressing his gratitude to Hitler for these assurances, Antonescu also mentioned that his position on the Transylvanian Question had been causing him trouble back home, given that until that point only Germany had upheld the Second Vienna Arbitration, an agreement that was never acknowledged by any of the Allies.[163] And indeed, on May 12, 1944, the British foreign ministry announced that nations continuing to fight alongside the Axis would suffer "disastrous consequences" proportional to the length and intensity of their collaboration with the German enemy.[164]

Even as Hitler and Antonescu were reaffirming their alliance, then, Ribbentrop and Mihai Antonescu were conferring about options for a separate peace with the Western Allies. On August 2, Mihai Antonescu received word from a contact in Bern urging him to effect the immediate severance of all ties with Germany. "Putting it off even for just a few days increases the risk that Hungary and Bulgaria will beat us to it."[165] One thing was certain, that occupation of Hungary did not improve the marshal's position, but rather increased fears that the same could happen to Romania. These fears fed the opposition, which finally managed to unite the Communist, peasant, liberal, and social democratic parties into the National Democratic Bloc [Blocul Naţional Democratic] in June 1944.[166] Shortly thereafter, the bloc announced to the Allies its plans to overthrow Antonescu.

Meanwhile the Red Army had advanced into Romanian territory. By mounting a major offensive on August 20, the Soviets forced the bloc to act quickly. On August 23, the Romanian King Mihai invited Ion Antonescu to his palace, where Antonescu was arrested together with Mihai Antonescu. That same day Mihai Antonescu sent an urgent message to a Romanian general: "Given what the king has done to me, I should have the sense to remain silent, but the [fate of] the country is at stake, the country I have served like a slave for four years. . . . Be vigilant with Transylvania so the Hungarians do not enter it. Tell me . . . that you have taken serious measures [to prevent it]?"[167] A few days later the underground Communists in Hungary published a propaganda pamphlet that read: "It is impossible to defend Transylvania by conducting a war in partnership with Hitler. This would only be a way of losing it altogether, for in the final instance Transylvania will belong to the state . . . that fights Hitler with courage and determination."[168]

The Real Thing

The belief—voiced repeatedly by the Hungarian leadership in particular—that war between Hungary and Romania was inevitable soon became a self-fulfilling prophecy.[169] Within days of Antonescu's arrest, Romania switched sides in the war, declaring war on Germany on August 25, declaring war on Hungary on September 7, and signing an armistice with the Allies on September 12. With the two countries no longer allied, conflict between them broke out almost immediately.

Initially, the Germans tried to hold back the Hungarian forces from invading Southern Transylvania, hoping to reach an agreement with Romania. Failing this, however, they planned a joint offensive into Southern Transylvania, such that by August 30, a newly created Hungarian Second Army was spread out along a three-hundred-kilometer-long line stretching across Northern Transylvania. On the other side of the border facing them was the Fourth Romanian Army.[170]

A series of border attacks by the Romanians were fought back by Hungarian forces during the days following Antonescu's arrest. On September 5, what became known as the Battle of Turda began when Hungarian and German forces started a major offensive into Southern Transylvania, occupying the city of Turda and advancing quickly as far as the Maros/Mureş River, gaining sixty-five kilometers in three days. By September 7, Romania had declared war on Hungary, and Soviet forces were less than one hundred kilometers away from the Hungarian positions.[171] Despite these early successes, the Hungarian leadership was quite aware that it was living on borrowed time and initiated yet another attempt to abandon the Axis that was, like the others, doomed to failure.[172]

For the Hungarian military command, the precedent of 1918 was a scenario to be avoided at all costs.[173] Just prior to Romania's defection from the Axis, the Hungarian military had initiated a massive mobilization of hitherto untapped human and material resources. By early September, the Hungarian army was over 950,000 strong. At no time during the war had mobilization been so high, and the losses sustained in the coming months overshadowed the magnitude of the Don catastrophe.[174] Romanian forces involved in the battle for Transylvania also suffered heavy losses.[175]

Nevertheless, one thing the military leadership on both sides noted as the two sides went to war with one another was an immediate improvement in the morale of their troops. A captain preparing his soldiers for what was to come reported on how much easier it was to motivate them to a battle with Romania than it had been to fight the Soviets. "The Hungarian soldier—who has been called up for service for the fourth, even the fifth tour of duty—completely snaps to when it comes to fighting the neighbor who caused his misfortune."[176] General Lajos Veress, who led the Second Army into battle that autumn, noted that the army was made up primarily of individuals born in Northern Transylvania. As such, "neither 'allied loyalty,' nor an anti-Russian or anti-Communist stance were the forces that invigorated and induced their readiness for battle, but rather the painful memory of 25 [*sic!*] years of Romanian occupation, which every single one of them wanted to escape at all costs."[177]

The Romanian military command was painfully aware that in Transyl-

FIG. 12. Romanian postcard, printed shortly after Romania's defection from the Axis, celebrating the new Romano-Soviet forces' penetration into Transylvania. From the collection of Dan Grecu; reprinted with permission.

vania it faced an enemy "determined to resist," reporting on battles "for every meter of terrain that went countless times from hand to hand, even in the course of a single day."[178] Nevertheless, Romanian military leadership noted the "highly combative spirit of our troops."[179] The new regime was very quick to make its designs on Transylvania clear to soldiers and civilians alike. Already on September 25, an article on the front page of the Romanian Communist newspaper *Scînteia* [The Spark] issued a call to arms for the liberation of Northern Transylvania. "The Hungarian Fascists must be made to pay mercilessly for all of the bestial crimes they committed against the Romanian population of Transylvania that has been enslaved for four years."[180] The punitive aspect of the counteroffensive was anticipated by the Hungarian military command. In the words of Chief of Staff János Vörös on September 4, "Only internal order and the untapped strength of the army can keep the neighboring small peoples (Romanians, Slovaks, Croats, Serbs) at bay. We must be aware that if we should stand defenseless in the face of them, our race will be exterminated."[181]

Nor did the Romanian troops need much encouragement to begin the fight with Hungary. The state-initiated propaganda had no trouble convincing the public that Transylvania should be reconquered, but it did face a challenge in explaining the necessity of Romania's new alliance with its former enemy, the Soviet Union. Hence the Romanian public was bombarded with statements from the new government glorifying the role of the Romano-Soviet "brotherhood-in-arms" in the liberation of Transylvania. On the occasion of the liberation of Kolozsvár/Cluj on October 11, Iuliu Maniu declared that "we bow our heads, with unfading gratitude in the face of the immense sacrifices of our beloved army, in the face of the unequaled prowess and skill of the glorious Soviet armies, who along with the victorious military advance have paved the road towards a lasting fraternity between our two peoples that nothing can dissolve."[182] The propaganda postcard depicted in Figure 12, which was printed shortly after Romania's defection from the Axis, celebrated the new Romano-Soviet forces' penetration into Transylvania.

Situation reports from the Romanian and Soviet military commands reported advances against the German and Hungarian forces, crossing into Northern Transylvania on October 10, and continuing westward.[183] By the end of October, the Hungarian and German forces had been pushed out of Transylvania entirely. Once the Soviet troops had occupied Transylvania, British diplomatic sources reported on the attitude of the Hungarian and Romanian populations toward the Soviet military presence. One such report from mid-January 1945 declared: "The Hungarians are trying to convince the Russians . . . that they make better Communists than the Rumanians."[184]

CONCLUSION

In the fall of 1944, the seventy-year-old former Hungarian prime minister Count István Bethlen was hiding from the Gestapo at the home of a count and countess in Herencsény. There he wrote an essay entitled "Hungarian Politics in World War Two: A Treatise or Indictment," in which he lamented the fact that Hungarian leaders had banked so heavily on a German victory. It was right and just, he argued, to reclaim territory with German assistance, but it was wrong to join the Tripartite Pact. "In a global political situation, such as it offered at the time, the only opportunity for Hungary's resurrection lay in Germany's avoiding yet another hazardous war, gradually recovering its domineering continental position in Europe, whereas Hungary, skillfully navigating in diplomatic waters at her side, might bounce on such chances as occurred, or even with arms in hand force one or the other of its neighbours to return some of the territories robbed at the end of World War I."[185] Toward the middle of the essay, Bethlen reflected on the Bolshevik menace and its significance for Hungary:

> Bolshevism is indeed a danger threatening the whole of Europe. It is not, however, the vocation of little Hungary, much tried and torn to pieces, to defend Europe against that danger at the sacrifice of the flower of its people. . . . For ever since Trianon, for the last 25 years, and quite a long stretch of time ahead, Hungary could and can have only one objective: to make one whole once more of our country ripped to bits and pieces and make it recover the weight and role in the Danubian Basin which befits it. And it is not the Great Powers which stand in our way on that road: it is our neighbors. They must never be left out of sight: nor must we allow ourselves to be deviated onto side-rails or slacken in our effort, for we might pay with our very lives for forgetting about this one and only and uppermost task.[186]

Communist regimes in East-Central Europe put their own spin on the history of World War II. The war was about Fascists and anti-Fascists battling it out at home and abroad, and the liberating force of the Soviet Red Army as it finally tipped the scales firmly in favor of the latter. Victims were of Fascism or of the exploitative upper classes; heroes were of the (working) people, and seeing oneself as one or both was not difficult given the hardship, losses, and deprivation suffered by most during the war.[187] The Communist version of the war gave the past a meaning many East-Central Europeans could live with in the postwar era, if not swallow whole.

Although this narrative does not require much in the way of historical probing to be discredited, this chapter has shown that even when Hungarians and Romanians were being anti-Fascists, it was generally not the case that opposition to the ideology of Fascism or the activities of Nazi Germany were foremost in their minds, but rather that being Communist became a means of achieving another, far more important goal, namely the recovery of Transylvania.

With the collapse of Communism, historians and politicians—often in the same person—tried to pick up where history had supposedly left off before the Communist ideological paintbrush had red-washed the war. The fighting forces and state leaders of Hungary, Romania, Croatia, Slovakia, and Bulgaria had not been Fascists and Fascist sympathizers, but anti-Bolsheviks with the foresight to recognize a real danger when it was heading their way, if not the strength to avert the impending national disaster.[188] Their alliance with Germany was incidental—or rather instrumental—rather than essential. (Who else was fighting Bolshevism? Not the Allies, certainly.) And the only ideological lens that distorted their vision was that of the "national interest." This version of the war gave the past a meaning many East-Central Europeans could live with in the post-Communist era, and many have swallowed it whole.

But even if the "national interest"—however defined—could be said to have been on the minds of leaders and soldiers during the 1941 and later 1942–43 offensives against the Soviet Union, this chapter has shown that the "Bolshevik menace," although a genuine concern, was not the primary preoccupation in Hungary and Romania. It certainly was not during the fall and winter of 1942–43, as increasingly ragged and depopulated armies pressed eastward to the Don River—and were pressed back westward by the Red Army—in an offensive that ended in tide-turning defeat of the Axis forces at Stalingrad. Instead, insofar as the political and military leadership and the rank and file in these countries could be said to have shared a common wartime preoccupation, it was with the possibility of losing or gaining territory, above all the territory of Transylvania.

Following the Second Vienna Arbitration, the quest for Transylvania was a mission shared by politicians and statesmen across the political spectrum—from extreme left to extreme right—who proposed different strategies for its achievement. Whatever the shape of the two governments' foreign policy and military mobilization strategy throughout the war, it was justified as the best means of winning Transylvania. For most of the war the struggle for control of that contested territory resembled a track race more than a boxing match. Instead of trying to defeat their opponent directly, the protagonists sought to outrun one another on the way to the inevitable reordering of Europe. But when the tide turned in the war to favor the Allies, the two states realized they were running in the wrong direction toward a dead end. This turn of events heightened the possibility that the track race would become a prizefight as leaders in both states scrambled to be the first to abandon the Axis and join the victorious Allies.

Yet if the military battles on the Eastern Front and in Transylvania were part of the contest over the fate of Transylvania, they were but one aspect of that contest, an aspect that should not be considered in isolation from a very different battle: the battle for the people of Transylvania.

CHAPTER THREE

People Between States

We must make Cluj Romanian, as this is the spine, the
vertebrae in the body of the Romanian state. Whoever is
the master of Cluj is the master of Transylvania.

—The first Romanian mayor of Cluj,
Iulian Pop, in March 1919[1]

Let us . . . pick up where we left off twenty years ago. . . .
[W]as it not a demented idea to try to turn Kolozsvár into
a Romanian city?

—Hungarian writer and critic Géza Laczkó in an article
entitled "Kluj," from October 1940[2]

On the afternoon of August 30, 1940, in the Transylvanian capital of Cluj,
a young boy could be seen "running like a madman, face red as a beet, covered with sweat" toward the house of his neighbor. Arriving at the gate, the
boy cried out in Hungarian, "Kolozsvár is ours!"[3] At about the same time in
another part of town, a forty-six-year-old man was listening to the radio as it
broadcast the outcome of the arbitration at Vienna. Upon hearing the news
that the Transylvanian capital would be ceded to Hungary, the man ran out
into the street shouting, among other things, "I'll see to it that the Hungarians
don't come! I'll drink the blood of the first Hungarian soldier I see!"[4]

Following the announcement of the Second Vienna Arbitration that day,
a new front opened in Transylvania. Although this was not a battlefront
in the traditional sense, it was, like the Eastern Front, an arena where the
struggle for control of the region played out. The soldiers in this battle were
ordinary people, civilians, whose weapons—in the form of laws, census
forms, permits, and testimonials—were forged by the state, distributed by
the state, and quite often, withheld by the state in the interest of achieving
what for Hungarian and Romanian leaders, politicians, statesmen and many
citizens was the foremost foreign policy objective: winning Transylvania.
Mobilization for this battle was immediate and had been a long time in the

making. Within hours of the announcement, the region began undergoing a rapid transformation precipitated by the movement of people, armies, and equipment. Already on the afternoon of August 30, people gathered in public parks, taverns, and private homes to protest, to celebrate, to mourn, and in many cases, to pack.[5]

The Battle Begins at Home

The Hungarian army's entry into Northern Transylvania was preceded, sometimes just hours before, by the withdrawal of Romanian army forces and government administrators.[6] On August 31, an order was distributed to the Romanian military command to inform its troops that if Romania failed to turn over Northern Transylvania, the country would be wiped off the map by a joint offensive to be carried out by Hungary, Bulgaria, Russia, Germany, and Italy.[7] "The organization of the decampment was perfect," carried out with "order and discipline," commented Ion Negoiţescu, a Romanian writer who was in the city at the time.[8] By order of the Romanian interior ministry, administrative offices and communal enterprises were to be left in such a state that they could continue to operate as they had before. On trucks loaded with personnel and equipment were also stacked boxes and bundles of paper.[9] Money, secret archives, and documents relating to the gendarmerie and police were to be removed, as were "statistical monographs, geographical volumes, charts and any studies which are of interest to us [Romanians] as an ethnic element in the ceded regions . . . libraries, museums belonging to villages, counties, territories, or the state, and only those rare ones that show us as the dominant people in Transylvania." The people, with the exception of government officials, "whose lives would be endangered due to their past attitude," were to stay where they were. Their task would be to "continue to assert the Romanian ethnicity."[10]

On September 1, a group of Romanian protesters stormed the German consulate in Oradea/Nagyvárad, climbing up to its third-floor offices and removing the sign from the wall. Later that same afternoon, Hungarians gathered around the building and sang the Hungarian national anthem, voicing their praise of Hitler and Mussolini.[11] Despite the ban on demonstrations imposed the following day, on September 3, a group of young men in Romanian military uniform stormed a radio station in Bucharest. Another young soldier stood before the royal palace and fired shots into the air. The German consulate in Bucharest had to be kept under constant guard to escape vandalism and attacks.[12] Despite Romanian claims to the contrary,

FIG. 13. Ad for Philips Radio published in the Hungarian daily *Népszava* [People's Word] on September 1, 1940 (*Népszava*, September 1, 1940, p. 2). In honor of the results of the Second Vienna Arbitration, the image shows the statue of King Matthias found on the main square in Kolozsvár with a broken border gate in the foreground. The text reads, "We greet you, brother!"

during the Romanian withdrawal from Northern Transylvania, there were numerous reports of looting and attacks on the Hungarian population.[13]

As Hungarian newspapers foreshadowed the advance of the Hungarian army into Northern Transylvania, demonstrators in Budapest showed their gratitude by celebrating in front of the German and Italian embassies.[14] Advertisements—for everything from light bulbs to radios to school supplies—hailed the reannexation, and the daily *Népszava* [People's Word] recommended in its weekly menu section that its readers prepare Kolozsvár cabbage and Transylvanian sweet cheese pudding to mark the occasion.[15] The Hungarian consulate in Bucharest was reportedly flooded with people asking how they could immigrate to the newly annexed territory, while trains departed toward Northern Transylvania "overstuffed with returnees."[16] In a special session of the upper house, Prime Minister Teleki declared: "Hungary never ceased voicing its revisionist demands. In vain did it turn to the League of Nations; the victorious powers tried to uphold a status quo that could not be upheld."[17]

On September 5, Hungarian troops crossed the border, and the follow-

FIG. 14. Photograph of spectators throwing flowers and waving Hungarian flags as the Hungarian army enters Kolozsvár on September 11, 1940. From the collection of András Fodor; reprinted with permission.

ing day they entered the city of Oradea/Nagyvárad, whence the Romanian administration had already removed statues of Romanian royalty and cultural icons.[18] Over the next week, an army over three hundred thousand strong advanced eastward toward the Carpathian Mountains, reaching their last outpost on September 13.[19] The largest, most symbolic celebration took place in the "heart of Transylvania," the city of Kolozsvár—formerly Cluj—which Hungarian soldiers entered on September 11.[20] For the festive parade on September 15, the streets were lined with flag-waving Hungarian patriots, houses were decorated with flags and banners, many of them faded and tattered from twenty-two years spent in attics or cellars, and groups of children and young men and women wore tricolor ribbons or dressed up in Hungarian national costume to welcome their liberators.[21] The city's largest café, which had borne the name "Regale" during the period of Romanian rule, featured a new sign out front that read "Hungária."[22] Hungary's military and civilian elite filed past, with Horthy riding in on a white horse. The parade was followed by a ceremony on the main square, where Horthy and a number of city officials and church representatives delivered speeches. Newsreels and photographs of the events were distributed throughout Hungary and could be seen in movie theaters, illustrated newspapers, and posters.[23]

FIG. 15. Hungarian regent Miklós Horthy speaking to a crowd of spectators gathered on the main square of Kolozsvár on September 15, 1940. Behind Horthy and to his right is Hungary's prime minister and Transylvania native Count Pál Teleki. From the collection of András Fodor; reprinted with permission.

Although Hungarian soldiers were told that they were "not entitled to initiate reprisals for the wrongs of the past twenty-two years," their entry into Northern Transylvania in 1940 was not without casualties.[24] As the troops entered the town of Bánffyhunyad[25] on September 10, two individuals—one an Orthodox priest—came out and reportedly began spitting at the soldiers, saying, "Go back to Asia where you belong!" and "These are not human beings!" According to a Hungarian source, at that point two hundred to three hundred individuals from the crowd started beating up, kicking, and throwing stones at the two men. Then two gendarmes and one soldier insisted on taking the two individuals to the edge of town, where they reportedly told those gathered, "You can do what you like now, because today there is still no [rule of] law."[26] Thereafter the crowd beat the two individuals to death and buried the bodies.[27]

Several other incidents of mistreatment, even murder of Romanians, were reported in communities throughout the region, starting with a border incident on September 4, when Hungarian soldiers opened fire on Romanian border guards at Diószeg.[28] Romanian sources place the total body count for the period from August 30, 1940, to November 1, 1941, at 919 individuals, with the greatest number of victims (436) in Szilágy[29] County during September 1940. In one village, Ipp,[30] 157 individuals were killed by Hungarian soldiers and collaborators in a single night (September 13–14).[31] Arrests of Romanians were also common during this period.[32]

Speaking to a group of Transylvanian and other Hungarian elites in mid-October 1940, Prime Minister Teleki condemned these actions of the Hungarian military. He said the "Transylvanian perspective" on the nationalities question was one of "conciliation." He continued: "We began with this conception. I use the word 'we' intentionally, because I am not saying that the Hungarian army and the Hungarian government came here with that intention. Sadly with their excesses [*uszitásokkal*] they spoiled the situation," thereby creating "the present press and diplomatic struggle."[33] Nevertheless, during a meeting with the German foreign minister on November 20, Teleki downplayed the scope of the atrocities, placing the blame for many of them—including the mass expulsion of Romanian intellectuals and professionals from Kolozsvár—on one "'clumsy' colonel." Of the stabbings and beatings that took place, Teleki purportedly explained that "there was always fighting and stabbing at a real wedding."[34]

The atrocities perpetrated against Romanians in Northern Transylvania were initially reported, and often exaggerated, in the Romanian press, causing trouble not only for Teleki and the Hungarian government but also for the Antonescu government, which had taken steps to silence anti-Hungarian and Romanian revisionist voices that opposed the Axis alliance.[35] Among these voices was that of Iuliu Maniu, a prominent Romanian statesman of the interwar period who had joined forces with Ion Antonescu to achieve King Carol II's abdication in early September of 1940.[36] Maniu and Antonescu nevertheless quickly parted political ways. Maniu's frustration with the failure of the Bucharest government for allowing Transylvania to slip away shifted readily from Carol II to Antonescu. Already on September 8, Maniu organized a meeting to protest the Second Vienna Arbitration, and on September 14 he told Ioan Hudiţa about the masses of Romanian refugees fleeing Northern Transylvania who "reproached the Regat for disappointing and abandoning them" and wanted to "break all ties with Bucharest."[37] In that same discussion Maniu laid the groundwork for a protracted political battle with Ion Antonescu around the Transylvanian Question.

A month later Maniu created an organization called "Pro Transilvania," the purpose of which was to lobby for Northern Transylvania's reannexation to Romania.[38] Additionally, in 1941, he actively sought the support of Romanians in the United States to "enlighten . . . public opinion and unmask the Hungarian false democrats who have flooded America."[39] The Antonescu government, fearing Maniu's Anglophile reputation would damage Romania's chances of gaining Axis support for the Romanian claim on Transylvania, banned "Pro Transilvania" on November 16, 1940, calling its activities incompatible with "the international obligations and interests of Romania."[40] In a letter to Antonescu from February 1941, Maniu confronted the Conducător, saying that the ban on "Pro Transilvania" had "impeded even those discreet initiatives" that had sought to win back the lost territories.

> In ceded Transylvania hundreds of thousands of Romanians are massacred or forced out of their homes, priests are murdered or thrown over the border, so that not even newborns can be baptized, and are buried in a manner better befitting animal corpses, void of all dignity and holy services. And the regime here does not register the smallest protest, nor are the newspapers permitted to speak of these matters. We cannot give our vote to a regime that assists passively in this or is incapable of obtaining justice and satisfaction.[41]

The reply from Antonescu came only in June 1941, but it was dozens of pages long. In it, he accused Maniu of making "perfidious" and "superficial" accusations. "What kind of attitude would you have seen us take to the change of borders? A front with the Axis, author of the Vienna arbitration of August 30 which was accepted by the Romanian state? Would it be politically desirable? Would it be smart? I am not so jealous of the likes of Yugoslavia that I regret not doing what they did."[42] Antonescu went on to say that "Pro Transilvania" was banned because making a public issue out of the sufferings of Romanians in the ceded territories (including Northern Transylvania) would upset internal order and peace and frustrate the regime's diplomatic actions in the interest of winning the territories back. Further, he argued, the organization would undoubtedly "be seen as—and rightly so—an organization secretly promoting your own [Maniu's] political initiatives."[43]

Maniu appealed the ban and won the appeal on February 18, 1942.[44] By then, the popularity of Romania's alliance with the Axis was on the decline, given that the territory Romania had lost to the Soviet Union had been recovered the previous summer, yet there was still Axis pressure to commit more to the war effort against the Soviet Union with no explicit guarantee that Northern Transylvania would be the reward for that commitment.[45]

Meanwhile, in newly annexed Hungarian Northern Transylvania, the Hungarian administration faced challenges of its own. The territory was initially placed under a military administration until November 26, 1940, when it was turned over to civil authorities.[46] During that time, the region's legal and government administrative structures had to be brought in line with Hungary's after a twenty-two-year divergence. "It is an unbelievably large task!" wrote one Hungarian commentator in October 1940; "the people should be made of steel to achieve it."[47] The process entailed a complete overhaul of the school system; the construction of transportation infrastructure; the re-relocation of the Hungarian university back to the Transylvanian capital from its exile in Szeged; the implementation of anti-Jewish legislation; the introduction of wartime rationing, conscription, and censorship measures; and the implementation of a wide range of restrictive policies and legal norms affecting religious groups, social, cultural, and political organizations, and privately owned businesses and factories. To discuss the many challenges facing the new administration, for two days starting on October 18 a group of local, regional, and national elites representing a variety of political, economic, and cultural institutions met secretly in Kolozsvár's city hall with Prime Minister Pál Teleki in what was known as the "Transylvanian Conference."[48]

Despite Teleki's assertion at the conference that the civilian administration posts would be filled with Transylvanians whenever possible, many of the higher-level state officials and most of the military officers who were to govern or assume command of troops in the reannexed territories came from Trianon Hungary.[49] These individuals were often labeled "parachutists" [*ejtőernyősök*] because "they dropped into positions of leadership from above with no knowledge of conditions in Transylvania." In fact, the Hungarian administration had anticipated the reannexation of Transylvania and prepared for it well in advance. In his memoirs, the former lord lieutenant [*főispán*] of two Transylvanian counties and later regional commissioner [*kormánybiztos*] of Northern Transylvania, Béla Bethlen, recalled that plans for the reannexation of the pre-Trianon territories were made long before the advent of the Second Vienna Arbitration and even included placement of specific officials in administrative positions in Southern Transylvania, a territory which was not reannexed.[50]

Northern Transylvania was initially represented in the Hungarian parliament by forty-five individuals, nominated by the government at the behest of Prime Minister Teleki. Most of these representatives soon became members of the so-called Transylvanian Party (Erdélyi Párt), a reincarnation of the State Hungarian Party of Romania (Romániai Országos Magyar Párt) that was the primary minority party of the Hungarians during the period of Romanian rule.[51] The party was supportive of Prime Minister Pál Teleki—himself of Transylvanian origin—and of the Hungarian government's policy more generally, on the condition that it be allowed to manage its own affairs. The party's program, adopted May 28, 1941, included "reparation for injustices committed by the Romanian authorities" and "no Party agitation in Transylvania, as this would weaken the Magyars against the Romanians." It also included a call for "social legislation in favor of workers and employees."[52]

In order to keep the Northern Transylvanian Hungarians politically united and to limit dissent within the government, the Transylvanian Party was the only officially recognized party in Northern Transylvania.[53] Furthermore, there were no elections in Northern Transylvania following the Second Vienna Arbitration, nor indeed in any of the other reannexed territories. Instead, members of parliament were appointed or "called up."

One thing became clear from the moment the Transylvanian representatives joined the parliament: Transylvania was different from the rest of Hungary. Its economic structure, its agricultural potential, even its people were in many respects unlike those of Trianon Hungary.[54] Prime Minister Teleki was among the first to draw out its uniqueness during a speech celebrating the recovery of Northern Transylvania. Transylvania, he said, was "more Hungarian" than other parts of Hungary.[55] "We learned over the course of twenty-two years what it means to live outside the Hungarian state and the Hungarian homeland," said one Transylvanian representative in a session of parliament. Experience had taught the Hungarians living there to venerate the "interests of statehood [*államiság érdekeit*] above all else." The need to build up the state was not a conclusion reached only recently by statesmen, but one reached long ago by the nation itself, which had refused to settle for the sentence of Trianon.[56] Prime Minister Teleki echoed this notion in his speech. "The nation itself [*maga a nép*] was the carrier of this spirit and will remain so in the future."[57]

Yet in addition to its particularly strong "Hungarian" credentials, Transylvania's leadership also emphasized the region's diversity as among its most prized features. The Hungarians therefore could not afford to be "closed in on themselves"; they had to be magnanimous, both individually and officially, vis-à-vis the nationalities. So it was that a significant portion of the discussions during the Transylvanian Conference of October 1940 revolved around the Transylvanian leadership's desire that all Hungarians should learn Romanian, and ideally also German.[58] Calvinist priest and member of parliament László Ravasz further stressed that Transylvanians were especially receptive to the idea that "public administration is not about empire, or giving orders, but about service."[59]

And Transylvanian Hungarians felt they had learned still other lessons that could benefit the state and the nation. The perceived need to form a united front in the face of Romanian state oppression, coupled with the leveling effect of the Romanian land reform of 1920–21 and other forms of economic advantage reversal, and the intellectual influence of Romanian rural sociology had eliminated much of the social stratification that was still a prominent and much-criticized feature of Trianon Hungarian society.[60] One Transylvanian representative proposed the "elimination of titles" [*címkorság megszüntetése*] in the interest of making "the whole of Hungarian life more social and more populist."[61] This was to be a recurring theme throughout the war, especially as putting workers on a "national" as opposed to an "international" base would not only strengthen the state and nation, but also have the parallel advantage of nipping Bolshevik tendencies in the bud.[62]

During a visit made by Hungarian prime minister László Bárdossy to the Transylvanian capital in January 1942, the president of the Transylvanian Party, Béla Teleki, gave a speech in which he said that "the simplicity and unmediated nature of public life we learned during our experience of being a minority should stay with us." Further, he added, if there is to be gain, "that gain should be shared by all magyardom. As regards the workers question . . . the only positive outcome of our oppression is the leveled Hungarian society that came into being as a result of the [Romanian] occupation. . . . The joy of liberation awoke in [the workers] a Hungarian national consciousness and self-esteem. . . . Transylvanian workers now stand on a 100 percent Hungarian base."[63] Bárdossy's successor, Miklós Kállay, restated this position during his visit to Transylvania in April 1942. "Transylvania has already been an example to all of magyardom countless times," he said, adding that he felt the Transylvanian approach to the workers question was just such an example.[64]

Yet what made Transylvania special in regard to the social question also made it potentially dangerous in the eyes of state leaders. During the interwar period in Trianon Hungary, following the Bolshevik revolution there in 1919, the Communist Party was outlawed and its members ruthlessly hunted by Horthy's regime in what became known as the "white terror." Meanwhile, however, the Communist Party of Romania—made up largely of Hungarians and Hungarian-speaking Jews from Transylvania—remained active. In fact, Transylvanian voters counted for the majority of votes cast for the Communist Party in Romania during the parliamentary elections of 1926, 1927, 1928, and 1931.[65] Many of these individuals felt Communism would ameliorate the plight of minorities by focusing on social as opposed to national inequality and oppression.[66] Thus the Hungarian state inherited some members of the (admittedly very small) Communist movement along with Northern Transylvania, which it immediately set out to crush.[67] The Kolozsvár-based leftist literary magazine *Korunk* [Our Time] was immediately banned, and the Hungarian secret police forces, known as the DEF, began rounding up and imprisoning thousands of suspected Communists in a series of raids. In July 1941, shortly after the Nazi attack on the USSR, the DEF established a headquarters in a village near Kolozsvár from where its operatives arrested hundreds of Northern Transylvanian Communists, effectively destroying the core of the movement there.[68]

Making the DEF's work easier was the fact that some Communists abandoned the cause once Northern Transylvania became Hungarian again, thereby eliminating its "minority advocate" appeal. In fact, one of the greatest successes of the DEF was convincing an important leader of the Communist movement in Transylvania, Júlia Szabó, that it was unpatriotic, given the success of the Axis alliance marked by the Second Vienna Arbitration, to subscribe to a transnational ideology along with "non-Hungarians."[69] Szabó then proceeded to denounce other key figures in the party.

The list of indictees from the 1941 roundup demonstrates the extent to which Hungarian workers formed an important core of the party at that time. Of the 127 inhabitants of Kolozsvár indicted, 75 were workers, 55 gave their nationality as Hungarian and 68 gave their mother tongue as Hungarian. By religion 66 were Jews, and of the remainder, 50 were either Calvinists, Roman Catholics, or Unitarians ("Hungarian"-coded denominations), many of whom considered themselves Hungarian patriots. In all, there were only four self-declared Romanians among the indictees.[70]

The regime was thus wrong to assume that the fate of Transylvania was a matter of indifference to Communists. The issue preoccupied even the Moscow-trained Stalinist Mátyás Rákosi, such that on December 5, 1942, Bulgarian Communist Georgi Dimitrov wrote in his diary: "Delayed publication of Rákosi's article about Transylvania in *Bolshevik* on the grounds that it is *pro-Hungarian!*"[71]

Beyond the Communists, there was another, quite different political force seeking to win over the inhabitants of Northern Transylvania and the other reannexed territories: extreme right-wing parties. The Arrow Cross, the Hungarian Party of Renewal [Magyar Megújulás Pártja], and the Hungarian Life

Party [Magyar Élet Pártja] saw opportunities for expansion in the new territories. Because these areas were generally considered less socially stratified
than Trianon Hungary, they were especially attractive to the extreme right
in Hungary, which was strongly populist in orientation. When the Felvidék
was reannexed, Hungary's prime minister at the time, Béla Imrédy (who later
became the founder and head of the Party of Renewal), said the Hungarians there were "more fresh-minded" and would endow the country with "a
deeper sense of social responsibility."[72] As for Transylvania, many among
the extreme right considered it "virgin" territory and made plans to set up
branches of their parties with the entry of the first Hungarian troops into
the region.[73]

Despite Teleki's attempts to keep party politics out of Transylvania with
the creation of the Transylvanian Party, the newly annexed territory became
a center of right-wing agitation, concentrated especially in the larger cities.[74]
The national socialist Arrow Cross Party, headed by Ferenc Szálasi, saw Transylvania as part of the key to their plan for the remaking of Europe.[75] Szálasi believed that society should be organized horizontally, eliminating class
boundaries through the creation of a national community.[76] The existence
of such a community nevertheless would not preclude cooperation with
members of other nationalities. The lord lieutenant of Nagyvárad, who was
charged with monitoring Arrow Cross activities in Northern Transylvania,[77]
said this of Szálasi:

> He imagines Hungary's role in the new Europe as the member of a confederation
> with the five bordering states, including Romania. With that the country borders
> will disappear, as will the nationality problem. . . . In order to realize this plan vis-à-
> vis Romania, the party has begun serious work there. The goal is to win members
> of the Romanian intelligentsia over to their cause. These will then initiate the lower
> classes into the plan as their spiritual leaders and guides.[78]

Although the Imrédyists agreed with Szálasi that "the fulfillment of the
Hungarian calling cannot take place in spite of Europe. . . . We must accommodate ourselves to Europe," they were very much opposed to the Arrow
Cross's proposed federation. The difference of opinion on this point was
apparent already in the summer of 1940: "Hungarism [the Arrow Cross
ideology] is unthinkable [because] it aspires to dissolve the Hungarian, the
German, the Slovak, the Ruthenian, and the Romanian into a unit. [We agree]
that we should all live in one state, but we should be the ones to lead and
govern it." In fact, their differences on the proper resolution of the Transylvanian Question and Hungary's place in a reordered Europe go a long way
toward explaining why extreme-right parties in Hungary were unable to put
together a shared platform, despite numerous attempts.[79]

Extremist political figures—from Communists to national socialists—nevertheless did share the view of the reannexed territories as potential laboratories for plans to try out new policies, remake the state, or redefine Europe.[80] The same was true in Romania, where Transylvanian-born legionnaire intellectual Emil Cioran argued in 1941 that Transylvanians "represent the perfect foundation and the human substance of a state" by virtue of their "respect for authorities" and "awkward modesty." He went on to suggest that all Romanians should be "Transylvanized."[81] Like the Hungarian leadership, Antonescu experienced similar challenges to his authority from Communists and Fascists in Romania, both of whom felt they had a superior vision for the reordering of Europe and the resolution of the Transylvanian Question. And like the Hungarian government, Antonescu made efforts to silence these and other critics.

The most serious challenge to Antonescu's authority prior to his arrest by King Mihai I in August 1944 came during the Legionnaires' rebellion of January 1941. The Legionnaires were members of an extreme right movement that had initially called itself the Legion of the Archangel Michael, later the Iron Guard. The movement was founded in 1927 by Corneliu Zelea Codreanu, a charismatic figure who advocated militant anti-Semitism, Orthodox spirituality, and glorification of the peasantry. The legion was active during the interwar period coordinating acts of political violence and public displays, the latter consisting mostly of funerals of fallen members. Its followers were mistrusted by Carol II, and Codreanu was arrested and killed in 1938, in what government spokesmen described as an escape attempt. After his death, Codreanu rapidly became a martyr of the movement, which gained strength as Carol lost credibility following the Second Vienna Arbitration.

When Ion Antonescu came to power, his cabinet was initially dominated by Iron Guardists, headed by the new vice president of the Council of Ministers, Horia Sima. Although the Legionnaires occupied only five of the nineteen cabinet positions in Antonescu's government, they wielded a power that was disproportionate to their numbers, and Romania was declared a "National Legionary State" by royal decree on September 14, 1940. There was nevertheless mutual distrust between Antonescu and the Iron Guardists, whose behavior became increasingly violent and unpredictable.[82] A small group of Legionnaires had been among the few to resist the incoming Hungarian army following the Second Vienna Arbitration, in defiance of Antonescu's insistence on adhering to its terms.[83] And on November 28, 1940, Legionnaires murdered and mutilated the bodies of Romanian historian Nicolae Iorga and an economist, Virgil Madgearu. Madgearu was targeted for his Hungarian roots and critical stance vis-à-vis the Iron Guard, which was expressly anti-Hungarian.[84] Two days later, on November 30, the guardists organized a belated funeral for their martyred leader, Codreanu. Representatives of all Axis allies were present at the funeral, except Hungary.[85] An Iron Guard flyer posted around the Transylvanian capital that fall called Hungarians "wild beasts who not so long ago ate raw meat!"[86]

In the weeks that followed the funeral, the division between Antonescu and the guardists grew more pronounced as the latter brazenly attacked political targets and Jews, with the violence often affecting passersby.[87] In January, the rebellion reached its peak when guardists tried to seize power by force. During that time, at a Legionnaire rally in the Southern Transylvanian city of Braşov, guardists swore to get Transylvania back.[88] Meanwhile, a list surfaced of the names of individuals targeted for assassination by the Iron Guard in the Southern Transylvanian city of Arad in the event of a successful coup. It included names of their political opponents, Jews, and local Hungarians.[89]

As Hitler planned the upcoming assault on the Soviet Union, the last thing he wanted was unrest in Romania, since he was counting on Romanian petroleum for the offensive. With Hitler's support, then, Antonescu was given a free hand to crush the rebellion.[90] The Romanian leader ordered the arrest and execution of many guardists in the months that followed, introducing a conservative military dictatorship with renewed legitimacy, especially following the successful reannexation of Bessarabia and Northern Bukovina during the offensive against the USSR.[91] In a propaganda publication of the presidency of the Council of Ministers from 1942, the Antonescu government sought to discredit the Legionnaires' activities and justify the move to eliminate them, saying they had fed the ambitions of Romania's revisionist neighbors, foremost among which was Hungary. The two-volume booklet, entitled *Pe marginea prăpastiei* [On the Brink of Calamity], drew out the Legionnaires' supposed ties to the Hungarian Arrow Cross movement, as well as the "internal weakness of Romania" that resulted from the rebellion.

> Already, from the moment of the installation of the Legionnaires in power, Hungary counted on disorder in Romania. The Hungarian general staff and government drew up a plan for conquering the whole of Transylvania, a conquest that would have been made possible as a result of some "bloody events that will inevitably come to pass in Romania following the Legionnaires' rise to power." . . . Anyone could have seen the danger to which our country was exposed as a result of the vanity of irresponsible, ambitious, and reckless [men] who wanted power at any price.[92]

Unlike the case of the Legionnaires, Antonescu's strategy vis-à-vis the Communists was one of zero tolerance from the very beginning. A very small force in Romania during the interwar period, the Communist Party became even smaller as a result of the loss of Northern Transylvania.[93] Part of the Communists' unpopularity between the two world wars was a product of their expressly antinational platform, which limited its appeal largely to minorities—among them Hungarians, Ukrainians, and Jews—who occupied key positions in the party throughout the interwar period.[94] In September 1941, however, the Romanian Communists came out with a program calling for the overthrow of the Antonescu government and the recovery of Northern Transylvania, opening up the possibility of forming a "united front" with other critics of Antonescu, among them the Legionnaires and liberals like Maniu.[95]

Condemning the Communists for their support of the USSR, which had taken vast areas of Romania's territory in the summer of 1940 and with whom Romania went to war in the summer of 1941 in order to recover that territory, was relatively simple. In addition, the Antonescu government executed some and interned other leading members of the minuscule Communist movement at a prison camp in Tîrgu Jiu.[96]

The Language and Science of Legitimacy

Beyond efforts to consolidate state power and eliminate sources of political opposition, state leaders and bureaucrats also built on a tradition of using language to project the legitimacy of their claims to Transylvania. Advocates for the two states thus developed mutually exclusive variants of the historical significance of the Second Vienna Arbitration and Transylvania's status. To the Hungarian administration, the territory of Northern Transylvania was a "liberated territory," or more commonly, a "reannexed territory," creating the sense of an interrupted continuity being restored.[97] This designation was complemented by the use of the term *occupation* in reference to the period of Romanian rule in the region and the phrase "not-yet liberated territory" or "the territory that stayed behind" in reference to Southern Transylvania.[98] The Romanian administration, on the other hand, tended to include the whole of Transylvania (Northern and Southern) under the heading "Greater Romania."[99] References to Southern Transylvania were as "the free part of Transylvania," whereas Northern Transylvania was "occupied" or "ravished [*răpit*]."[100]

These divergent takes on the nature of the Second Vienna Arbitration were supplemented by references to the barbarity and backwardness of the other state and its people.[101] A Romanian academic thus referred to certain actions of the Hungarian state as those of "barbarians of the Middle Ages."[102] In a popular song among refugees from the Transylvanian capital to Romania, "Homesick for Cluj," one of the verses lamented:

> We raised magnificent churches for you
> We made you into a center of culture
> We built you fairy-tale palaces
> And now the barbarians have come to steal them![103]

Beyond these efforts to portray the other nationality as "barbaric," there was also considerable sensitivity, especially on the Romanian side, about being *perceived* as uncivilized by Hungarians and their sympathizers.[104] Antonescu, for example, said that some Transylvanian Romanians "continued to have relations with Hungarians, spoke Hungarian, and—so as not to lose it—read Hungarian newspapers, went to Budapest for Easter and Christmas, instead of coming to Bucharest, because [to them] we were gypsies, good only for spilling our blood and giving them our gold."[105]

Arguments for why Transylvania should be given to Romania thus emphasized the extent to which Romania was more "modern" than Hungary. In his December 1940 letter to Mussolini, Iuliu Maniu stressed how twenty-two years of Romanian rule had brought "progress" and "civilization" to the region by means of eliminating "feudalism," introducing agrarian reform, reforming the system of sanitation, and "incorporating the entire Danubian Basin and the Carpathian region into a modern network of communications," all of which showed Romania operated according to "modern principles of statehood."[106]

And to reciprocate charges of Romanian backwardness and barbarism, Romanian commentators drew on the supposed links between the Hungarians and the Huns. One informer for the Romanian government living in Northern Transylvania made references in his letters to the "Hun culture" that prevailed in Northern Transylvania under Hungarian rule.[107] In internal correspondence of the Romanian military from August 10, 1943, the chief of the General Staff, General Ilie Şteflea, declared that twenty years of Romanian rule had not succeeded in eliminating the "hun-like habits"—which included "theft, burglary, degeneracy, etc."—of the Hungarian population of Transylvania. Even worse, the "degrading moral decay" that he claimed typified the Hungarian rule of Transylvania from 1867 to 1918 had "infected our Romanians."[108] Şteflea concluded with the recommendation that soldiers in Transylvania be forbidden any contact with the Hungarian population, "so that we can cleanse the youths' fresh spirits of the rude habits they picked up from the foreign atmosphere in which they have lived till now."

On the Hungarian side, the belief that twenty-two years of Romanian rule had had a corruptive influence on the population of Transylvania was widespread and frequently mentioned. In a speech before the Hungarian parliament on June 13, 1941, Transylvanian Party representative Baron Antal Braunecker lamented that "over the course of twenty-two years public morality . . . has been greatly corrupted."[109] Hungarian newspapers regularly published articles decrying the blow Romanian rule had struck to Transylvania's economic and social health, arguing that high rates of illiteracy, child mortality, infectious disease, and the deplorable state of public sanitation and transportation were the direct result of Romanian backwardness and mismanagement.[110] In a report on criminal behavior in Hungary since the outbreak of the war, one statistician concluded that the higher crime rate in the reannexed territories was attributable to the fact that the population of these regions "has been more corrupted over the past twenty years than the population of [Trianon Hungary], which has enjoyed more ideal public and legal security."[111]

It also often happened that "parachutist" administrators and military commanders bawled out their Transylvanian Hungarian subordinates by calling them "Romanian," or worse, "*oláh*." In the army the practice was so common and created so much tension between Transylvanian soldiers and their Trianon-Hungarian commanders that on more than one occasion specific orders had to be issued forbidding such name-calling.[112] A 1942 episode in Kolozsvár, in which a passenger called a city bus driver and a ticket taker "*oláh*" resulted in a major investigation and a spate of testimonies and accusations.[113] In general, the "corruption" of the Transylvanian Hungarian population was presumed to be the result of overexposure to the uncivilized, even unclean Romanians. The first verse of a popular Hungarian song, entitled "For Transylvania," went as follows:

> Morning, evening, after nightfall, or at noon,
> One day we will indeed go to Transylvania
> The girls will smile, and we will smile back
> No one will cry save the wimpy *oláhs* glistening with grease.[114]

In general, the term *oláh* (meaning Vlach) implied a rejection of the notion of Romanians' Daco-Roman descent in favor of a different theory claiming the Romanians are the descendants of the pastoral Vlachs who migrated north into the Carpathian Basin from the Balkans in the thirteenth century (i.e., *after* the arrival of the Magyars).[115] Romanians were called *oláh* by Hungarians in private contexts, and occasionally even in official correspondence.[116] It is noteworthy that Hungarian soldiers, upon entering Northern Transylvania in the first days of September 1940, were expressly warned *not* to use the world *oláh* in the presence of Romanians as it was considered especially offensive.[117]

In order to lend these linguistic distinctions a material reality, researchers on both sides of the border searched for a scientific basis for racial differentiation in Transylvania. Their efforts entailed locating biological differences between Hungarians and Romanians, but also claiming that the purest of each race could be found in Transylvania.[118] The work of racial anthropologists and serologists was thus inextricably bound to the politics of legitimating territorial claims. In a 1938 issue of the Romanian *Bulletin of Eugenics and Biopolitics*, racial eugenicist Iordache Făcăoaru wrote: "In our national politics, anthropology has the role of clarifying some of the most important issues concerning our political rights over the territory we possess and over the territories we do not possess."[119]

Less than two years after the appearance of Făcăoaru's article, on the eve of the Second Vienna Arbitration, a Romanian scientist at the university in Cluj published a paper in which he "proved" through examination of blood types that "from the racial standpoint Hungarians have no right to Transylvania" and that a territorial revision could be demanded by Romania more readily than by Hungary, since so many Romanians had been "absorbed" by the Hungarians.[120] The annual year-end report of the Transylvanian Scientific Institute from 1943 included an article on the work of a Hungarian professor at the university in Kolozsvár, Lajos Csík, who undertook "blood type and other eugenic examinations" on over twenty-five hundred Romanians and seventy Hungarians during the course of the year. The stated goal of these examinations was to determine the extent of racial difference between Hungarians and Romanians, which Csík and his team concluded was considerable.[121] Another group was occupied with aptitude tests that accounted for "Hungarian racial traits."[122] Such research projects, and their less institutionalized spin-offs, resulted in a report concluding that 50 to 55 percent of the "Romanian" population of Northern Transylvania consisted of romanianized Hungarians. Echoing the standards laid down in the Nuremberg Laws, the report suggested that everyone with at least two Hungarian grandparents should be remagyarized, which one employer proposed to do by informing individual employees (one by one and in closed-door consultations) that they were actually Hungarians.[123]

The People as Territory

Race science was only one component of Transylvanian people's centrality to territorial claims. The people's historical and contemporary identity, their experience under "foreign oppression" or "occupation," their relationship to the state in which they lived and the state that laid claim to them and the property they owned were all presumed to have value in the struggle to win Transylvania. As such, the rhetoric of minority rights and arguments regarding the general well-being of Transylvania's inhabitants were as prevalent in official and popular discussions of the Transylvanian Question in the two states during the war as they had been during the interwar period. In 1941, a Hungarian commentator went so far as to conclude that Romania's loss of Bessarabia, Bukovina, Dobruja, and Transylvania was the direct result of its leaders' misguided minority policy.[124] This is not to say that these states were categorically protective and sympathetic toward their own "ethnic base" in Transylvania. Indeed, appearances were often much more important than reality, but ordinary people were the ones called to do the appearing, while the state held a virtual monopoly on the manufacture of reality.[125]

One group of people with special status in this hierarchy of value were refugees, or optants. Articles 3 and 4 of the Second Vienna Arbitration gave individuals who were—or would soon become—members of the minority nationality six months to opt for the state where they would belong to the majority.[126] Reports on the numbers of refugees, or optants, fleeing to and from Hungary and Romania offer a sense of the scale of the resultant cross-border migration. In the case of Hungary, from the Second Vienna Arbitration up to 1943, the interior ministry's Ninth Social Work Division reported providing aid to around two hundred thousand refugees, and the government spent 36 million pengő on various forms of aid and support for them.[127] From September 1 to December 31, 1940, the Romanian state reportedly provided aid to 234,714 refugees in the amount of around 200 million lei.[128]

The numbers of refugees fleeing to and from Northern Transylvania were thus undeniably significant, and the two states felt an obligation to make special accommodations for them. Although many refugees presumably went uncounted, staying with relatives and making their own way, the ones who crossed the border with no support network were put at the mercy of state aid agencies. Refugees fleeing to Northern Transylvania in 1940 received a daily allowance from the Hungarian state of two pengő forty fillér and were initially housed in refugee camps.[129] The challenge, then, was to find jobs for them. Many refugee heads of households wrote letters to the mayor's office asking for work, but the city could rarely offer anything but promises to consider them for future positions.[130] Although official statistics showed that, of the nearly five thousand individuals seeking jobs in the Transylvanian capital after August 30, 1940, 4,402 had been placed as of June 1941, there were still 1,345 unemployed individuals seeking work in June 1941.[131]

The Romanian government provided aid to its refugees in a variety of ways. On December 31, 1940, Antonescu boasted that by November 15 of that year, 152,159 professionals, students, workers, and peasants who had fled across the new border were placed in jobs and schools.[132] Lawyers were given grants of between twenty thousand and forty thousand lei to establish themselves, and medical professionals were placed through the Ministry of Labor and Sanitation. Other economic resources—mostly expropriated from the Jews—were earmarked for refugees, including 163,181 hectares of arable land, 14 breweries and distilleries, 49 commercial mills, and 178 agricultural mills.[133] During the first months of his tenure as head of state Ion Antonescu repeatedly emphasized his government's efforts to provide for the refugees.[134]

In general, the combination of the war, refugee traffic, and the two states' policy of reciprocating slights to the other state's minority had a considerable effect on the labor force throughout the region. The Dermata leatherworks in the Transylvanian capital employed around three thousand men and women at full capacity, but due to material shortages caused by the war, in 1942 there were probably only around two thousand people working there.[135] At that time the factory mainly produced army boots, which rendered it essential to the Axis war effort. Following the Second Vienna Arbitration, nearly 90 percent of the factory's seven hundred Romanian employees either opted for Romania or were dismissed from their positions.[136] The same was true of other factories in Northern Transylvania, including the porcelain and tobacco factories in Kolozsvár. Nor was this rapid change in the national character of the workforce unique to the factories of Northern Transylvania. In Romania, too, particularly in Southern Transylvania and Bucharest, hundreds if not thousands of Hungarians were fired from their jobs, ostensibly to reciprocate atrocities and slights against the Romanian minority in Northern Transylvania. Many chose or were forced to flee across the border into Hungary.[137]

The placement of refugees in homes and jobs raised the question of *whose* homes and *whose* jobs they should have. In Hungarian Northern Transylvania, taking over the property of Romanians who had fled to Romania was one option.[138] In countless appeals to municipal and state officials, Hungarian refugees from Southern Transylvania and the Regat asked for everything from furniture to arable land that had once belonged to Romanians.[139] Poorer

Hungarian refugees who could not find work and had no relatives to shelter them once the refugee camps were closed settled in slums in Kolozsvár, which the new Hungarian administration had plans to demolish.[140] The city's mayor asked the interior ministry to allow him to reopen the refugee camps to accommodate the displaced refugees, but his request was denied. By way of an alternative, the president of the Transylvanian Party in Kolozsvár, József Nyirő, proposed that the Hungarian refugees living in slums be relocated to the houses of Romanian government officials who had left their homes without an overseer.[141]

Opposite the Transylvanian capital, about thirty kilometers to the south on the Romanian side, was the city of Turda. The border ran between two cities—Kolozsvár on the Hungarian side and Turda on the Romanian side—making Turda a popular departure, stopover, and settlement location for refugees fleeing to and from Northern Transylvania.[142] When the Romanian administrative and other government offices evacuated the capital after the announcement of the Second Vienna Arbitration, the police headquarters relocated to Turda, operating under the title "Inspectoratul de Poliție Cluj" [Inspectorate of the Cluj Police] for the duration of the period of Hungarian rule.[143] It was in Turda that the Romanian government experimented with housing Romanian refugees with Hungarian families.[144] There and elsewhere in Romania it was common practice to place refugees in the homes of Hungarians who had fled or owned more than one residential property, or more commonly, in the homes of Jews that had been expropriated.[145] In fact, the government office charged with distributing aid to refugees was part of the same one that oversaw the material disenfranchisement of the Jews.[146]

Romanian officials also considered settling Transylvanian refugees in the territory they would reannex from the Soviet Union following their participation in Operation Barbarossa. On June 17, 1941, Mihai Antonescu spoke of this possibility, but rejected the idea on the grounds that would-be refugees should above all be discouraged from fleeing Northern Transylvania. Moving refugees to Bessarabia, he argued, would constitute "a serious encouragement to Hungarian politicians and a shameful action with regard to our aims and rights in Transylvania."[147]

The idea that refugees should stay in Transylvania, indeed should not have become refugees at all, was voiced repeatedly by both state administrations, especially as refugees continued to cross into both countries even after the border officially closed on December 16, 1942.[148] It was costly and difficult to find work and homes for them once they arrived, but more importantly, voluntary population transfers of this sort reified the borders established by the Second Vienna Arbitration, which both sides found untenable. Since most statesmen in Romania and Hungary wanted their state to have control over Northern *and* Southern Transylvania, they made it a priority to gain control over the border—control meaning the ability to decide who and what could come and go, when, and on what terms. This entailed discouraging members of their own national groups from defecting to the "homeland."

The Romanian Consul in Kolozsvár admonished the Romanians of Northern Transylvania to remain in their homes, sell none of their property, and wait for the forthcoming reannexation.[149] Similarly, the leader of the Romanian minority in Northern Transylvania, Emil Haţieganu, told his fellow Romanians: "Stay where you are! You have a duty to perform here!"[150] One Hungarian who lived in Northern Transylvania during the war suspected that the Romanians who stayed in Northern Transylvania following the Second Vienna Arbitration did so in order to lend credence to the idea that the border was provisional.[151]

To keep Romanians from fleeing Northern Transylvania to Romania, a Romanian police official went so far as to propose that some refugees be imprisoned and deported back to Hungary.[152] A Romanian writer reported on the case of one Romanian refugee fleeing Northern Transylvania into Romania who was brought before Romanian courts for illegally crossing the border and under suspicion that he was a spy.[153] Indeed, as time went on and the refugee problem refused to go away, records from Ion Antonescu's Council of Ministers reveal how the marshal became increasingly frustrated with the refugees. In a meeting on March 13, 1942, he called the refugees from Transylvania "the scum of Romanian society. They did not flee here out of fear of the Hungarians, but for other reasons. They need to be put to work. In the Romanian state it cannot be that some work while others profit, doing nothing at the expense of those who work. . . . I think they should be put in prison."[154]

The Hungarian administration also sought to keep Hungarian refugees from Southern Transylvania at arm's length.[155] Despite the fact that each day the interior ministry received thirty to forty requests from Hungarians for permission to enter the country from Southern Transylvania, most such requests were denied. Secretary to the Interior Minister Géza Sükösd commented in late 1941 that the Hungarian administration's policy was to give permission only to individuals who had no means of survival if they stayed in their Southern Transylvanian homes. "[I]t is a matter of top priority that those individuals whose livelihood is in any way insured be made to stay in [Southern] Transylvania."[156] Only indispensable state employees, those who could prove their permanent residence was in Northern Transylvania or Trianon Hungary, or who, due to their Hungarianness, had already suffered oppression at the hands of the Romanian state which made their continued presence there impossible were granted permission to enter the country with intent to immigrate.[157]

The Hungarian Consul in Braşov noted that "a great many pure Hungarian families of refugees await the permit required to return home."[158] Their eagerness and numbers made it easier for the Romanian leadership to confound the Hungarian administration's efforts to keep Hungarians from leaving Southern Transylvania. Reports surfaced that Romanian officials encouraged, even forced some Hungarians to flee Romania with death threats and the issuance of "one-way" passports allowing them to leave Romania but not to reenter.[159] Minority Hungarians were similarly encouraged or forced to flee to Hungary by a variety of means. The Romanian government fired many Hungarians from government jobs with the railroad and large factories and drafted Hungarian men into the military, where they could expect abuse at the hands of Romanian officers and fellow soldiers.[160] Newspaper articles openly suggested Hungarians should leave Romania, and the Hungarian defense minister even reported on rumors that a secret office had been set up in Braşov by Romanians who sold fake entry permits to Hungarians seeking to enter Hungary from Southern Transylvania.[161]

Despite the fact that the Second Vienna Arbitration made provisions for would-be optants to take their property, money, and belongings with them across the new border, there were numerous reports of personal items and money being confiscated by border officials. In a meeting of the Romanian Council of Ministers on October 11, 1940, the minister of Foreign Affairs, General Petrovicescu, reported on his conversations with refugees from Northern Transylvania. "At the border all their cash was taken away and they were each given a receipt stating the number of pengő or lei that were withheld there. Some of the expellees have a receipt; others were not given one but made a statement at customs recording the sums confiscated."[162]

Testimonies such as these were collected by both states and soon constituted yet another front in the battle for Transylvania. On Christmas Day 1940, the newly formed Romanian Association of Refugees and Expellees from Occupied Transylvania [Asociaţiei Refugiaţilor şi Expulsaţilor din Ardealul Ocupat] called on readers of its newspaper to submit detailed descriptions of any losses or humiliations they had suffered at the hands of the Hungarian authorities or photographs of refugees "with serious injuries" or "in cattle cars" or "other aspects of the Calvary they were forced to endure."[163] On November 28, 1941, the president of the Transylvanian Party, Count Béla Teleki, gave a speech before parliament in which he called on the Hungarian government to take the offensive in the propaganda war with Romania and to severely punish members of minorities who "bring propaganda here, take news over there." The proposition received strong support from all sides of the House.[164]

The relationship between refugees and state propaganda was thus taken for granted in both states. In a meeting of his Council of Ministers on March 13, 1942, Ion Antonescu told those present that the government needed to compile comprehensive statistics on the refugees. "This is not just a matter of domestic policy," he argued, "but one of foreign policy. I will have to go and discuss and defend the rights of the Romanian nation at the green table. If I can present [our case] there with clear data and well-designed graphics, my assertions will [more likely] be taken into consideration." The emphasis should thus be on arguments "that cannot be refuted by the Hungarians."[165] Consequently, on June 16, 1942, when Mihai Antonescu called together a group of statesmen and intellectuals to discuss how to "win the peace," one of the foremost items for consideration was how to improve the propaganda efforts of the state in lobbying for Romania's territorial claims. The Romanians had made a mistake during World War I, Antonescu argued. Romanian delegates to the peace conference went in "without prepared material, without the possibility to report, without documentation to facilitate action and response." These oversights would not be repeated, he told those present. "The problem of Transylvania and of the Romanians from beyond the border" must be studied, and "we must prepare documentary material so that we have it already written up for the moment of the peace."[166] The documentary material should include "complaints" that "reflect the Romanian drama in Northern Transylvania." The Hungarians had come prepared to the peace conference of 1918, he said, and their documentation had "enormously served the Hungarian revisionist struggle" from 1918 to 1940.[167]

The results of Mihai Antonescu's initiative were almost immediately apparent. A report to the Romanian secret police from July 1 includes 358 pages of testimonies of Romanian refugees from Northern Transylvania offered in response to a query the secret police had placed to the gendarmerie in June of that year.[168] Also, in an attempt to invalidate testimonies of Hungarians who fled to Northern Transylvania, Romanian officials introduced a "declaration" that had to be signed by individuals planning to leave the country. Many of these declarations included clauses such as "I declare that I depart of my own free will and am not forced by anyone and that I did not suffer any form of difficulties [*neplăceri*] from the Romanian authorities, and I renounce all my legal rights with respect to the Romanian state."[169]

By the late fall of 1942, Hungarian authorities had become savvy to Mihai Antonescu's plans for a propaganda offensive. The Hungarian ambassador in Bucharest reported that the Romanian government "in the future would use the situation of the Romanians fleeing from Northern Transylvania even more so than before for purposes of anti-Hungarian propaganda and recriminations." The ambassador expressed concern that the Hungarian government was not doing the same and suggested that "to compensate for the Romanian refugee propaganda, we, too, should outline the sufferings of our refugees from Southern Transylvania to the world as much as possible."[170]

RECIPROCITY

The notion that states should answer every provocation, or that what one state did with its minorities should be reciprocated by the other—called reciprocity—was a declared policy almost from the moment Hungarian troops entered Northern Transylvania. Indeed, the very premise of the reannexation from the Hungarian standpoint was to undo the slights perpetrated against the Hungarian minority in Transylvania under Romanian rule. As such the principle of reciprocity was written into the program of the Transylvanian Party.[171] Romanian leaders and officials in turn claimed that Hungary had initiated the slights, while their own actions against the Hungarian minority in Southern Transylvania were implemented only in response to "all the atrocities and illegalities committed by Hungarians."[172]

Leaders and politicians in both states periodically decried the practice of reciprocating harsh treatment of minorities on numerous occasions. "We do not approve of the current brutal idea and position of reciprocity and return-reciprocity," said Transylvanian Party president Béla Teleki in a speech before parliament on November 28, 1941. "But nevertheless," he continued, "we must demand that they [minorities] be kept under surveillance and that no one should abuse the mild treatment [they enjoy here]."[173] Almost a year later, in the summer of 1942, the head of the nationalities division of the prime minister's office, Tibor Pataky, commented: "Foreign policy interests and the future demand that our nationalities policy be a positive one and that it satisfy the just wishes of the domestic nationalities. . . . The Hungarian government will . . . steer away from the principle of reciprocity and in its domestic affairs will not allow itself to be influenced by the situation of the Hungarian minority in Romania and Slovakia."[174]

Part of the motivation behind attempts to temper reciprocity was the fact that reciprocal action had a way of aggravating the refugee problem and confounding state efforts to force minority populations on the other side of the border to stay put. In July 1941, the Hungarian foreign ministry noted the dizzying political calculus involved in weighing the positive and negative effects of reciprocity. "Considering that our rights regarding Southern Transylvania—which are supported by historical, geographical, and economic factors—can only really be validated while there is a significant Hungarian population there, from the national standpoint it is in our interest to adopt such provisions as will make the lives of the Hungarians living in Romania at least tolerable."[175] Such "provisions" would include treating the Romanian minority in Northern Transylvania better. The threat of reciprocity and the inevitability of the postwar negotiating table thus lent staying power to minority rights rhetoric.

During a meeting with his Council of Ministers on February 3, 1942, Ion Antonescu explained why he felt moderation in the application of reciprocity was in order:

> Whenever I am asked by foreigners: What are you doing about the Hungarians? My response is: I let them make mistakes, but I'll abstain and keep myself from making the same mistakes they are making. You have no idea what kind of struggle I have within myself to keep from doing what the Hungarians do: to imprison them, to take away their freedom, to kill them. . . . We won't resolve the problem if we kill a hundred Hungarians, nor if we close schools and churches, just as they cannot solve the Romanian problem that way.[176]

On February 26, Antonescu repeated his position, this time linking the practice of reciprocity to Romania's chances for recovering Transylvania through a future peace settlement in the event of an Axis defeat. "So as not to weaken our position in the West, let us close our eyes and be conciliatory."[177]

Despite these assertions, however, reciprocity was practiced by both states throughout the period of their uneasy alliance, resulting in reciprocal policies on a variety of issues, ranging from newspaper publication to the status of clergymen, to the payment of police pensions.[178] Already in September 1940 the Antonescu government undertook reciprocal action against the Hungarian minority in Southern Transylvania, and Mihai Antonescu retrospectively confirmed that, from the spring of 1941 until February 1944, all slights against the Romanian minority in Northern Transylvania had been reciprocated.[179]

Even Romanian civilians threatened to reciprocate violence against Romanians in Northern Transylvania vigilante-style, especially after hearing news of the atrocities in September 1940.[180] In November 1940, the leader of the Hungarian minority group, Elemér Gyárfás, met with both Ion Antonescu and Maniu. Antonescu spoke of the atrocities against the Romanian minority committed by Hungarian military and civilians. "The easiest thing to do would be to satisfy the desire to kill 1,500 Hungarians, after which the Hungarians will kill 3,000 Romanians, and so on," he said. "The Romanian people expect that the Axis powers will give them satisfaction, but if they don't get it, they'll take it for themselves at my expense because I was the one who kept them from exacting revenge. But the next victims will be you [Hungarians], and I will no longer be in a position to protect you."[181]

Threats of reciprocity began early in Hungary as well. An article from October 8, 1940, in the daily *Népszava*, for example, suggested that the Hungarian administration planned to respond to abuses against the Hungarian minority in Romania with "reprisals."[182] In August 1942, the Hungarian Consul in Braşov wrote to the central Hungarian administration: "If the Romanian government sees that with the last Hungarian driven out of Southern Transylvania the last Romanian will be driven out of Northern Transylvania, perhaps it will stop the planned persecution of the Hungarians. . . . Lenient behavior . . . *modus vivendi* cannot succeed."[183] The fact that Hungary was now home to over 1 million self-declared Romanians also gave comfort to Hungarians living in Southern Transylvania, many of whom reasoned that "according to the principle of equal treatment, our situation and fate should in any event improve because now there is someone upon whom to reciprocate the blow of the whip that lashes our body."[184]

Reciprocity also affected the function of a variety of state-run institutions. Already on September 3, 1940, for example, the Hungarian postal service brought a new stamp into circulation printed with the words "The East Returns!" Romanian postal officials proceeded to write "Retour, non admis" [Returned, not admissible] on letters with the stamp and sent them back where they came from.[185] Hungarian officials immediately started the search for an appropriately offensive Romanian postage stamp so they could retaliate.[186]

The Romanian postal service also did not accept letters addressed in languages other than Romanian, German, French, or Italian. That this policy amounted to a ban on letters addressed in Hungarian was clear to the Hungarian administration. Though a reciprocal provision was not proposed, the Hungarian Ministry of Foreign Trade suggested that mailings from Romania could be regulated by the military authorities to achieve the same effect.[187]

COUNTING AND BEING COUNTED

Not only were minority populations subject to reciprocity measures; they could also be policed by other members of their own nationality. National defections, or assimilation to the majority population, were criticized and duly punished from within national communities. Such defections had a long tradition, as did criticism aimed at potential defectors. In 1870, Romanian poet Mihai Eminescu referred to those Romanians who had been magyarized following the Compromise of 1867 as "renegades" and "the venom that the benefactress nature has eliminated from our body. . . . I always had to laugh at the attempts of renegades to return to the bosom of the nation."[188] The same message was delivered at a meeting of the Romanian agricultural society in Kolozsvár, Plugarul [ploughman], on July 27, 1944, where members and sympathizers listened to a speech by Emil Haţieganu. A former professor, politician, and at the time representative of the Romanian minority in Hungary and editor of the one remaining Romanian-language daily newspaper in Northern Transylvania (*Tribuna Ardealului*), Haţieganu admonished those in attendance to be and stay Romanians: "Despite the fact that there are some who have left [our] ranks, farewell to them. There will come a time when those who distanced themselves will wish to return to the Romanian ranks, but they will not be allowed in."[189]

Hungarian minister of religion and education Bálint Hóman made a similar statement in a speech he delivered at a meeting of the extreme-right Hungarian Life Party in Székesfehérvár in March 1941:

> Apparently there are those who separate themselves from the circle of magyardom and on the basis of ancestry declare themselves to be of a different nationality. Those [people] should go ahead and leave! Whoever dissimilates was never Hungarian, and whoever just claimed they were Hungarian is also not a Hungarian. Hungarianness must be felt with inner conviction. To be conscious of one's Hungarianness is not enough, because it could be merely a sense of ambition [*törekvés érzése*]. Whoever lives with conviction in their heart and soul does not dissimilate, and can be nothing but Hungarian until the closing of his coffin.[190]

The case of Mrs. Stanciu offers a concrete illustration of what could happen to Hungarians who left—or threatened to leave—the national fold. In 1942, Mrs. Stanciu asked the Hungarian state to find her Romanian husband—who had fled to Romania following the Second Vienna Arbitration—and force him to pay child support. The foreign ministry sent her request to the leader of the Hungarian minority in Southern Transylvania, Elemér Gyárfás, who composed a lengthy reply explaining why he could not possibly fulfill the request. He concluded his reply with the following admonition:

> [The] petitioner belongs to the group of Hungarian women who *ignored* the repeated advice and warnings of their spiritual leaders *not to marry a Romanian*. . . . [Instead she] chose the easiest path, broke away from [the Hungarian spiritual community], and when the very same thing happens that we had warned her about before, *she has only herself to blame for the consequences.* Neither the Hungarian leaders here nor the Hungarian state should feel in any way ethically obliged to assist her.[191]

Some cases were more complicated, however, as the following document from the Hungarian prime minister's office from November 1941 reveals. It deals with the request of a Calvinist pastor for an entry permit for his son-in-law (who was of Romanian nationality) so that the latter could return to his family living in Northern Transylvania. The officials called upon to consider the request were perplexed.

> The request puts the department in a difficult position, because if we grant permission for [the Romanian son-in-law] to enter Hungary, we raise thereby the number of Romanians and deny a Hungarian the opportunity to enter while letting a Romanian through. On the other hand, . . . if we do not allow him to return to his wife and children, then the man could take the Hungarian woman and children to Romania and romanianize them.[192]

In the above case, the decision ultimately affected at most four or five individuals, but the Hungarian administration anguished over it nonetheless. Indeed, statistically, their suspicions regarding the likely fate of the family if it moved to Romania were largely accurate. According to data gathered in mixed rural communities by Hungarian officials during the war, speakers of Hungarian in Northern Transylvania who entered into mixed marriages with speakers of other languages (mostly Romanian) were more than twice as likely to assimilate to the Romanian nationality than those who married within their language group. Furthermore, women were more likely to adopt the mother tongue and religion of their husbands for use with their children.[193]

These probabilities emerged—albeit belatedly—from a massive survey undertaken between 1942 and 1944 by the Hungarian administration. The survey, from which over 12,500 completed forms survive, was apparently designed to determine the extent to which the Hungarian population living in mixed rural areas of Northern Transylvania had been threatened by forced or opportunistic romanianization during the interwar period.[194] In their eagerness to understand the mechanisms of romanianization—presumably in order to reverse the process—the survey's authors demanded extremely detailed information, including the mother tongue, religion, and occupation not only of immediate family members but also of more distant relatives (grandparents, resident relatives), even the nationality of neighbors. The survey also inquired into the financial situation, education level, health, and reading habits of family members, as well as the distance to the nearest clergyman of the family's chosen faith.[195]

In general, population statistics were presumed to be essential in deciding the fate of Transylvania.[196] Both states produced statistics "proving" their national group to be in the majority in Northern Transylvania, Romanian sources claiming the population to be 50.2 percent Romanian, Hungarian sources as 52.1 percent Hungarian.[197] Demographic anxiety, or the fear that one nationality could gain converts at the expense the other, pervaded discus-

TABLE I

Population of Northern Transylvania (territory ceded to Hungary with the Second Vienna Arbitration) according to the Hungarian census of 1910, the Romanian census of 1930, the Hungarian census of 1941, and Romanian estimates from ~1941

| | Hungarian census (1910) (by mother tongue) | Romanian census (1930) (by nationality)[a] | Hungarian census (1941) (by nationality)[b] | Romanian estimates (~1941)[c] | |
				[Simion]	[Golopenția]
Magyar	1,125,732[d]	911,550	1,347,012	886,235	911,000
Romanian	926,268	1,176,433	1,066,353	1,199,165	1,173,000
German	90,195[e]	68,694	47,501	64,497	68,000
Jewish	—	138,885	45,593	—	199,000
Other	52,059	99,585	70,832	238,877	38,000
TOTAL	2,194,254	2,395,147	2,577,291	2,388,774	2,389,000

[a]These figures are slightly different from those given by F. Burgdörfer, the president of the Bureau of Statistics in Bavaria. In his 1942 article, the total population for Hungarian Northern Transylvania (using data from the 1930 Romanian census) was 2,387,778 (1,171,457 Romanians and 912,098 Hungarians). Of interest in his study is the division between rural and urban populations, which shows that individuals in both parts of Transylvania who declared themselves to be of Hungarian nationality were far more likely to live in urban areas, whereas the self-declared Romanian population was much more rural. F. Burgdörfer, "Recensământul general al României din 1941, dare de seamă," in *Analele Institutului Statistic al României*, vol. 1 (Bucharest, 1942), 323–53, esp. 340, 350–53.

[b]In 1940, Béla Bulla made estimates for 1930 and 1940 population figures based on the 1910 Hungarian census. For 1930, an estimated total population of 2,370,000, of which Hungarians constituted 47.1%; Romanians, 44.5%; others, 8.4%. For 1940, an estimated total population of 2,578,000, of which Hungarians constituted 47.4%; Romanians, 44.4%; others, 8.2%. See Béla Bulla, "Az új országgyarapodás," in Magyar *Szemle* 39 no. 4 (158.) (October 1940): 230–40, 239.

[c]The figures at left are from Simion (1996), cited in Ottmar Trașcă, "Relațiile româno-ungare și problema Transilvaniei, 1940–1944 (I)," *Anuarul Institutului de Istorie* "A. D. Xenopol," 41 (2004): 311n. In an earlier edition of his book on the Second Vienna Arbitration, Simion cited statistics from 1945 giving the total population as 2,600,000 and the size of the territory as 42,243 square kilometers. A. Simion, *Dictatul de la Viena* (Cluj, Romania: Editura Dacia, 1972), 200. The figures on the right are from Anton Golopenția, "Populația teritoriilor românești desprinse în 1940" in *Opere Complete*, vol. 2, *Statistică, demografie și geopolitică* ([Bucharest]: Editura Enciclopedică, 2002), 549. These figures, first published in the fall of 1941, were derived from projections based on the 1930 Romanian census.

[d]Includes Hungarian-speaking Jews.

[e]Includes Yiddish-speaking Jews.

sions of strategies for securing control of the region. In his strategizing for "winning the peace," Mihai Antonescu emphasized the collection, "scientific" interpretation, and propagation of ethnographic information, "so that we can support, on the basis of that, the official claims of the administration."[198]

The presentation of statistics, including nationality statistics, was in fact part of the arbitration process leading up to the Second Vienna Arbitration. Each state had presented data on Transylvania from its own census, Hungary from its last census before Trianon (1910) and Romania from its most recent (1930) census.[199] There were also some individuals who declared themselves to be of Hungarian nationality living in the Regat, and some living in Trianon Hungary who declared themselves to be of Romanian nationality, but their numbers were, relatively speaking, insignificant.[200]

TABLE 2

Population of Southern Transylvania (the part of Transylvania that remained under Romanian state control following the Second Vienna Arbitration) according to the Hungarian census of 1910, the Romanian census of 1930, and the Romanian census of 1941

	Hungarian census (1910) (mother tongue)	Romanian census (1930) (nationality)[a]	Romanian census (1941) (ethnic origin)[b]
Magyar	533,004[c]	441,720	363,206
Romanian	1,895,505	2,031,447	2,274,561
German	465,814[d]	475,158	490,640
Jewish	—	138,885	—
Other	152,820	150,934	204,491
TOTAL	3,047,143	3,099,259	3,332,898

[a]Again, Burgdörfer's figures are slightly different, giving the population in the parts of Transylvania left to Romania as 2,843,559 (442,774 Hungarians and 1,940,155 Romanians). F. Burgdörfer, "Recensământul general al României din 1941, dare de seamă," in *Analele Institutului Statistic al României*, vol. 1 (Bucharest, 1942), 323–53, esp. 344–46.

[b]*Recensământul din 1941: Transilvania* (Cluj, Romania: Editura Presa Universitară Clujeană, 2002), ix. Here "Transylvania" includes Transylvania, Banat, and Crişana. On how the census determined nationality using a combination of three criteria (mother tongue, religion, and ethnic origin), see Burgdörfer, "Recensământul general," 327. For discussions of this method's implications, see E. Árpád Varga, *Fejezetek a jelenkori Erdély népesedéstörténetéből* (Budapest: Püski Kiadó, 1998), 36, 57–58 (footnote 85).

[c]Includes Hungarian-speaking Jews.

[d]Includes Yiddish-speaking Jews.

The narrow margin by which either nationality held the majority in Northern Transylvania meant that the battle for national converts—generally cast as conversion *back* to an individual's "original" nationality—was fierce and took a variety of forms. State officials and nationalists employed a number of methods to "win over" or coerce individuals into declaring themselves a certain way on the census, while nationalist demographers sought means to make the numbers match their preferred image of reality.

Acts of government fiat and ways of formulating census questions made a certain outcome more or less likely.[201] In any case, 1941 was a peculiar year for a census, given that there was a war going on and that conducting a census that year constituted an oddity in the pattern of census-taking intervals for both states.[202] Upon hearing the news that the Hungarians were preparing a census, a Romanian newspaper expressed concern that Hungarian officials would use the new data to seek to invalidate the 1930 Romanian census, the results of which were only published several years after the data had been gathered.[203] The Hungarian government had encouraged such anxiety by drafting a propaganda brochure in English entitled "The Desperate Fight of the Romanians with Statistics." The brochure claimed that "the Rumanians are nervous, because they are afraid of the truth, and want to distract attention from the turpidity [*sic*] of their statistical data."[204]

The two state administrations gave considerable power to census authorities at the lower level, many of whom were free, or even encouraged to make their own judgments about who was what.[205] Under the circumstances, it is not surprising that suspicions of foul play abounded on both sides.[206] As a result, both states tried to undertake censuses on the other state's territory.[207] In the Hungarian case, questionnaires were distributed secretly through consulates to minority leaders, who passed them on to religious leaders. The latter had to memorize the questionnaire so as not to leave a paper trail. From a surviving example copy, we learn that the questions covered nationality and religion but were mostly about jobs, minority institutions, property, and Hungarians who fled the country.[208]

Meanwhile Romanian demographers used interwar Romanian censuses to extrapolate their own population statistics for Northern Transylvania.[209] The Romanian administration also included a page on the official 1941 census form for refugees from ceded territories. The form included mainly questions about property and businesses left behind, their approximate value, and their exact location.[210]

TITLES AND ENTITLEMENT

Making sure that property was in the hands of people who embodied the state as members of the nation, or nationality, was a primary preoccupation of the Hungarian and Romanian administrations. Policy relating to property took a variety of forms, from the more or less ad hoc confiscation of minority property for housing refugees, to crafting more far-reaching legal provisions to achieve advantage reversal by redistribution of property on a large scale. Both states sought to "own" Transylvania, and it was therefore of utmost importance that "national" property remain in the hands of reliable elements.[211]

Ministerial Decree 1,440/1941[212] formed part of the Transylvanian Party's efforts in the interest of "reparation for injustices committed by the Romanian authorities," among which was the redistribution of property. In a session of the Hungarian parliament on November 14, Imre Mikó of the Transylvanian Party argued that "Romanian rule deprived the mid-level Hungarian landowners of the bulk of their property and deprived the Szekler people of their common landownership rights." He went on to declare that "this huge amount of property cannot remain in the hands of those to whom the Romanian regime distributed it."[213] Four days later, on November 18, another representative of the Transylvanian Party, Baron Antal Braunecker, explained that land and property were currently "in the hands of those who were able to unjustly acquire Hungarian land through various national gifts and manipulations and through the spawn of a variety of corrupt systems." He concluded by emphasizing that "these lands were earlier all Hungarian."[214]

The 1,440/1941 was designed to reverse the advantage achieved by Romanians by making provisions for the recovery of land and property bought and sold during the period of Romanian rule.[215] Its primary targets were the transfers made during the course of the Romanian land reform of 1920–21, and as such it was crafted to undo interwar Romanian attempts at advantage reversal.[216] Nor was this the only measure adopted to that end in Northern Transylvania.[217] Within less than two months after the introduction of the 1,440/1941, 4,333 individuals in Northern Transylvania had already petitioned to recover or be duly compensated for the loss or sale of property, not all of whom were of self-declared Hungarian nationality.[218] In Kolozsvár County alone, 1,013 such petitions were submitted to the Kolozsvár District Court by the end of 1941.[219]

In the meantime, the Romanian government compiled lists and testimonies of Romanians who had lost property as a result of such policies. As the number of claims based on the 1,440/1941 grew, the Romanian consulate, foreign ministry, and police kept records of the submitted petitions whenever possible. The resultant state propaganda trumpeted the injustice of Hungarian policies vis-à-vis the Romanian minority before the international community.[220]

The Romanian administration also sought and often found ways to reciprocate the effects of advantage reversal in Northern Transylvania, as well as increasing the advantage enjoyed by Romanians in Romania. "Romanianization" began officially with a series of decree-laws introduced just after the loss of Northern Bukovina and Bessarabia, and later intensified by means of a spate of similar laws in the wake of the Second Vienna Arbitration.[221] On May 2, 1941, the National Center of Romanianization and the State Undersecretariat for Romanianization, Colonization, and Inventory came into being as part of a government effort to coordinate and centralize romanianization activities.[222] Its primary task was the romanianization of the Romanian economy and society, beginning with the economic and cultural disenfranchisement of the Jews and expropriation of their property, but often extending to other minorities as well, most notably Hungarians.[223] The National Center of Romanianization and the Undersecretariat mandates also included the distribution of aid to Romanian refugees from the territories the country had lost, and the latter had among its sub-organs the Directorate of Refugees and Evacuated Populations.[224]

Beyond land and real estate, however, one of the most valuable pieces of property an individual owned was his or her name. Names were presumed to carry essential information about national identity and thus formed a basis for states' claims on people, and through people, territory.[225] The relationship between names and claims was well known to members of the two administrations, as well as to ordinary people, who were voluntary and involuntary players in the zero-sum name game.

Despite the assertion of Hungarian minister of religion and education Bálint Hóman that "we cannot follow the example of some politicians from the last century who simply called everyone Hungarian who spoke a different language and considered themselves to belong to a different nationality," magyarization of names was a common practice in Northern Transylvania.[226] In both parts of divided Transylvania, people's names were frequently changed as a matter of course whenever individuals had contact with the state bureaucracy. Birth certificates, marriage, hospital and school records, not to mention legal documents and identification papers all afforded opportunities for the state to bestow a name—and oftentimes a religion—on an individual. Some chose to change their names voluntarily, or under pressure from their employers or peers.[227] In Hungarian Northern Transylvania, there were numerous name-change applications submitted by individuals with all kinds of names (Slavic, Romanian, Germanic, etc.).[228] Applications for name changes from Jews were repeatedly denied. Applicants representing *other* religious and national affiliations, however, were categorically approved, including those with Romanian-sounding names of the Romanian Orthodox and Greek Catholic faiths.[229]

The link between name, faith, and nationality was often viewed as implicit. A Hungarian name was presumably coupled with the Roman Catholic or Protestant (Calvinist or Unitarian) faiths, while a Romanian name was presumed to belong to an individual of the Greek Catholic (Uniate) or Eastern (Romanian) Orthodox faiths. Naturally, these presumptions were often misleading, but the power of presumption meant that a name change likely foreshadowed or was foreshadowed by a change of religion as well. József Hlavács [Hlavaciu], for example, wrote to the office of the public registry in Kolozsvár in May 1942 to request that the last-name entry for his two-year-old daughter, Maria, be changed from the Romanian-sounding "Hlavaciu" to the Hungarian-sounding "Hlavács."[230] He argued that "the name change [to 'Hlavaciu'] was an act of the Romanian officials' imperiousness and did not reflect my own desire." Furthermore, he wrote, his religion at the time of his daughter's birth was given as Romanian Orthodox "because on April 1, 1935, I was obliged to convert to Romanian Orthodoxy in order to keep my job. On October 4, 1940, I converted back to my original religion, Lutheranism."

Another man, János Pakurár (Juhász), appealed to the office of the public registry for a similar reason. When in 1920 his wife bore a child, his name as the father was given as Pacurar. János wanted this last-name entry to be replaced with his "real" last name, Juhász, which he had adopted in 1913.[231] His case is comparable to that of another János, who requested that the registry entries for his children be changed from "Rațiu" to "Rátz."

> For although I was born Greek Catholic, I converted to the Roman Catholic faith in 1916. The Romanian authorities did not acknowledge my conversion, and in 1923 they ordered that the entries for both myself and my children be changed to Greek Catholic. Naturally, as soon as I could I gave witness to the fact that I feel myself to be of the Roman Catholic faith, and in 1940, I converted back to Roman Catholicism. For this reason I respectfully ask that both my religion and my name be changed back to their original form [on the registry].[232]

Name-change requests of this sort were looked upon with approval by the Hungarian administration of Northern Transylvania, which had resolved to "absorb" the strayed "Hungarian families back into the national circulatory system."[233] Indeed, already by the end of 1940, 774 individuals had converted from the "Romanian"-coded religions of Greek Catholicism and Orthodoxy to the "Hungarian"-coded Roman Catholic and Protestant faiths.[234]

It was not only ordinary *living* people whose names could be changed, but also famous dead people. A Renaissance king claimed as their own in both Hungarian and Romanian national histories offers a prime example. His statue—erected in 1902—on the main square in the Transylvanian capital, was repeatedly renamed. Under Hungarian/Habsburg rule, the orthography of his name (Mátyás Király) emphasized two things: that he was king of Hungary and that he was a Hungarian king. After the territory was ceded to Romania, he was given another name, "Matei Corvinul," which stressed not so much his status as ruler as his presumed Romanian ethnolinguistic origins.[235]

Finally, in addition to the names of people, the names of places were hotly contested as well. In the words of historian Irina Livezeanu, "in Transylvania the cultural conquest of the cities was more than a metaphor, it was a physical process."[236] That process involved changing street and place names, shifting the spiritual "center" of a city or region from one place to another, erecting or demolishing monuments, plaques, and statues, and more generally trying to nationalize space by drawing out historical continuities and eliminating signs of rupture in the nationalist metanarrative.

The "Renaming" of Kolozsvár

If Transylvania was the ultimate prize, then Kolozsvár was understood as the key to winning that prize.[237] The battle for the city—which took place during the interwar period and later during the war itself—was a microcosm of the battle for Transylvania and of the war between allies. In addition to absorbing the demographic and cultural realms, the struggle also saturated local politics, public health, labor policy, transportation, communication, and city planning and colored interactions among the city's inhabitants.

Nearly 87 percent of the city's population declared itself Hungarian by nationality on the 1941 census.[238] With the return of Hungarian rule, street names were officially changed back to their Hungarian forms, forms that many inhabitants of the city had in fact never ceased using. A number of the city's inhabitants had grown up learning the Hungarian names of streets, squares, parks, and other landmarks regardless of how they appeared on most maps.[239] Consequently, many of these individuals also took a personal interest in the city's Hungarian makeover.

A letter to the editor in the leading Hungarian daily newspaper on May 2, 1942, complained that all of the movie theaters seemed to have "foreign" names, like Royal, Capitol, Urania, Rio, and Edison. "And there is not a single Árpád movie theater, or a Mikes, Rákóczi, Kossuth, Bólyai, Mózes Székely, or Petőfi, etc."[240] "Brother Hungarians, . . . the final hour is about to strike. . . . Let us wake up at last! Let us shake off the mark of the alien spirit that has been thrust upon us. Let us want and let us dare to be Hungarians at all times and in all places. And let us safeguard, let us cherish all that is ours." Shortly thereafter, all but one of the movie theaters in the city were renamed. Their new names were Árpád, Mátyás király (King Matthias), Rákóczi, Erdélyi (Transylvanian), Corvin, and Egyetem (University).[241]

A group of residents along Donáth Road in a mostly Romanian part of Kolozsvár were equally eager to see their part of the city given a more "Hungarian" name.[242] In the spring of 1941, they issued a complaint to the mayor regarding the city's plan to change the name of their street to Képalatti. Their spokesman argued that Képalatti, meaning "under the picture," was an "*oláh*" name derived from the local Romanians' lack of sufficient Hungarian vocabulary. In their ignorance, the spokesman asserted, these Romanians called a statue in the area a "kép," or "picture," designating their own part of town as "*képalatti*," or "under the picture." "We [therefore] request the quickest possible removal of the *oláh* '*képalatti*' street signs, because not only do the individuals of good Hungarian disposition not like the name, but they

FIG. 16. Postcard from 1941 showing Miklós Horthy Road (once called Franz Joseph Road, later King Ferdinand Road), leading from the train station to the center of Kolozsvár. Visible on the left are the "tasteless, Romanian-looking urns," which were "remodeled" in response to a complaint submitted to the municipal authorities by a Calvinist minister. From the collection of András Fodor; reprinted with permission.

also find it insulting and condemning of themselves because the city thinks to connect thereby this Hungarian quarter to the *oláh* quarter."[243] The mayor's office sympathized with the residents' concern and agreed not to change the name of their road to "Képalatti."

In a similar incident, a local Calvinist minister drew the municipal administration's attention to the presence of some "tasteless, Romanian-looking stone urns" that had been placed in the island dividing the two directions of traffic at the beginning of the recently renamed Horthy Road.[244] The minister wrote to the Office of Public Order to request the removal of the offending urns. "It is with great sadness that I see that these by no means beautiful and by no means Hungarian-looking things are still there where visitors to our city are called upon to be awed by them from the moment of their arrival. I respectfully ask that . . . this beautiful street be restored to its former state and that those most uncharming reminders of the Romanians be removed." By the spring of 1942, by order of the mayor himself, the "vases" in question were not removed, but "remodeled" to look less "Romanian."

The wartime fate of the Házsongárd cemetery demonstrates how the zeal

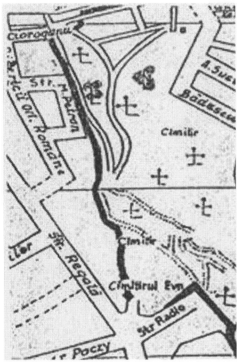

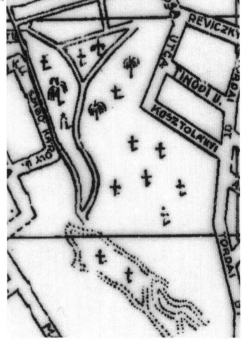

FIG. 17. Fragments of two maps showing the Házsongárd cemetery in Kolozsvár. The map on the left dates from the interwar period of Romanian rule; the one on the right from 1941, when the city was under Hungarian state control. Petru Bortes, "Harta generală a orașului municipal Cluj" (Cluj, 1937); and Gusztáv Cseh, "Kolozsvár thj. sz. kir. város átnézeti térképe" (Kolozsvár: László Zsombory, 1941). The different crosses—Orthodox crosses with bulges on the extremities versus the standard Catholic/Protestant "straight" crosses—are a testament to efforts to "nationalize" the dead as Romanian or Hungarian respectively. The Romanian map also shows a "Jewish Cemetery," which cannot be found on the Hungarian version, showing that Romanian officials tended to view Jews as Jews, whereas the Hungarian regime did not distinguish them from Hungarians.

for renaming extended far beyond the grave. Here the struggle for national, religious, and linguistic hegemony marked the graves of the city's past generations. One essay written by a Hungarian in 1942 complained that the Romanian "rulers" of the interwar period had "stolen into the cemetery and scattered the crypts and mausoleums of the new rulers among the collapsing, centuries-old Hungarian crosses."[245] A city map from the interwar period shows the great blank hillside cemetery dotted with ostentatiously Orthodox crosses, the trademark of the Romanian dead. In a later version of the same map from 1941, the Orthodox crosses are replaced by Catholic/Protestant ones, indicating the presence of Hungarians and Germans in the cemetery. The other key difference between the two maps is the status of the "Jewish cemetery," which is labeled as such on the interwar Romanian map, but entirely absent from the Hungarian one. The maps thus provide visual confirmation of interwar Romania's policy of identifying Jews as Jews rather than as Hungarians, and the Hungarian policy of folding them in with Hungarians.[246]

The mayor's office developed a less subtle means of reclaiming some of Házsongárd's dead. It resolved to revamp the Heroes' Cemetery, where the fallen soldiers of World War I were buried. In its late–World War I incarnation, the Heroes' Cemetery had featured equal numbers of gravestones (thirty-five) for each of four nationalities represented among the dead: Austrians, Germans, Hungarians, and Romanians. The city administration during World War II, however, determined that 1,185 of the total 1,700 soldiers who had died in the area had been Hungarians, so they determined to double the size of the Heroes' Cemetery to include four more plots of thirty-five gravestones each, all of which would bear the names of fallen Hungarians.[247]

A similarly ambitious component of the "renaming" of Kolozsvár was the plan to convert an unfinished Romanian school building into a new military headquarters for the Ninth Division of the Hungarian army stationed in the city.[248] The planned complex was to be called Miklós Horthy Square and required the demolition of several dozen houses, to be replaced by a massive park bracketed by two mirror-image buildings. The architect's plan was to transform the "imitation classical, columned" school into a "military headquarters in the Szekler style."[249] In fact, the plan for the complex was superimposed, literally drawn over, an interwar blueprint of the city prepared by the Romanian administration. On the blueprint, streets appear with their Romanian names, which the Hungarian architect did not bother to cross out; he simply wrote in the new names next to them in dark ink. As for the buildings and park, they were set off from the "Romanian" background by their stark colorfulness, drawn in bright yellow, red, blue and green directly over existing buildings.[250]

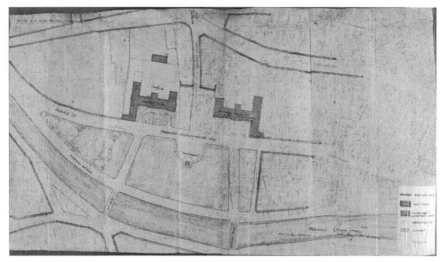

FIG. 18. Planner's sketch of the future Miklós Horthy Square in Kolozsvár, featuring the new military headquarters for the Ninth Division of the Hungarian army that was stationed in the city. The plan was drawn over a blueprint of the city from the period of Romanian rule. The names of the streets in Romanian (Calea Traian, Calea Decebal) are faint but still visible in the background. MOL, K150 1941 - IV. kútfő - 30. tétel. [MOL, K150, 3542. csomó, 30. tétel., 255].

FIG. 19. The completed first building of the Ninth Division headquarters as featured on a 1941 postcard. Construction of the building began during the interwar period. The Romanian administration had intended it to be a school. Hungarian authorities made plans to turn it into a military headquarters and add another building (see planner's sketch). Only the first was completed. After the war, the Szekler ornamentation added to the building's exterior by the Hungarian builders was knocked off. Remnants of it are still visible today. After the Second World War, the building housed the offices of the infamous Securitate, or Romanian secret police. Today it houses the Securitate's successor, the so-called SRI (Romanian Information Service). From the collection of András Fodor; reprinted with permission.

The first of the two planned buildings was completed in December 1941 and was dedicated during a ceremony attended by Prime Minister László Bárdossy in mid-January 1942.[251] A newspaper article in the local daily *Ellenzék* [Opposition] described both the exterior as well as the interior features of the building in great detail. The gates to the building included two statues of ancient Hungarian warriors, there to "stand watch at the entrance to the new military complex so that everything that happens here will be undertaken in the spirit of the ancients."[252] Inlays in the tables portrayed scenes from the Hungarian revolution of 1848, wherein Hungarian soldiers beat back "an easily recognizable enemy," most likely a reference to the Romanian "counterrevolutionaries," but also to the Russians, with whom Hungary was again at war. Finally, in the commander's room there was a table impressed with a newspaper from August 30, 1940, and under it the names of cities in Southern Transylvania still under Romanian state control, "a constant reminder to the Hungarian soldier" who looks upon it. The building along with its furnishings, the author concludes, "is in all respects capable of keeping the national idea and the Hungarian mission alive."[253]

During his speech at the ceremonial opening of the building the lieutenant general commander of the army corps declared: "As the bricks of this building were laid, the walls plastered, the doors and windows installed, humanity came to understand that the world, too, was being rebuilt. History is again carefully measuring each of the nations to cast off the feeble and reward the serious."[254] With these words the commander wove the Hungarian-Romanian struggle into the larger Axis narrative of the "New European Order." The building, which symbolized how the "serious" Hungarian nation had prevailed over the "feeble" Romanian one, was thus a battleground of history. That both nations fought for the Axis as allies was a fact that could not be denied in words but could be effectively subverted by assigning certain meanings to space, as with the Hungarian army headquarters. The commander concluded his speech by calling on the audience to spread the Szekler architectural style "so that Transylvania's exterior will get that Hungarian character which so typifies its internal way of thinking." The nationalization of space, then, was to be the solemn obligation of all.

One Too Many

Despite claims from both the Romanian and Hungarian sides that Kolozsvár was and had long been a "city of schools," in the fall of 1940, Kolozsvár was a city with ten times as many taverns as schools.[255] Nevertheless, schools seemed to be a more pervasive point of reflection and locus of intervention for the Hungarian and Romanian administrations. Concerns about the numbers of majority and minority students attending schools; whether to allow minority religious and parochial schools to operate; language of instruction; curriculum; and slights to minority schools, teachers, and students in the other state were common themes. They consumed much of the discussion during the Transylvanian Conference and resurfaced repeatedly in everything from municipal correspondence to parliamentary debates to public speeches.[256]

Yet taverns could also play host to the convergence between foreign and domestic policy, where ordinary people became representatives of the national interest, and where the "enemy" was confronted. Perhaps this was why, during the evacuation of the Romanian troops from the regional capital in the first two weeks of September 1940, authorities decreed that taverns could operate for only two hours in the afternoon and two in the evening.[257] Even thereafter the only pub that could operate past 1 a.m. was the one at the train station, and then only to serve passengers.[258]

Drunken men in particular could, and did, say incredible things while sitting in taverns or on their way home from them. Some of their comments were meant to upset people, and succeeded therein. But perhaps an even more significant aspect of their verbal attacks is how and when the state came to take an active interest in the words of men who had had one too many.

One such man was Lajos Cseh, a resident of Turda in Romanian Southern Transylvania who, on September 19, 1940, after stopping in to the county seat to declare his intention to opt for Hungary, went out to celebrate with a few drinks. On his way home, he was arrested for "insulting the honor of the nation" after reportedly telling a city official that Miklós Horthy would soon arrive to occupy Turda. While in prison, he reportedly was beaten and robbed by Romanian police, who blamed both on his drunkenness at the time of arrest. Within a month he had crossed the border to Kolozsvár, where he reported the incident to Hungarian military authorities on October 26.[259]

In Romania, insults to the nation's honor—including singing Hungarian irredentist songs, making revisionist statements, even flying a faded or torn Romanian flag—were prosecuted in military courts.[260] Hungarian officials complained that 1,284 Hungarians had been tried for insulting the nation's honor and related crimes in one of three Transylvanian military courts during 1942 alone, estimating the total number of those tried in all three courts at around 4,000.[261] The reason for all these indictments, the Hungarian officials claimed, was "to break the resistance of magyardom through aggravating methods, systematic depredation, and constant intimidation."[262]

Reciprocity was not slow in coming. During this time Hungarian courts were also active trying presumed slanderers of the nation.[263] Furthermore, the prime minister's office insisted that a copy of the proceedings of these cases be sent to Budapest for review, presumably to determine whether slanderers posed a serious threat to national security.[264] In over half of the cases whose proceedings I examined most thoroughly—all tried in Hungarian courts in Kolozsvár from 1940 to 1942—the accused was either in a tavern or on his way home from one when the slanderous comments were said to have been made.[265]

Among the latter was a man who, despite his Hungarian-sounding name (perhaps made so by the court official preparing the indictment), was of self-declared Romanian mother tongue and nationality. On April 29, 1942, the man, who was at the time "drunk, but not so drunk that he had passed out," reportedly threatened to "shit in the mouth of every Hungarian." The public prosecutor [*kir. ügyészségi elnők*] in the case considered this statement slanderous of the Hungarian state and nation because "under Hungarians is understood the Hungarian nation, and the Hungarian nation is the people who created the Hungarian state, thus the slanderous statement made about the Hungarians is slanderous of the Hungarian state and nation as well."[266] This delineation of the links between Hungarians, the Hungarian nation, and the Hungarian state was common in cases of this sort and was symptomatic of a shift in understandings of statehood and the nation's role in and for the state, as discussed in Chapter 1.[267]

Yet not all "slanderous" remarks were uttered in and around taverns by drunken men, nor was it only the abstract mass of "Hungarians" who could stand in for the nation and state as they did in the case of the aforementioned defendant. Individuals could stand in for the state as well. On April 21, 1941, a sixty-one-year-old woman who considered herself Romanian was in her apartment when a uniformed ensign came to ask about renting an apartment there.[268] Upon learning the reason for the ensign's visit, she purportedly said the following: "No way that I'm renting my room to a Hungarian, much less to an army officer; I'd rather burn it. It's not enough that the Hungarians stole Transylvania from the Romanians, now they want to give orders in my apartment. But you won't be ruling for long because our Mihai [King of Romania] is coming back!" When the officer returned later, she also was said to have called him a "stinking Hungarian" and a "Hungarian Gypsy" and told him: "I won't be ordered around by a stinking Hungarian or by Hungarian laws!" The district attorney in the case declared that referring to the ensign as "stinking" was slanderous of the Hungarian state, since "under Hungarians is understood the Hungarian nation, and the Hungarian nation is the people who created the Hungarian state, thus the slanderous statement made about the Hungarians is slanderous of the Hungarian state as well."[269]

Finally, it was not only state officials and soldiers—like the ensign—who could legally stand in for the state. Ordinary people, including women, could as well. Early in 1942, Julianna Pató, a twenty-one-year-old woman of self-declared Romanian nationality, had had a run-in with another woman who was apparently visiting her at home. As the woman was preparing to leave, Julianna was said to have called after her: "Stop, you stinking Hungarian! Thief! Moocher! You'll see what will become of you in a few days!"[270] The district attorney was clearly aware that, even out of context, Julianna's statement was basically a personal insult directed at the woman visitor, for he stressed that "the defendant's expressions were not directed *solely* at [the visitor] but against all Hungarians, and since under Hungarians is understood the Hungarian nation, and since the Hungarian nation makes up the Hungarian state, her expression . . . is defamatory of both the Hungarian state as well as of the Hungarian nation."[271]

Of significance in these cases is the fact that the confrontation between Hungary and Romania in the struggle for control of Transylvania had many side effects, one of which was making it possible for ordinary people to stand in for the state, another example of how people had become tied to territory in very concrete ways with real consequences.

Whose Uniates?

Despite the firm link between people and territory, the question of *which* people could stand in for *which* state was hardly straightforward. One group in particular was regularly caught in the orbit of *both* states, namely the Greek Catholics, or Uniates. Greek Catholicism, first adopted in some areas of Transylvania during the early eighteenth century, was a "compromise" religion that allowed members of the Orthodox Church in Habsburg East-Central Europe to gain the recognition and protection of the crown. It was a religion that accepted the primacy of the Pope in Rome but ran the liturgy according to the Eastern, or Byzantine, rite. In Transylvania, most of the church's early adherents were speakers of Romanian.

In the early spring of 1942, József Mosolygó, a Greek Catholic priest, wrote to the lord lieutenant of Kolozsvár County in Northern Transylvania with a request. Mosolygó had recently published a book entitled *The Eastern Church in Hungary* and wanted the lord lieutenant to purchase two hundred copies of it for use in "high schools, vocational schools, teaching colleges, state elementary schools, etc." The book's overarching claim was that there were as many as three hundred thousand "romanianized Hungarians" among the Greek Catholics. "In Transylvania," he wrote, "it is not so much a matter of importance to keep Hungarians Hungarian, but rather to lead the romanianized Hungarians back to the community of Hungarian life."[272] A good place to start, he argued, was with the romanianized Greek Catholics.

In an effort to determine whether it was worth state revenue to purchase the requested two hundred copies of Mosolygó's book, a copy was sent to the Ministry of Religion and Education for review. "In connection with the problem at issue, the author has nothing worthwhile to say, and it appears doubtful that he has the requisite knowledge of the Eastern Church," the review began. "The Committee therefore does *not* recommend the purchase of this well-meaning, but dilettantish work for use in Transylvanian schools."[273]

The book was also sent to András Sztankay, a Hungarian Greek Catholic priest, for his opinion. He sent back a glowing review, recommending that Mosolygó's work be purchased for "every library, especially for the isolated Hungarians of Transylvania." His concluding remarks echoed Mosolygó's thesis as he reminded the ministry that "there are 300,000 romanianized Greek Catholic Hungarians in Transylvania." In the end, the prime minister's office decided to buy one hundred, as opposed to the requested two hundred copies of *The Eastern Church in Hungary*, since, as stated by Sztankay, "the work is valuable not from the pedagogical standpoint, but rather in its political implications."

The case of *The Eastern Church in Hungary* epitomizes the problem of special treatment versus discrimination. By pointing to an unlikely intersection between religion and nationality, Mosolygó's book challenged the Hungarian administration to choose between its short-term policies of reciprocity and advantage reversal, and its long-term goal of assimilation. Reciprocity and advantage reversal required favoring Hungarians over Romanians, even punishing Romanians to avenge slights to the Hungarian minority in Southern Transylvania. Significantly, on both sides of the border, many of these slights and the reciprocal oppression they set off were meted out to religious institutions, including "Hungarian" Roman Catholic or Protestant, and "Romanian" Greek Catholic and Orthodox schools, churches, and clergy.[274] Advantage reversal also affected religious institutions through the confiscation of church property and foodstuffs.[275]

These two features of the Hungarian nationalities policy—advantage reversal and reciprocity—were both subjects of discussion at the Transylvanian Conference in October 1940. Those present expressed general agreement that the state should do all in its power to help Hungarians, especially those in majority-Romanian areas. Nevertheless, Hungary's former prime minister

István Bethlen warned that "a part of Transylvania remains on the other side [of the border], and all that we do here, if the Roman government does the same over there with regard to Hungarians, could be disastrous."[276]

Two years later, in a speech that Hungarian prime minister Miklós Kállay gave before parliament in the fall of 1942, these themes were revisited. Kállay announced that it had been his intention to implement a benign policy towards the nationalities, "but to this I received an answer of an entirely different nature from across the border," implying that Hungary's nationalities policy could only reflect Romania's policy toward its Hungarian minority (i.e., be based on reciprocity). On advantage reversal, Kállay said, "We must first occupy ourselves with Hungarians and make up for what we have lost in the past." Yet the ultimate goal, he declared, was "to win [the nationalities] over to the Hungarian idea."[277]

Since part of the "Hungarian idea" was to favor and promote Hungarians, winning the nationalities over to the "Hungarian idea" suggested that nationalities should assimilate, or *become* Hungarians.[278] And in fact, voluntary and coerced changes in names and religion in both Hungary and Romania had taken "assimilation" out of the realm of ideal and into the realm of practice. Kállay's policy complicated the process of advantage reversal and reciprocity still further by problematizing distinctions between the two nationalities. Favoring a Hungarian Roman Catholic over a Romanian Greek Catholic, for instance, would likely frustrate any subsequent attempt to win the latter over to the "Hungarian national idea."

In any case, the story of Mosolygó's book neither began nor ended with his request to the lord lieutenant. Greek Catholicism remained linked in the minds of many to Romanians. In May 1942, for example, the buildings of the Greek Catholic Bishopric in Northern Transylvania were visited by vandals who wrote anti-Romanian slogans on the walls and windows. Just above the main entrance, they wrote "Woe is you" in half-meter-tall letters. On the side of the building was written "Blow this spies' nest sky high," and on the windows "*Oláh*'s out." A few days later, on the night of May 15, vandals wrote "Run to your brothers" on the same building. [279] Yet in July the Northern Transylvanian daily *Ellenzék* reiterated a view similar to Mosolygó's. "In Transylvania, it is far from being the case that every Greek Catholic Hungarian is of foreign extraction," the author declared, and only "false prejudice" could lead someone to conclude that "whoever is Greek Catholic cannot be Hungarian."[280]

The prejudice, however false, was nonetheless commonplace, and at least partially confirmed by the 1941 Hungarian census data.[281] In 1940, Hungarian historian László Makkai wrote:

It is common knowledge that in [Transylvania] a person's denomination also determines his nationality. The Romanians are Greek Orthodox and Greek Catholic, the Hungarians are Roman Catholic, Calvinist, and Unitarian, the Germans are Roman Catholics and Lutherans, and vice versa; Greek Orthodox and Greek Catholics are for the most part Romanians, Calvinists and Unitarians are exclusively Hungarians, Lutherans are exclusively Germans. Acknowledging this situation, the Romanian authorities [during the period of Romanian rule] made efforts to win over as many converts as possible to the Greek Orthodox and Greek Catholic faiths, because conversion to one of the Romanian religions generally meant certain romanianization.[282]

The solution, then, was to convert those who had converted to Greek Catholicism (and Eastern Orthodoxy) *back* to the "Hungarian" denominations.[283]

György Papp, a professor of Eastern Theology at the Péter Pázmány University in Budapest, assailed this approach to Transylvanian Greek Catholics in a book published in Kolozsvár in 1942 entitled *Greek-Rite Magyardom*. In it he decried "the indifference with which Hungarian public opinion has for centuries [looked upon] and continues to look upon the denationalization of our pure Hungarian brethren from the racial, ancestral [*származás*], and sentimental [*érzés*] perspective." Even worse, he wrote, the Hungarian public had not only watched this denationalization take place, "rather it has many times taken an active part in driving pure Hungarians out of the national community, thrusting them over into the ranks of foreign nationalities to be absorbed as booty."[284] Papp concluded that "Magyardom is hardly in a position today to bear this huge loss of blood," and he proposed a shift in attitude toward acceptance of Greek Catholics as Hungarians.[285] Meanwhile, the Romanian authorities suspected that "the Hungarian government is trying to set up a Hungarian Eastern Church in order to push the Romanian Eastern Church into the background."[286] To reciprocate, they proposed the creation of a Romanian Calvinist episcopate on the grounds that "there are many communities of the Calvinist faith in Romania . . . whose inhabitants speak only Romanian."[287]

As states laid claim to territory through Transylvania's people, the attraction of opening up a new identity category, "Hungarian Greek Catholics," was strong for many in the Hungarian administration who felt the demographic pinch, made still more palpable by the hotly contested matter of which nationality constituted the majority in Northern Transylvania. But despite sporadic efforts to pay lip service to the plight of the Hungarian Greek Catholics, many Hungarian authorities continued to look on Greek Catholics in general with distrust, performing background checks on Uniate priests, compiling statistics on the number of individuals who converted from Greek Catholicism to Roman Catholicism, denying trade permits to individuals of the Uniate faith, requisitioning food for the Hungarian army from the Uniate church, and a variety of other more or less oppressive practices and measures.[288] Meanwhile, Makkai's assumption that Greek Catholics were Roman Catholics or Protestants who had been forced to convert under Romanian rule was partially confirmed by the fact that a number of individuals in Northern Transylvania petitioned to convert *back* to Protestantism or Roman Catholicism from the Eastern-rite denominations.[289]

Nor did the Romanian leadership view the Greek Catholics as unproblematically loyal to the Romanian state. Marshal Antonescu declared in May 1943: "We have far fewer difficulties with Roman Catholics [in Romania] than we do with Greek Catholics." He went on to commend the Greek Catholic priests in Northern Transylvania for making common cause with the Romanian Orthodox priests, calling it "the most Romanian action for the protection of our interests and rights," suggesting that the two denominations should try to get along as well in Romania proper.[290]

TRANSCENDING BOUNDARIES

Many institutions and demographic groups—like the Greek Catholics and their institutions—spanned the border between Hungary and Romania. Their instant fragmentation following the Second Vienna Arbitration highlighted the awkwardness of Transylvania's division into North and South, a division that many in Hungary and Romania considered provisional. In his memoirs, Miklós Kállay, who became prime minister of Hungary in March 1942, recalled that during the first ceremony celebrating the Second Vienna Arbitration, Prime Minister Pál Teleki whispered to him that "this decision . . . cannot be final; it will only be the source of new problems."[291] Similarly, in a report on the situation in Northern Transylvania, a Hungarian official observed with concern "*the ever-increasing self-assurance, often provocative and offensive behavior of the Romanian population* of the annexed territories, who, by their impatience, want to make it felt that the current situation is temporary and everyone knows it, and that the reestablishment of '*Greater Romania*' is no more than a technical issue or a matter of time."[292]

And in fact, after the reannexation of Northern Transylvania by Hungary, Romanian politicians, demographers, and economists mounted a propaganda assault on the Second Vienna Arbitration. They argued, as Hungarian politicians and statesmen had done after Trianon, that the annexation was disastrous for the entire region, disrupting business and trade networks and causing large-scale demographic turmoil.[293] Meanwhile, in Romanian schools,

FIG. 20. Cover of a revisionist Hungarian board game called "Let's Reclaim Greater Hungary." Players were to plant Hungarian flags in all the counties of pre-Trianon Hungary as they moved across the board. BMF, RW 50, 286 (or BArch RW 50/286); reprinted with permission.

children continued to see maps in their geography textbooks showing "our homeland's natural and political boundaries," including Northern Transylvania. Those children also learned that the Second Vienna Arbitration had resulted in the creation of "forced, unjust, and temporary boundaries," and that the goal of restoring "the old borders" should "spur on the youth."[294]

The introduction to a Hungarian atlas published in 1942 asserted that despite temporary changes in "state territory" the "territory of the country remains unchanged." Accordingly, the atlas covered the geography "not of the state territory of today, but of the entire country," including territories still under Romanian state control.[295] In Romania, authorities noted with outrage that in Northern Transylvania revisionist maps (showing Hungarian claims to Southern Transylvania) were posted in cities and towns, and that police and soldiers sang revisionist songs, one of which called for the decapitation of Antonescu.[296] Another source of agitation was a board game sold in Hungary called "Let's Reclaim Greater Hungary," which required players to plant Hungarian flags in all the counties of Greater Hungary, noting the attributes of each as outlined on playing cards.[297] At the Transylvanian Conference in October 1940, István Bethlen admonished those present: "No one sees this border as permanent. This is a temporary border and we must carve that into the consciousness of every Hungarian."[298]

The presumed provisional nature of the Second Vienna Arbitration resulted in a variety of policies and practices crafted to overcome or extend the boundaries of state policy to include the other part of Transylvania. Some of these were mentioned earlier, like the policy of encouraging would-be optants and refugees to hold their ground, or reciprocity itself, which was understood as a means of influencing what happened on the other side of the border. But there were other, more subtle ways to reach across the border and stake a claim on the population there. Among these was radio.

Although only about 2 percent of the population in Romania and 6 percent in Hungary owned radios, both regimes recognized the power of this relatively new medium to stretch invisibly across borders and into people's homes.[299] When Hungarian troops entered Northern Transylvania, they were repeatedly told that "up until now, the Hungarian soul and world only reached us by radio."[300]

Already in early 1941, the Antonescu government ordered the creation of a mobile clandestine radio station to transmit propaganda into Northern Transylvania. The station, initially called "Ardeal" [Transylvania] and then "Greater Romania," later began broadcasting from a fixed station located in the building of the Romanian General Staff, with broadcasts in Romanian, Hungarian, and German starting in February 1942. The station even broadcast "Szekler Radio" in Hungarian, which claimed to be the "brave voice of the Transylvanian Szekler-Hungarian people's true interests and rights." Among those preparing the broadcasts were a handful of refugee intellectuals from Northern Transylvania.[301] Although the broadcasts ranged in length from just a few minutes to at most a few hours a day, once Hungarian government officials became fully aware of the content and scope of the Romanian radio propaganda, they were horrified.[302]

It proved convenient for the clandestine Romanian radio stations that the city of Kolozsvár was cut off from the nearest radio tower by the new border.[303] The proximity of Romania to Kolozsvár, the "the old, populous city of culture, [and] Transylvania's recognized center," nevertheless inspired the Hungarian administration to reach into the center of still-Romanian Transylvania by means of a new radio transmitter.[304] Despite early Hungarian claims that the Hungarians would not sink so low as to respond to Romanian radio propaganda, in 1943 and 1944 two clandestine Hungarian radio stations were reportedly transmitting anti-Romanian propaganda.[305]

Concerns about the power of radio to influence listeners gave rise to bans and periodic confiscation efforts.[306] In Hungary, listeners who tuned in to the

BBC's special news broadcast, for example, risked confiscation of their radios and a possible criminal indictment.[307] Minority populations were seen as particularly susceptible to the influence of propaganda broadcasts from abroad. At the beginning of 1941, the radios of many Hungarians living in Southern Transylvania were confiscated by Romanian authorities.[308] In October, Hungarian officials ordered the confiscation of some Romanians' radios.[309]

Other strategies for stretching across the border centered around the village of Feleac, which overlooked the city of Kolozsvár from the Romanian side. This area was one of intense border activity with regular crossings, both legal and illegal. During a visit there, Romanian writer Miron Paraschivescu observed the phenomenon of the "*vorbitorul*," or "parlance," that border officials arranged for residents living on either side. Every Sunday citizens of the two countries—oftentimes family members, some traveling from considerable distances for the occasion—could approach the border to talk to one another, maintaining a certain required distance between them.[310]

A group of women from Feleac found a more indirect, but nonetheless powerful means of communicating with their Romanian brethren on the other side; they erected a large cross that could be seen from the city. The cross was dedicated during a ceremony in early April 1942, attended by various local and national leaders and celebrities, including the mayor of Turda and Princess Alexandrina Cantacuzino, president of the Romanian Orthodox Women's Society. In her speech at the dedication, the princess called the cross "a symbol of unity of all Romanians under one scepter." Another commentator writing in June 1942 dubbed it a sign that for Northern Transylvania "the day of national liberation is nigh."[311]

An article in the Romanian newspaper *Ardealul* [Transylvania] on June 27, suggested that the cross was too small and should be made bigger, into a "monument of gigantic proportion worthy of Romanian conception." Over the course of the months that followed the erection of the cross, several border incidents took place at the Feleac crossing, and on July 1 a group of Hungarians demonstrated on the streets of Kolozsvár, where Romanian witnesses claimed they heard chants of "We want to go through Feleac and on to Predeal and Bucharest! Down with foul Wallachia! Let's go to war with the Vlachs and destroy everything that is Romanian!"[312]

CONCLUSION

The struggle for control of Transylvania was a battle with many fronts, involving people and places on the Transylvanian home front as well as soldiers on the Don. Here, as on the Eastern Front, winning the peace seemed more important than winning the war. The contest was based on a particular understanding of the factors most likely to influence the fate of Transylvania, an understanding that was shared by leaders and administrators in both states. According to this shared understanding, among the standards for legitimate rule of the territory was the relative capacity of the two states to represent the interests of the people of Transylvania. Demonstrating demographic and cultural predominance was part of this calculus, but hardly sufficient in itself.

On August 30, 1940, the day the Second Vienna Arbitration was announced, Iuliu Maniu published a series titled "Declarations to the Crown Council on the Occasion of Discussions Relating to the Arbitration at Vienna." In them he wrote: "The unification of Transylvania with the Mother Country is not based on the Treaty of Trianon, but springs from the right of self-determination of the Romanian people of Transylvania, manifest voluntarily on December 1, 1918."[313] A Hungarian district attorney in a slander case made a similar argument about Hungary's right to Transylvania, saying that "the motivating factor behind the Second Vienna Arbitration and its dominating principle was to ease the situation of the population living under Romanian occupation and, in correspondence with their wishes, to annex them to the mother country."[314] Thus both states' territorial aspirations vis-à-vis Transylvania were presumed to derive from a mandate from the masses, linking the territory to the will of the people.

It is nonetheless clear that the will or desire of the people, although a matter of rhetorical emphasis, was not always behind state policy in Hungary and Romania. Because ordinary people could and did represent the state, the attention they received from the state was often limited to their perceived utility as part of number sets, as mouthpieces for state interests, or as stewards of national territory and property. Furthermore, because interactions between "ordinary" people often served as channels through which state policies were manifest, and because the people themselves provided the justification for states' territorial aspirations, disproportionate power was often stacked behind individual interests—in courtrooms, at border crossings, in taverns, in movie theaters, and even in private homes. Hungarian and Romanian leaders and officials found ways to do battle with one another and found many "soldiers"—both willing and reluctant—to assume positions on the front lines.

So it was that in census declarations, refugee testimonies, court appearances, property purchases and exchanges, and other state-elicited venues, individuals were thought to help legitimate a state's claims to territory, often by delegitimating the claim of the other state in the eyes of the forces that were remaking Europe. The presumption was that an international panel of judges would ultimately decide boundaries based on an assessment of which state best represented the interests of the Transylvanian people.

Yet there were many ambiguities when it came to defining those interests. With the slander cases, for example, Hungarian authorities often faced defendants who considered themselves Hungarians, yet who had made negative or pessimistic remarks about the state of affairs under Hungarian rule.[315] Ion Antonescu's love/hate relationship with Romanian refugees from Northern Transylvania similarly highlighted the official tension between national and individual interests. Uncooperative national "clients" could too easily belie what both the Hungarian and Romanian states had depended on for legitimacy: the support of a willing populace.

In a 1928 propaganda publication in English, Hungarian member of parliament György Lukács said of Trianon, "Hungary can never accept these losses, because she is convinced that should the peoples with whom she lived in close community be consulted they would declare for the maintenance of political and economic union with Hungary."[316] In Mihai Antonescu's 1942 meetings with Romanian intellectuals on how to win the peace, he emphasized the need to document "[our] treatment of [minority groups] from 1918 until today," with special emphasis on "the freedoms accorded them by Romania, the rights they had, the way in which they exercised those rights; in other words, what Romania did from 1918 to 1940 for its nonmajority population."[317] In general, both states' leaderships considered it crucial to show how their governments had brought improvements to the region's infrastructure and opened up social, cultural, economic, and political opportunities to *all* its inhabitants.

Even during the Second World War, then, the interests and well-being of the two states' Hungarian and Romanian minorities also had to be considered. "We must do all in our power so that we only undertake actions that will not frighten off the Romanians on the other side," said former Hungarian prime minister, István Bethlen at the Transylvanian Conference in October 1940. "If we do what they do," mused Ion Antonescu during a Council of Ministers session in February 1942, "when it comes to a general peace, the Hungarians will say that we did the same to others. We must be prudent."[318]

Of course the matter of *which* powers would be arbitrating at the "general peace" would depend on who won the war. Nevertheless, Hungarian and Romanian leaders banked on the assumption that *regardless of who won the war* the *criteria* by which states would be judged in the final evaluation would prove more constant. A state's record in securing minority rights was among those criteria.

CHAPTER FOUR

A League of Their Own

Europe is not merely a military front, but a civilization
which must be preserved by all means.

—Mihai Antonescu to Andreas Schmidt, leader of the
ethnic Germans in Romania, March 30, 1943[1]

In 1940 Hungary joined the Berlin Tripartite Pact, and this
mature nation knew even then that it did not join a pack
of Avars and Huns, but the great European peoples who
live next to us.

—Right-wing Hungarian politician and publicist Ferenc
Rajniss in a speech before parliament, November 26, 1943[2]

On June 23, 1942, a daily newspaper in Kolozsvár ran a story about the trial
and sentence of a local woman named Irina for slander against the Hungarian
nation.[3] The venue for her purportedly slanderous statements was a letter
she wrote in July of the year before, addressed to a friend living across the
border in Romania. In the letter she had commented disparagingly on "local
conditions."[4] The Hungarian court record of her indictment from April 15,
1942, provides more detail regarding the content of the letter: "Here, as you
know, everything is expensive," she wrote. "It is very hard to get flour and
fat. . . . They set up commissions that go from house to house and gather up
flour and ham for the soldiers. Of course they only take from the Romanians
and the Jews." In another part of her letter she mentioned the mandatory
outfitting for air defense: "If you don't buy it, they fine you up to 500 pengő,
because they fined some poor Romanian as much."[5]

In justifying the indictment, the district attorney drew attention to how
Irina's words "make it appear as though life is very expensive in Hungary [and
that] in Kolozsvár it is impossible to obtain items of even the most basic and
necessary sort." He further commented that "in the entire content of the letter it would appear as though the extent of justice delivered were dependent

on a person's nationality, that is, that the Romanians under Hungarian rule suffer oppression." Another problem was Irina's tone in the letter, which the district attorney described as "of an utterly bad-natured disposition" in her presentation of the facts. Even worse, Irina's letter was addressed to a friend living in Romanian Southern Transylvania. It was intercepted by Hungarian authorities and never reached its destination, but the fact that its ultimate audience was someone beyond the border and that it thus could have fallen into the hands of a "foreign citizen (perhaps citizens)" was given as an "aggravating circumstance" in her sentence. "The accused wished to send the letter . . . abroad by diplomatic means and was desirous of offering a biased and slanderous characterization of the conditions brought on by the hardships of war to a foreign citizen (perhaps citizens)."[6]

The article in the Hungarian newspaper reported that Irina expressed no regrets to the court and even "continues to stand by what was written in the letter." She was sentenced to one year in prison and a three-year suspension of her political rights, to be carried out immediately.[7] She appealed the decision, but the appeal was denied on October 5. By that point she had served three months and twelve days in prison. Her remaining sentence was reduced to an additional two months and four days.[8]

The concern of the Hungarian court that Irina's letter and its contents could fall into the hands of "a foreign citizen (perhaps citizens)" was justified. In fact, following her indictment and sentence, three foreign governments became involved in her case: Romania, Germany, and Italy. In their effort to prevent Irina's complaints from being trumpeted abroad, Hungarian justice officials had facilitated the realization of their own worst-case scenario.

The Romanian government was quick to take up her cause through their legation in the Hungarian capital of Budapest. But instead of issuing a complaint directly to the Hungarian government, the legation petitioned the Axis powers to intervene on Irina's behalf.[9] They also included her name, along with the names of twenty-five other individuals, on a list of "Romanians from Northern Transylvania sentenced for slander against the nation and the Hungarian state."[10] The list was translated into German and submitted to the offices of the German-Italian Commission responsible for mediating between Hungary and Romania in minority questions. The list joined thousands of other such lists and petitions sent by the Hungarian and Romanian governments, groups, and individuals to the commission.

Shortly after Irina was sentenced by a Hungarian court, a special commission of international observers went to visit several labor camps in different parts of Romania to report on conditions there. During a series of visits in mid-August 1942, the commission observed "unbelievable conditions," with inmates lying on "primitive wooden pallets" dressed in "rags and covered with rags."[11] Another report stated that inmates received regular beatings and that, on the whole, "the social and hygienic conditions in the camp inspected by the commission can only be described as insufferable for any person."[12]

The result of the special commission's investigation was an eighty-four-page report and another sixty or so pages of recommendations to the governments in question. The inmates in these camps were not Jews for the most part, but Hungarians and Romanians. As for the report of the special commission of international observers, it was prepared in Berlin during the fall of 1942 by the officers and staff of the German-Italian Officers' Commission and later distributed with recommendations for improving the treatment of the Hungarian minority in Romania and the Romanian minority in Hungary to the governments of the two countries.

So it was that Nazi Germany and Fascist Italy were playing the role of minority rights watchdog for both states, in a sense picking up where the League of Nations had left off. Their mediation efforts implicitly confirmed the claim that formed the basis for the League system, namely, that minorities constituted "obligations of international concern."

Unlikely Protectors

Germany's relationship with the League of Nations had been a troubled one from the beginning. Yet despite the fact that the League was created in part to prevent Germany from becoming as powerful as it once had been, Germany was on the League Council from 1926 to 1933 and frequently petitioned the League on behalf of the German minority living in Poland, Czechoslovakia, and other East-Central European states.[13] Even before Hitler became chancellor of Germany in January 1933, however, German interest in the League depended on the League's ability to advance German interests, foremost among which was territorial revision. By 1932, the League seemed more of a barrier than a facilitator to German revisionism.[14] In October 1933, just months after Hitler came to power, Germany withdrew from the League. In a speech justifying this move, Konstantin Freiherr von Neurath, Germany's minister of foreign affairs, said:

> Concern for the fate of national groups that were separated from their nation-state by the boundaries drawn in 1919 was a first-order political obligation of the League of Nations. Will anyone honestly claim that it has even remotely fulfilled this obligation? . . . Thus the League of Nations is, in this respect as well, merely the executor of the will of the victorious powers, although according to the text of

the proclamations of 1919 there should have been at least some correctives of the territorial dictates of Versailles.[15]

Thereafter Germany's relationship to the League was openly antagonistic, and later Nazi Germany and Fascist Italy lobbied the states of East-Central Europe to withdraw as well.[16] When approached in May 1938 about the possibility of withdrawing from the League, the Hungarian ambassador to Rome responded that "we are not able to withdraw because the minority rights treaties are under the jurisdiction of the League of Nations for the consideration of all complaints submitted on behalf of minorities." Count Galeazzo Ciano, the Italian minister of foreign affairs, countered that "after the dissolution of the League of Nations, the Reich and Italy will be so powerful that they will be able to do much more for the minorities than the biased and impotent institution in Geneva."[17] The Axis, Ciano hinted, would assume the function of the League as far as Hungary was concerned, with the difference that it would be more effective in doing so.

The notion that Germany and Italy could play the role of League of Nations in minority rights protection during World War II seems as paradoxical as the Red-Cross-like concern the German officers expressed for the situation of labor camp inmates in Romania. Germany had, after all, provided a model for cruel and inhumane treatment of labor camp inmates and espoused an ideology of "Deutschland über alles" that left little room for the concerns of other states and peoples. But Germany's self-interested policy of maintaining peace in the Danube region (mostly to facilitate the flow of oil for the German war machine from the Romanian oil fields[18]) produced relationships and situations for which the term *ironic* seems euphemistic. Furthermore, since German leaders generally believed that the best way to improve the lot of the German minority was to revise the borders to include them in the German state, revisionism was a form of minority rights protection, and the promise or potential for revision or reciprocity brought out strange tensions between minority rights and territorial claims, as demonstrated in the Chapter 3.

This chapter explores how and why the German-Italian Officers' Commission came into being, what its activities were, how its role in the region was understood by the leadership in Germany, Romania, and Hungary, and how effective it was in mediating between Hungary and Romania on minority issues. The analysis draws out parallels with the interwar period international "justice" system and seeks to explain how these parallels reflected ideas about Europe's future that, as far as leaders in Hungary and Romania were concerned, had changed little since World War I.

The Terms of Mediation

The agreement between Hungary and Romania signed in Vienna on August 30, 1940, included provisions for the evacuation of Romanian troops from Northern Transylvania, the creation of a Romanian-Hungarian Commission to decide on the exact line of the border and see to an orderly transfer of state control, affording citizenship to all those who lived in or opted for either Hungary or Romania following the transfer, and protection of the property of optants and refugees.[19] Other provisions mandated the equality of minority populations in both states, "unmediated" negotiations between the two states in matters relating to the transfer, and finally, in Article 7, German-Italian mediation in the case of a failure of direct negotiations. It did not take long for last-resort Article 7 to be invoked.

Already on September 7, a small contingent of three German officials arrived in Bucharest and were later sent to Transylvania as "observers." The Germans called on the Italians to make a similar contribution.[20] On September 20, the Romanian foreign minister Mihail Sturdza met with the Italian ambassador in Bucharest and requested that a commission be created to investigate the "violence committed by the Hungarians with the complicity of the occupying authorities."[21] When Sturdza met again with the Italian ambassador on October 6, he announced the Romanian government's intention to explicitly invoke Article 7.[22]

The following day the Romanian government wrote a memo to the Hungarian government outlining its frustrations with the direct negotiations (or lack thereof) and called for German-Italian mediation.[23] Despite numerous attempts to initiate negotiations—specifically on the resolution of the minority question as essential for the establishment of good relations—the Romanian government's overtures had met with repeated resistance from the Hungarian side, the memo claimed. Another reason for invoking Article 7, the memo went on, was the extent and brutality of the atrocities committed by the Hungarian military and police following the transfer of sovereignty. "Every Romanian suggestion for an investigation of the incidents through mixed Hungarian-Romanian commissions, to be carried out on the basis of reciprocity and thus to improve the situation of the Romanian population, has been categorically denied by the royal Hungarian government."[24]

The Hungarian government denied the allegations put forward by the Romanian memo, but also requested German-Italian mediation on October 11.[25] So it was that a commission was established to investigate the claims of minority abuse on both sides. At the head of the commission were Count

Altenburg for Germany and Count Roggeri di Villanova for Italy, who began their investigation into reports of atrocities later that same month.[26] Over a period of eleven days, the commission covered thirty-five hundred kilometers in Northern and Southern Transylvania and conducted interviews with over five hundred individuals.[27]

In the report of the commission from October 31, both states were criticized, although it stressed that "the Hungarian side carries a greater share of the guilt than the Romanian."[28] Among other things, the commission established that over three hundred Romanians had been killed by Hungarian military and civil authorities and civilians since August 30.[29] Neither Ciano nor Hitler were inclined to make a big issue out of these "events."[30] Already on October 14, before the commission's formal investigation had even begun, German foreign minister Joachim von Ribbentrop told Romanian minister Valer Pop that "when territories changed hands, and especially in cases where national antagonisms were as intense as they were between Hungary and Romania, it was inevitable that incidents should occur at the time of the transfer." Nevertheless, the foreign minister assured Pop that "this matter would be looked into" and "Germany and Italy would not tolerate any systematic persecution of minorities." Of utmost importance "was first of all to have tranquility in the territories affected."[31] In a conversation with Hungarian prime minister Teleki on November 20, the German foreign minister again stressed in connection with the atrocities that "tranquility had to be restored and conditions had to return to normal, in order that peace in the section of Europe might not again be disturbed."[32]

The recommendations put forward by the commission were the same for both states and included the following: that violence and expulsions should be halted, that the press and radio war should cease, that refugees and expelled individuals should be given the right of return, that expelled or otherwise tormented individuals should be compensated, that negotiations for the establishment of the border and economic matters be reinstated, that the two states should reach an agreement regarding the treatment of minorities and the establishment of a permanent German-Italian commission to prevent expulsions and acts of violence.[33]

Despite the German and Italian leadership's willingness to overlook the atrocities, Hungarian leaders were uncomfortable with the commission and opposed its permanent presence in Northern Transylvania on the grounds that it "would perpetuate uncertainty and anxiety."[34] On October 24, the leader of the Hungarian minority in Romania, Elemér Gyárfás, proposed the creation of a mixed Romanian-Hungarian commission instead.[35] Nevertheless, the German-Italian Commission set up two permanent offices in

January 1941. One office was located in Kolozsvár (Northern Transylvania), and the other in Braşov (Southern Transylvania). The offices were staffed by German and Italian military personnel and diplomats until September 1943, when, following Italy's capitulation to the Allies, only German officers served on the commission.[36] At the suggestion of Romanian negotiator Valer Pop, Hungary and Romania were each permitted to send one permanent delegate to the commission to "be at its disposal to supply information on local conditions."[37]

The offices received individuals and minority representatives with grievances against the state or municipal authorities, including anything from job discrimination to unlawful confiscation of property to outright physical abuse. The commission also sent out "special missions" to investigate reported or potential abuses of minorities in both parts of Transylvania and prepared reports on their findings. The "special mission" entourage generally consisted of six or seven people, including three men in civilian dress, one or two each of German and Italian officers, a translator, and a scribe (the latter two were often women).[38]

The backgrounds of the commissioners who led the special missions— Günther Altenburg, Andor Hencke, and Delfino Roggeri—point to considerable continuity with pre-Nazi interwar diplomacy in the German case, as well as to the importance assigned to the commission's work as a matter of foreign policy concern. All three commissioners were career diplomats with considerable experience in the region prior to the war, and the careers of the two Germans began well before the Nazis' rise to power. Both joined the NSDAP (a day apart) only in January 1935, and in fact they were good friends.[39]

Of the three, Hencke was the most experienced in handling delicate foreign policy and mediation matters. He had been attached to the German legation in Prague before, during, and just after Munich (1936–1939) and participated in the negotiations between Germany and the USSR in Moscow during August and September 1939.[40] Thereafter he led the German delegation to the German-Soviet Mixed Central Commission for Border Questions [Gemischte Zentralkommision des Deutschen Reichs und der UdSSR für Grenzfragen] from August 1939 until April 1940.

The commissioners were thus knowledgeable about the region and experienced in matters of mediation and international diplomacy. Germany's leadership took the task of mediating between Hungary and Romania especially seriously, at the investigative level as well as at the level of endogenous Axis diplomacy. As a result, the commissioners' reports were not submitted directly to the governments in question but first to the governments in

Rome and Berlin, which evaluated them and submitted recommendations for reversal of certain policies or decisions or compensation for confirmed material losses. These recommendations would then be passed on to the Hungarian and Romanian legations. The special missions of the commission thus did not have "official" exchanges with leaders and diplomats in either country.[41] The permanent offices of the commission, however, did make inquiries into reported slights and sent out requests and recommendations to the two governments through the German consulates in Northern and Southern Transylvania.[42]

Besides the "special mission" assigned to investigate slights and atrocities in the wake of the Second Vienna Arbitration in fall 1940, there was another "special mission" dispatched in the summer and fall of 1942.[43] This time the request came from both sides in mid-June; the Hungarian ambassador to Berlin, Döme Sztójay, cited the recent requisition of foodstuffs from the Hungarian minority in Southern Transylvania, and the Romanian deputy prime minister, Mihai Antonescu, cited the situation of the Romanians in Northern Transylvania as requiring the investigation and opinion of the Axis powers.[44] Shortly thereafter, on June 19, Ribbentrop wrote to the legations of both countries announcing the formation of the second mission, headed by German commissioner Andor Hencke and the Italian Roggeri.[45] The two investigators relied heavily on material acquired and processed by the two permanent commission offices in Northern and Southern Transylvania.[46] The final report of the second special mission came out on February 8, 1943, and like the first, distributed the blame between the two states, offering recommendations to both.[47]

HIGH-STAKES MEDIATION

The commission's approach to investigating minority rights abuses invited comparison with its interwar predecessor in the region, the League of Nations. After learning of the commission's rigorous structure and procedures, the Slovak ambassador to Romania concluded in mid-December 1942 that "not even the much-criticized League of Nations was so careful" in gathering evidence and enforcing a "double blind" review process of purported abuses.[48] But how effective was the commission in either preventing or rectifying abuses? And what motivated such care on the commissioners' and their respective governments' part?

When speaking of the effectiveness of the German-Italian Commission and its German-only successor, a distinction must be made between its explicit and implicit missions. The commission's explicit mission was to protect Hungarian, Romanian, and German minorities in both states from oppressive state policies and practices. Its implicit mission was to maintain peace between the two countries in the interest of the Axis war effort. Insofar as German leaders could ill afford to permit Hungarian-Romanian relations to boil over into open conflict, the success or failure of the commission's activities, and indeed of the Axis-brokered Second Vienna Arbitration more generally, reflected directly on the viability of the New European Order.

As discussed in Chapter 1, since the World War I peace treaty negotiations, both the Hungarian and Romanian leaderships had focused a major part of their propaganda efforts on casting the Transylvanian Question as an issue with extra-regional—indeed Europe-wide—ramifications. The international politics surrounding the work of the commission provide strong evidence that this propaganda had successfully convinced many in both the Axis and the Allied countries that the exigencies of the Hungarian-Romanian regional dispute served as a gauge measuring the workability of the going European system. The commission's presence meant that, like the victorious Allies before them, the Axis leaders recognized in Transylvania a problem requiring both vigilance and mediation.

As with the League of Nations before it, Hungarian and Romanian leaders thus understood the commission's role as first and foremost of a political as opposed to an impartial and disinterested "juridical" nature. For despite the care and conscientiousness with which commissioners gathered testimonies from informants on the ground, once the commission had completed its work and retired to Berlin to draft its report, the matter became one of German foreign policy and the politics of conflict aversion took precedence over the assignation of guilt.

In early November 1942, the Hungarian consul in Braşov, Zoltán Sztankay, commented on the effectiveness of the German-Italian Commission. He protested against the notion that the commission was nothing more than a "puppet," claiming that "world-shaping forces are at work here."

> The Axis powers do not want to do justice to one or the other side, but rather to keep the two enemies from going at one another. . . . Here no one expects justice; everyone just looks after the interests of his own country. . . . It seems certain that the Axis's position between Hungary and Romania has decreased the chances of an escalation to some degree. The question is, is that what we want?[49]

While Hungarians and Romanians could argue about whether peace between them was desirable or not, German statesmen could not afford to be so cavalier about the possibility of war between the two nations as they generally believed that keeping peace between Hungary and Romania was not *merely*

"Quiet, children, I'm looking for a nice quiet place for
a summer vacation."

FIG. 21. Cartoon by Romanian-born Saul Steinberg showing Hitler as a woman in a rocking chair with two children labeled "Hungary" and "Romania" fighting in the background. The image shows how conflict between the two states was used as evidence of Axis weakness. The caption reads: "Quiet, I'm trying to find a nice place for a summer vacation!" Cartoon by Saul Steinberg in *American Mercury* 15, no. 224 (August 1942): 223. © The Saul Steinberg Foundation/Artists Rights Society (ARS), New York; reproduced with permission.

practical for purposes of the war effort, but also a *necessary* precondition for the maintenance of Germany's status and power. From a 1942 report on Hungary's attitude toward the Second Vienna Arbitration, the commission pointed to how relations between Hungary and Romania were linked in the minds of many to the "reputation [*Ansehen*] of the German Reich as guarantor for the [Second Vienna] Arbitration." "By no means is it the case," the report continued, "that this matter involves the domestic, private affairs of the two hostile states alone. If allowed to continue, the possible effects [of these affairs] will extend far beyond the frame of private disputes."[50]

For their part, the Allies were keen to portray tensions between Hungary and Romania as signs of Axis weakness. An article published in the Soviet daily *Pravda* on December 7, 1941, with the headline "Conflict in the Hitler-allied Camp" chronicled tensions between Hungary and Romania with unmistakable schadenfreude. "To the extent that Hitler's troubles [with Hungary and Romania] grow, so does the unavoidable failure of his bloody adventures become palpable."[51] A cartoon published in *The American Mercury* in August 1942 revisited the same theme.

The commission was very sensitive to such propaganda. It took notice when an "inflammatory anti-German radio transmitter" tied the effectiveness of German mediation between Hungary and Romania to the reputation of the Reich. In an evening broadcast on July 21, 1942, the "Deutsche Volkssender" [German People's Radio], an instrument of Allied propaganda transmitted from Moscow, noted the increased tensions between Hungary and Romania over Transylvania. "How instructive it was for us, then, [to see that] as long as Hitler seemed strong, he could suppress the unwanted tension between Hungary and Romania. Is there better proof of his current hopeless situation than the fact that now the antagonism between Hungary and Romania can be displayed so openly against Hitler's will?!"[52]

Under the circumstances, it is hardly surprising that German officials suspected Allied money was behind Romanian revisionist agitation, just as the Allies had earlier seen German interests feeding Hungarian revisionism.[53] In the words of the Slovak ambassador to Romania in a report from April 15, 1942, the problem of tensions between Hungary and Romania would be among the most difficult to solve after the war, and would in fact serve as a "litmus test [skušební kámen] for the so-called new Europe." [54]

The challenge was indeed great, for the German-Italian Commission had to outperform its predecessor in mediation, the League of Nations. This was made all the more difficult by fervent resistance to the commission's activities couched in terms of violation of state sovereignty. So it was that the lord lieutenant of Szolnok-Doboka complained in a letter to the commission from August 1942 that Hungary's reputation with its own minorities was harmed by the presence of the commission. "Because it is today unusual for a special commission to have a say in the domestic affairs of a country, the reputation of the state is harmed in the eyes of the agitated citizens of Romanian nationality."[55] The lord lieutenant lamented that Romanians circumvented the legal means already in place for addressing grievances by going straight to the commission with their complaints. Hungary's minorities were a "domestic affair," not to be interfered with by other states. Such arguments echoed almost verbatim those of the interwar Romanian state in its objections to League of Nations mediation attempts.[56]

And indeed, although Romania had been the first to request Axis mediation, the Romanian leadership also soon resented the commission's presence, linking its interventions to those made by the League on the basis of the post–World War I minority treaties.[57] In a response to a proposal for yet another special commission investigation on the part of the German and Italian governments on June 19, 1943, the Romanian government outlined its dissatisfaction with the commission's activities. The report informed the Italian and German governments that Marshal Antonescu "could not easily accept that foreign officers were asserting their will [*să facă lege voință*] on sovereign Romanian territory." Romania had long resisted such encroachments on its sovereignty in the interest of minorities, he argued, first by refusing to sign the minority treaties following the Treaty of Paris in 1856, "with its offensive interference in favor of the Jews," and later by its initial refusal to sign the minority treaties after World War I.[58]

RECIPROCITY VS. MEDIATION

In some respects, mediation was built into the very nature of the Second Vienna Arbitration insofar as the arrangement left significant minority populations in both "halves" of divided Transylvania. The initial Axis mediation that produced the division thus made it possible for both states to pursue a politics of reciprocity which had been impossible both during the pre–World War I era (because there were effectively no Hungarians living in Romania), as well as during the interwar period (because there were very few Romanians living in Trianon Hungary). The Second Vienna Arbitration itself can thus be considered a mediation strategy, one designed to operate on autopilot.

The ever-present threat of reciprocity—and the fact that both countries (especially Hungary, given its underdog demographic status) wanted their minority populations on the other side of the border to stay where they were to legitimate further claims on the other's territory—rendered outright oppression of minorities risky.[59] In the summer of 1941, officials in the Hungarian foreign ministry opined that persecuting Romanians in Hungary would only provoke abuses of ethnic Hungarians in Romania. This would in turn cause Hungarians to flee Southern Transylvania and thereby weaken Hungarian claims to the territory.[60] Similarly, in May 1943, Mihai Antonescu sent out a resolution to the effect that the commemoration of the death of Romanian right-wing politician Octavian Goga was not to be accompanied by demonstrations. In justifying the decision, he wrote:

> It is not the time to throw gas on the fire. Any demonstration with a boisterous irredentist character will give the Hungarian[s] a new opportunity to let loose acts

of terror against the subjugated Transylvanian [Romanians]. It would not be those who organize such demonstrations (in which I would myself wholeheartedly participate) who will carry the moral and historical responsibility [for the consequences], but those who authorize them. I do not want to take that responsibility.[61]

Nevertheless, reciprocity did not offer a surefire means of preventing minority rights abuses, especially given that acts of reciprocity could also be interpreted as provocations to open conflict of the sort some individuals in both states expressly desired. This view was held by a member of the Hungarian minority in Southern Transylvania, who concluded that "the Romanian [state's] treatment of the Hungarians is perhaps only a provocation by means of which they want to force Hungary to intervene forcefully on our behalf."[62] And indeed, a direct conflict did appeal to some members of the Hungarian administration as an option superior to mediation. This is evident from Hungarian consul Sztankay's question regarding whether the commission's mission to prevent open conflict between the two states was in the Hungarian interest. In a draft response to one of the commission's reports such frustration was still more blatantly expressed:

> I see it as necessary to remind the Axis powers' governments that Hungary was not the one who asked for Axis arbitration in the Transylvanian Question. Hungarian public opinion and the late Count Pál Teleki's government had already decided in the late summer of 1940 to solve the Transylvanian Question by force of arms, and it was only out of respect for the interests of the Axis powers that we did not take that step. . . . I take the [Hungarian] minister of defense as a witness, who just after the [Hungarian troops'] entry into Sepsiszentgyörgy, correctly noted that "the Hungarian army would be in Sepsiszentgyörgy even if there had been no Second Vienna Arbitration."[63]

The author of the response also mentioned that the "spirit" of the Second Vienna Arbitration called for "the rectification of the injustices created by the Versailles-Trianon order."[64] It was thus natural that the Hungarian state should seek to reverse the privileging of the Romanians at the expense of the Hungarians that had taken place over the twenty-two years following Trianon.

Reciprocity did not then necessarily *prevent* abuses, but rather was used to *justify* them. In fact, using reciprocity to justify oppressive policies was a common response made by representatives of both states to commission charges and queries. This rhetorical strategy rendered "justice" around the issue of minority rights a matter of transnational rather than domestic consideration. In the summer of 1941, for example, the Hungarian minority leader in Romania Elemér Gyárfás complained that the Romanian administration had denied him a passport, that members of the Hungarian minority group's leadership in Southern Transylvania were forbidden to travel even within Romania, and that their telephone connections were cut off. In the fall, when the German-Italian Commission wrote to the Hungarian administration requesting that it grant the Romanian minority representation in Northern Transylvania, the Hungarian prime minister's office replied that it would allow such an organization to operate as soon as the Romanian government lifted the restrictions on the Hungarian minority group in Southern Transylvania. The Hungarian prime minister's office drew the commission's attention to the "organization lacking content and value" that was the magyar minority group in Romania, adding that the creation of an equally restricted Romanian organization on Hungarian soil would only result in "ever more and more insults and accusations."[65]

Following the mass requisitions of foodstuffs from Hungarians in Southern Transylvania in the summer of 1942, Romanian officials justified the policy as reciprocating slights against the Romanian minority in Northern Transylvania.[66] The Romanian government's December 4, 1942, response to the report and recommendations of the Altenburg-Roggeri Commission mentioned several misdeeds perpetrated against the Romanian minority in Northern Transylvania, arguing that Hungary had learned nothing from Trianon.[67]

Complicating the effects of reciprocity was the fact that Hungarian state officials regularly practiced both geographical and historical reciprocity, meaning that it sought to reciprocate not only slights against the Hungarian minority in Southern Transylvania, but also to reverse slights committed by Romanian authorities during the period of Romanian rule. The Hungarian leadership protested against the report of the commission following its 1942 special mission, for example, on the grounds that Hungarian policies that *appeared* to discriminate against Romanians were merely the "indemnification of the injustices [we had] repeatedly complained of to the League of Nations," and "the Hungarian government not only felt it was entitled, but also that it was bound to act to put a stop to the institutionalized discrimination against the Hungarians, at least within a very modest framework."[68] Hungarian officials repeatedly stressed to the commission that policies—such as the 1,440/1941—which targeted Romanians were means of undoing the wrongs of the Romanian regime of twenty-two years.[69]

Because the rhetorical landscape was such that the two states were responsible for the fates of their own minorities living beyond their respective borders, leaders in both sought through those minorities to project their states' effective sovereignty onto each other's territory, even across time. Hence when the commission completed its second mission in the fall of 1942, its achievements must have seemed meager. The question of the exact border between the two states was still not fully resolved, oppressive policies were still being reciprocated, and the flow of refugees continued such that in two years' time the commission estimated that 7.5 percent of the total population of Transylvania had changed residences.[70] Nevertheless, Hungary and Romania were not at war with one another, mass killings had ceased, and the commission had become the target of both small- and large-scale persuasive propaganda efforts initiated at all levels of both states' bureaucracies, and occasionally even by interested civilians.

MANIPULATIONS

The extent to which the Hungarian and Romanian state leaderships took the commission and its special missions seriously is evident from the myriad ways in which the two states sought to influence the opinions and decisions of the commission's members, and through them the foreign policy of the Reich and Italy. Such efforts included attempts by state authorities and civilians to intimidate minority individuals who wished to report to the commission, state efforts to "prime" individuals on how to present their situation to the commission, sending or attempting to send spies—in the form of secretaries, building overseers, translators, and so on—to keep an eye on and potentially influence the commission's activities and decisions, and centralizing the collection of testimonies from refugees and minorities, as well as the gathering of press clippings and transcripts of radio broadcasts for the purpose of demonizing one another in the eyes of the commission.

In January 1941, when the commission visited towns and cities in Northern Transylvania, the authorities in both countries were on the lookout. During the visit, a Hungarian police captain reported that "since the Romanians found out the German-Italian Commission is here, they have supposedly begun to keep records on every person leaving Hungary for Romania. In these records the optants mention unprecedented atrocities as the reason for their departure."[71]

The similarity between the accounts of Romanian refugees did not escape the notice of commission members. In November 1942, a commissioner in Brașov reported on the testimony of a man who had recently arrived in Romania in a group of twenty refugees fleeing Northern Transylvania. The man testified that Romanian authorities had informed the refugees "that we should appear before the German-Italian special commissioners to give a report of our escape." The commissioner noted that "almost every one of those interrogated explained that they had been driven from their homes by Hungarian authorities and thus were forced to flee to Romania. . . . It seems unlikely that these unanimous and consciously counterfactual statements (that so happen to correspond exactly to the official Romanian position) are the product of the tactical sense of these simple people."[72]

Even when the commission did not suspect that states were coaching minority refugees directly, commissioners noted patterns in the content and presentation of Romanian and Hungarian refugee testimonies. "In the case of Romanian refugees there is often an apparent tendency to exaggerate the tale of suffering. In the case of Hungarian refugees, the reason for their flight always begins with the oppression they suffered from the Romanians in the year 1919, and then goes into a long-winded presentation of the difficult fate [they have endured] over the past twenty years."[73] In the same report the commissioner concluded that "intellectuals" were more likely than "peasants" to try to make an impression through exaggeration.[74] The head of the Romanian delegation to the commission, Lieutenant Colonel Virgil Bichiceanu, also believed that many Romanian refugees' complaints were "untrue" or "exaggerated," a fact which "decreases the value of the claims we are making." He proposed the testimonies be checked and more strict questioning be introduced to eliminate specious claims. [75]

Officials and leaders in both Hungary and Romania thus worked hard to shape the content of the commission's reports by various means. It was part of the job description of the Romanian delegate to the commission, for example, to "warn interested parties regarding the arrival of the commission," and in general to "present the facts in the most favorable light for the Romanian cause."[76] In a circular to the prefects of counties in Southern Transylvania from August 1942, Mihai Antonescu admonished district authorities to collect declarations from Hungarians that they had not been mistreated by the Romanian state or authorities, as well as to collect anti-Hungarian testimonies of Romanian refugees, and to prevent members of the German-Italian Commission from speaking with the Hungarian minority leadership in Southern Transylvania.[77] At the same time in the Northern Transylvanian city of Szatmárnémeti, the Romanian consul in Kolozsvár and a Romanian lawyer (Aurel Socol) arrived to confer with Romanian leaders there. When the commissioners appeared in the city, they were met by thirty-two Romanians queuing up to submit complaints, all of them dressed in national costume.[78]

The gathering of testimonies and trumpeting of slights and atrocities was thus assumed to have ramifications for the future of the region. In a report to a government minister in Bucharest, also from August 1942, a

Romanian professor in Turda wrote that "for the days that are to come, it is good that [the extent of the tragedy] be known by as many good Romanians as possible, especially by former and future leaders."[79] And it was not only for "good Romanians" to know, but also the commission and other foreign powers. In fact, efforts to provide the commission with documentation of Hungarian abuses were coordinated with international propaganda initiatives undertaken by the foreign ministry.[80]

Because the stakes were presumed to be so high, authorities in both states employed various strategies not only to influence, but also to hinder the activities and fact-gathering efforts of the commission. Hungarian government officials and minority representatives regularly complained to the commission that members of the Hungarian minority in Southern Transylvania were harassed or intimidated by Romanian authorities if they approached the commission or the minority representatives with problems.[81] The result was that many withdrew their complaints or "kept all national grievances to themselves, since every disclosure can bring upon them still worse injustices."[82]

Nor did Hungarian authorities shy away from coming between the commission and the Romanian minority in Northern Transylvania. In April 1942, Hungarian intelligence intercepted a letter from the Romanian Captain Negulescu to the German-Italian commission in which he wrote that "since the Romanians of the annexed territories cannot gather in any kind of organization or club which would enable them to come into contact with their leaders . . . only the priests can give [members of the commission] information regarding the situation of the Romanians." Having learned this, the Hungarian regional commissioner of Northern Transylvania suggested that "we notify the organizations within the realm of our authority of the potentiality that priests will be receiving instructions from the other side [Romania]. We should furthermore tell these authorities to keep an eye on the priests and report anything even slightly suspicious to me immediately."[83]

That both states kept a close watch on the commission, to the point of spying on its members, is clear from the amount of detailed information provided in reports on the commission's activities. One such Hungarian report from the Hungarian royal gendarmerie in Márosvasárhely includes information on the commission's visit to the city and detailed references to nearly all of their conversations with plaintiffs.[84] Romanian police similarly noted the tiniest details of the commission's activities—which individuals it visited and where, how many minutes it spent consulting with a given plaintiff, what the likely outcome of the consultation would be, the license plate number on the commission's car, where it was parked during consultations, and what mood commissioners were in when they left.[85]

The commission also complained that the Hungarians repeatedly called up their translator for military service (despite appeals for an exemption), ostensibly so they could replace him with one who better represented Hungarian interests.[86] Hungarian authorities considered a similar intervention relating to the building occupied by the commission in Kolozsvár. The Tataru villa at 17 Bercsényi Street had been the home of a professor at the local university who opted for Romania following the boundary shift.[87] The villa was an exceptionally high-class residence, featuring a tennis court on a terrace over the servants' quarters, a swimming pool, and two hundred fruit trees on the property. "From its location it reigns over all of Kolozsvár," remarked one observer.[88] Its prime location and posh surroundings made it attractive to the German-Italian Commission, which took up residence there on the basis of a rental agreement with its absentee owner. In mid-1942, the commission apparently began making inquiries about buying the villa from the owner, but the Hungarian liaison officer to the commission, László Dunszt, had a better idea.

Dunszt thought the Hungarian state should purchase the property and allow the commission to use it rent-free. In this way, he opined, "it would come into Hungarian hands," and "the Hungarian state could keep its own person there as an overseer." Dunszt's proposal implied that this would be a good way to keep an eye on the activities of the commission and also make it more dependent on the goodwill of the Hungarian state. The ambassadorial adviser at the Hungarian foreign ministry reacted favorably to Dunszt's suggestion, adding that he thought the purchase would have the supplementary advantage of discouraging "those Romanian circles who still have not ceased to speculate about the return of Romanian rule" to the region. The temporary withdrawal of the commission to Vienna in 1943 rendered the question moot, however.[89]

The Tataru villa affair was but one of several of Dunszt's attempts to keep close tabs on the commission or sabotage its fact-finding initiatives. In July 1942, the commission made mention of 235 unanswered queries it had addressed to Dunszt since January of that year, thirty-two of which were considered "urgent." On another two occasions, Dunszt failed to show up to scheduled meetings with officers of the commission in villages and towns where the commission was taking testimonies, and he also instructed officials in those towns to give no information to the commission unless he (Dunszt) was present. Finally, the commission suggested that Dunszt be removed from office on the grounds that he had "systematically sought to hinder the work [of the commission]."[90]

Providing more cause for suspicion was the fact that the Romanian consulate was very near to the commission's headquarters in Kolozsvár. In May 1941, the Hungarian consul in Braşov wrote to Jenő Ghyczy, head of the Hungarian foreign ministry's political section, to warn him that "a reliable confidential source" had discovered that one of the commission's female scribes was having "intimate relations" with one of the clerks of the Romanian consulate. "There are grounds for the suspicion that the woman regularly informs the clerk about the confidential findings of the commission."[91]

A further strategy employed by authorities in both states was to draw the commission's attention to the other state's antagonism toward the German minority and hostility to German interests. Hungarian authorities regularly reported Romanian slights against ethnic Germans in Southern Transylvania.[92] The lord lieutenant of Szolnok-Doboka County, Béla Bethlen, wrote to commissioners about "bloody confrontations" between Romanians and Saxons when the latter tried to reclaim lands they had lost to Romanians under the Romanian regime.[93] In another report to the German-Italian Commission from August 1942, the head of the Hungarian minority in Southern Transylvania, Elemér Gyárfás, linked oppression of Hungarians in Romania to the oppression of Germans.[94]

Beyond the German minority issue, Hungarian commentators also sought to demonstrate Hungary's loyalty to Germany in their contact with the commission. One Hungarian report on the commission's visit to the city of Nagyvárad highlighted a demonstration in favor of Hitler and Mussolini by Hungarian refugees there on the day of the commission's visit.[95] In July 1942, the Hungarian president of the Transylvanian Hungarian Economic Association[96] in Southern Transylvania reminded commissioners of how "the entire Hungarian nation bled in the 1914–1918 world war. Here there still live many people who fought out the world war together with the Germans. Many of them had to suffer through—with only one leg or one arm—all the indignity and unjust struggle that fate has dealt us through the conduct of the Romanian government over the course of twenty years."[97]

The German minority and German interests were indeed among the preoccupations of the commission. A confidential Hungarian report detailed a session between Commissioner Hencke and a member of the Hungarian minority who had a German-sounding name. Hencke wondered whether the man had been harassed in Romania for his name, which the man denied. "That's all I wanted to know," Hencke reportedly said, "because in Hungary magyarization is being undertaken with fire and iron, and they barely allow a person to go around with a German name."[98]

Statements such as Hencke's gave Hungarian authorities the impression that the commission was biased in favor of the Romanians.[99] In another conversation with a Hungarian minority leader in Aiud, a commissioner reportedly showed him a dossier of the complaints issued by Romanians in Northern Transylvania against the Hungarian state and asked, "how can [you] expect [the Romanians] to treat the local Hungarians with understanding when such crimes are being committed across the border? Are [you] not afraid that the patience of the Romanians will run out and the Northern Transylvanian Romanians will massacre the Hungarians living there?"[100] In a meeting with Hungarian ambassadorial councillor Ervin Vladár on November 6, 1942, commissioners told Vladár that Romanian revisionism was not the real cause of the tensions between the two states. The real cause was "the brutality of the [Hungarian] gendarmes. . . . The gendarmes . . . behave very brutally, and they treat the Romanians like second-class citizens, slapping them in the face right at the start of an interrogation. In general their entire approach and manners are such that they evoke revulsion."[101]

In the Hungarian response to the recommendations offered by German and Italian governments following the commission's second special mission of the summer and fall of 1942, the charge of favoritism is very nearly explicit. Indeed, it is quite explicit in the internal memo of the Hungarian foreign ministry relating to the response, which concludes that the German National Socialist government had taken a "divide and conquer" strategy in its foreign policy vis-à-vis Hungary and Romania. "German foreign policy has aimed at keeping Hungary and Romania in check with one another, achieving this—within the framework of a carefully thought out policy of equilibrium—by favoring by every means possible the state that is of greater importance to [Germany], Romania."[102] Further evidence of Romania's favored status, the memo asserted, was the Second Vienna Arbitration itself. Given the circumstances in Romania just prior to the negotiations at Vienna, the author speculated that Hungary could easily have taken what it wanted from Romania without Axis intervention.[103] As it was, however, the Second Vienna Arbitration left the bigger, "more valuable" part of Transylvania to Romania, giving Hungary the smaller, "poorer," more "economically passive" northern section.[104] Since then, Germany—through the commission's activities—had maintained its "pro-Romanian policy of equilibrium."[105] Hungarian authorities speculated that Romania was the favorite not only due to its "geographical position" as a point of departure for the offensive against the Soviet Union, and "natural treasures," most notably oil, but also for the "lightning-fast transformation of its foreign policy orientation," which entailed the adoption of all Hitler's views in domestic policy, and a heavy commitment to the war against the Soviet Union.[106]

In general, the commission's assessment of the situation in Transylvania indeed stressed that Hungarian authorities were harsher toward Romanians in Northern Transylvania than their Romanian counterparts were toward Hungarians in Southern Transylvania.[107] Nevertheless, in informal interactions with commissioners, Hungarian authorities were encouraged when the officers seemed to share the Hungarian view that Romanians were less civilized and "western" than Hungarians. In December 1942, the Hungarian consul in Arad told Lieutenant Colonel Dehmel—head of the commission office in Brașov—that Hungarians, who carried a "western worldview," resisted going back to being ruled by "nations with an eastern mentality." Dehmel reportedly concurred, adding that "the Romanian administration . . . has proved that it is incapable of governing foreign nationalities."[108] Similarly, in one commission report on Hungarian police brutality—specifically beatings of interned Romanians—the commissioner wrote that "the envoys are aware that in southeastern countries slaps in the face come more readily and are also more necessary than in the West," but said that nevertheless Hungarian gendarmes should be punished for excesses.[109]

For as much as the Hungarian leadership felt the commission could and would play favorites, the Romanian leadership also hinted that the commission was biased against Romania.[110] The head of the Romanian delegation to the commission, Lieutenant Colonel Virgil Bichiceanu, felt the commission responded more enthusiastically to reports of slights against Hungarians and complained that one member of the commission fraternized with the Hungarian elite in his area.[111] For his own part, Ion Antonescu was frustrated when the commission attributed equal blame and gave similar recommendations to both sides following the special mission investigations of 1940 and 1942, "as if the civilized and lawful treatment of the Hungarian minority in Romania can be equated with the arbitrary arrests and subjugation, the starvation and the abasement of the Romanians in Northern Transylvania."[112] When the commission's special mission was doing the rounds in Southern Transylvania in the summer of 1942, the police inspector for the Romanian secret police in Turda reported on the anger of the local Romanian population:

> The people ask in astonishment how it is that the Romanian government takes no measures against the propaganda being created by the Hungarians here, who never miss an opportunity to spread vicious rumors—intended to provoke panic among Romanians—that soon all of Transylvania will be theirs. And [they wonder] how it is that no reprisals are made to compensate for the misdeeds committed against Romanians in ravished [Northern] Transylvania.[113]

A mirror-image report was filed by Hungarian police in August 1942, during the visit of the commission to Northern Transylvania. As Hungarian civilians in one town noted the Romanians going to submit complaints to the commission, they shouted, "We tried to complain under Romanian rule. If we had made such processions they would have mowed us down with machine guns," and "We don't understand the passivity of the police—these people should be hung up by their feet in front of the police station as a deterrent."[114] The author of the report commented that the protestations against the Romanian hubris would have been still larger had the weather been better.

The Little Man

Despite hostile rhetoric, the ongoing competition between the two states for a favored position in the international political arena may have helped along the commission's explicit mission of protecting minorities in both states. Although it was clear enough to the German foreign ministry in the summer of 1942 that many previous efforts of the commission to smooth out tensions between Hungary and Romania had been in vain,[115] the efforts of the two states' leaderships to keep the commission from accessing information, coupled with efforts to influence the quantity and type of information the commission received, is evidence of its perceived power. Consequently, "the mere existence of the commission, or rather the possibility that rights violations can be brought before the commission, makes the situation of the Hungarians easier," wrote a representative of the Hungarian minority in Southern Transylvania in a report on the situation of the Hungarians in Brașov. "In many cases the local Romanian authorities remedied slights when threatened that the case would otherwise be taken before the commission."[116]

There was nevertheless much frustration with the commission from both sides, and not only due to the presumed unfairness or "political" motivations of the commissioners. A Hungarian document from 1942, for example, lists the "cases in which it could be determined that either as a result of the plaintiff's testimony or of the response of the commission, the commission's proceedings proved harmful to the plaintiff." The document names seventeen such cases, mainly harassment and intimidation of individuals and a school closing, and speculates that there were many more such cases about which the Hungarian consulate was not informed. Another document lists "consular memos submitted for more severe cases that were never answered by the German-Italian Commission, or only very late." These included 14 reports of murders, beatings, and other serious offenses, followed by an inventory of 135 lesser slights that had not been addressed by the commission.[117] There was even speculation from the Hungarian side that "neither the uninterrupted oppression of the Hungarians, nor the anti-Hungarian propaganda undertaken with the full force of the state apparatus domestically and abroad could have been undertaken by the Romanian government without the approval and endorsement of the German government."[118]

Similarly, in correspondence between Romanian foreign minister Mihai Antonescu and Germany's ambassador to Romania Manfred Killinger in June 1943, Antonescu complained that, insofar as the commission's primary mission was to "avoid expulsions and frontier incidents . . . the commission was not able to prevent the wave of thousands of refugees from continuing each month to be thrown into Romania." He concluded that these organs of the Reich and Italy, although they were "well-meaning institutions," nevertheless "could not hold back the acts of persecution unleashed [*deslănțuită*] in Hungary."[119] When the commission visited Southern Transylvania in the summer of 1942, Romanian security police claimed that the visit had raised the indignation of the Romanian population to such an extent that "it could all too easily lead to excesses against Hungarians" and that the Romanian population was calling for "double reciprocity" (two eyes for an eye) to be exercised against the Hungarians who "pretend" to suffer at the hands of the Romanian authorities and population.[120]

There is no doubt that the situation of minorities in both states was made difficult—sometimes impossible—by incensed civilians, overzealous local officials, and oppressive state policies. They faced forced name and religion changes; were often harassed if they used their own language in public; had property, foodstuffs, and radios confiscated by authorities; were denied trade permits, pensions, and education in their own language; were often interned and mistreated by police and judges for minor offenses or for no reason at all; were drafted into labor service battalions where they worked under conditions the Germans described as "impossible"; had their clubs, newspapers, and other publications banned or shut down; and suffered intimidation and obstruction in public offices, and some were even murdered.[121]

The German-Italian Commission documented many of these slights, and in some cases the only record that exists of them can be found among the surviving documents of the commission. Ironically, it was often copies of these same documents—submitted to the commission by Hungarian and Romanian officials—that fattened the dossiers both states had begun compiling in preparation for the peace. Indeed high-ranking officials in both Hungary and Romania believed that the commission's successor, be it Axis or Allied, would be mediating on the same terms as the commission and *its* predecessor, the League of Nations, had done.

CONCLUSION

When Romania pulled out of the Axis in August 1944 and joined the Red Army in the fight against Nazi Germany, the German foreign ministry sent its Balkan correspondent in a special plane to Kolozsvár to consult with the commission. During the meeting, those present debated whether the commission still had a role to play in the region under the circumstances. They concluded that its role, should it continue to have one, would depend on whether and to what extent "the government of the Reich gives a free hand to the Hungarians with regard to Southern Transylvania, so that if need be the Reich can declare the Second Vienna Arbitration as no longer binding (insofar as it was unilaterally abandoned [*aufgekündigt*] from the Romanian side)."[122] The commission staff was also instructed to burn all documents in the event of an evacuation. With Romania now an enemy state and the border just a few kilometers to the south of the city, the last remnants of Germany's awkward role mediating between the two states came to a fiery end on September 1, 1944, when the complete collection of documents held by the commission office in Kolozsvár was burned, together with all of the secret documents of the German consulate there. Only the contents of the commission's receipts and personal files were retained to be evacuated—together with the commission's staff, vehicles, typewriters, pistols, and picnic basket—back to the Reich.[123]

The legacy of the German-Italian Commission is difficult to disentangle from the political interests of both past and present. Historians' assessments of the commission's role and effectiveness have been almost categorically negative. During the Communist period, Hungarian historian Dániel Csatári emphasized the harmful nature of its activities.[124] More recently, Romanian historian Vasile Puşcaş has said that the commission not only failed to stop expulsions, loss of property, and other minority abuses, but also "contributed to an even greater aggravation of relations between Hungary and Romania, with consequences for them as well as for this part of Europe."[125]

German activities during the war are ready examples for what happens when minority rights rhetoric loses all power. It is nevertheless striking to note how the goals and expectations for the commission's work were so similar to those for the League of Nations during the interwar period, and disappointment at its apparent failure to administer "justice" was cast in nearly identical terms. That the Axis could be seen as assuming the role the League of Nations had set out to play shows that ideas about what "Europe" stood for and how it should operate had not undergone such a radical overhaul in the eyes of these two states' leaders and officials. Although Mark Mazower notes that "the essential feature of [Hitler's] 'New European Order' is that it was a German order," all parties involved in the drama around Transylvania *appeared* to be operating under the assumption that minority populations—and not just German minorities—and their suffering mattered.[126]

Recall, for example, the statement of the district attorney in Irina's case: "In the entire content of the letter it would appear as though the extent of justice delivered were dependent on a person's nationality, that is that the Romanians under Hungarian rule suffer oppression"; or Ion Antonescu's mention of "the civilized and lawful treatment of the Hungarian minority in Romania." The moral outrage is palpable: the language of minority rights retained its power. In fact, putting a positive spin on Romania's interwar minority rights record was among the "problems to be resolved by the 'Peace Bureau'" of Mihai Antonescu.[127]

For state authorities in Hungary and Romania, the promise and threat of national self-determination and minority protection held out by the post–World War I peace were being fought through during World War II. In February 1940, an article in a public affairs journal in Hungary cited the Duke of York as having said, "It cost us a war to set up the League of Nations, and it will cost us another war to see its prestige recognized."[128] The citation was untrue to the spirit of the original, but indeed telling in its own right, just as discussions of Hitler's "New European Order" tended to be in these states.

The extent to which the work of the German-Italian Officers' Commission and its recommendations were taken seriously—evident from the two states' efforts to manipulate the information the commission received— demonstrates how state leaders in Hungary and Romania believed that the minority question would help determine the outcome of the peace. To understand how deeply ingrained was this assumption, we move now to the one issue that made the Axis and Allied visions of a reordered Europe very different as far as Hungary and Romania were concerned: the so-called Jewish Question.

CHAPTER FIVE

The "Jewish Question" Meets the Transylvanian Question

I fully share the opinion that liberalism must be practiced, but one should part ways with it if the well-conceived interests of the nation so require.

> —Pál Teleki's speech before the Upper House of the Hungarian parliament, March 13–14, 1928[1]

I, too, am a democrat except when it comes to policies related to nationality.

> —Ion Antonescu to the Military Cabinet of the Romanian Council of Ministers, fall 1940[2]

In mid-May 1941 the Soviet and Bulgarian ambassadors stationed in Budapest sat down to discuss Hungarian politics. During the course of the conversation, the Bulgarian ambassador, Dimitar Toshev, observed: "Hungarians can be Anglophiles or Anglophobes, Germanophiles or Germanophobes, but they are all Romanophobes to the extent that even the Jewish population forgets about its anti-German feelings when it comes to revisionist aspirations."[3]

Although Toshev's statement was certainly not true of all Transylvanian Jews, it is nonetheless the case that many were among the cheering crowds that came out to greet Hungarian troops as they entered towns and cities in Northern Transylvania.[4] It is also true that some Jewish families living in Southern Transylvania and the Regat opted for Hungary following the announcement of the Second Vienna Arbitration, and many submitted claims under the (in)famous 1,440/1941 ministerial decree by means of which Hungarian citizens could (re)claim property or compensation from individuals who they felt had exploited them during the period of Romanian rule.[5]

One of the most high-profile compensation cases was that of Jenő Janovics, who had been the director of the Hungarian Theater in Cluj during the interwar period. Under Romanian rule the Hungarian Theater received no assistance from the state, and Janovics sold some of his own property to sustain the struggling institution.[6] When Hungarian rule returned, Janovics filed a claim against a Romanian couple who had bought one of his properties in 1930 at half its appraised value.[7] He demanded compensation and legal expenses from the couple, who had since fled to Romania, on the grounds that his sacrifice had been made for the Hungarian Theater. This claim was submitted just as the anti-Jewish legislation implemented in Hungary, and by extension in the reannexed territories, forbade Jews from taking part in the artistic life of the nation, and Janovics was forced to withdraw from involvement in the theater.[8] The Hungarian state thus allowed Jews to make claims against Romanians, because "correcting the injustices of the interwar period" was the primary element in the platform of the Transylvanian Party, but it did not allow them to retain their positions in public life.

Further traces of the paradox that simultaneously empowered and disenfranchised the Hungarian Jews of Northern Transylvania is offered by the Hungarian census of 1941, which allowed, even encouraged, Jews to declare themselves Hungarians by nationality, and many did.[9] Nevertheless, practically speaking, they could not *become* Hungarian, even by changing their names to Hungarian-sounding ones. Individuals with Christian backgrounds (Lutheran, Orthodox, Greek Catholic) and German or Romanian names could officially adopt Hungarian-sounding names, and indeed they often had such names thrust upon them. But Jews were denied this opportunity (sometimes obligation).[10]

The field of recruitment for the national franchise thus included Romanians and Germans, but Jews—the traditional allies of magyardom—were permitted only part-time membership. Some Hungarian leaders were self-conscious about this shift, which put them in the unsavory position of lobbying for converts among their national enemies (Romanians and Germans) while alienating their only minority allies, the Jews.[11] Just after the Second Vienna Arbitration, Miklós Horthy argued in a letter to Prime Minister Teleki against the radical solutions to the Jewish Question propounded by the Hungarian extreme right: "We need [the Jews]. . . . They are tied to us by mutual interest."[12]

In Transylvania, political rhetoric relating to the Jews often focused on the question of whether the interwar symbiosis between Jews and Hungarians should be taken into account. "Looking at the Jewish Question with Transylvanian eyes," some argued, meant recognizing and rewarding the loyalty many Transylvanian Jews (like Jenő Janovics) had shown to Hungarian culture and political interests during "hard times."[13] But as Jews were being edged out of businesses and proprietary and management positions throughout Northern Transylvania, the justification voiced by the right-wing press, as well as the administration, was that the Transylvanian Jews had aided the Romanian regime in the oppression of magyardom during the period of Romanian rule. One member of the Transylvanian Party commented in the fall of 1942 that "under Romanian rule the majority of Transylvanian . . . Jews became extraordinarily rich, as did the Romanians. At the same time the Hungarians were driven to total poverty."[14] In a letter to Hitler, Regent Horthy confided that "the Transylvanian Jews . . . were all satisfied with the Romanian regime, because they all figured out soon enough how much bribe money was needed, how much will be won in the course of a transaction, and whether it's worth it to make the trip to Bucharest."[15]

This sentiment was repeated in a newspaper article of May 9, 1942, from Kolozsvár. The article offered a commentary on the exodus of Jewish shop owners following enforcement of anti-Jewish legislation that forbade the presence of Jewish merchants on the main square:

> Until now . . . the main square was ruled by the Grüns and the Cohens. The nouveau riche of the Romanian world, the occupying Romanian upper classes, were the most frequent visitors to these shops. The upper-class women who came here from the Regat bought silk and fine "English" fabrics, fur coats, jewels, snakeskin shoes—the finest and most fashionable of everything. . . . That millions of Hungarian masses starved and went without at that time, while they weighed silk and jewels, was of no interest to them.[16]

Forcing the Jews off the square was thus cast as an extension of the same policy that forced the Romanian administration and many individual Romanians out of Northern Transylvania.

MORE QUESTIONS THAN ANSWERS

The threads binding the Transylvanian to the Jewish Question stretch back to the mid-nineteenth century, to the origins of both "questions." By the Second World War, the fate of the Jews in Hungary and Romania and the fate of Transylvania were so inextricably linked that a change in policy regarding one necessitated a change in policy regarding the other. The policies affected were both domestic and foreign and, like the minority issue, involved several states. Unlike the minority question in Hungary and Romania, however, assumptions about how Jews should be treated and what role they should play in the state and society (if any) were very different on the two sides of the war effort. That difference helps reveal how the fates of ordinary people were presumed to influence the way the struggle for control of Transylvania would ultimately be resolved.

It is not a coincidence that the benchmark dates for Hungarian Jewish history are the same as those for Hungarian history more generally (i.e., 1848, 1867, 1919, 1920, 1938–40, 1944, 1956). Nor is it a coincidence that these same dates resonate in the national metanarratives of the other nationalities of the region, including the Slovaks, Serbs, and Romanians. In the words of one historian, "Historically, ideas on Jewish emancipation and assimilation were interrelated in Hungary," and "Jewish emancipation and assimilation were also intertwined with the larger issues of non-magyar nationalities"[17] The links between the rise of the Hungarian national idea, the Jewish Question, and the nationalities question can be understood by means of a close examination of the origins and evolution of the struggle for control over Transylvania between two emerging would-be nation-states, the Kingdoms of Hungary and Romania.

Among the religions represented in early nineteenth-century Transylvania were Roman Catholicism, Greek Catholicism, Eastern Orthodoxy, Lutheranism, Calvinism, Unitarianism, and Orthodox Judaism. Only four of these were legally recognized and protected by the state—Roman Catholicism, Lutheranism, Calvinism, and Unitarianism—while other religions, including Eastern Orthodoxy, Greek Catholicism (Uniates), and Judaism, were "tolerated."

The 1848 Hungarian revolution proved a critical moment in Hungarian-Romanian relations as much as for the Jews of Hungary. Among the excesses committed just prior to the revolution were pogroms in Pozsony (Bratislava), Pest, and elsewhere. In Pozsony, acts of violence were perpetrated by artisans—many of them German-speaking—who feared emancipation of the Jews would result in unwanted competition. In Pest, on the other hand, during the period leading up to the revolution, the city's Jews had been labeled "better Germans than magyars."[18] Thus the pogroms were directed against a largely German-speaking Jewish population by which artisan classes felt threatened, while during the revolution itself Jews in some areas with large non-magyar populations were accused of collaborating with the Hungarian revolutionaries.[19] These pogroms took place in the midst of an ongoing debate in Hungarian political circles regarding the desirability of emancipating the Jews.

Although idealists like the reformer József Eötvös and the revolutionary poet Sándor Petőfi lobbied for the emancipation of the Jews in the spirit of liberal reform, emancipation was also considered in light of the Jews' potential role in the Hungarian state's struggle to achieve national independence and greater homogeneity. In 1842, a piece entitled "Jewish Emancipation" was published in Pest. Its author, István Gorove, argued that if the Jews were emancipated, they would become Hungarian and facilitate assimilation among other minority populations.[20]

During the revolution, this position was reiterated by Ignác Einhorn, a young Jewish activist in Pest, who argued that an emancipated Hungarian Jewry "would not only not prevent, but would actively promote the spreading of the [Hungarian] nationality" among the other nationalities living in Hungary.[21] Some Jews claiming to represent "Hungarian and Transylvanian" Jewry accordingly issued a declaration on March 17, 1848, during the heady March days of the nascent revolution: "We are Hungarians and not Jews, not members of another nation."[22] Belatedly, the besieged revolutionary Szeged parliament offered the Jews emancipation on July 28, 1849, the same day it passed a bill granting considerable ethnic rights to the other groups in an effort to win them over to the revolutionary cause.

The revolution was crushed, however, and it was not until 1867, following the Ausgleich, that Jewish emancipation became a practical reality. Act 17 of 1867, granting political and civil equality to Jewish inhabitants of the Hungarian Kingdom, was followed closely by the formal and full integration of the formerly autonomous province of Transylvania into the Hungarian Kingdom. These, among the first acts of the post-Ausgleich Hungarian leadership, were followed a year later by the much-debated nationalities law in 1868. The temporal proximity of the three decisions reflected the intensification of the strategy of assimilation and centralized national consolidation designed to check the growth and activism of the nationalities (in Transylvania, this meant the Romanians and Saxons in particular). In this venture the Hungarian leadership sought and found willing support from an emancipated—and thus grateful and rapidly assimilating—Jewish population.[23] During the period between the Ausgleich and the outbreak of the First World War, as the Hungarian state undertook a rigorous policy of magyarization, the Jews played an important role. Jews were among the most tenacious Hungarian nationalists and apologists for assimilationist policies, proudly associating themselves with Hungarian culture, oftentimes even with the Hungarian bureaucracy, and assuming middle-class status. So it was that Hungarian anti-Semitism during this period was markedly more intense in places where Hungarians were in the solid majority, while in mixed areas voters were less likely to vote for candidates with an anti-Semitic platform.[24]

After Hungary lost two-thirds of its territory with the Treaty of Trianon, much of it to Romania and the new state of Czechoslovakia, the country was flooded with tens of thousands of refugees who had fled to Hungary.

Many of these refugees were former state employees whose livelihoods had disappeared with the change in state sovereignty. They thus remained vocal advocates of territorial revision and were, initially at least, largely unemployed.[25] Since the loss of territory meant there was no longer any need to assimilate the Jews in order to bolster the number of Hungarians vis-à-vis other nationalities, the Jews came to be seen as outsiders who were occupying positions to which the refugees thought themselves entitled. The refugees' anger was compounded by the failure of the Hungarian Republic of Soviets of 1919—which many refugees originally supported—to retake the lost territories as it had promised, and the general unpopularity of the Communist experiment in Hungary, which had come to be associated with the Jews.[26]

Refugee politics and the events of 1919 thus served to intensify already existing strains of Hungarian anti-Semitism of the sort that had been mobilized in the course of nineteenth-century political discussions of the role of the Jews in Hungarian society.[27] In 1920, just months after the signing of the Trianon treaty, what amounted to the first piece of anti-Jewish legislation in Europe was implemented in Hungary. It was called the *numerus clausus*, and it limited the number of individuals (by religion) who could obtain a university education to a number proportionate to the percentage of adherents to that religion living in Hungary. Although the law did not mention Jews specifically, it is clear from the debates surrounding its implementation that they were its intended targets.[28] As such, the *numerus clausus* was in a very real sense a response to Trianon.[29] And when in 1928 the Bethlen government proposed to soften the terms of the *numerus clausus*, many—including the later prime minister Pál Teleki—opposed the change, arguing that the threat posed by the Jews to post–World War I Hungary was comparable to the one posed by the Slav and Romanian minorities *prior* to World War I, and that implementing a milder version of the *numerus clausus* could have Trianon-like results.[30]

But Hungarian Jews' resistance to the *numerus clausus* was minimal, partly because its effects were softened by the Bethlen government, but also because resistance would suggest the Jews had indeed failed to fully assimilate. When western Jewish organizations submitted a formal complaint to the League of Nations regarding the legislation, the Hungarian Jewish leadership was critical of what it perceived as unwarranted intervention. "We do not consider ourselves a national minority, seeking the protection of Geneva," one member of the Jewish leadership commented in 1924.[31]

The one issue in Hungarian interwar politics on which there was a nearly universal consensus was that of the need for a revision of Trianon. In the words of one historian, "Any variations of approach to this goal were due almost entirely to considerations of tactics and expediency."[32] The Jewish leadership remaining behind in Romanian Transylvania expressed solidarity with the goals of the revisionists. "Our national sentiments are those of magyardom," one Transylvanian rabbi stated in the name of the Jews of the territories lost. "Under this new rule we remain Hungarian Jews, and we will remain true to our Hungarian sentiments to the end."[33] The Hungarian revisionists were also aware of the important role Jews could play in achieving territorial revision. Delegates to the peace negotiations commented on the national identity of the 460,000 Jews in the lost territories, saying "from the ethnic [*faji*] standpoint the Hungarian Jews are no longer Jews, but Hungarians."[34] In order to make an effective argument on the basis of national self-determination, Hungary had to prove that a significant number of Hungarians lived in these severed areas. As a result, not only were Jews in these territories accepted as Hungarians, but in Transylvania they were even given leadership positions in the State Hungarian Party during the interwar period.[35]

Back in rump Hungary, however, the status of and official attitude toward the Jews were undergoing rapid changes. Like their coreligionists in Transylvania, many Jews in Trianon Hungary supported the goal of revision, going so far as to make appeals to world Jewry to aid Hungary in the interest of achieving it.[36] Yet anti-Semites cited the Jews' involvement in the bloody Bolshevik revolution instigated by Béla Kun in 1919.[37] The fact that Romanian troops had been called in to secure areas as far west as Budapest to oust the revolutionaries was an added humiliation in a state that had so recently lost so much territory to Romania. The Jews remaining in Hungary after the revolution were hard hit by the so-called white terror, during which many were arrested, sentenced to forced labor, or executed.[38]

Nor was the situation of the Jews in Transylvania less precarious during the interwar period, for although many professed loyalty to the goals of Hungarian revisionism, they made no friends under Romanian rule doing so. The Romanian administration was incredulous of their loyalty to Hungarian culture and the Hungarian language, and Jews were often openly criticized for their affinities with magyardom. Nevertheless, though Romanian officials coordinated efforts to separate Jews from Hungarians, these initiatives were not accompanied by official or unofficial mandates for them to assimilate to the Romanian nationality.[39] Nowhere is this more evident than in the area of population statistics. The Romanian census of 1930 showed 192,833 persons of the Jewish faith living in Transylvania. Of these 178,799 declared themselves to be of Jewish ethnicity, while a fantastic 111,275 (or around 60 percent) declared their mother tongue to be Yiddish, despite the fact that in 1918, 80 percent of Transylvanian Jews considered Hungarian to be their mother tongue.[40] In the words of one historian, "The obviously exaggerated number of persons with Yiddish as their mother tongue can be explained by the struggle, in the field of statistics, between Hungary and Rumania for the possession of Transylvania."[41]

Forbidden to attend Hungarian schools and criticized for speaking Hungarian on the streets, a number of Jews in Transylvania became Zionists. In 1927, the president of the Jewish National League [Zsidó Nemzeti Szövetsége], József Fischer, stated that the Jews of Transylvania "consider themselves neither Hungarians nor Romanians, just Jews."[42] Romanian politicians sympathetic to Jews—like Iuliu Maniu in this 1934 speech—similarly sought to reinforce the division between Jews and Hungarians in Transylvania by appealing to their sense of uniqueness:

> Being unable to bring together enough of a bourgeoisie for a single city, Hungarians have sealed off [the cities] and forcibly populated them with the Jewish element, who according to Hungarian statistics are Hungarian, in spite of the well-known reality that this industrious and entrepreneurial element is neither Hungarian, nor Romanian, but Jewish, belonging in every country to the nation that constitutes the State.[43]

Increasingly the Hungarian right wing in Transylvania came to share the view that Transylvanian Jews and Hungarians should go their separate ways, arguing that Jews were hostile to Nazi Germany, a state that was expected to facilitate the revision of Trianon boundaries.[44]

CASUALTIES OF THE WAR BETWEEN ALLIES: 1940–1944

As we have seen in earlier chapters, the leadership in Hungary and Romania initially sought to outdo one other in showing loyalty to the Axis. Such displays took many forms, most notably troop commitment to the Axis war effort, but also in the implementation and enforcement of anti-Jewish legislation and deportations. Each state kept a keen eye on what the other was doing in these two areas.

Hungarian leaders monitored not only anti-Jewish policy in Romania but also Slovakia's treatment of its Jewish population, given that Hungary had claims to territory in both states. Historians have observed that the implementation of anti-Jewish legislation in Hungary—specifically the First, Second, and Third Jewish laws of 1938, 1939, and 1941—was timed to demonstrate Hungary's willingness to cooperate with Nazi Germany in return for territorial compensation.[45] When Romania introduced a bundle of anti-

Jewish legislation in the autumn of 1940, on the heels of the Second Vienna Arbitration and Antonescu's rise to power, the Hungarian army's chief of staff opined that "the Romanians are thus making great efforts . . . to align themselves with the direction represented by the Axis."[46] Later, on October 8, 1942, the personal secretary of Hungarian prime minister Kállay, v. Fáy, had a conversation with Dieter Wisliceny, the SS officer in charge of organizing the deportations of Jews from Slovakia, Hungary, and Greece, "in which [v. Fáy] took a particular interest in the solution to the Jewish Question in Slovakia" and then asked "if it is true that the Jews were also to be deported from Romania."[47]

As for the Jews of Transylvania themselves, many of whom still had strong ties to magyardom, but had been watching events in Hungary with suspicion, the Second Vienna Arbitration was greeted with a mixture of excitement and apprehension. A number of Hungarian-speaking Jews shared Hungarians' joy. As bureaucrats and officials who had worked for the Romanian administration and educational institutions in Northern Transylvania prepared to leave, thousands of Hungarian families, as well as several hundred Hungarian-speaking Jews, left Southern Transylvania and moved north to be under Hungarian rule.[48] Approximately forty thousand Jews remained in Southern Transylvania, most of whom spoke Hungarian.

During the war, Jews in both Southern and Northern Transylvania were often targeted as members of or collaborators with the opposing national group (i.e., Hungarians or Romanians). The Jews in Northern Transylvania under Hungarian rule were frequently criticized for their interwar disloyalty to magyardom. In June 1942, a representative of the Transylvanian Party, Baron Antal Braunecker, said in parliament that "the rank of magyardom was abandoned first by the Jews of all the minorities. They negated any company with magyardom and set off in the track of the enemy."[49] The Transylvanian Party secretary, György Páll, voiced the conviction in a speech delivered in Kolozsvár in the fall of 1942 that "the Jews [of Transylvania] were never Hungarian and never will be Hungarian . . . they are unassimilable."[50]

The Romanian press from the fall of 1940 onward often placed responsibility for the loss of territory on the Jews.[51] A study of Jewish organizations in Transylvania prepared by the Romanian Office of Military Statistics in Cluj in August 1940, just prior to the reannexation of Northern Transylvania by Hungary, reported: "Jews from Transylvania were always Magyarophiles and are at present, for the most part, magyarized. They have never shown a *sincere* desire to draw nearer to the Romanian element, in which they saw only an element to be exploited in one form or another."[52] A Romanian police report from the Southern Transylvanian district of Turda from May 1941 complained that "the greater part of the Hungarian Jews from Transylvania and Bucharest declared themselves on the census to be of Hungarian nationality."[53] Another police report from Alba Iulia dated March 16, 1942, claimed that Jews had "become the most enthusiastic propagandists for Hungarian revision, nourishing the Hungarian population with the hope that soon they will get all of Transylvania."[54]

The Jews were even accused of deliberately contributing to the intensification of the struggle between Hungarians and Romanians. In one report distributed to regional police headquarters throughout Romania in 1942, officials claimed that the Jews of both Hungary and Romania had conspired to speak Hungarian in Romania and Romanian in Hungary. "Insofar as the conflicts between Hungarians and Romanians will multiply [as a result], so will the situation of [the Jews] improve, to the point where at a certain moment even the authorities will depend on the eventual aid of the Jews, be it material or moral."[55]

SINGLED OUT

Among the first anti-Jewish policies introduced by the Romanian state was Decree-Law No. 2650 of 1940, which made all Jews living in the territories annexed with the post–World War I treaties—and under separate provisions most Jews living in Romania as a whole—into de facto "foreigners."[56] Marshal Antonescu also issued an order as of April 15, 1942, to the effect that Jews crossing into Romania from Hungarian Northern Transylvania be deported to Transnistria.[57] And already in the late summer and early fall of 1942, the Antonescu government, at the suggestion of German political and military organs, had developed plans to deport Southern Transylvania's Jews. Their deportation was to be followed by a series of deportations that would wipe out all of Romania's Jews.[58] According to a separate Romanian plan for the deportation of the Jews formulated in the summer and early autumn of 1942, the economic positions and homes of the deported Jews were to be given to Romanians who had fled Northern Transylvania.[59]

Jews in Romania came under direct attack during pogroms in Bucharest in late January 1941 as part of the Legionnaires' rebellion, and in Iași in late June during the offensive against the Soviet Union.[60] When Bessarabia and Bukovina were retaken and Transnistria was occupied by the Romanian army in the wake of Operation Barbarossa, large-scale killings of Jews ensued. These were perpetrated largely by Romanian military and gendarmes, whose activities were occasionally—but not always—coordinated with similar initiatives of German Einsatzgruppen.[61] Romanian military officers at various levels, from Ion Antonescu down to regional commanders, took advantage of the war against the Soviet Union to charge Jews in the region with large-scale collaboration with the Soviets, despite knowing that many Romanians had also welcomed the Red Army and had been pleased to see the Romanians driven out of the territories.[62] The results were devastating. Between 45,000 and 60,000 Jews were murdered in reannexed Bessarabia and Northern Bukovina, and another 220,000 to 300,000 lost their lives during expulsions to Transnistria or in the occupied territory itself between June 1941 and October 1942.[63]

In Hungary, the three successive anti-Jewish laws marginalized and disenfranchised the Jews. Following the Hungarian takeover of Carpatho-Ukraine, Jews from that territory were deported, while another group of around 7,500 Jews was left trapped between the new Hungarian-Slovak border.[64] Starting in March 1939, Jewish men between the ages of ages of 20 and 48 were drafted into labor service battalions. The labor service regime radicalized following the Second Vienna Arbitration, when Hungarian Jewish policy took what Randolph Braham has called "a sharp turn to the right in response to internal political pressure and the general realization that the country's further revisionist ambitions could be achieved only in closer cooperation with the Third Reich." Approximately 42,000 men would die or be killed while working in these battalions.[65]

Another 20,000 "foreign" Jews—many of them refugees from occupied Poland—were deported and killed in 1941, and in January 1942, Hungarian gendarmes massacred over 3,000 Jews and Serbs in Hungarian-controlled Bácska. Yet by far the most intense period of mass deportations and killings of Hungarian Jews began in the spring and summer of 1944 following the German occupation. In addition to the tens of thousands of Jews who died or were killed in Budapest and elsewhere following the occupation, over 440,000 Hungarian Jews—including the Jews of Northern Transylvania—were deported to Auschwitz and other labor and death camps during that time; most of them did not survive.[66]

The "singling out" of Jews in Hungary and Romania had a much milder, but nevertheless noteworthy corollary in the treatment of minority populations in the two states. For although the Hungarians of Southern Transylvania and the Romanian minority in Northern Transylvania were often spared harsh treatment due to the threat of reciprocity and the presence of the German-Italian Officers' Commission, the two states found both legal and extralegal means of restricting the rights and freedoms of non-Jewish minorities living within their states. Furthermore, many of these policies and practices mirrored those implemented against the Jews. The Romanian state policy of "romanianization" of property, for example, was not limited to Jews but often extended to Hungarians as well.[67] Hungarians in Romania also had their radios confiscated, lost jobs and property, and saw their schools and cultural institutions shut down; a number of Hungarians were also drafted, along with Jews, into labor service battalions instead of into the regular Romanian army.[68]

In Hungarian Northern Transylvania, it was the Romanians who were drafted into labor service battalions, and several laws and ministerial decrees were passed that effectively limited Romanians' right to own property, retain trade and manufacturing licenses, find work, and attend certain schools.[69] Also, anti-Jewish laws in Hungary and Romania made it mandatory for individuals to declare their religion when seeking a job, trade permit, or passport, making it easier for officials in both states to discriminate not only against Jews but also against minority populations in both states.

Nor were deportations and violence against minorities beyond consideration. In 1942, a Hungarian official wrote that if Hungary were to emerge from the war with sizable military and political capabilities, "the expulsion of the 3 million Romanians [in Transylvania] can be recommended. Whoever stays in the country in spite of this—and I repeat, if we are strong—we will have a free hand to deal with the masses, deprived of their leaders, or to assimilate them."[70] In 1941, Henrik Werth, chief of staff of the Hungarian army, went so far as to propose the expulsion of *all* non-magyar and non-German elements from Hungary, a total of about 8 million individuals (mostly Slavs and Romanians).[71] Hungarian historian Krisztián Ungváry has noted the links between the Holocaust and plans to expel other minorities from Hungary.[72]

Historians Vladimir Solonari and Andrej Angrick have recently drawn attention to Romanian government ambitions to get rid of *all* the country's national minorities as outlined in three distinct plans from 1941 to 1943, and how these plans related to the Holocaust in Romania.[73] A 1942 plan, derived with the help of demographer Sabin Manuilă, emphasized the importance of clearing the state of "minorities with centrifugal tendencies," foremost among which were the Hungarians.[74] Policy and practice vis-à-vis the status of the Jews in these states were thus often inextricably bound to minority policy more generally, and ultimately to territorial considerations.

COMPETING TO WIN

The relationship between territorial claims and Jewish policy is most starkly evident in the two states' treatment of their respective Jewish populations living abroad. These provided the governments of Hungary and Romania yet another area in which to compete, for not only did the two states keep close track of each other's *domestic* policies vis-à-vis the Jews, but they also monitored the way *other countries* treated Jews from Hungary and Romania.

In March 1942, Romanian Jews living in Germany and Austria were required to wear the yellow star, whereas Hungarian Jews were not. This differential treatment incensed Romanian diplomats and officials, who protested to German authorities that Romanian Jews "should be treated as the equals of Jews from Hungary." (This protest was lodged despite the fact that the Romanian military was engaged in large-scale killings and deportations of Jews in Romanian-controlled Bessarabia, Northern Bukovina, and Transnistria at the time.[75]) Again in the spring of 1943, Constantin Karadja, an official in the Romanian Ministry of Foreign Affairs, appealed to Mihai Antonescu, the deputy prime minister of Romania, to "instruct our legation in Berlin to insist that our citizens of the Israelite race be given treatment identical to that of Jews from other countries and, in the first instance, to those of Hungary." Karadja concluded his appeal with a tone of urgency, saying the matter should be addressed "promptly, otherwise it will be too late."[76]

For as long as Nazi Germany was at the very peak of its power, both Hungary and Romania competed for status and favor in the eyes of the Axis. Consequently, there was a very clear understanding within the German leadership that if the deportation of Jews from one of the two countries could be undertaken successfully, the other would soon commit to the same action.[77] In the fall and early winter of 1942, Mihai Antonescu began criticizing Kállay to the German leadership for his unreliability and relative friendliness to the Jews.[78] But in fact it was *Romanian* policy that had undergone the more drastic reversal. Romanian leaders had their own plan for deporting the country's Jews to Transnistria, which they scrapped in the autumn of 1942. The exact reason why the Romanian leadership changed its policy cannot be ascertained with absolute certainty from the archival record, but territorial considerations undoubtedly played an important role.

On August 20, a group of Romanian intellectuals had signed a memorandum opposing the deportation of the Jews from Romania. In it they made an explicit link between the deportations and the territorial settlement that would follow the end of the war.

> We must bring ourselves in line with international law and guarantee the right to
> life and legal protection of every Jew in the territories which we claim, because no-
> where have territories been awarded, nor are they awarded except with the popula-
> tions which live in them. Our national interests must be defended in time through
> a policy of foresight by which not one principle upon which our rights could be
> based could be attacked or disturbed.[79]

And indeed, when explaining why Romania's leadership was reversing its
policy on the deportations, Mihai Antonescu told the Council of Ministers on
October 13, 1942, that the reversal came about "because of the international
situation and because of the fact that in other countries the treatment of the
Jews is different from that in Romania."[80] Hungary was one such country.

In the meantime, the German foreign ministry continued to pressure the
Kállay government into going through with the planned deportation of the
Jews from Hungary. On October 20, 1942, the secretary of state in the German foreign ministry, Ernst von Weizsäcker, had the Hungarian ambassador
in Berlin, Döme Sztójay, in for a talk. Weizsäcker warned the ambassador
that Germany was dissatisfied with the way Hungary was handling the Jewish
Question. He added: "The Romanians are committing everything they have
to the present struggle against Bolshevism, while Hungary holds back a part
of its forces for a conflict with Romania."[81]

Yet by January 1943 it was clear to those outside Romania that the Romanian leadership was stalling on the deportations. The Undersecretary of
State in the German foreign ministry, Martin Luther, sent a note to the German embassy in Bucharest calling on the ambassador to "let the Romanian
government know that . . . the positive stance of the Romanian Government
with regard to the Jewish Question to date has led us to hope that it will
continue to act as a good example for our mutual interests."[82] Hungarian
leaders also came under fire from Edmund Veesenmayer in a secret report
composed some months later in April 1943. Veesenmayer, a brigadier-general
in the SS, made a direct link between Hungary's Jewish policy and its flirtation
with the Allies.

> [The Hungarian leadership] sees in Jewry a guarantee for the protection of "Hun-
> garian interests" and believes it can prove with the help of the Jews that [Hungary]
> was forced to join this war on the side of the Axis powers, while in practice con-
> tributing to the cause of the enemies of the Axis with subtle and indirect acts of
> sabotage. . . . Kállay himself has recently offered proof of this, saying that, from
> the perspective of foreign policy, he will consider . . . all measures against the Jews
> as crimes against Hungary.[83]

There can be little doubt that the "Hungarian interests" Veesenmayer mentioned included territorial concerns.

At about the same time, the German foreign ministry sent a memorandum to the Hungarian government containing numerous accusations regarding Hungary's plans to extract itself from the war, and thereby from the Axis, and make contact with the Allies.[84] The message to the Allies from Prime Minister Kállay had been that "he [Kállay] continually speaks against the Jews, but in fact does nothing, and was protecting seventy thousand Jewish refugees in Hungary. He can follow no other political course at present, as Germany will otherwise occupy Hungary and all the Jews would be destroyed."[85]

Kállay's fears of German occupation were well founded. The Germans did indeed occupy Hungary less than a year later. One of their first demands to Horthy was that Kállay be dismissed and replaced by someone more amenable to the Reich's policies and interests, among them the deportation of Hungary's Jewish population. The choice for the new prime minister ultimately fell on Sztójay, who took office on March 22, 1944. Once this was done, the plans for the deportation of Hungary's Jews were implemented almost immediately. Around 131,000 Jews of Northern Transylvania were among the first to be ghettoized and deported in May and June 1944.

The Allies, the Jews, and Jewish Allies

As it became increasingly clear that the Germans could not win the war, protection of Jews became a more critical consideration for leaders in both states. As early as June 18, 1941, a Romanian police report from Alba Iulia in Southern Transylvania speculated that the Hungarian administration was instructing the Hungarian minority in Transylvania to collaborate closely with the Jews as "it is still not certain who will obtain the final victory" in the war. "Of the collaboration between these two minorities one thing is certain: that daily their hatred for our country emerges from the shadows."[86] Another such report from July 25, 1941, claimed that Hungary "wanted to gain a moral reserve for the eventuality of an Anglo-American victory" by helping out the Jews in Southern Transylvania. "Thus Hungarian policy is 'anti-Semitic' whenever it is necessary and philo-Semitic whenever possible."[87] In yet another report from the Romanian Regional Police Inspectorate in Transylvania, dated August 19, 1942, the author wrote that the Jews in Southern Transylvania "have hope that in the case of either an Allied or an Axis victory, Transylvania in its entirety will belong to Hungary, which is executing a policy of duplicity for either eventuality in the future."[88]

Indeed both states were trying to keep their options open. On July 29, 1943, just after the Italian defection from the Axis camp, Kállay made a brief reference to the Bácska massacre during a speech to members of parliament. The mass killing of Jews and Serbs, he said, "should not have been allowed to happen.... Hungarian politics did not begin with the Axis, but with Trianon."[89] In Romania too the manner of viewing the "Jewish Question" was tied to the exigencies of territory-related foreign policy calculations.[90] Furthermore, the rhetorical landscape around the "Jewish Question" increasingly took on a different tone in Romania as the tide of war shifted to favor the Allies.

In July 1944, the Romanian consulate in Kolozsvár prepared a report on the situation of the Jews in Hungary. The author of the report commented on the ghettoization and deportation of the Jews: "The measures taken against the Jews were executed by local authorities mercilessly and in the most brutal manner. This brutality, otherwise characteristic of Hungarians, is nothing new for us Romanians; we have had numerous occasions to feel it every day since 1940."[91] The author was careful to link the suffering of the Jews to the suffering of the Romanians, lumping together the two groups as victims of Hungarian oppression.

The consul's valuation of the situation is complementary to the Hungarian administration's lumping of Jews and Romanians together as oppressors or subversive elements. Indeed, just as the Jews of Northern Transylvania were being ghettoized and deported, the Hungarian administration began sending Romanians (men and women) either to the front or to work in Hungary or Germany. They purportedly justified this move to the Germans by declaring that the Romanians in question "had worked hand in hand with the Jews."[92]

The rhetoric of victimization by association with the Jews was also deployed in a May 1944 report submitted by the Romanian border police stationed outside Kolozsvár. The agent reported that "among the ethnically Hungarian inhabitants of Kolozsvár, it is said that after they finish sending the Jews to the camps, they will send the Romanians."[93] A report from the Romanian consulate in Nagyvárad from about the same time pointed out that the Jews from the territories formerly under Romanian state control were treated with particular cruelty, not only during the deportations, but since the Second Vienna Arbitration in August 1940. The report concludes: "[It is] incontestable that the attitude of the Hungarian government toward the Jews of Northern Transylvania was dictated not by anti-Semitic considerations, but by well-known political motives, in close connection with the future destiny of Transylvania and of the Romanians from Transylvania."[94]

Accusations of Hungarian foul play also centered around the demographic implications of the deportations. In reports of the Romanian Army Supreme General Staff dating from the period during which Jews in Northern

Transylvania were being ghettoized and deported (May/June 1944), Romanian officials indignantly noted how the number of Jews in ghettos proved that there were not as many "Hungarians" in Northern Transylvania as the Hungarian census had indicated. In one such report on the ghettoization of Jews in Nagyvárad, the author (D. Coltofeanu) observed: "On the census, the majority of Jews were entered as being of Hungarian origin, and only a very few of them were entered as being of Jewish origin. As a result of this operation the number of Hungarians from Oradea was greatly increased and the city of Oradea was presented to all as a city with a predominantly Hungarian population with an overwhelming majority."[95] In another report on the ghettoization of Jews in Kolozsvár, Coltofeanu concluded: "It is known that in the matter of their claims on Northern Transylvania, Hungarians have always used false statistics presenting the majority of Jews as Hungarians."[96]

Like their Romanian critics, Hungarian statesmen were also keenly aware of the likelihood that persecuting the Jews would have an adverse effect on their chances at a future peace settlement. On July 11, 1944, Hungary's acting foreign minister complained to Edmund Veesenmayer, now official representative of the Third Reich and German envoy to Hungary:

> How difficult the position of the Hungarian government has become due to the differential treatment of the Jewish Question through the responsible German outposts in Hungary, Romania, and Slovakia. While [the German officials] here [in Hungary] demand of the government the strictest action against the Jews, the Romanians and Slovaks are allowed to treat their Jews much more mildly. . . . This is obviously done in order to make a good impression on our enemies. Observed from outside one thus gets the impression that the Romanians and Slovaks have taken a completely different position on the Jewish Question than the Hungarians, against whom the hatred of the enemy and neutral states has been turned. This has a very unfavorable effect on the position of the Hungarian government.[97]

In another piece of correspondence to the German foreign ministry in Berlin from July 29, 1944, Veesenmayer reported that "the recent stiffened stance of the Hungarian government in Jewish matters—specifically also in the continuation of the evacuation of Jews from Budapest—is quite obviously grounded in no small part in the Slovak and Romanian stance. From the Hungarian side one is justified in pointing out that . . . the action against the Jews in Hungary outstrips by far what has taken place in Romania or Slovakia."[98] On June 6, 1944, in a meeting with Hungary's prime minister Döme Sztójay, Hitler reminded the Hungarian that "without the support of the German Reich, which had pushed Hungary's revisionist interests, Hungary would still today have the borders of Trianon." He went on to say that the

Slovaks had managed to completely remove Jews from the economic life of their country, while Hungary had as yet failed to do so.[99] Either way, by September 1944, with Germany's defeat on the horizon, Hungarian regent Miklós Horthy was well aware that "in the coming peace settlement it will be significant how Hungary treated its Jews."[100]

The Romanian leadership in Bucharest and its diplomatic personnel abroad were also cued to the links between the Jewish Question and the Transylvanian Question. The Romanian ambassador to Switzerland, Vespasian V. Pella, saw in Hungary's intensified persecution of the Jews a window of opportunity for reopening the Transylvanian Question. In a message to the Ministry of Foreign Affairs in Bucharest, Pella argued:

> With the means now at our disposal we should undertake a special action to protect the Jews of Northern Transylvania. . . . In this way we could attract the sympathy both of the world Jewish organizations and of the Anglo-Americans, while in the same stroke consolidating our rights to the territories lost with the so-called Second Vienna Arbitration. Of course in order to achieve the best results from this action, it . . . should appear to be initiated, or at least favored, by the Romanian government.[101]

Certainly by the time Hungary was occupied, some Jews in Transylvania and elsewhere in Hungary knew what German occupation and deportation of the Jews meant. As a result, several hundred fled across the border into Romania to escape deportation. There they told stories of the anti-Jewish measures in Northern Transylvania.[102]

In response, Jewish leaders and other politicians who opposed Antonescu's policies, encouraged by recent events which showed the Allies were winning the war on all fronts, started putting pressure on the Romanian leadership—specifically Ion Antonescu—not only to protect the Hungarian Jewish refugees fleeing from Northern Transylvania, but to contact Hungary directly regarding the ruthlessness of the anti-Jewish undertakings in Transylvania: "[We] must show the [Romanian] government that it is in the political interest of Romania to give asylum to the Jewish refugees from Hungary just as the Hungarians are taking anti-Semitic measures."[103]

In fact, it seems that many Jews in Romania, particularly those in Southern Transylvania, shared the belief that their own fates were tied to Romania's territorial aspirations. In a mid-May 1944 Romanian police report on the attitude of the Jews regarding the anti-Jewish measures being taken in Hungary, the reporting official noted that the Jews of Alba Iulia were talking about the ultimate victory of the Anglo-American forces over Germany. They were also purportedly spreading rumors that the measures taken by the Hungarian government would be avenged by the Allies at the conclusion of peace and that the Jews would not forget the relatively "mild" treatment they had received at the hands of the Romanian state. As a reward, the rumor went, "Jewry from America would support the interests of Romania following an eventual American victory."[104]

Another report from the same area prepared in July 1944 asserted that the Jewish intellectuals of the community were discussing the future of Transylvania: "After the end of the war, Hungary will not exist. Romania will get Transylvania up to the Tisza, or perhaps even up to the Danube."[105] Yet another report from police officials in Aiud related that the Jews there were of the opinion that "if Germany loses the war, Hungary will be the definitive loser."[106]

But despite predicting an Allied victory, the Jews of Southern Transylvania also feared they might be next after the Hungarian Jews, should Germany succeed in occupying Romania as well.[107] As a result, many Southern Transylvanian Jews sought a way out of Romania. According to the General Directorate of the Romanian Police, about thirty thousand Hungarian Jews had applied through the Turkish legation for permission to emigrate from Romania to Palestine by late July 1944.[108]

Antonescu proved willing to accommodate the Hungarian Jews' desire to emigrate through Romania. Although initially, in response to German pressure, he agreed to have all Jews illegally crossing the border into Romania shot on sight, the law remained unenforced.[109] The Jews who crossed into Romania from Hungary were even treated as political refugees; nevertheless, Antonescu insisted that they not stay in Romania.[110] They were given transport to Palestine, many on ships tellingly named after the territories Romania had lost to Hungary and the USSR during its alliance with the Axis. So it was that a number of Jewish refugees sailed to Palestine on a ship called the "Transylvania."[111]

Although King Mihai of Romania arrested Antonescu and effected the country's defection to the Allies on August 23, 1944, it was not until November 7—months after the Jews of Northern Transylvania had all been deported, and weeks after the Northern Transylvanian city of Kolozsvár had been taken over by combined Red Army and Romanian troops—that the Romanian government sent a note to the Hungarian government via Switzerland. The note criticized the Hungarian government for targeting, in cooperation with German forces, the Jews of Northern Transylvania, the "Romanian" Jews living in Hungary, and the Romanians in Germany and Hungary.[112] It threatened to target, in turn, Hungarians and Germans living in Romania if the oppression of the three above-named groups continued.

In response to the note, the Hungarian foreign ministry denied the accusations of mistreatment of Jews and Romanians from Romania and Northern Transylvania, but made a couple of very telling comments. The first, in connection with the Jews in Northern Transylvania, was an expression of surprise at the sudden concern for the fate of the Jews, "for whom only now the Romanian government has shown any interest."[113]

> The Royal Hungarian Government cannot escape the impression that all of the accusations and threats brought forth from the Romanian side are to serve merely as pretexts to publicly justify the previously planned and partially already carried out anti-Hungarian measures in Transylvania, and to distract the attention of the interested governments and organizations away from the desperate state of the Transylvanian Hungarians.[114]

In case there was any doubt as to the identity of the "interested governments and organizations," the final clue is a document issued by the American government, also through the Swiss embassy, in late October 1944, warning the Hungarian government not to mistreat the Jews. The note further explained that such atrocities would not go unpunished.[115]

That the threats issued by the Allies were taken seriously by the Hungarian leadership is evident from a report on the progress of the deportations in Hungary by Veesenmayer from early July 1944. Sztójay was purportedly "left cold" by the accusations and threats of the Anglo-American legations. "He explained to me that he would see the matter as uninteresting if we were to be victorious, but if not, his life is over."[116] Sztójay communicated to Veesenmayer that Regent Horthy, in collusion with the Hungarian government, had put a stop to the deportation of the Jews. By that time, all but the Jews of Budapest had already been deported from Hungary. Sztójay outlined the reasons why the Hungarian government had decided to halt the deportations. First, the Hungarian government had discovered that "in Romania no particular measures were being taken against the Jews there." The second, related reason was that Slovakia had also begun to protect its remaining Jews.[117] That the Hungarian government was so closely following the policies of precisely these two countries with regard to the Jewish Question is a further indication of the tightly woven links between territorial concerns and treatment of the Jews.

CONCLUSION

Recently, the well-known theorist of nationalism Rogers Brubaker and three coauthors published a book on "everyday ethnicity" in the city of Cluj. The work is an impressive piece of scholarship that applies Brubaker's theoretical insights on ethnicity and nationalism to a case study in present-day Transylvania. One of the many images in the book is a photograph of a gravestone from Házsongárd cemetery bearing the names of Jenő Janovics and his wife, Lilly. In the caption the image is described thus: "Gravestone with ribbon in Hungarian national colors." The authors note that "groups of Hungarian students, some led by their teachers, visit the graves of famous Hungarians and light candles in their memory. The cemetery is also visited during the summer months by tourist groups from Hungary; they sometimes leave ribbons or wreaths in national colors on the graves, such as this one on the grave of an early twentieth-century theater director and his wife, an actress."[118]

Neither Jenő Janovics nor his wife—who was not Jewish—died in the camp system. In May 1944, when a ghetto was established in a brick factory in Kolozsvár, they were visiting Budapest, where they stayed on in hiding and thus survived the deportation of over 131,000 Jews from Northern Transylvania.[119] Janovics was able to return to Kolozsvár (which again had become Cluj) and resume his position as head of the Hungarian theater in 1945, but he was unwell. His last wish was that—come what may—the Hungarian theater should open its 154th season with a performance of József Katona's *Bánk Bán* on November 16. He died that same day.[120]

Bánk Bán was not the only drama Janovics was wrapped up in to the very last. In the drama of the Transylvanian Question, he was assigned many roles, some of which he has continued to play even beyond the grave.

Hungarian and Romanian leaders gambled with the fates of millions of people in the interest of resolving the Transylvanian Question in their favor, betting with the lives of front soldiers, minorities, and their own presumed ethnic constituencies on the outcome of a future peace settlement. But by far the most extreme form of this type of gambling with ideologies and the fates of the region's inhabitants was the treatment of the Jews, who since the nineteenth century were variously nationalized, denationalized, renationalized, marginalized, murdered, and "saved," all according to Hungarian and Romanian state leaders' sense of whether and how the Jews might figure into the resolution of the Transylvanian Question.

Anti-Semitism, a common feature of European politics more generally since the late nineteenth century, was thus localized and domesticated in modern Hungary and Romania by passing through the Transylvanian Question, and pro-Jewish activism was also cast as an expedient to achieving states' territorial ambitions. The two states' varying ties with Germany, their contributions to the Axis war effort, the relationship they had with one another, as well as the ebb and surge of anti-Jewish legislation were all factors these countries' leaders felt could influence the territorial reshuffling that would inevitably follow close on the heels of the peace. As such they monitored each other's moves very closely and acted according to their assessment of who would win the war, and by extension, who would have the power to effect territorial revision in their favor following the peace.

For statesmen and political elites in Hungary and Romania, the "Jewish Question" was the one issue that highlighted the irreconcilable difference between Hitler's "new Europe" and the "new Europe" that would be created by an Allied victory. It constituted an awkward inconsistency in the rhetoric of those "European" interests and ideals that seemed otherwise unshakable—national self-determination and dedication to a more justly ordered, peaceful, and secure Europe of the future. Perhaps in an attempt to overcome this clear divergence, those who spoke of the "Jewish Question" as a "problem" for the state argued that its "settlement" was a Europe-wide project, something that "Europe" was doing and approved of, rather than simply a local, national, or Axis interest.[121] Yet it is revealing that the Jewish Question was not discussed in the international propaganda publications relating to the Transylvanian Question—in German, English, French, or Italian—of either state during the interwar period or World War II. Bringing it up would have been to admit that one or the other side in the conflict was not operating according to the true tenets of what "Europe" is, does, and means. In short, it would require choosing a side, acknowledging that playing both sides to win was ideologically, if not practically, impossible.

In his book on Hungary covering the interwar period and World War II, C. A. Macartney argued that the Jewish Question was the most prominent issue in interwar Hungary.[122] At the beginning of his essay "Fascism, Communism, and the Jewish Question in Romania," published in 1974, historian Stephen Fischer-Galați wondered: "Why . . . did the Jewish Question rather than the Magyar or the Russian, become paramount in inter-War Romania? . . . In reality, the Jewish Question was infinitely less significant than the Magyar or Russian."[123] Yet Macartney's claim and Fischer-Galați's question both assume that the so-called Jewish Question was distinct from minority and territorial concerns. In fact, these issues were intimately and inextricably linked. The branching phenomena of population politics, demographic anxiety, refugee and religious policy, minority policy, and Jewish policy all share a common trunk in the problems of territory and sovereignty embodied in the Transylvanian Question, and common roots in the second half of the nineteenth century.

One effect the events of the Holocaust had on historiography of the region was that it challenged scholars to explain how the Holocaust could happen given that the Jewish Question had not figured prominently on the radar screen of historians of Hungary and Romania prior to the war. Histories of the region from the interwar period focused almost exclusively on the problem of territorial claims and national unity and unification, at most emphasizing the minority grievances of state-enfranchised nationalities, as these were the presumed battlegrounds of future conflicts.[124] The events of the Holocaust seemed to suggest that historians had missed something, so after World War II they went back to the primary sources and found plenty of discussion about Jews during the interwar period and before. They came to the conclusion—as Macartney and Fischer-Galaţi did after the war—that the Jewish Question *had* been the primary interwar obsession in these states.[125] This conclusion was based on the assumption that the Holocaust could only have unfolded as it did if the status and fate of the Jews were the most all-consuming issues during the interwar period and the war. Yet it seems rather the opposite is true. The events of the Holocaust in Hungary and Romania were heavily influenced by the fact that the Jews were *not* the primary policy preoccupation in these states either before or during the war. Instead, the "Jewish Question" was frequently viewed in light of its relationship to territorial matters, and for that reason Hungarian and Romanian policy vis-à-vis the Jews was shockingly inconsistent.

One long-standing impediment to seeing how the history of the Jews and the history of territorialized statehood and state-enfranchised nationalities in the region are related has been the way historians of the Holocaust have focused on the events of the cataclysm as they unfolded within "national" contexts. This approach has yielded a tremendous amount of important work. But studying the Holocaust only within individual national contexts—or on the other extreme as a pan-European transnational phenomenon—leaves many questions unanswered.[126] For example, how did Jews figure into the foreign policy objectives of states? And how did relations *between* neighboring states—not just relations with Germany—affect the timing and outcome of the Holocaust? In examining the Holocaust in light of the Transylvanian Question, I have sought to offer what Mark Mazower calls "the role of historic contingency both in time—the catalytic impact of wars, civil wars, and other upheavals—and space—geopolitical location, the proximity of disputed borders" to the study of the Holocaust.[127]

The two countries' inconsistent Jewish policies reveal the multiplicity of roles and functions the Jews of Hungary and Romania played in this territorial struggle. At times enfranchised, at others subject to the harshest restrictions, at times protected, at others brutally persecuted and murdered, the Jews in these two countries never enjoyed a stable status either as national allies or as national enemies. The Hungarian tricolor ribbon adorning the grave of Jenő Janovics is both an ironic memorial and a powerful symbol of that inconsistency.

CHAPTER SIX

A "New Europe"?

The entry into Europe or the construction of Europe, of which Romania has always been a part, has been a burning preoccupation of the Romanian nation. Even under the most difficult circumstances of the great world conflagrations of the twentieth century, Romanians have sought the path to Europe.

—From the introduction to a 1991 Romanian publication edited by historian Ion Ardeleanu containing documents relating to Mihai Antonescu's 1942 initiative to prepare for the postwar peace conference[1]

Is it possible that what was lost at Trianon in 1920 and in Paris in 1947, and what during the course of the temporary territorial revision of the Second World War was doomed to failure, can perhaps now succeed by other means, in a different dimension of political space?

—Hungarian literary historian Béla Pomogáts in a 2005 article on European integration and Hungarian national politics[2]

After the fateful August 23, 1944, over the next several days the Romanian leadership imposed a series of "security measures" affecting Hungarian and German minorities. Their weapons, radios, automobiles, and bicycles were confiscated, individuals were forced to register with the police and were issued personal documents identifying them as members of a particular nationality.[3] Nevertheless, leaders in German-occupied Hungary took one last opportunity to win back Southern Transylvania in the late summer of 1944. The action was swift and initially successful. One Hungarian colonel noted in a letter dated September 13, the day his unit entered the city of Arad: "It is impossible to describe the sincere enthusiasm of liberation after twenty-six years; you had to see it. My car was a pile of flowers, full of cigarettes and [the locals] reached for my hands such that I fell out of my slow-moving car. The people were frenzied, even though out of eighty thousand inhabitants around forty thousand had fled (Jews and Romanians)."[4]

Many of those who fled did so for good reason, as several dozen Romanians and Jews in some of the occupied towns and villages were killed by Hungarian soldiers.[5] When the Romanian army reentered the area, and later Northern Transylvania with the Red Army in October, these atrocities were reciprocated when bands of volunteers calling themselves the Maniu Guards killed Hungarians in some localities.[6] The call to join the guards had been issued by the head of the Transylvanian Refugees Association operating in Bucharest. Volunteers were a mix of individuals and interests ranging from senior officers to women hoping to serve as nurses. The guards' battalions were named after sites of atrocities committed by the Hungarian army upon its entry into Northern Transylvania in 1940: "Ip," "Trăznea," and "Beiuş."[7] According to a British diplomat who was in Transylvania at the time, the guards "kept the Hungarian population . . . in a state of terror for some weeks."[8]

On September 12, 1944, Romania signed an armistice with the Soviet Union that ensured the return of Northern Transylvania to Romania in the event that the Allies won the war.[9] Thereafter, the Red Army, along with Romanian troops, steadily advanced through both Southern and Northern Transylvania. All "presumed Germans and Hungarians" were declared "internable," and as many as four thousand were interned in a camp near the city of Braşov, where many died of disease and starvation.[10]

The confidence of the Romanian army was high in late October 1944 as the territory of Northern Transylvania came completely under its control. A general proclamation of the minister of war, Mihai Racoviţă, dated October 26, declared: "Holy Transylvania, the beloved cradle of the Romanian people, snatched away by an odious arbitration [*dictat*], generously offered to the Hungarian magnates for the completion of their estates by the dictators of Europe, has returned today, through a just struggle and worthy sacrifice, to the country from which it was torn."[11] Incidentally, this was the same Mihai Racoviţă who had earlier been reprimanded by the German command because his troops reported they were fighting on the Eastern Front for the recovery of Transylvania rather than to deliver a crushing blow to Bolshevism.[12]

The job of regional commissioner of newly reoccupied Northern Transylvania was initially given to Ionel Pop, a relative of Iuliu Maniu. In one of his first statements as commissioner, he called on members of the Hungarian minority to recognize that Transylvania would forever be a part of Romania and to abandon their irredentist strivings and "fantasies." Otherwise a more "radical solution" would be sought in the form of their expulsion from Romania.[13]

In the late summer and fall of 1944, another exodus from Northern Transylvania had already begun, this time of Hungarian officials, educators, and others who could not face the prospect of living under Romanian rule. In one area of the Szekler Land, less than 50 percent of the 1941 population remained as of December 1944.[14] Despite the presence of the Soviet army, the first several years of the postwar period in Transylvania saw an overt continuation of the nationalities conflict on the ground, but also ongoing maneuverings on the part of several states in the interest of resolving the Transylvanian Question diplomatically and militarily.

This chapter is not meant to offer a comprehensive account of what took place in Transylvania after the war, but rather to track some of the events and phenomena that drew on wartime and prewar conceptions relating to the future of Transylvania. In so doing, it seeks to explain how and why the Transylvanian Question has persevered, and what forms it has taken since the collapse of Communism.

AFTER THE WAR

The interwar Hungarian prime minister István Bethlen was right when he said that the victors of World War II would "reorder" Europe and redraw its boundaries, just as the victors of World War I had done.[15] Hungarian and Romanian statesmen, politicians, demographers, historians, and others had invested enormous energy in convincing both sides of the rectitude of their claims. But neither Hungarian nor Romanian leaders had counted on the eventuality that neither "side"—as they understood it, Nazi Germany or the Western Allies—would be the force to reorder Europe.

Although the Soviets had made clear their animosity toward the Versailles system already in the 1920s—in addition to sharing revisionist aims with respect to Romania—only in 1934 did Hungary take up diplomatic relations with the Soviet Union.[16] During the war itself only very limited diplomatic efforts were made by either state in the interest of convincing the Soviets of the justness of their respective claims to Transylvania.[17] As the Nazi defeat loomed, both the Hungarian and Romanian state leaderships sustained the unrealistic hope that they could negotiate to surrender to the Western Allies rather than face Soviet occupation.[18] Yet it was Stalin who—in March 1945—ultimately promised Transylvania to Romania.

Shortly after the Romanian and Soviet armies had taken Northern Transylvania, a provisional Soviet administration was installed that lasted from mid-November 1944 until mid-March of the following year. The fate of the province remained uncertain during that time, and consequently it experienced a kind of de facto autonomy. Just prior to the creation of the pro-

visional Soviet administration, on November 10, General Nicolae Rădescu
wrote to the Soviet commander Marshal Malinovsky requesting permission
to install Romanian authorities in the region. In his request, he linked the
appeal explicitly to the Romanian military efforts on the side of the Soviets:
"In view of the fruitful collaboration between the Soviet and the Romanian
forces in the common fight of the battle-front, . . . I ask Your Excellency to
approve and make provisions so that the reestablishment of Romanian civil
authorities in Cluj and in Oradea might proceed unhampered."[19]

In fact, many Romanian officials had already assumed positions, including several recent evacuees from Soviet-occupied Bessarabia and Northern
Bukovina.[20] A report prepared by a county branch of the Communist Party
and the Hungarian Democratic Union [Magyar Demokrata Szövetség] complained to the county lord lieutenant on November 11 that administrators who
had come to claim posts in the area did so "with the thought of revenge."[21]
Among the first acts of the Romanian Commissariat for the Administration
of the Liberated Regions of Transylvania—the members of which included
Emil Hațieganu and Sabin Manuilă—was to extend Romanian legislation
over Transylvania, annul the consequences of the Hungarian ordinance
1,440/1941, and grant amnesty to individuals charged with any crime against
the Hungarian state.[22]

Another commission was established to review the names of streets and
squares and make changes to eliminate the names of "Fascist and reactionary"
individuals. This resulted in an awkward provisional situation wherein home-
owners, overseers, and tenants were required to take down old signs themselves and fashion new ones out of available materials—generally cardboard
or tin. But these concerns were small in comparison to the problem of massive displacement of people and tensions around property. Many Hungarians
who initially fled the region were overtaken by Soviet and Romanian forces
and returned home, only to find their homes occupied or their possessions
looted.[23] Confusion was compounded by the fact that some functionaries of
the Hungarian administration remained at their posts and continued to use
the Hungarian language and Hungarian state letterhead and stamps in their
official correspondence.[24] The general befuddlement was such that one Romanian official reported at the end of December that "Northern Transylvania
currently does not belong to either Hungary or Romania."[25]

The new Romanian premier as of March 1945, Petru Groza, promised that
the country's minorities would be treated well. In general, Groza had the reputation of being a Magyarophile, but in the words of a Romanian foreign ministry official, "Groza's Magyarophilia stops at the border question, for the Groza
government is sustained by the fact that it won back and retains Transylvania

for Romania. Groza knows this perfectly well and therefore above all clings to Transylvania's western border."[26] In the absence of a formal agreement, however, technically the matter was not yet resolved and would remain in the air until August 23, 1947. On that date, symbolically set to coincide with the three-year anniversary of the successful King Mihai coup and Romania's defection to the Allies, Northern Transylvania was formally returned to Romania. In the meantime, the Soviet leadership took advantage of the two states' preoccupation with the fate of Transylvania to consolidate its position in both.[27]

In opposition to the Soviet preference, U.S., British, and French delegations to the London talks of September 20, 1945, called for limited territorial revision in favor of Hungary according to the ethnic principle, meaning that Hungary should receive some seventy-eight hundred square kilometers of territory just east of the Hungarian-Romanian border, while Romania should retain the rest. But by the following spring's negotiations, both the United States and Great Britain backed away from their earlier positions with the understanding that the Transylvanian Question could be resolved by granting autonomy to part of the region rather than shifting borders.[28]

The new Hungarian coalition government, consisting of Communists, Socialists, Peasant Party members and Smallholders, presented Stalin with their territorial claims on April 8, 1946. The claims consisted of two options, one more ambitious (22,000 square kilometers of the Partium), another considerably less so (11,800 square kilometers). When Stalin registered the claims, he joked that if the Soviets accepted them, the Romanian king would abdicate. The Hungarian prime minister Ferenc Nagy countered that at least then Romania would be a republic like Hungary.[29]

The special department within the Hungarian government charged with compiling materials to present at the peace conference also drew up a list of atrocities and slights suffered by the Hungarian minority at the hands of the Romanian administration in Transylvania since the territory had been retaken by Romanian-Soviet forces.[30] The report, much like the material presented by the Romanian delegation, was similar in format and content to inventories drawn up for consideration by the Axis arbiters of the German-Italian Officers' Commission. Meanwhile, Romanian delegates sought to convince the British in particular that, far from being a "matter between Axis allies," the Transylvanian Question should be considered one between an Axis ally (Hungary) and an Axis satellite (Romania), arguing that Romanians never willingly fought alongside the Axis.[31]

After the spring of 1946, in a reversal of the run-up to World War II, Hungarian foreign policy aims shifted to the question of minority rights protection for Hungarians in the neighboring states, but without accepting that the matter of territorial revision was entirely closed. On September 2, the head of the Romanian delegation to the peace conference, Gheorghe Tătărescu, revisited a series of old tropes in a speech before the conference's Political and Territorial Commission for Hungary and Romania. He argued that Romanian claims to Transylvania were based on historic, ethnic, and economic factors and that any attempt to alter the Hungarian-Romanian border in Hungary's favor would constitute an assault on Romanian sovereignty and independence and disrupt European peace and security.[32] That day the Romanian foreign minister as well as the Council of Ministers rejected Hungarian proposals, arguing that the Trianon border was in fact an "ethnic" border. With this conclusion the Romanian leadership suggested that Hungarian leaders' efforts in the interest of securing minority rights for Hungarians would also meet with resistance.[33]

During the run-up to the peace, the matter of minority rights protection and the interest of the Hungarian state in the status and well-being of the Hungarian minority in Transylvania and the other lost territories remained a constant preoccupation of the Hungarian leadership.[34] Meanwhile, Romanian politicians were busy arguing that the period of Hungarian rule in Northern Transylvania had been a disaster for *all* the territory's inhabitants, Hungarians and Romanians alike, and that it was only within the framework of the Romanian state that Transylvania's people could thrive. On July 4, 1946, in a speech to fellow National Peasant Party members, Iuliu Maniu declared: "Whenever Transylvania has been closely tied to the Regat, everything has gone well; both Romanians and Hungarians from Transylvania profited. From the moment that Northern Transylvania was kidnapped from us, there came a period of great want and misery." Maniu decried what he saw as the excessive tolerance the Groza government displayed toward the Hungarian minority, calling it a "government estranged from the soul of the Romanian nation" that would "bring ruin on the country."[35]

Despite such claims of excessive tolerance on the part of the postwar Romanian provisional government, in March 1947, the Hungarian foreign ministry's Political Section compiled a pessimistic report on the situation of the Hungarians in Romania. The report outlined slights against the Hungarian minority, ranging from the postwar equivalent of slander cases (whereby individuals caught wearing national colors or singing the Szekler Hymn were charged with "upsetting public order"), to prejudicial treatment against Hungarians in the Romanian land reform and during the People's Tribunals set up to punish war criminals. It also described a variety of other official and unofficial means by which members of the Hungarian minority experienced economic, cultural, and political abuse and discrimination.[36]

One method some Hungarians—as well as Jews—found of countering the punitive and nationalist impulses of the returning Romanian administration was to seek protection in the ranks of the Communist Party. A disproportionate number of Jews and Hungarians joined the party, such that in January 1946, only about 10 percent of Communist Party members in the Transylvanian capital of Cluj were Romanian.[37] What were in many respects the worst years of Communism for many parts of East-Central Europe—the period of "high Stalinism," from about 1948 to 1955, were in fact some of the "best" years for minority rights in Transylvania. Soviet nationalities policy ensured bilingual signs, education, and cultural venues—including a university—for Hungarians.[38] Furthermore, the 1952 Romanian constitution made provision for an autonomous Hungarian region in the four counties where Szeklers constituted a majority.[39]

The atmosphere changed in 1956, however. In the fall of that year Hungarian demonstrators gathered in Budapest to protest Soviet hegemony and ultimately pressured their chosen leader, Imre Nagy, to divorce Hungary from the Warsaw Pact. Many Hungarians in Transylvania expressed solidarity with the Hungarian cause. This gave the Romanian Communist government the opportunity to crack down on Hungarian institutions, among them the university, which was closed in 1959. Hundreds of Hungarian intellectual leaders and students were imprisoned and interrogated by the Securitate (Romanian secret police) and the Romanian Communist leadership under Gheorghe Gheorghiu-Dej.[40]

But it was only later, following the ascent to power of Nicolae Ceaușescu in 1965, and especially in the 1970s and 1980s, that partisan battles in the nationality conflict again came out into the open.[41] Historiography of the Ceaușescu era drew on interpretations of the Transylvanian Question that had been prominent during the interwar period and World War II, and the continuity was both personal and political. Constantin C. Giurescu, a Romanian historian who published a number of works on Romanian history during the interwar period and who served in the Historical Section of Mihai Antonescu's commission to prepare evidence for the postwar treaty conference, remained active within the Romanian Academy almost until his death in 1977.[42] Writing in 1967, Giurescu opined: "Transylvania has proved to be an integral and essential part of the Romanian territory and people. It is thus natural and legitimate that in the two international treaties of the greatest significance—those treaties by which the First and Second World Wars were concluded—Romanians' right to Transylvania was sanctioned by repeated international recognition as the basis of that right."[43]

Beginning in the mid-1970s, in an ironically competitive gesture, Hungarian historians openly criticized Romanian historians for making the nationalistic turn. In 1976, historian Zsigmond Pál Pach announced that the Hungarian Academy of Sciences was undertaking the preparation of a Marxist history of Transylvania that would "tear down the last vestiges of nationalist historical thinking."[44] Pach asserted that it was essential for Hungarian historians to avoid the trap of "counter-nationalism" when preparing the three-volume history. Nevertheless, the outrage at Romanian historians' elisions of the Hungarian presence in Transylvania was eminently palpable. So while Pach acknowledged the political reality of the postwar borders, he added, "We also see our thousand-year history as an objective reality, and we will not allow our history to be changed."[45]

Émigré historians and advocates, particularly Hungarians, seized on the Transylvanian issue with less reserve. The Hungarian congress that met in Cleveland in 1972 repeated the interwar claim that European security and peace depended on altering the "status quo" in accordance with the will of the Hungarian minorities living in neighboring states.[46] Some even claimed that Ceauşescu's invasive reproductive policy amounted to a "biological super Trianon" against the Hungarian minority.[47]

From the mid- to late 1970s through the 1980s the anti-Hungarian rhetoric of the Ceauşescu regime was at its most shrill, and traces of the Transylvanian Question were evident in the historiography in both Hungary and Romania.[48] But sympathy for the Ceauşescu regime was also at an all-time low during those years. One Hungarian woman recalled that, from the perspective of the 1980s, the nationalist tensions of the 1990s seemed impossible. "We were all depressed, we were all oppressed, we were all exploited, and so we were all in it together."[49]

In 1991, the transcript of Mihai Antonescu's meetings with Romanian intellectuals, statesmen, and politicians from 1942 was published in Cluj under the title "If You Want to Win the War, You Have to Prepare the Peace." The volume included a preface by Romanian historian Ion Ardeleanu, who reflected on why the subject of those meetings was topical in 1991. The wartime propaganda minister's initiative, he argued, revealed how Romania had always been preoccupied with "the entry into Europe or the construction of Europe."[50] In a postscript, Ardeleanu praised the achievements of those who participated in the 1942 meetings as displaying "an impressive patriotism." "The Romanian government of the time proved itself to be aware of the importance of the initiated program and allocated the necessary funds. Will our government of today, while the international political context resembles that of the period after 1941 (especially the revisionist outpourings), do the same? It would be good if it would do so now."[51] Ardeleanu thus saw the Romanian government of 1991 as facing a set of challenges similar to those faced by the government of 1941 and felt that Romania had a role to play in the Europe of 1991 similar to the one it had played in 1941.[52]

"If You Want to Win the War" was not the only publication to draw out the connections and continuities—either implicitly or explicitly—between the World War II and post-Communist eras.[53] In addition to the publication (or republication) of primary works, a mass of monographs has been published on the subject of the Transylvanian Question, the Second Vienna Arbitration, and the governments of Horthy and Antonescu since 1989.[54] Furthermore, the institute founded in 1942 to produce propaganda material relating to Transylvania for Mihai Antonescu's peace intiative, the Centrul de Studii Transilvane [Center for the Study of Transylvania], was revived in 1991.[55] Among its first publications were books and document collections on the Second World War, Hungarian-Romanian relations, and the work of Sabin Manuilă.[56]

Much of this activity is due to the opening of the archives and a general desire to reexamine issues and put forward views that had earlier been considered taboo under the Communist regimes of Hungary and Romania. Many recent publications on the Transylvanian Question and the war have betrayed an undeniably right-wing slant.[57] Yet only a few are the work of the successor groups to the Legionnaires, the Hungarian Revisionist League, or the Arrow Cross. A number of statesmen, politicians, and intellectuals (among them historians) are involved in its creation, popularization, and dissemination.

THE "NEW EUROPE," THEN AND NOW

In 1994, a collection of speeches by the then-president of Romania, Ion Iliescu, was published in German entitled *Romania in Europe and in the World*. It contains a speech entitled "Protection and Loyalty," which Iliescu gave as part of a parliamentary colloquium in Bucharest on September 15, 1994. The speech addressed the status of national minorities in Europe, evoking the example of the interwar period as proof that "national minorities [could be used] as a pretext for territorial claims and expansion." In a thinly veiled response to Hungarian minority calls for regional autonomy, Iliescu went on to argue that "the isolation of minority groups in the form of territorial ethnic autonomy" would not only threaten "the territorial integrity of states," but also serve to destabilize the entire region. Furthermore, autonomy "is by no means a democratic and European solution, as some are now seeking to justify it," but rather runs counter to the spirit of European unity.[58]

Many—if not most—of the ideas that were meant to typify the new Europe of the interwar period and World War II remain entrenched in the political thinking of both states' diplomatic, intellectual, and political elites today. Although Hungary formally renounced its revisionist claims on Romania in 1996, the issues that earlier informed proposed solutions to the Transylvanian Question remain among the most predominant driving forces behind interpretations of Europe's past and future in these countries. Consider, for instance, the following assertion made in a Romanian newspaper from the summer of 1942: "In order to serve Europe's interest," the state must take responsibility for "all of the national elements living outside the borders" of Romania.[59] Sixty years later, in 2002, the former prime minister of Hungary and current leader of the opposition commented for a Hungarian daily that "the future of Hungarians resides in a nation of 15, not 10 million Magyars," which includes the approximately 5 million Hungarians living beyond Hungary's current borders, around 1.6 million of whom live in Transylvania.[60]

Also, during World War II, it was Transylvanian Party member Gyula Zathureczky's belief that being part of the new Europe of the early 1940s "means that we have to keep, nurture, and develop our Hungarianness." This statement was echoed almost verbatim in a Hungarian editorial from 1990, in which the author declared that "we can only truly be Europeans if we are good Hungarians. . . . Thus with the strengthening of our national essence we must knock on the doors of Europe so that we can get back in after a forty-year detour."[61] A still more self-conscious borrowing from the new European ideas of the 1940s can be found in a recent essay in the Hungarian journal of literature, art, and society, *Hitel* [Credit], in which the author laments that throughout history, and especially in 1943, "we never succeeded in making our own concerns into European concerns. Now is our chance. We want to be strong, united . . . members of a Europe made up of nation-states. . . . How can we validate, but above all represent, those values whose preservation is a prerequisite not only for the continued existence of Hungarians but, we believe, of Europe as well?"[62]

Even the European Union itself can be and is viewed as a means of achieving long-standing goals of national unification. With the integration of ten formerly East-Bloc states—Poland, the Czech Republic, Slovakia, Hungary, Slovenia, Estonia, Latvia, and Lithuania in May 2004, and Romania and Bulgaria in January 2007—into the European Union, "Europe" again moved toward a "new order," much as it had after World War I and during World War II.

In a 2002 speech, former Hungarian prime minister and current opposi-

FIG. 22. Keychain purchased by the author in a Budapest shop in 2005. The full text on the medallion reads "Éljen a magyar EU—Erdéllyel Uniót" [Long live the Hungarian EU—Union with Transylvania], linking Hungary's accession to the European Union to the recovery of Transylvania. Photo by Heidi Fancher; reproduced with permission.

tion leader Viktor Orbán declared that "the ultimate goal and significance of the European Union is the dissolution of borders, not the dissolution of nations and the flowing together of peoples. . . . This is in the Hungarian interest, for if we join the European Union, . . . many millions of Hungarians can feel themselves to be that much closer to us."[63] In June 2003, Orbán declared to a Transylvanian Hungarian audience that "our home, Hungaria Magna—our lost paradise" could be recovered within the framework of an enlarged European Union.[64] A keychain I found in a shop in Pest during the summer of 2005 is much more explicit in this regard. It reads: "Long live the Hungarian EU," where *EU* stands for "Erdéllyel Uniót" [Union with Transylvania].

Nor is the goal of national unification within an EU framework the purview only of political outsiders. The current Socialist government of Hungary has a "Renewed Nation Policy," as espoused by the country's Ministry of Foreign Affairs, which states: "Our diplomatic strategy is focused on the reunification of the Hungarian nation in the framework of the European Union."[65] On a number of occasions in 2006, Romania's current president, Traian Băsescu, called for a similar EU reunification of Romania with Moldova.[66]

Meanwhile, the argument that the state has but one nation is codified today—as it was in 1923—in the Romanian constitution, the first line of which reads as follows: "Romania is a sovereign, independent, unitary, and indivisible National State." Article 2 states that "national sovereignty belongs to the Romanian people."[67] This line was evoked recently by Băsescu in a discussion with minority Hungarian representatives as a constraint on granting full autonomy to some areas of Transylvania with a significant Hungarian population.[68] And despite gesturing toward the need for minority rights, Ion Iliescu, echoing the words of Sabin Manuilă from 1938, has held that "there is no historical province of the country where, overall, the Romanian population should not make up the majority; the biggest concentrations of Hungarians, for instance, are to be found in only two counties in central Romania, which are also among the smallest in point of population."[69]

Neither has there been a shortage of statements on either side claiming that the other country is acting counter to the interests of the most recent new Europe. A Hungarian publication from 1992 asserted that "Romania's road to Europe goes through Transylvania, and if it does not wish to recognize Transylvania as an intermediary, it has no chance of making it as far as the gate of the 'European house.'"[70] In a 2004 visit to Transylvania, the president of the Foreign Affairs Commission in Hungary called Romania "the rear courtyard of Europe," capable of bringing chaos to the European Union (in specific reference to Romania's treatment of its Hungarian minority in Transylvania).[71] Similarly, in a complaint issued to the Council of Europe in 1995, members of the Romanian National Party of Unity called Hungary "the force behind the destabilization of Romania and Europe whose goal it is to destroy the Romanian nation-state."[72]

Thus "Europe" itself has remained in the eyes of Hungarian and Romanian statesmen what it was during the interwar period and World War II—namely, the watcher and standard-setter for interstate interaction around contested issues. With the overhaul of the Romanian constitution in 2003 to meet EU expectations, for example, minority rights were a key issue.[73] The revised constitution contains several provisions for the protection of national minorities and their languages, a response to both Hungarian and EU pressure.[74] Furthermore, the Hungarian and Romanian proposed minority amendments to the (now defunct) EU constitution can be construed as efforts to raise the two states' concerns to the level of European concerns.

The "Transylvanian Question"—which embodies issues ranging from the nature of the state and the status of minorities to the problem of sovereignty—is thus in many respects still an open question, because those issues have yet to be resolved and are currently being renegotiated within the context of today's "new Europe." In this respect, there is not much that is "new" about the Europe of today any more than there was about the new Europe of World War II, as far as Hungary and Romania are concerned.

The one apparent exception, attitudes and policies relating to the Jewish Question, remains a locus for the expression of unresolved tensions around sovereignty and ideals of statehood, especially in reflections on the events and significance of the Holocaust in the two states.

THE TRANSYLVANIAN QUESTION AND THE HOLOCAUST SINCE WORLD WAR II

Among the first acts of the new, post–World War II Romanian government was to set up a people's tribunal in Transylvania to try those suspected of having committed war crimes. Romanian-language newspapers began reporting on the atrocities of the Hungarians against the Romanians as far back as 1940 in preparation for the trials. "[The criminals] will be tried here in Transylvania, here in the place where they committed their crimes. Eighty-seven wooden crosses in Sălaj demand justice."[75] The author's mention of Sălaj—where eighty-seven Romanians were murdered by Hungarian soldiers on September 9, 1940—points to early assumptions that the crimes the court was most interested in were those committed by Hungarians against Romanians. Early attempts to add the Jews to the inventory of the victims were influenced by the struggle between Hungary and Romania (indeed often between Hungarians and Romanians) for greater postwar legitimacy.

In what he called an "Open letter to a Hungarian friend in Romania," a Jewish survivor of the Holocaust, Jenő Király, attacked not only the Hungarian administration, but the Hungarian bystanders who allowed the deportations from Hungarian Northern Transylvania to take place. Only with the cooperation and encouragement of the Hungarian population of Cluj, he argued, could "this bestial act [the deportations] be carried out so perfectly [by] our Hungarian 'fellow citizens'—scrambling for the property of the Jews which had been put out for the taking—making great efforts to be sure that no Jew escaped death."[76] Király also noted that the Hungarian regime under Regent Miklós Horthy, during its four-year rule of Northern Transylvania, "inflicted terrible wounds, both on the Jews and on the Romanians." In the opening paragraphs of the letter, Király explained that he was writing in response to those Hungarians who saw in the vindictiveness of the Romanian regime a "Romanian reaction." In his next article, which was similarly critical of Hungarians' treatment of the Jews during the Horthy era, Király's byline gave his first name in romanianized form, "Eugen," instead of the earlier Hungarian form (Jenő).[77]

Thus in the response of the immediate postwar Romanian press, helped along by some Jewish survivors of the Holocaust, the Jews and the Romanians were cast as the two victims of Hungarian rule, and of Hungarians more generally. This trend was continued unofficially by Jewish émigrés and later by the Romanian state, but by the spring of 1946, the official line in Communist Romania was increasingly intolerant of nationalist agitation of the sort the Romanian press was undertaking against the Hungarians.

Jews from the region played a role in this transformation as well. Already in February 1946, Hillel Kohn said at the meeting of the democratic Jews in Cluj that it would be "a mistake to equate Fascism with the Hungarian people."[78] Yet another push was given in this direction by the new prime minister of Romania, Petru Groza, who, in a speech delivered on March 6, 1946, called for an end to national chauvinism and peace with the national minorities, including Hungarians.[79] Just over a month later, an April 9 issue of *Tribuna Nouă* [New Tribune] asserted that "the Fascist idea knows no national differences, only class differences."[80] In this valuation, the victims of Fascism were no longer Jews and Romanians but the lower classes, while the perpetrators were no longer Hungarians, but the ruling upper classes of the old semifeudal order.

The change was not immediate and did not proceed without regressions to the old national rhetoric, but it gained ground unmistakably from the spring on, especially as the People's Tribunal began its proceedings.[81] "This trial has particular significance: the group of criminals of war is made up of all the nationalities of Transylvania. The Saxon Boschner sits together with the Jew Chaim, the colonel Vitou together with the Hungarian lieutenant Dr. Barna Győri, etc. This is proof that Fascism is not typified by nationalities when it is a question of crimes and cruelties."[82] Despite the efforts of the state to dampen the national struggle, or perhaps because of them, hard feelings about the fate of Transylvania and the fate of the Jews found other outlets.

In 1947, a report of the Romanian gendarmerie in Cluj County documented "chauvinist and racial manifestations" in Transylvania during and since the war. The author(s) expressed concern that "Hungarians and Romanians have signed up for different democratic organizations in the framework of which they are continuing their insidious work, thereby sabotaging the genuine interest in a pure democracy." The report described incidents that took place in 1946 in which Hungarians in one village refused to celebrate a state holiday, while in another village Hungarian schoolchildren ripped up a Romanian flag. Even the report itself is symptomatic of the failure to move beyond national factions, as it outlines chauvinist acts of the Hungarian population while speaking of Romanian dislike for Hungarians only in terms of revenge.

"One thing is certain—that the Hungarians cannot forget Transylvania, and the Romanians cannot forget the massacre of 157 Romanians from Ip and 86 Romanians from Trăznea."[83]

At the same time the Hungarian and Romanian elements were struggling with the legacy of the nationalities conflict in Transylvania during World War II, the Jews of Transylvania were involved in a struggle of their own, to reestablish themselves in a much-changed society. Remnants of the Transylvanian Jews' ties with Hungarians—in the form of a shared language, culture, even in some cases a shared religion—were being reevaluated. In late January 1945, for example, the head rabbi of Romania, Alexandru Şafran, forbade all Jews who had converted to Roman Catholicism (a "Hungarian" religion) in order to escape persecution during the war to convert back to Judaism. In a statement similar to Emil Haţieganu's regarding Romanians who had abandoned the national fold, Şafran declared: "Let them stay where they are, indifferent to the trafficking of sacred things through which Jews have suffered for nearly six thousand years."[84]

While some—particularly Southern Transylvanian—Jews sought to maintain their ties with magyardom, a few even going so far as to change their names to Hungarian-sounding ones, they were often criticized by their fellow Jews for doing so.[85] A Jewish man living in Timişoara wrote to a friend who had left for Cluj and taken a Hungarian name: "After all we have been through, it seems ridiculous to discuss the viability of making a Bodrossy out of Kraus, a Lányi out of Lippner, a Popescu out of Khon. We can do anything we like, except shed our own skin."[86] The author went on to criticize the name change of his friend in more direct terms, saying it was particularly inappropriate to take a Hungarian name "after all the Hungarian baseness" the Jews had been exposed to.

Just as some chose to affirm their Hungarian identity, other Transylvanian Jews sought and found ways to distance themselves from their former Hungarianness during the immediate postwar period. This they did by using Romanian instead of Hungarian as their main language, or in more subtle ways, like using Romanian place names even in the body of a letter written in Hungarian.[87] There were also more overt gestures, such as appealing to the Romanian state to demand restitution of confiscated property from the Hungarian state, which the surviving Jews of Northern Transylvania did in October 1947.[88]

Nevertheless, most of the arguments for or against assimilation or cooperation with one or the other nationality lost their edge as a large number of Jews left Romania for Palestine during this period. By 1948, the number of Jews who had emigrated reached thirty-two thousand, and by 1950 an estimated additional seventy-five thousand had left the country.[89] In 1960, Moses Rosen, the head rabbi of Romania at the time, commented that "if things continue as they are, in five years I'll be the last Jew in Romania."[90]

The exodus of the Jews—for the most part to Palestine (later Israel) and the United States—had a considerable impact on the creation of the legacy of the Holocaust in Hungary and Romania. During the late 1960s, partly as a result of massive emigration of Jews to Israel, the first writings on the Holocaust in Transylvania began to appear. The first memory book to be published on Cluj appeared in 1968 in Israel. In a Hungarian-language summary of the book, Tibor Simon reflected on the glorious cultural and other achievements of the city's Jewish population, concluding that "four lines' worth of laws were enough to bury and destroy the entire legacy of an undeniably significant cultural center, enough to turn against us, or even to intensify the already harmfully developed anti-Semitic feelings of the Hungarian population."[91] He recalled returning to the city after the Holocaust: "There I stood on the King Mátyás Square and looked at the engraved writing on the beautiful statue by János Fadrusz: 'Mátyás, the just.' I laughed cynically."[92] This was among the first of many attempts to "renationalize" the Holocaust as the product of Hungarian ruthlessness, a process that began with the work of these émigré historians.

In the 1970s, another Jewish émigré historian working in the United States, Stephen Fischer-Galaţi, went beyond condemning the Hungarians for their role in the extermination of Northern Transylvania's Jews. He effectively praised the wartime Romanian regime for "saving" the Jews on its territory. "It is a tribute to Antonescu and to the Romanian population at large that the Romanian Jews alone were saved from the physical extermination through the 'Final Solution.'"[93] The demonization of the Hungarians for their role in the Holocaust soon resonated with the Romanian state's desire to demonize the Hungarians for persecution of the Romanians during the war.

In the mid-1980s, the Ceauşescu regime made common cause with some émigré survivors of the Holocaust and their descendants. In 1986 two books appeared, one in Israel, one in Romania, both in English. One was the eleventh volume of a series of document collections entitled "Concerning the Fate of Romanian Jewry during the Holocaust." It included an English summary of the first ten volumes of documents. At the end of the summary of volume 10, the author explained how the documents were obtained from Romanian archives: "These documents show that in Romania a new generation of historians has come forth. They attempt to understand the events of the past by flexible thought patterns and a readiness to conceive a true picture of the Jewish tragedy. They naturally expect that the Romanian problem, too, be understood in the light of the burdens that the Romanian state and people suffered during the period."[94]

Belonging to this "new generation" of historians were the authors of the other book published in 1986, this one in Romania, entitled *Horthyist-Fascist Terror in Northwestern Romania*. In this volume the suffering of the Jews is given extremely short shrift in favor of detailed descriptions of the suffering of Romanians at the hands of Hungarians. Furthermore, the title itself denies that Northern Transylvania had ever been part of Hungary; instead, the area is called "Northwestern Romania."[95]

Following the collapse of Communism, the battle continued. In 1993, a collection of documents was published relating to the emigration of Jews from Romania during the war. Its tone, set in the introduction, proceeded in the same vein as the 1986 collection. The documents contained in the volume, it claims,

> testify to the constant willingness of the Romanian government to allow the emigration of the Jews in Romania as well as of those arrived here from other countries—and for whom Romania represented a safe place or at least a temporary shelter while waiting to emigrate—in order to escape the "Final Solution." We hope this book . . . will contribute to the elucidation of certain moments from the history of secular cohabitation of Romanians and Jews on Romanian soil.[96]

The strategy of victim lumping, that is, associating the suffering of Romanians or Hungarians with the victimization of the Jews during the Holocaust, did not become obsolete with the collapse of Communism in either Hungary or Romania. As part of a protracted debate surrounding the comment of a famous Hungarian literary figure (Sándor Csoóri) that the Hungarian Jews were "assimilating" the Hungarians, one of Csoóri's defenders, Rezső Döndő, complained about the excess of "propaganda" surrounding Holocaust commemoration in Hungary.

> The Jewish Holocaust is an essential part—but only a part—of the Hungarian holocaust, of the Hungarian genocide. To us, who live in this country, the Holocaust of six to seven hundred thousand Jews is also painful, *but so is the planned genocide of 3 million Hungarians*. The fact is that the Jewish Holocaust has been repeatedly mentioned since the 1970s. But the fact that for decades there has been a constant elimination of magyardom—not just fifty years ago, but today, as well!—has received not a word in the mass media.[97]

The "holocaust" to which Döndő refers in his article is the plight of the Hungarian minorities in Romania, (Czecho)Slovakia, Croatia, and Serbia (Yugoslavia).[98] This conflation was repeated by the former Hungarian foreign minister, Géza Jeszenszky, four years later.[99]

Victim lumping across time is another strategy by which the fate of the

Jews has been linked to the fate of Transylvania. Anti-Semitism in post-1989 Hungary, for example, returns to the image of the Jew as Communist, implicated in the persecution of Hungarians under Stalinism, but also in the loss of Transylvania. One article written in 1990 complained of the "bespectacled Marxist Freemasonic intellectual who sold Transylvania and brought the Communists to power."[100] The House of Terror museum in Budapest also famously begins the story of the Holocaust with the tragedy of Trianon and casts Hungary as the victim first of Nazi Germany and then of the Soviet Union.[101]

In Romania, too, commemorations of the Holocaust have been overshadowed by aspects of the Transylvanian Question. This has been particularly true in the city of Cluj, the former mayor of which, Gheorghe Funar, was a member of the ultranationalist Greater Romania Party.[102] In June 1992, during a commemorative ceremony for the victims of the Holocaust, Funar commented that, unlike in Hungary, no one had persecuted the Jews in Romania during World War II. An article on the event in the local Hungarian paper *Szabadság* quoted the head Rabbi Moses Rosen's condemnation of growing anti-Semitism in Romania, as well as his special thanks to the Democratic Alliance of Hungarians in Romania [Romániai Magyar Demokrata Szövetség, RMDSz] for holding a commemorative ceremony in the Catholic Church.[103] The article itself is demonstrative of how the commemoration of the Holocaust has been bound up in the political struggle for legitimacy between Hungary and Romania.

During yet another commemorative ceremony in June 1995, Funar warned that the RMDSz was following a political platform that could lead to atrocities against Romanians and remaining Jews.[104] Funar's effort to nationalize guilt for the Holocaust by casting the Hungarians in the role of the eternal and essential perpetrators—whether their victims were Romanians or Jews—was mirrored a month later by a Romanian journalist who wrote that it was indeed fair to set a sign of equation between Hungarian Fascism and the Hungarian people. "The Romanians who lived under the Horthy regime for four years came to the conclusion that the Hungarians and the Horthyists were . . . like twins."[105]

On the fifty-fifth anniversary of the Second Vienna Arbitration (August 30, 1995), Funar attacked the Organization for Security and Cooperation in Europe's high commissioner on national minorities, Max van der Stoel, during the latter's visit to Romania. The mayor was incensed that Stoel had not attended the Romanian commemoration events, instead choosing to fraternize with members of the RMDSz. He asked that Stoel be present at the ceremony in which the audience would remember that the parents of RMDSz members had committed atrocities against 150,000 Jews and several hundred thousand Romanians. A statement by the Romanian far-right Romanian Hearth Party regarding the anniversary asserted that the Hungarians in Northern Transylvania during World War II had "'celebrated' their victory over the defenseless Romanians and Jews with violence and murder."[106]

Some days later, at a commemoration ceremony in the village of Ip, where as many as 157 Romanians had been murdered by Hungarian soldiers during the war, Funar called on Hungary to apologize to Romania for its World War II crimes against the Romanians, just as Germany had done with the Jews.[107] In a similar vein, still today the Romanian Wikipedia site for "The Ip Massacre" refers to the "holocaust" perpetrated by Hungarians against Romanians.[108] Funar's use of perpetrator lumping—linking Nazi crimes against the Jews to Hungarian crimes against the Romanians—shows how the struggle for control of the region's World War II historical legacy borrows skillfully from the postwar narrative of German guilt and the Holocaust.

Statues and memorials of World War II figures have in recent years expanded the field of competition for control over the legacy of the war. Two figures in particular—Romanian wartime leader Ion Antonescu and Albert Wass, a Hungarian literary figure convicted during the 1946 tribunal in Cluj of atrocities against Romanians and Jews—have been the objects of attempts to exonerate, even to glorify, individuals implicated in wartime atrocities.

During a 2002 parliamentary debate surrounding memorials to Antonescu, Senator Adrian Păunescu of the governing Social Democratic Party declared that "if there is a nation in Europe that must be condemned for the Holocaust, it is Horthy's Hungary."[109] Senator Corneliu Vadim Tudor, president of the Party of Greater Romania, added that "while Hungary killed [Jews], Romania protected its own Jews." Meanwhile, Romanian schoolchildren are taught that "it is to Antonescu's credit that he opposed the implementation of the 'Final Solution' and the destruction of Romania's Jewish population. Unlike in Horthyist-occupied Northern Transylvania, where the Jews were subjected to numerous atrocities and ultimately deported, the 'Final Solution' was not implemented in Romania."[110]

A year later, following the decision to remove a statue of Albert Wass from the courtyard of the Roman Catholic Church in Reghin,[111] the Hungarian press criticized the administration for its double standard. At the core of the complaint was the fact that, just as the display of the Wass statue was condemned, a street in Tîrgu Mureș[112] bearing the name of Antonescu had still not been changed, despite promises to do so a year before.[113]

Conclusion

Communism's collapse was preceded and followed by a sharp resurgence in discussions about the situation of the Hungarian minority in Transylvania and the legitimacy of Romania's claim on the region.[114] Again, as during the interwar period and World War II, such discussions were tied to how these states and their inhabitants understood their place in Europe, and especially the issue of European integration.

In trying to make sense of the parallels between the rhetoric surrounding the fate of Transylvania during World War II and since the collapse of Communism, the temptation is to see in post-1989 manifestations of wartime rhetoric a resurgence of right-wing extremism. And indeed, anyone looking for signs of such a resurgence need look no further than the Internet, where the latest incarnation of the Legionnaire movement dedicates a Web page to the Transylvanian Question and where the successor to the Hungarian Revisionist League is still alive and well.[115] But although these issues may find expression through the extreme right, they are not uniquely bound to a right-wing position. It is after all the Socialist government of present-day Hungary that has adopted the so-called Renewed Nation Policy, and Ion Iliescu—only recently replaced as president of the Social Democratic Party—whose rhetoric most mirrored that of interwar and wartime politicians on the Hungarian minority question.

As this work has shown, in fashioning answers to the Transylvanian Question, twentieth-century state leaders mobilized myriad systems, institutions, and ideologies at both the national and European levels. Consequently, European institutions and ideas about Europe were forged in the fire of unresolved issues around minority rights, the nation-state, territoriality and sovereignty left over from the nineteenth century, and the attempt to re-make Europe after World War I. Statesmen and politicians in Hungary and Romania today have thus retained one of the most long-standing objectives of their predecessors: transforming the Transylvanian Question into a European concern.

Conclusion

⌒

An Aberration?

In his memoir—published in 1990—entitled *The Battle for Transylvania*, Romanian statesman Valer Pop opens with the words, "From the beginning of 1919 up until the summer of 1940, irrespective of the governments that succeeded one another, Romania had a rectilinear attitude, characterized above all by the sincere and unreserved adoption of the politics of peace of the League of Nations."[1] Along this continuum, the subtext reads, the period between 1940 and 1944 was an aberration. This thesis is built into the very organization of Pop's memoir, which deals with the events leading up to the Second Vienna Arbitration and then jumps straight to August 23, 1944, when Romania switched sides to join the Allies.[2] Indeed, Pop's thesis was the primary narrative strategy employed by Romanian delegates to the Paris Peace Conference in 1946, and the way Romanian historiography has dealt with the period ever since.[3]

A History of Transylvania, published in Hungary in the mid-1980s, also elides the 1940–44 period, dedicating three volumes and over seventeen hundred pages to Transylvania's history up until 1918, with only seven pages on World War II.[4] One Hungarian historian, Gábor Egry, has referred to this period as a "mere grey fleck" in Hungarian historiography, a "peculiar four years" that historians have only recently begun to try to make sense of in light of what came before, and what came after.[5]

There is no doubt that the years 1940 to 1944 were peculiar, but their peculiarity stems not from their presumed aberrational qualities. They are strange because we expect to find a more or less radical discontinuity of ideas and practices once the critical war-line is crossed. In fact, however, a particular understanding of the essential features of national statehood in the European context stretched largely untransformed across the two critical war thresholds (1939–40 and 1944–45), survived in a muted form under Communism, and has emerged more or less intact since 1989–90. This understanding continues to color domestic politics and foreign policy in Hungary and Romania, finding expression in efforts to reconcile minority rights with concerns about sovereignty.

The European Union, which was created in part to negate the national chauvinism that brought on both the First and Second World Wars, nevertheless borrows attributes from earlier visions for a "new Europe." It inherited from the League of Nations system the necessity of limited or shared sovereignty, especially for the purpose of minority rights protection, a necessity that Hitler's "new Europe" also negotiated (indeed quite literally, in the case of the Second Vienna Arbitration). And in the World War II "new Europe," nations were called upon to remain or become more national within a European framework, a feature "new Europes" of the interwar and post-1989 periods were quite comfortable accommodating.[6]

Despite these similarities, however, the "new Europe" of the post-1989 watershed has made it possible for sovereignty to become a local or a regional, as opposed to a foreign policy issue. Hungarians can believe themselves to be united in a single state because in some sense, they are. Romanians can believe they are still the sole possessors of Transylvania because in some sense, they are. And the problem-word *self-determination* is, in the present context of both states being members of the European Union, much less meaningful than previously. In his New Year's speech of January 1, 2007, Hungary's president, László Sólyom, noted the significance of Romania's accession to the European Union. "As of today, Romania is a member of the European Union. Thus the greater part of the Hungarian nation—more than 12 million—are now a part of the same political, economic, and legal territory. . . . Every Hungarian can love the Carpathian Basin in its entirety, each land to which he or she is tied by history and culture. And all the other peoples living here can do the same."[7]

This is not to say the European Union has definitively "solved" the Transylvanian Question. It is clear that the status and fate of Transylvania and its inhabitants will continue to be central to debates in this region about what it means to be European, as well as to debates about what Europe's role in the region should be. And it is in places like Transylvania that the "new European" notion of regionalism is being tried and tested, together with strategies for the preservation of minority communities. As renewed tensions around the issue of Hungarian autonomist aspirations in Transylvania in the wake of Kosovo's independence reveal, Hungarian and Romanian leaders and spokespersons will continue to influence the debate on these issues by drawing on their understanding of what Europe represents and how it should be manifest within and between states.

WHAT WAS THE TRANSYLVANIAN QUESTION AND WHAT COMES NEXT?

The Transylvanian Question encompassed myriad issues during its life span. It took on many of the characteristics of an ideology in that it accounted for, justified, excused, and explained everything that was done in the interest of addressing it, from the failure of the 1919 Bolshevik revolution to the crushing of the Legionnaires' rebellion in 1941. But it also proved more flexible than an ideology, moving across the political spectrum from left to right, quite at home on both extremes as well as in the middle. It pointed to gaps and openings in ideas, ideologies, policies, and practices, allowing those who addressed it to shape the terms of interstate relations, domestic policy, and everyday human interaction.

Like nationalism, the Hungarian and Romanian preoccupation with the fate of Transylvania provided a line to power for individuals as well as states, a means of acquiring agency, a venue for activism, a way of setting the terms for belonging in and being excluded from communities, states, and even supranational political orders. And like nationalism, it also provided a distraction, a means of deflecting responsibility, denying agency, ignoring other problems, creating scapegoats, explaining failure, excusing violence and mistreatment, silencing critics.

Yet the Transylvanian Question has something to teach us about the nature of nationalism. It forces us to recognize the counterintuitive fact that—like the Transylvanian Question itself—Hungarian and Romanian nationalism were born out of interactions *between states*, at the same time and for the same reasons "Europe" was being created to oversee and to moderate between them. As such, nationalism in this region has always inherently been *trans*national.

The analysis of the preceding chapters has shown that neither the ebb and surge of extremist ideologies, nor Hungarian and Romanian nationalism, nor the events of the Holocaust and other episodes of mass violence lend themselves to being categorized solely as "national" phenomena. The fact of their "national" character and significance indicates *only* that they were by some means nationalized and localized, and it is the task of the historian not only to study them *within* the "national" context, but to understand the processes by which the *domestication* of ideas and practices takes place. In the case of Hungary and Romania, modern anti-Semitism, Communism, right-wing extremism, liberalism, nationalism and ideas about Europe were all "domesticated" at least in part by passing through the Transylvanian Question.

Thus the Transylvanian Question has been neither an ideology nor merely an instrument for the expression of nationalism and nationalist goals, for it has subsumed and colored nationalism as readily as it did anti-Semitism and political extremism. And for as much as it channeled extremism and violence, it also got in the way of individual, collective, and official efforts to adopt violent means of achieving nationalist goals like unmediated sovereignty and ethnic homogeneity. It raised questions about the legitimacy of nation-state aspirations and the desirability of their fulfillment. It demanded moderation, restraint, and a degree of tolerance, as well as flexibility and patience. In the words of Hungarian prime minister Teleki, the two states had to prove "that we deserve" Transylvania.[8]

The perceived necessity of states to "prove" their worthiness is a recurring theme in the history of the Transylvanian Question, since all of the actions and reactions, all of the maneuvering around the matter of Transylvania's fate, were undertaken in the surest knowledge that someone was watching and that the observers would have the power to shape the future European order. In this respect, the post-1989 period is profoundly typical of these states' experience of "European-ness"—here being European has meant watching others and being watched.[9]

Like nationalism, the Holocaust, and ideologies, then, ideas of Europe are generally not intelligible or historicizable either from within a single "national" context or as pan-European phenomena. Commentators within Hungary and Romania and abroad have nevertheless sought to understand conceptions of Europe from within national frameworks or as manifestations of a universal culture. Hence the myriad works that draw out one or the other nation's troubled relationship with "Europe" and its own "European-ness," works that tend to see this relationship as the by-product of power struggles between different domestic interests. The recurring trope in this narrative synopsis is the heated battle between the modernization- and reform-minded Europhiles and those who glorified the indigenous peasantry, "Asiatic" militarism, or Eastern Orthodox mysticism.[10]

The close resemblance between both domestic and "European" political rhetoric of the 1930s and 1940s and today has been touted recently by historians.[11] In 2003, Hungarian historian Ervin Csizmadia remarked in an interview that "what we have conceptualized up until now as a 'Fidesz project' is certainly at most mere plagiarism. Things happened between the then-left and then-right of the 1930s that are similar to those that have been happening in recent years. We need to find a common explanatory principle!"[12]

Such a "common explanatory principle," I would argue, must account for discussions about Europe and the nation's place within it emerging from interactions *between states*, rather than in hermetic national isolation. Taking this into account, we can observe how these discussions are not so much a product of left-right *conflict* within these states, but are the legacy of a political *consensus* on issues like the Transylvanian Question that emerged in the second half of the nineteenth century, and within which the left and the right sought to stake out territory on the same field to gain legitimacy by addressing the question more effectively than their opponents. In the process and over time, the consensus itself has been transformed—the Transylvanian Question has given shape to an idea of what Europe does in this region, and "Europe" has in turn become the object of a *new* consensus, one over which the right and left are fighting new battles to determine who is more "European" and what that means. Participating in a European project thus has become part of the nationalist repertoire—or rather, being "European" has become a constituent component of being Hungarian or Romanian.

This transformation from Transylvania to Europe as the locus of political consensus has its origins in World War II, when the various strands of the old consensus on the Transylvanian Question converged on the position that the question could be resolved only within the framework of a "new Europe." It remained merely to determine what that "new Europe" would look like. It is not surprising that "Europe" rhetoric of the World War II era has been revived since the collapse of Communism; after all, that was the last time a reordering of Europe was on the table in this region, and indeed the last time Europe itself was "between states." Furthermore, as this book has shown, the structural and rhetorical similarities between the interwar League of Nations system, Hitler's "New European Order," and the "new Europe" of post-Communism and EU enlargement are striking from the standpoint of Hungarian and Romanian domestic and foreign policy objectives.

It is nevertheless true that some forces in Hungary and Romania remain uneasy with the new consensus around "Europe" as manifested by the European Union, which in their minds has strayed too far from the original nexus of issues that formed around issues of national independence and territorial integrity. These groups, largely representing the extreme right, wax nostalgic about the politics of World War II leaders and right-wing parties, attack European Union symbols, and try to force the focus back onto national unification as a zero-sum game in which there can be but one winner. Such voices are most audible in debates around the Holocaust and minorities. But as anthropologist Douglas Holmes has pointed out, these groups—like many of their World War II counterparts—see their own brand of extremist xenophobia as part of a Europe-wide movement, suggesting that the "Europe" consensus might still be construed as pervasive.[13]

In these states, then, the terms of the debate around Europe were set during World War II, and subsequently the record of their origins has been obscured. I have sought here to recover a part of that record, and in so doing to make a larger claim about the importance of small-state interactions to the way Europe functions—both as a field of perception and as a political entity—still today.

On March 19, 1942, Mihai Antonescu made a speech entitled "Why we fight." In it, he declared that "if Europe did not exist today, it would have to be invented."[14] In some respects, that is precisely what leaders and politicians in Hungary and Romania have been doing since the second half of the nineteenth century. Realizing that the European Great Powers had an interest in the region, leaders in the two states fought to focus and channel that interest and make it conform to their own geopolitical visions.

Were their efforts successful? There is perhaps no greater proof of their success than the phenomenon of the German-Italian Officers' Commission whose role it was to investigate minority rights abuses in Transylvania. Nazi Germany played the role of the League of Nations there not because it *wanted* to, but because it *had no choice*. The terms and standards of minority rights had already been set and Hungarian and Romanian statesmen held the Germans and Italians to them. So it was that out of interactions between these two small states there emerged an increasingly fixed template for "Europe's" involvement in their ongoing territorial dispute. In the process, important precedents were set that have shaped broader understandings of what "Europe" is and what it can do.

Taking Exception

The power to set precedents for how Europe functions derived in part from the uniqueness of the Transylvanian Question as a contest for territory. That uniqueness lay in the fact that the two states competing for control of Transylvania occupied a fairly level playing field during the Second World War. Unlike other conflicts involving states and minorities in East-Central Europe—Serbs and Croats, Germans and Czechs, Poles and Ukrainians—no one state or "nation" in this conflict had an obvious advantage for most of the war, in the form of either a powerful ally or an abundance of human or material resources. Furthermore, neither state was a serious target of German expansionism, and neither Hungarians nor Romanians were positioned as low on the German racial hierarchy as were the Slavs. And both states had something Nazi Germany needed—grain, oil, and support for the campaign against the USSR. Cumulatively, these conditions meant that occupying Hungary and Romania was an unattractive option for Germany, and having the two states at war with one another was equally undesirable. The relative equality of the two states as Axis allies explains why the Allied and Axis war aims and visions for a reordered Europe did not seem entirely distinct. The hobbyhorse of the Atlantic Charter was, after all, equality of states, something Hungary and Romania experienced as much or more *during* the war as before it.[15]

It was thus much easier for the two states' leaders and inhabitants to sustain the belief that the key elements of the post–World War I order had remained intact, and that the same criteria—self-determination according to the demographic principle and the "worthiness" of states as judged by their economic, social, and cultural achievements and viability, as well as by their minority treatment record—would shape the coming peace settlement. Wartime leaders in both states hoped that those criteria would be more "justly" applied in a Europe reordered following a Nazi victory, and only transferred that hope to the Western Allies when it was clear there was no chance the Germans could win.

Nor were Hungary and Romania the only states for which the contrast between Allied and Axis interests and platforms seemed similarly vague. Perhaps an even more extreme case in this regard is Bulgaria, whose leaders felt their state's territorial acquisitions had been sanctioned by Great Powers in *both* the Axis *and* the Allied camps, and which did not participate in the war against the Soviet Union.[16] Furthermore, the line between interwar and wartime principles and aims was blurry enough to many in Bulgaria, among them a Bulgarian specialist on international law, Georgi Genov, who wrote in 1941 that "the idea . . . of a so called Pan-Europe, that [Europe] should turn into a single federation, stressing the solidarity of European nations [is] precisely what Germany is calling for today."[17] It is also worth noting that in the case of Hungary, Romania, and Bulgaria, their leaders were careful not to seek or accept territorial expansion beyond the maximum extent their states had already achieved in the past, which set them apart from the more imperialist and expansionist Germany and Italy.[18]

One area of future research this parallel suggests is a comparative exploration of states' competition for territory around "questions," such as the

Transylvanian and Macedonian questions. The states and statehood aspirations of Ukraine, Poland, Lithuania, Slovakia, Croatia, Serbia, and Greece would also highlight what national elites and state leaders considered to be the "rules of engagement" regarding such competition and the understood standards for legitimacy and viability of states in the European context.

One way an analysis of the Transylvanian Question may prove especially instructive for such a comparison is in stressing regional as opposed to Europe-wide preoccupations. Whereas traditional narratives of Europe's twentieth-century focus on the nearly simultaneous appearance of extremist ideologies or embattlement of delegitimized democracies, here the emphasis is on the specific content and historical baggage these ideologies and political systems bore and how they affected clusters of states. This is not an argument for continual disaggregation and regional specificity, but rather a plea for resetting the terms of generalization when we speak of twentieth-century European history. Perhaps the conflicts of the twentieth century were not about ideological incompatibilities, but about a consensus around the standards for legitimate statehood that produced mutually exclusive conceptions of Europe's future boundaries. Careful examination of these cases might therefore reveal not only why *particular* strategies were mobilized by different states in the interest of realizing these conceptions, but also what informs thinking about European statehood in general.

Do mutually exclusive conceptions of Europe's internal and external boundaries still exist and have influence on interstate relations in Europe? Certainly. Yet there is one crucial difference between the European Union and earlier multiethnic systems, states, and utopian projects, from the Habsburg Empire to the League of Nations to Pan-Europe or the Nazi New European Order—namely, that the latter were all explicitly or implicitly built on, and indeed depended on, maintaining antagonisms between different groups within them in order to function. To the extent that equality between groups and entities was achieved, it was done by spurring competition and mistrust of other groups.

The European Union, by contrast, has outlived many of the Cold War antagonisms between "East" and "West" that lay at its foundation and seems committed to diffusing antagonisms between groups within it by allowing antagonistic ideas and visions of Europe and the nation to coexist, while preventing antagonistic practices on the part of member states and substate groups. In 1870, Romanian romantic poet Mihai Eminescu wrote an essay entitled "Transylvania Under Austro-Hungarian Rule," in which he aptly described the problem posed by the nineteenth-century map of Europe. "The impenetrability of a physical body makes it impossible for two bodies to occupy the same place at the same time," he wrote.[19] Achieving national unification and independence thus had to be achieved at the expense of other states' aspirations. Yet in today's European Union, not all such idealized maps of national boundaries need occupy the same page, so to speak. Like an anatomy book with transparent overlays, the European Union can allow states and peoples to maintain their projections of national unification, as long as there is no presumption that a single definitive map of Europe's internal and external boundaries need be drawn.

To return, then, to the question of "why we fight," one answer might be that the Europe forged out of friction between states seemed to require it. Perhaps the Europe of today occupies "a different dimension of political space," wherein state boundaries never truly touch, and such friction is therefore impossible. But that remains to be seen.

REFERENCE MATTER

Notes

Abbreviations

The following abbreviations are used in the Notes:

ADAP   *Akten zur Deutschen Auswärtigen Politik* [Documents of German Foreign Policy]

ANIC   Arhivele Naţionale Istorice Centrale [Central National Historical Archives] (Bucharest, Romania)

ASFJC   Arhivele Statului Filiala Judeţului Cluj [Cluj County Division of the Romanian State Archives] (Cluj, Romania)

BMF   Bundesarchiv-Militärarchiv Freiburg [State and Military Archive
(or BArch)   Freiburg] (Freiburg, Germany)

DDI   *I Documenti Diplomatici Italiani* [Italian Diplomatic Documents]

DGFP   *Documents on German Foreign Policy, 1918–1945*

DIMK   *Diplomáciai iratok Magyarország külpolitikájához* [Documents of Hungarian Diplomatic History]

HDA   Hrvatski Državni Arhiv [Croatian State Archive] (Zagreb, Croatia)

HIWRP   Archives of the Hoover Institution on War, Revolution and Peace (Stanford, California)

MOL   Magyar Országos Levéltár [Hungarian State Archives] (Budapest, Hungary)

MVRI   Ministerstvo na Vŭnshnite Raboti i Izpovedaniiata [(Bulgarian) Ministry of Foreign Affairs and Religion]

MZV   Ministerstvo Zahraničných Veci [(Slovak) Ministry of Foreign Affairs]

NDH   Nezavisna Država Hrvatska [Independent State of Croatia]

OHA   1956-os Intézet Oral History Archívuma [Oral History Archives of the 1956 Institute] (Budapest, Hungary)

SNA   Slovenský Národný Archív [Slovak National Archive] (Bratislava, Slovakia)

TsDA   Tsentralen Dŭrzhaven Arkhiv [Central State Archive] (Sofia, Bulgaria)

USHMMA   United States Holocaust Memorial Museum Archives (Washington, D.C.)

BOOK EPIGRAPHS: Péter Vida, *Magyarország és Románia: két ország Európa színterén* (Budapest: Hornyánszky Viktor Könyvnyomda, 1940), 3; Mihai Antonescu, *Warum wir kämpfen* (Bucharest, 1942), 25.

INTRODUCTION

1. A 1974 analysis of nine survey histories of twentieth-century Europe shows Germany received the most attention (on average, 28 percent in survey books), with Britain, France, and Russia nearly tied for "second place," but with only just over half the amount of coverage Germany received. The countries of Eastern Europe combined were tied with Italy, followed by Spain, the Netherlands and Switzerland, and Scandinavia. R. A. H. Robinson, "Histories of Twentieth-Century Europe (Review Essay)," *History* 59, no. 197 (October 1974): 407–13, 412.

2. See Bradley Abrams, *The Struggle for the Soul of the Nation: Czech Culture and the Rise of Communism* (Lanham, Md.: Rowman & Littlefield, 2004); Paul Hanebrink, *In Defense of Christian Hungary: Religion, Nationalism, and Antisemitism, 1890–1944* (Ithaca, N.Y.: Cornell University Press, 2006); Jan Gross, *Neighbors: The Destruction of the Jewish Community in Jedwabne, Poland* (Princeton, N.J.: Princeton University Press, 2001).

3. See Kim Munholand, "Wartime France: Remembering Vichy," *French Historical Studies* 18, no. 3 (1994): 801–20; Robert G. Moeller, "Sinking Ships, the Lost *Heimat* and Broken Taboos: Günter Grass and the Politics of Memory in Contemporary History," *Contemporary European History* 12, no. 2 (May 2003): 147–81; Peter Schneider, "The Germans Are Breaking an Old Taboo," *New York Times*, January 18, 2003, B7.

4. See Eric D. Weitz, "From the Vienna to the Paris System: International Politics and the Entangled Histories of Human Rights and Forced Deportations," unpublished paper (cited with permission of the author); Tara Zahra, "The 'Minority Problem' and National Classification in the French and Czechoslovak Borderlands," *Contemporary European History* 17, no. 2 (May 2008): 137–65; C. A. Macartney, *National States and National Minorities* (London: Oxford University Press, H. Milford, 1934), 286–94.

5. I borrow this concept from Rogers Brubaker's theory of nationalism. Rogers Brubaker, "Ethnicity Without Groups," *European Journal of Sociology* 43, no. 2 (2002): 163–89, 164.

6. See Jan T. Gross, *Revolution from Abroad: The Soviet Conquest of Poland's Western Ukraine and Western Belorussia* (Princeton, N.J.: Princeton University Press, 1988); Mark Mazower, "Violence and the State in the Twentieth Century," *American Historical Review* (October 2002), http://www.historycooperative.org/journals/ahr/107.4/ah0402001158.html (accessed August 6, 2006); István Deák, Jan T. Gross, and Tony Judt, eds., *The Politics of Retribution in Europe: World War II and Its Aftermath* (Princeton, N.J.: Princeton University Press, 2000), vii–xii.

7. Mark Mazower, *Dark Continent: Europe's Twentieth Century* (New York: A. A. Knopf, distributed by Random House, 1999), xii.

8. See Jürgen Habermas and Jacques Derrida, "February 15, or, What Binds Europeans Together: Plea for a Common Foreign Policy, Beginning in Core Europe," in *Old Europe, New Europe, Core Europe: Transatlantic Relations After the Iraq War*, ed. Daniel Levy, Max Pensky, and John Torpey (London; New York: Verso, 2005), 3–13.

9. Márta Font, *1100 év Európában: Fejezetek Magyarország történetébol* (Budapest: Nesztor, 1996); Balázs Sipos and Pál Pritz, eds., *Magyarország helye a 20. századi Európában: Tanulmányok* (Budapest: Magyar Történelmi Társulat, 2002); Ferenc Glatz, ed., *Magyarok Európában*, vols. 1–3 (Budapest: Háttér Lap- és Könyvkiadó, 1990); Domokos Kosáry, *Magyarország Európában* (Budapest: Nemzeti Tankönyvkiadó, 2003); Adrian Neculau, *Noi și Europa* (Iași: Polirom, 2002); Győrgy Ránki and Attila Pók, eds., *Hungary and European Civilization* (Budapest: Akadémiai Kiadó, 1989); J. C. Dragan, ed., *România și Europa* (Roma: Nagard, 1991); Ion Iliescu, *Rumänien in Europa und in der Welt* (n.p.: 1994); Al. Husar, *Ideea europeană, sau, Noi și Europa: istorie, cultura, civilizație* (Iași: Institutul European; Chișinău: Hyperion, 1993); Dan Berindei, *Românii și Europa: istorie, societate, cultura* (Bucharest: Ed. Museion, 1991); Ivan Pfaff, *Česká prináležitost k Západu v letech 1815–1878 k historii českého evropanství mezi vídenským a berlínským kongresem* (Brno: Nakl. Doplnek, 1996); Miloš Knežević, *Srbija i Evropa: evropski kulturni identiteti i nacionalni identiteti evropskih naroda—položaj i perspektive srpskog kulturnog identiteta u evropskoj kulturi: Zbornik* (Belgrade: Dom kulture Studentski grad, 1996); *Polska w Europie* (Warsaw: Osrodek Studiów Miedzynarodowych 1990s- [Monthly serial]); Andrzej Koryn, *Rola i miejsce Polski w Europie 1914–1957: w 75 rocznice odzyskania niepodległości: materialy z sesji naukowej w Instytucie Historii PAN, 8–9 listopada 1993 r.* (Warsaw: Instytut Historii PAN, 1994); Janusz Stefanowicz, *Polska w Europie na przelomie wieków* (Warsaw: Instytut Studiów Politycznych PAN, 1997); Henryk Samsonowicz, *Miejsce Polski w Europie* (Warsaw: Wydawn. Bellona, 1995).

10. See Berindei, *Românii și Europa*, 3.

11. In the case of Transylvania, this kind of thinking was facilitated by the recent publication and translation of the work of Samuel Huntington (*Clash of Civilizations*) into Hungarian and Romanian. Huntington's "fault lines between civilizations" cut directly through the region. Samuel P. Huntington, "The Clash of Civilizations?" *Foreign Affairs* 72, no. 3 (Summer 1993), http://www.georgetown.edu/faculty/irvinem/CCT510/Sources/Huntington-ClashofCivilizations-1993.html (accessed August 6, 2006). See also Gusztáv Molnár, "The Transylvanian Question: In Memory of Gelu Pateanu," in *The Hungarian Quarterly* 39, no. 149 (Spring 1998), http://www.hungarianquarterly.com/no149/49.html (accessed November 3, 2007); Gabriel Andreescu, "The Transylvanian Issue and the Issue of Europe," *Hungarian Quarterly* 39, no. 152 (Winter 1998), http://www.hungarianquarterly.com/no152/056.html (accessed November 3, 2007); Sorin Mitu, "Illusions and Facts about Transylvania" *Hungarian Quarterly* 39, no. 152 (Winter 1998), at http://www.hungarianquarterly.com/no152/064.html (accessed August 6, 2006).

12. Michael Ignatieff, "Nationalism and Toleration," in *Europe's New Nationalism: States and Minorities in Conflict*, ed. Richard Caplan and John Feffer (New York: Oxford University Press, 1996), 220–21; Milica Bakic-Hayden, "Nesting Orientalisms: The Case of Former Yugoslavia," *Slavic Review* 54, no. 4 (Winter 1995): 917–31.

1. The "Transylvanian Question" and European Statehood

1. Magda Ádám and Győző Cholnoky, eds., *Trianon: A magyar békeküldöttség tevékenysége 1920-ban* (Budapest: Lucidus Kiadó, 2000), 116.

2. *23 August 1944, Documente*, vol. 3 (Bucharest: Editura Ştiinţifică şi Enciclopedică, 1985), doc. 928, p. 107.

3. László Kürti, *The Remote Borderland: Transylvania in the Hungarian Imagination* (Albany: State University of New York Press, 2001), 15.

4. Lucian Boia, *History and Myth in Romanian Consciousness* (Budapest: Central European University Press, 2001), 181.

5. Paul Schmidt, *Hitler's Interpreter* (New York: Macmillan, 1951), 206.

6. Vasile Stoica, "Studiu elaborat de Vasile Stoica, diplomat, funcţionar superior în Ministrul de Externe al României, 25 februarie 1942," in *Din istoria Transilvaniei: Documente, 1931–1945*, ed. Mihai Fătu (Alexandria: Editura Tipoalex, 1999), doc. 30, pp. 172–73. Thirty years later, Romanian historian/statesman Constantin Giurescu referred to the "Transylvanian stronghold" as "the central region of the country, its nucleus." Constantin C. Giurescu, *The Making of the Romanian People and Language* (Bucharest: Meridiane, 1972), 11.

7. László Gáldi, "Az Erdélyi Album," *Magyar Szemle* 39, no. 6 (160) (December 1940): 354–61, 361.

8. Aladár Szegedy-Maszák, *Az ember ősszel visszanéz* (Budapest: Európa Kiadó, 1996), 321.

9. Ádám and Cholnoky, *Trianon*, 428.

10. Cited in Kürti, *Remote Borderland*, 90.

11. "Szekler" refers to a group of Hungarian-speaking people of the so-called Szekler Land (*Székelyföld*) in eastern Transylvania. Though their origins likely differ from those of the Magyars, their Hungarianness has often been considered especially authentic.

12. A significant portion of the discussions during the Transylvanian Conference of October 1940 (see Chapter 3) was consumed with this issue. See especially discussions about how administrators in Transylvania should know Romanian. "Az Erdélyi értekezlet jegyzőkönyve," MOL, K28 [Miniszterelnökség], 267. csomó., 36–38, 48, 51, 58.

13. Former Romanian prime minister Iuliu Maniu alluded to this the day after the Second Vienna Arbitration was announced, referring to "all the injustices imposed [on Transylvania] by the government in Bucharest." Ioan Hudiţă, *Jurnal politic*, vol. 1 (Iaşi: Institutul European, 1998), 303.

14. Rogers Brubaker, Margit Feischmidt, Jon Fox, and Liana Grancea, *Nationalist Politics and Everyday Ethnicity in a Transylvanian Town* (Princeton, N.J., and Oxford: Princeton University Press, 2006), 339, 342. See also "Kétfarkú kutyás hülyeség,"http://www.mkkp.hu/ (accessed March 5, 2007).

15. On the emergence of population politics, see Eric D. Weitz, "Germany and the Young Turks: Remaking the Eastern Question from Diplomacy to Population Politics," paper delivered at the Fourth Turkish-Armenian Workshop, Salzburg Seminar, April 14–17, 2005 (cited with permission of the author); Eric D. Weitz, "From the Vienna to the Paris System: International Politics and the Entangled Histories of Human Rights and Forced Deportations," unpublished paper (cited with permission of the author); Peter Holquist, "New Terrains and New Chronologies: The Interwar Period through the Lens of Population Politics," *Kritika: Explorations in Russian and Eurasian History* 4, no. 1 (Winter 2003): 163–75.

16. *Oxford English Dictionary Online*, 2nd ed., 1989 (Oxford University Press, 2006); "state, n." def. 24, 26, 29, 30 (accessed August 19, 2006).

17. On the historical relationship between states and territoriality from a social science perspective, see Peter J. Taylor, "The State as Container: Territoriality in the Modern World System," in *State/Space: A Reader*, edited by Neil Brenner, Bob Jessop, Martin Jones, and Gordon MacLeod (Malden, Mass.: Blackwell Publishing, 2003):101–13, esp. 101–6.

18. Cited in Peter Hanák, "The Image of Neighbors in the Hungarian Mirror," in *Vampires Unstaked: National Images, Stereotypes, and Myths in East Central Europe*, ed. Andrew Gerrits and Nanci Adler (Amsterdam: North-Holland Publishing Company, 1995), 57.

19. *Pierer's Universal-Lexikon der Vergangenheit und Gegenwart, oder Neuestes encyclopädisches Wörterbuch der Wissenschaften, Künste und Gewerbe*, XVI. Band (Altenburg: Verlagsbuchhandlung von H. A. Pierer, 1863), 618. Pieter Judson convincingly argues that German-speakers in the Habsburg Monarchy did not develop a sense of themselves as a territorial nation until even later, in the 1880s, with the conceptualization of a "language frontier." Pieter Judson, *Guardians of the Nation: Activists on the Language Frontiers of Imperial Austria* (Cambridge, Mass.: Harvard University Press, 2006), 15–16.

20. Állam, in "A Pallas Nagy Lexikona" (Budapest, 1893–1897), http://www.mek. iif.hu/porta/szint/egyeb/lexikon/pallas/html/003/pc000315.html#6 (accessed October 30, 2007).

21. C. Diachonovici, *Enciclopedia Română* (Sibiu: Editura W. Krafft, 1904), 3:1007–8.

22. Judson, *Guardians of the Nation*, 25–33.

23. Additionally, Article 63 of the Austrian penal code from 1852 made it a crime to violate "the reverence for the emperor, whether done by personal insult, by abuse, slander or mockery." Daniel Unowsky, *The Pomp and Politics of Patriotism: Imperial Celebrations in Habsburg, Austria, 1848–1916* (West Lafayette, Ind.: Purdue University Press, 2005), 120.

24. "1848. évi III. törvénycikk független magyar felelős ministerium alakításáról," 1. §, http://www.1000ev.hu/index.php?a=3&param=5271 (accessed November 26, 2007).

25. "1878. évi V. törvénycikk a magyar büntetőtörvénykönyv a büntettekről és vétségekről," 141. §, 173. §. http://www.1000ev.hu/index.php?a=3&param=5799 (accessed November 26, 2007). The law stipulates two years' imprisonment for oral slights, three for written ones, five for utterances made at public gatherings.

26. "1913. évi XXXIV. törvénycikk a király megsértéséről és a királyság intézményének megtámadásáról," 3. §, http://www.1000ev.hu/index.php?a=3&param=7230 (accessed November 26, 2007). The reason given for these changes was that "the legal system had not anticipated the kind of proliferation of violations that have surfaced in the course of the past few years' unbridled and blind agitation." Gyula Térfi, ed., *1913. évi törvényczikkek* (Budapest: Franklin-társulat, 1914), 397.

27. Térfi, *1913. évi törvényczikkek*, 397. The wording of this explanation leaves it unclear whether it is insults to the king or on the Hungarian nation which must be "beaten back and prevented."

28. "1920. évi I. törvénycikk az alkotmányosság helyreállításáról és az állami

főhatalom gyakorlásának ideiglenes rendezéséről," 14. §. http://www.1000ev.hu/index. php?a=3&param=7416 (accessed November 26, 2007).

29. "1921. évi III. Törvénycikk az állami és társadalmi rend hatályosabb védelméről," 7.–8. §. http://www.1000ev.hu/index.php?a=3&param=7459 (accessed November 26, 2007).

30. *Büntetőjogi döntvénytár,* vol. 24 (Budapest: Franklin-Társulat, 1932), határozat sorszáma 214, 136.

31. During the last part of the nineteenth century, acts that would later fall under the category of "slander against the nation" were prosecuted under different laws (against abusing the flag, inciting riot, etc.). Seton-Watson estimated that from 1898 to 1908, 503 Slovaks were indicted on such charges and received sentences averaging a month or two. Seton-Watson is cited in Andrew C. Janos, *The Politics of Backwardness in Hungary, 1825–1945* (Princeton, N.J.: Princeton University Press, 1982), 105.

32. Diachonovici, *Enciclopedia Română,* 3:643–44, 1007–8.

33. D. Gusti, "Individ, societate și stat in constituția viitoare," in *Constituția din 1923 în dezbaterea contemporanilor* (Bucharest: Humanitas, 1990), 581–607, 598. Gusti would later serve as Romania's minister of education (1932–33).

34. This was likely the work of Romul Boilă, a professor from Cluj. Article 33, *Constituția din 1923,* 618, 543.

35. Gusti, "Individ, societate și stat," 581–607, 606.

36. The mayor's office of the (Southern) Transylvanian city of Arad, for example, went so far as to issue a decree in 1938 that all new buildings be constructed in a "unified . . . Romanian style." MOL, K63 [Külügyminisztérium, Politikai osztály], 252. csomó., 1939–27. tétel./7/E, 180. See also Irina Livezeanu, *Cultural Politics in Greater Romania: Regionalism, Nation Building, and Ethnic Struggle, 1918–1930* (Ithaca, N.Y., and London: Cornell University Press, 1995), 166–73.

37. Most notable in this regard is the work of well-known interwar historian and statesman Nicolae Iorga, who famously downplayed the Hungarian historical presence in Transylvania. See, for example, Nicolae Iorga, *În luptă cu absurdul revizionism maghiar* (Bucharest: Editura Globus, 1991); Nicolae Iorga, *A History of Roumania: Land, People, Civilisation* (London: T. Fisher Unwin Ltd., 1925); Imre Mikó, "Iorga kultúrpolitikája és a római egyezmény," in *Huszonkét év: az erdélyi magyarság politikai története 1918. december 1-től 1940. augusztus 30-ig* (Budapest: Studium, 1941), 107–9.

38. Nicolae Bălășescu cited in Ambrus Miskolczy, "Transylvania in the Reform Era, 1830–1848," in *History of Transylvania, from 1830 to 1919,* ed. Zoltán Szász (New York: Columbia University Press, 2002), 165.

39. "Uniți-vă în cuget, uniți-vă-n simțiri," from the poem, "Un răsunet" [Echo]. This poem later became the Romanian national anthem, "Deșteaptă-te, Române" [Romanian, Awake!].

40. V. Curticăpeanu, *Mișcarea culturală românească pentru unirea din 1918* (Bucharest: Editura științifică, 1968), 59–162; Miskolczy, "Transylvania in the Reform Era," 151, 165. On the Liga Culturală, see Benedek Jancsó, *A román irredentista mozgalmak története* (Máriabesnyő-Gödöllő: Attraktor, 2004), 120–24.

41. Mihai Eminescu, "Transilvania sub stăpânire dualistă austro-ungară," in *Statul, I. Funcțiile și misiunea sa* (Bucharest: Editura Saeculum I.O., 1999), 94.

42. This was mostly done through one of the subplots, telling the story of Romanian poet and budding nationalist Titu. Liviu Rebreanu, *Ion* (New York: Twayne Publishers, 1967), 181–90, 205–8, 403–12, 429–32.

43. Zsuzsanna Török, "Planning the National Minority: Strategies of the Journal *Hitel* in Romania, 1935–44," in *Nationalism & Ethnic Politics*, 7, no. 2 (Summer 2001): 57–74, 60. Furthermore, Hungarian grievances against the Romanian state during the interwar period generally took two forms: property claims, and the preservation of cultural symbols and institutions, including churches and schools. See József C. Urbányi, *Erdély vérző kultúrája* (Budapest: Stephaneum Nyomda, 193[?]); Imre Mikó, *Huszonkét év: az erdélyi magyarság politikai története 1918. december 1-től 1940. augusztus 30-ig* (Budapest: Studium, 1941), 303–8.

44. M. Take Jonesco, *The Policy of National Instinct: A Speech Delivered by M. Take Jonesco in the Roumanian Chamber of Deputies during the sitting of the 16th & 17th December, 1915* (London: Sir Joseph Causton & Sons, Ltd., 1916), 33–34.

45. Sándor Makkai, "Nem lehet," in *Nem lehet: a kisebbségi sors vitája*, Gusztáv Molnár, ed. (Budapest: Hét Torony kiadó, 1989): 106–11, 109. Italics in the original.

46. Ion Antonescu, *Generalul Antonescu către țară 6 septemvrie 1940–22 iunie 1941* (Bucharest, 1941), 189.

47. Ibid., 160. For Antonescu's notion of collective guilt for the loss of territory, see pp. 26, 40–41. He also stressed that the future of the nation could only be secured through dedication to culture (191–93).

48. "Constituție din 27 februarie 1938," published in *Monitorul Oficial*, no. 48 (February 27, 1938), http://www.cdep.ro/pls/legis/legis_pck.htp_act_text?idt=9206 (accessed September 24, 2007).

49. Marius Turda, "The Nation as Object: Race, Blood, and Biopolitics in Interwar Romania," *Slavic Review* 66, no. 3 (Fall 2007): 412–41, 415.

50. Sándor Bölöni Farkas in 1835, on the occasion of the dissolution of the Hungarian diet, cited in Miskolczy, "Transylvania in the Reform Era," 139. See also Gabor Vermes, *István Tisza: The Liberal Vision and Conservative Statecraft of a Magyar Nationalist* (New York: Columbia University Press, 1985), 7.

51. Based on figures from Miskolczy, "Transylvania in the Reform Era," 8. In the Hungarian Kingdom as a whole in the mid-nineteenth century there were around 5 million Magyars and over 11 million non-Magyars (ibid., 138).

52. See Lajos Kossuth, *Írások és beszédek 1848–1849-ből* (Budapest: Európa Könyvkiadó, 1994), 56–57, 70, 131, 133, 246, 319, 410. Deák notes that in 1848, "Hungarian leaders never felt that their treatment of the national minorities was ever anything but enlightened and progressive." István Deák, *The Lawful Revolution: Lajos Kossuth and the Hungarians, 1848–1849* (New York: Columbia University Press, 1979), 315.

53. Cited in Sorin Mitu, *Transilvania mea: istorii, mentalități, identități* (Iași: Polirom, 2006), 134.

54. Eminescu, "Transilvania sub stăpânire dualistă," 96.

55. Cited in Miskolczy, "Transylvania in the Reform Era," 319.

56. Cited in György Spira, *A nemzetiségi kérdés a negyvennyolcas forradalom Magyarországán* (Budapest: Kossuth Könyvkiadó, 1980), 216; Miskolczy, "Transylvania in the Reform Era," 320.

57. Kossuth, *Írások és beszédek,* 202, 368, 404, 437, 451, 456, 467, 526.

58. Cited in Mitu, *Transilvania mea,* 132.

59. Cited in Spira, *A nemzetiségi kérdés,* 216.

60. Miskolczy, "Transylvania in the Reform Era," 319. See also Ambrus Miskolczy, "The Dialogue among Hungarian and Romanian Exiles, 1850–1851," in *Geopolitics in the Danube Region: Hungarian Reconciliation Efforts, 1848–1998,* ed. Ignác Romsics and Béla Király (Budapest: CEU Press, 1999): 99–129.

61. The word *minority* was not often used by representatives of either Hungary or Romania in reference to the Romanians in Transylvania. In a Hungarian encyclopedia from the 1890s, the word *minority* is defined in strictly political terms and includes no reference to ethnically based groups. See definition of *Kisebbség* in "A Pallas Nagy Lexikona," http://www.mek.iif.hu/porta/szint/egyeb/lexikon/pallas/html/058/pc005830.html#8 (accessed August 18, 2008).

62. Cited in Janos, *Politics of Backwardness,* 125.

63. Zoltán Szász, "Political Life and the Nationality Question in the Era of Dualism, 1867–1918," in *History of Transylvania, from 1830 to 1919,* ed. Zoltán Szász (New York: Columbia University Press, 2002), 644.

64. There is, not surprisingly, considerable divergence of opinion on the nature and extent of "magyarization" policies between some Hungarian and Romanian historians. Romanian nationalist historians and historians representing other nationalities of the former Hungarian Kingdom often describe it as a "violent" process. See Ion Dulamă-Peri, *Ardeal: Pământ, cuvânt și suflet românesc* (Bucharest: Editura Ministerului de Interne, 1995), 74–76; Titus Podea, *Transylvania* (Bucharest: Editura Fundația Culturale Române, 1936), 45–93. The most extreme Hungarian historiography, on the other hand, insists that Hungary had a liberal, tolerant nationalities policy and that the nationalities flourished under Hungarian rule. See Sándor Biró, *The Nationalities Problem in Transylvania, 1867–1940* (New York: Columbia University Press, 1992), 369–73. This historiographical drama is reversed for coverage of the interwar period, after Transylvania came under Romanian rule. Hungarian commentators and historians charged the Romanian state with aggressive "romanianization," while Romanian historians, statesmen, and commentators protested that no state treated its minorities better than Romania did. Ibid., 377–664, see esp. 443–58; Ioan Scurtu, ed., *Minoritățile naționale din România, 1918–1925: Documente* (Bucharest: Arhivele Naționale, 1994), 225–26; Margit Feischmidt, *Ethnizität als Konstruktion und Erfahrung: Symbolstreit und Alltagskultur im siebenbürgischen Cluj* (Münster, Hamburg, London: LIT Verlag, 2003), 46–57. On Romania's treatment of minorities during the interwar period as better than any other state's, see "Ședința consiliului de cabinet din 4 octombrie 1940," in *Stenogramele ședintelor consiliului de ministri: Guvernarea Ion Antonescu,* vol. 1 (Bucharest: Arhivele Naționale ale României, 1997), doc. 8, p. 160.

65. On magyarization policies generally, see the sources listed in note 64 and Livezeanu, *Cultural Politics,* 143–55. On the privileged social position of Hungarians in Transylvania, see Katherine Verdery, *Transylvanian Villagers: Three Centuries of Political, Economic, and Ethnic Change* (Berkeley, Los Angeles, London: University of California Press, 1983), 222–29.

66. In the interwar period, Hungarian statesman István Bethlen blamed the post-Ausgleich bonds of foreign policy and the military that Hungary continued to share

with Austria for the fact that "the integrity of Hungary's independence [had been] obscured in international public opinion" such that many Great Power statesmen saw Hungary as "a province of Austria," rather than a "thousand-year-old independent state" during the post–World War I peace negotiations. István Bethlen, *Magyarország az új Európában* (Budapest: "Kelet népe, Das junge Europa R.T." Kiadványa, 1925), 6.

67. Louis Kossuth, *Memories of My Exile*, trans. Ferencz Juasz (New York: D. Appleton and Company, 1880), viii.

68. See Nicolae Căzan și Șerban Rădulescu-Zoner, *Rumänien und der Dreibund, 1878–1914* (Bucharest: Editura Academiei Republici Socialiste România, 1983), 117. Nevertheless, Romania's reasons for joining the Triple Alliance were largely dictated by a balance-of-power arena divided along "Russian" and "anti-Russian" lines. Corneliu-Mihail Lungu, *Transilvania în raporturile româno-austro-ungare, 1876–1886* (Bucharest: Editura Viitorul Românesc, 1999), 115.

69. See Kürti, *Remote Borderland,* 29; József György Oberding, *A bukovinai magyarság településtörténeti és társadalomrajzi vázlata* (Kolozsvár, 1939); Enikő Sajti, *Hungarians in the Voivodina 1918–1947* (New York: Columbia University Press, 2003), 250. The resettlement—largely to the Banat—was hardly a success, however, and many would-be settlers wound up back in Bukovina. Erdmann Doane Beynon, "The Eastern Outposts of Magyars," *The Geographical Review,* 31, no. 1 (Jan, 1941): 63–78; esp. pp. 73–74.

70. Cited in Căzan și Rădulescu-Zoner, *Rumänien und der Dreibund,* 115.

71. Cited in Lungu, *Transilvania în raporturile româno-austro-ungare,* 184.

72. Cited in Eugen Brote, *Die rumänische Frage in Siebenbürgen und Ungarn: Eine politische Denkschrift* (Berlin: Puttkammer & Mühlbrecht, 1895), [see Beilage 42].

73. Lungu attributes the internationalization of the Transylvanian Question to the work of the Romamian National Party (in Hungary), founded in 1881, most notably around the fallout of the "Memorandum" affair. Lungu, *Transilvania în raporturile românoaustro-ungare,* 184–85.

74. Brote, *Die rumänische Frage,* v. The pamphlet was written by Brote from "exile" in Bucharest, where he fled, according to his own testimony, to escape the "blind wrath of my political opponents" (ibid., vi).

75. Ibid., 125–29.

76. Jancsó, *A román irredentista mozgalmak,* 239–47. The subventions became all the more controversial when Hungarian authorities discovered in 1896 that the Romanian government had invested some capital in Budapest financial institutions and had used the interest earned to support organizations like the Liga Culturală in Transylvania. Zoltán Szász, ed., *Erdély Története, 1830-tól napjainkig* (Budapest: Akadémiai Kiadó, 1987), 3:1666–67.

77. Szász, *Erdély Története,* 3:1691–95.

78. This did not mean up to the Tisza at all points, but mainly near Szeged. The border agreed upon during these secret talks would have lain between the present border and the Tisza.

79. Szász, *Erdély Története,* 3:1730.

80. Kálmán Benda, *Magyarország történeti kronológiája, 1848–1944* (Budapest: Akadémiai kiadó, 1983), 3:873.

81. György Gaal, "Kolozsvár kétezer esztendeje dátumokban," in *Szabadság Évkönyv 2002* (Kolozsvár [Cluj]: Minerva Művelődési Egyesület, 2001): 196–253, 228. A searing fictional account of their arrival, which documents Hungarian bitterness on the occasion, was written by Transylvanian Hungarian author Dezső Szabó shortly thereafter. Dezső Szabó, "Az öreg asszony karácsonya," *Keletmagyarország*, 1, no. 3 (November 22, 1920): 2–3.

82. Szász, *Erdély Története*, 3:1724–28. For Hungarian reports of atrocities committed by Romanian troops and officials in Transylvania during and after the occupation, see Sándor Tóth, *Erdély 22 éves rabsága* (Budapest: Magyar Géniusz Kiadása, 1941), 62–74.

83. HIWRP, Sabin Manuilă, box 11, folder 6, Iuliu Maniu to Benito Mussolini, December 28, 1940.

84. In a 1942 speech entitled "Why We Fight," Mihai Antonescu noted that, in 1919, Romania, unlike Hungary, had not gone Bolshevik, and instead had fought against Bolshevism. Mihai Antonescu, *Warum wir kämpfen* (Bucharest, 1942), 15, 19. In the fall of 1943, Ion Antonescu also told Hitler that he thought Hungary was ripe for social revolution. Andreas Hillgruber, ed., *Staatsmänner und Diplomaten bei Hitler: Vertrauliche Aufzeichnungen über Unterredungen mit Vertretern des Auslandes, 1942–1944, II. Teil* (Frankfurt am Main: Bernard & Graefe Verlag, 1970), doc. 50, p. 394. For an interwar Hungarian perspective on the effect of the 1919 Romanian occupation of Transylvania and part of Trianon Hungary, see György Lukács, "The Injustices of the Treaty of Trianon," in *Justice for Hungary: Review and Criticism of the Effect of the Treaty of Trianon* (London, Bombay, Calcutta, and Madras: Longmans, Green and Co. Ltd, 1928), 157.

85. The National Convention of Transylvanian Romanians met in Alba Iulia (Gyulafehérvár) on December 1–2, 1918, to draw up a statement declaring "total national freedom" to the cohabitating nationalities. Keith Hitchins, *Rumania, 1866–1947* (Oxford: Clarendon Press, 1994), 287–88.

86. The official number of registered refugees from Romania in Hungary as of 1920 was 154,000, with the total number of individuals born in Romania at about 197,000. István Mócsy, in his book on the subject, suggests that both of these figures are low, as many refugees did not register and the total decline in the Hungarian population of Transylvania from 1910 to 1921 could not be accounted for solely in terms of national conversions. He estimates the total to be around 222,000. István.I. Mócsy, *The Effects of World War I: The Uprooted: Hungarian Refugees, and Their Impact on Hungary's Domestic Politics, 1918–1921* (New York: Columbia University Press, 1983), 11–13.

87. Otto Szabolcs, *Munka nélküli diplomások a Horthy-rendszerben, 1919–1944* (Budapest: Kossuth Könyvkiadó, 1964), 19. In 1922, the government experienced a fiscal crisis and was forced to lay off twelve thousand state officials. The following year another 18 to 20 percent lost their positions. See government correspondence of 23.II.17 and 24.II.4 in Pál Pritz, ed., *Iratok a magyar külügyi szolgálat történetéhez, 1918–1945* (Budapest: Akadémiai Kiadó, 1994), 47, 52, 147–48, 155–62.

88. Despite initial hardship, many refugees did find positions in the state bureaucracy, education, or the professions. As a result, Mócsy concludes, "The refugees made certain that the issue of revision was never lost from the view of the Hungarian public. . . . Using their positions, they were able to exercise an exceptionally strong influence on

the minds of the population; to exercise a virtual veto over Hungary's foreign policy." Mócsy, *Effects of World War I*, 194.

89. Hitchins, *Rumania*, 347. For the wartime Hungarian take on the land reform, see Tóth, *Erdély 22 éves rabsága*, 102–8.

90. It is nonetheless true that, in the wake of the Romanian land reform, Transylvania still had by far the highest percentage (14.6 percent) of large landowners in all Romania. Norman L. Forter and Demeter B. Rostovsky, *The Roumanian Handbook* (New York: Arno Press & New York Times, 1971), 133.

91. C. A. Macartney, *National States and National Minorities* (London: Oxford University Press, H. Milford, 1934), 298.

92. For a more detailed discussion of this phenomenon, see Andrew Behrendt, "Dreams of Geneva, Schemes of Trianon: Hungary and the League of Nations, 1922–1939" (M.A. Thesis, University of Chicago, 2008), 14–20.

93. *Some Opinions, Articles and Reports bearing upon the Treaty of Trianon and the Claims of the Hungarian Nationals with regard to their Lands in Transylvania* (London: Old Bailey Press, [1929?]), 1:3.

94. Vladimir Ortakovski, *Minorities in the Balkans* (Ardsley, N.Y.: Transnational Publishers, 2000), 85–88.

95. Mikó, "A Nemzetek Szövetsége előtt," in *Huszonkét év*, 114–25, esp. 125. See also Frank Koszorus Jr., "The Forgotten Legacy of the League of Nations Minority Protection System," in *Total War and Peacemaking: A Case Study on Trianon*, ed. Bela K. Kiraly, Peter Pastor, and Ivan Sanders et al. (New York: Columbia University Press, 1982), http://www.hungarian-history.hu/lib/tria/tria41.htm (accessed December 12, 2007).

96. *Some Opinions*, 1:27–28.

97. Christoph M. Kimmich, *Germany and the League of Nations* (Chicago and London: University of Chicago Press, 1976), 131–49.

98. Mikó, "A Nemzetek Szövetsége előtt," 114–25, esp. 115–16. Just under a quarter of all the petitions submitted to the League of Nations in the interest of the Hungarian minority in Transylvania during the interwar period were submitted—either officially or unofficially—by the Hungarian state (i.e., eleven out of a total of forty-seven). All of these were submitted prior to 1923. Most of the remainder were submitted by Hungarian minority organizations—political and cultural—in Romania proper (ibid., 303–8). Of the thirty-four submitted by Hungarian minority organizations, only two were ultimately considered by the council. Incidentally, Romania did have a seat on the council from 1926 to 1929, and again from 1935 to 1938, which Hungarian commentators argued made objective consideration of complaints against the Romanian state all the more difficult (ibid., 115).

99. Ortakovski, *Minorities in the Balkans*, 83.

100. See Carole Fink, *Defending the Rights of Others: The Great Powers, the Jews, and International Minority Protection, 1878–1938* (Cambridge: Cambridge University Press, 2004), 232–33.

101. TsDA, MVRI, F176K, op. 4, a.e. 2921, 24–24g.

102. Bethlen, *Magyarország az új Európában*, 13.

103. Article 5, for example, states that "Romanians, regardless of their ethnic origin, language or religion, enjoy freedom of conscience [libertatea conştiinţei], freedom

of education, and freedom of the press." *Constituția din 1923*, 611. Hungarian commentators of the time were especially critical of this formulation. See Zsombor Szász, "Rumanian Constitutionalism," *Hungarian Quarterly* 7, no. 1 (Spring 1941): 32–46, 32.

104. The manner of obscuring the presence of ethnic minorities had a precedent in the Hungarian law of 1868 relating to the "equality of nationalities." The law declared Hungary to be a nation-state (an "indivisible unified Hungarian nation") in which citizens, "regardless of the nationality to which they belong" enjoy equal membership. "1868. évi XLIV. törvénycikk a nemzetiségi egyenjogúság tárgyában," http://www.1000ev.hu/index.php?a=3&param=5366 (accessed November 27, 2007).

105. *Desbatorile Deputaților*, April 27, 1923, cited from MOL, K63, 256. csomó., 1940–27. tétel./7.III, 46.

106. *Constituția din 1923*, 611. Article 3 asserts: "The territory of Romania cannot be colonized with populations of foreign extraction." These articles appeared more or less in the same form in the 1866 Romanian constitution and are based loosely on similar provisions in the 1831 constitution of Belgium, another state that felt it had cause to believe its sovereignty was threatened by its neighbors. See "Constituția României din 1866," *Monitorul Oficial*, no. 142 (June 1, 1866). Such provisions were notably absent from the 1919 German constitution, which in Article 2 made provision for territorial *expansion* to absorb ethnic kin according to the right of self-determination. See *Verfassung des Deutschen Reichs*, August 11, 1919, Art. 2, http://www.verfassungen.de/de/de19–33/verf19-i.htm (accessed November 27, 2007).

107. *Roumania Ten Years After* (Boston, 1928), 7.

108. Richard Coudenhove-Kalergi, founder of the "Pan-Europe" movement, described European states as "twenty-six human beings" living "within a narrow space." Richard Nicolaus Coudenhove-Kalergi, *Pan-Europe* (New York: A. A. Knopf, 1926), 105–6.

109. Representations of this sort have a long history, dating back to Plato, through early modern Absolutism and Thomas Hobbes's *Leviathan* and Jean-Jacques Rousseau's *Social Contract*, according to which the person of the monarch is replaced by the collectivity of the people, which arguably yields the French emphasis on "the nation" as sovereign.

110. Count Albert Apponyi, *The Struggle for a Just Peace* (Budapest: Hungarian National Confederation, 1933), 7–9; from the introduction by Baron Zsigmond Perényi, president of the Hungarian National Alliance.

111. Ibid., 12–13.

112. See Kossuth, *Írások és beszédek*, 56–57, 70, 131, 133, 246, 319, 410. This notion was reinforced in the second half of the nineteenth century by Károly Csemegi, who claimed that "only the greatest extent of civic freedom can be the force that corresponds to the interests of the peoples in question." Károly Csemegi, "A nemzetiségek Magyaroszágon," *Jogállam jog- és államtudományi szemle* (Budapest, 1902): 681–90, 684.

113. Sándor Makkai, "Nem lehet," *Láthatár*, 5 (1937): 49–53.

114. György Ottlik to Lajos Walko, Geneva, May 3, 1928. Pritz, *Iratok a magyar külügyi szolgálat történetéhez*, 241, 365. In 1927, the Hungarian ambassador to Great Britain, Iván Rubido-Zichy, wrote that "the dominant political and power relations do not allow us to achieve [revision of the treaties] at this time" (ibid., 242, 367).

115. During the period leading up to the Anschluß and the Munich Agreement, Hungary's interventions were mostly related to minority rights. See, for example, László Zsigmond, ed., *Diplomáciai iratok Magyarország külpolitikájához, 1936–1945* (hereafter cited as *DIMK*), vol. 2, *A Müncheni egyezmény létrejötte és Magyarország külpolitikája, 1936–1938* (Budapest: Akadémiai kiadó, 1965), 57, 72b, 82, 83, 84, 85a, 90, 156, 159. The shift to territorial claims was facilitated by Germany's successful lobbying on behalf of the German minority in Czechoslovakia, which meant that Hungary could argue that the Hungarian minority in Czechoslovakia should be treated just as well as the German minority (ibid., 206, 212, 283, 315, 341, 351, 359, 363, 374, 385, 405, 408, 416, 417, 443, 444). When Germany also managed to revise the Versailles Treaty with the Munich Agreement on September 29, 1938, this grafting of the Hungarian onto the German cause opened up the possibility for Hungary to make territorial claims as well (ibid., 351, 380, 437, 457, 515).

116. László Zsigmond, ed., *DIMK*, vol. 1, *A Berlin-Róma tengely kialakulása és Ausztria annexiója, 1936–1938* (Budapest: Akadémiai kiadó, 1962), 83.

117. László Zsigmond, ed., *DIMK*, vol. 3, *Magyarország külpolitikája, 1938–1939* (Budapest: Akadémiai kiadó, 1970), 156, 368.

118. Zsigmond, *DIMK*, 1:120, 153, 453; Zsigmond, *DIMK*, 2:11, 147.

119. On Hungary's withdrawal from the League on April 11, 1939, see László Zsigmond, ed., *DIMK*, vol. 4, *Magyarország külpolitikája a II. világháború kitörésének időszakában, 1939–1940* (Budapest: Akadémiai kiadó, 1962), 67, 72.

120. This began with negotiations between the Little Entente and Hungary leading up to the Bled conference on August 23, 1938. The Bled Agreement included mutual nonaggression, a mitigation of the demilitarization clauses of the Treaty of Trianon, and a minority protection protocol. Zsigmond, *DIMK*, 2:294, 298. Shortly thereafter, Romanian statesmen tried to get the Great Powers to include a provision in the Munich Agreement that Germany's annexation of the Sudetenland would be the last territorial adjustment made in the region. Zsigmond, *DIMK*, 3:71.

121. Zsigmond László, ed., *DIMK*, vol. 5, *Magyarország külpolitikája a nyugati hadjárattól a szovjetunió megtámadásáig, 1940–1941* (Budapest: Akadémiai kiadó, 1982), 129, 218, 249, 275, 280, 295, 299, 300, 301, 317, 325.

122. Zsigmond, *DIMK*, 4:529, 695. During this time Romania also sought closer economic and political ties with Germany in hopes of mitigating the revisionist cooperation of Hungary with Germany. These efforts were marked by the signing of the "Treaty for Promoting Economic Relations between the Romanian Kingdom and the German Reich" (or the so-called Wohltat Convention) on March 23, 1939, the "Öl-Waffen-Pakt" [oil-weapons pact] in Bucharest on May 27, 1940, and Romania's own withdrawal from the League of Nations on July 11, 1940, shortly after the Soviet annexation of Bessarabia and Northern Bukovina. Constantin C. Giurescu, ed., *Chronological History of Romania* (Bucharest: Editura Enciclopedică Română, 1972), 319, 321.

123. Mihai Antonescu, *Dacă vrei să câștigi războiul, trebuie să pregătești pacea* (Cluj-Napoca: Muzeul Etnografic al Transilvaniei, 1991), 6, 15, 22.

124. Among these was a three-volume work entitled *The Organization of the Peace and the League of Nations* (1929–1930), and a book entitled *The Crisis of the League of Nations* (1936). See Mihai Antonescu, *Dacă vrei să câștigi războiul*, 4.

125. *Recensământul General al populației Romaniei. Rezultate definitive precedate de o intro-ducțiune cu explicațiuni și date comparative de Leonida Colescu* (Bucharest: Institutul de Arte Grafice Eminescu, 1905), http://uk.geocities.com/imjhsourcebook2/Table01b.htm (accessed October 31, 2007).

126. Cited in Fink, *Defending the Rights of Others*, 10.

127. On Romanian resistance to the minority treaties of 1919, see Ortakovski, *Minorities in the Balkans*, 79–81. The most recent manifestation of this dynamic has come in the form of EU pressure for constitutional reform in Romania to improve the status of minorities (to be discussed in Chapter 6).

128. Florin Constantiniu, ed., *Antonescu-Hitler: corespondență și întîlniri inedite, 1940–1944*, vol. 2 (Bucharest: Gozia Ed., 1991), 96–97, 103–4.

129. Carol Iancu, *Jews in Romania, 1866–1919: From Exclusion to Emancipation* (Boulder, Colo.: East European Monographs; New York: distributed by Columbia University Press, 1996), 43, 55–56, 169.

130. Fink, *Defending the Rights of Others*, 18, 25, 232–33.

131. Cited in R. W. Seton-Watson, *A History of the Roumanians: From Roman Times to the Completion of Unity* (Archon Books, 1963), 351.

132. Fink, *Defending the Rights of Others*, 28–35.

133. Csemegi, "A nemzetiségek Magyarországon," 683–85.

134. *Die Debatte vom 27. Januar 1882 im ungarischen Abgeordnetenhaus über die deutsche Bewegung* (Kronstadt [Brașov]: Johann Gött & Sohn, 1882), 4.

135. Ibid., 5–6.

136. Ibid., 32.

137. Ibid., 8–9.

138. Kimmich, *Germany and the League of Nations*, 131–49, esp. 138.

139. Ibid. See also István Bethlen, *The Treaty of Trianon and European Peace* (New York: Longmans, Green and Co., 1934).

140. Zsigmond, *DIMK*, 1:120, 153, 453; Zsigmond, *DIMK*, 2:11, 147.

141. Zsigmond, *DIMK*, 5:92.

142. Ibid., 1:156, 264, 313, 427.

143. Several such cases from the 1930s—relating to efforts on the part of the Germans to resist magyarization by changing their magyarized names back to German ones—are cited in Viktor Karády and István Kozma, eds., *Név és nemzet: Családnév-változtatás, névpolitika és nemzetiségi erőviszonyok Magyarországon a feudalizmustól a kommunizmusig* (Budapest: Osiris Kiadó, 2002), 230–31.

144. Mark Pittaway, "Confronting War and Facing Defeat in the Austrian-Hungarian Borderland, 1938–1945," paper delivered at the American Association for the Advancement of Slavic Studies (AAASS) 39th National Convention, November 15–18, 2007, New Orleans. Cited with permission of the author.

145. Grigore Gafencu, *Last Days of Europe: A Diplomatic Journey in 1939* (New Haven, Conn.: Yale University Press, 1948), 68–69.

146. Zsigmond, *DIMK*, 4:170.

147. For Trianon Hungary in 1930, see C. A. Macartney, *October Fifteenth: A History of Modern Hungary, 1929–1945* (Edinburgh: Edinburgh University Press, 1956), 1:70. For Transylvania, including the still-Romanian part of the Banat and Partium: according

to the census of 1910, there were 565,000 Germans living in Transylvania. The 1920 and 1930 censuses gave this number at 539,000 and 544,000 respectively. See John F. Cadzow, Andrew Ludanyi, and Louis J. Elteto, eds., *Transylvania: The Roots of Ethnic Conflict* (Kent, Ohio: Kent State University Press, 1983), 305.

148. Macartney, *October Fifteenth,* 2:153n. Note that only 550,000 individuals declared themselves to be of German nationality, most of whom were from Trianon Hungary (as opposed to the reannexed territories).

149. *The Trial of German Major War Criminals Sitting at Nuremberg, Germany, February 2 to February 13, 1946,* vol. 6 (London: His Majesty's Stationery Office, 1946), 286. In December 1942, Romanian diplomat Raoul Bossy also feared that Germany might have its own plans for Transylvania, specifically the creation of a "Danube province destined to enter into the great German family." ANIC, Arhivele Ministerului de Externe, Fond 71/Germania, vol. 90, f. 391. German plans to assume control were a perennial concern. See Jean Ancel, ed., *Documents Concerning the Fate of Romanian Jewry during the Holocaust,* vol. 9 (New York: Beate Klarsfeld Foundation, [1986]), docs. 125, 153, 172, 207, pp. 339–40, 413, 441, 559–60.

150. For the text of the Second Vienna Arbitration, see *DGFP,* series D, vol. 10 (Washington, D.C.: U.S. Government Printing Office, 1953), doc. 413, 584–86. Romania also had to sign a separate document relating to the German minority in Romania, but it was considerably less rigorous and detailed than the Hungarian one.

151. Magda Ádám, Gyula Juhász, and Lajos Kerekes, eds., *Magyarország és a második világháború: titkos diplomáciai okmányok a háború előzményeihez és történetéhez* (Budapest: Kossuth Könyvkiadó, 1959), 295–97, 304.

152. See Karl M. Reinerth, "Zu den innenpolitischen Auseinandersetzungen unter den Deutschen in Rumänien zwischen den beiden Weltkriegen," in *Siebenbürgen zwischen den beiden Weltkriegen,* ed. Walter König (Cologne, Weimar, Vienna: Böhlau Verlag, 1994), 149–67.

153. Béla Bethlen, *Észak-Erdély kormánybiztosa voltam* (Budapest: Zrínyi katonai kiadó, 1989), 31–32, 38–40. Bethlen was at the time lord lieutenant of Szolnok-Doboka and Beszterce-Naszód counties, the latter having a significant German-speaking population.

154. Institutul central de statistică, *Anuarul statistic al României 1937 şi 1938,* 58–61 (cited in Livezeanu, *Cultural Politics,* 10).

155. In the county of Cernăuţi the number of German-language schools dropped from seven to two from 1918 to 1922, with the number of classes dropping from thirty-one to seven. Livezeanu, *Cultural Politics,* 64. For a more general treatment of interwar romanianization practices, see Mariana Hausleitner, *Die Rumänisierung der Bukowina: die Durchsetzung des nationalstaatlichen Anspruchs Grossrumäniens 1918–1944* (Munich: R. Oldenbourg, 2001).

156. Othmar Kolar, *Rumänien und seine nationalen Minderheiten, 1918 bis heute* (Vienna, Cologne, Weimar: Böhlau Verlag, 1997), 80. The party won nineteen deputy and seven senatorial seats in 1919, and after 1927 voted in a minority block with the Hungarian party.

157. Cited in Kolar, *Rumänien und seine nationalen Minderheiten,* 181–82.

158. In arguing the case for Hungarian control over Transylvania at the 1920 peace

conference, the Hungarian delegation relied heavily on statements of support and petitions in favor of continued Hungarian rule submitted by Transylvanian Saxon minority
organizations and individuals. See Ádám and Cholnoky, *Trianon*, 201–12.

159. Stefan Sienerth, "Kunstlerisches Selbstverständnis und Zugehörigkeitsdilem-
ma deutscher Schriftsteller in Rumänien während der Zwischenkriegszeit," in *Deutsche
Regionalliteraturen in Rumänien, 1918–1944: Positionsbestimmungen, Forschungswege, Fallstudien,*
ed. Peter Motzan and Stefan Sienerth (Munich: Verlag Südostdeutsches Kulturwerk,
1997), 96–99; Hans Beyer, "Geschichtsbewusstsein und Nationalprogramm der sieben-
bürger Sachsen," in *Studien zur Geschichtsschreibung im 19. und 20. Jahrhundert,* ed. Paul
Philippi (Cologne and Graz, Austria: Böhlau, 1967), 103–4; Wolfgang Knopp, *Multikul-
turelle Wegzeichen in Ostmitteleuropa* (Pfaffenweiler: Centaurus, 1995), 41; Johann Böhm,
Die Deutschen in Rumänien und die Weimarer Republik, 1919–1933 (Ippesheim: Verlag des
Arbeitskreises für Geschichte und Kultur der deutschen Siedlungsgebiete im Südosten
Europas e.V., 1993), 240–41; Scurtu, *Minoritățile naționale,* 206.

160. See Weitz, "From the Vienna to the Paris System."

161. See Gyula Juhász, *Uralkodó eszmék Magyarországon, 1939–1944* (Budapest: Kossuth Könyvkiadó, 1983), 238. István Bethlen, *Hungarian Politics During World War Two:
Treatise and Indictment,* ed. Ilona Bolza (Munich: Rudolf Tofenik, 1985), 7. Indeed, not
only Hungary and Romania were impressed by Masaryk's success. In 1922, British historian R. W. Seton-Watson called Masaryk "the leader of a new political school and of
new diplomatic methods" who had "beat the Ballplatz and the Wilhelmstrasse at their
own game, and set us all that measured ideal . . . upon which alone the new Europe
and the new Society of Nations can build." R. W. Seton-Waton, "The Historian as a
Political Force in Central Europe," an inaugural lecture delivered on November 22, 1922
(London: The School of Slavonic Studies in the University of London, King's College,
1922), 33. For an excellent discussion of Czechoslovak leaders' efforts to propagate
their vision of Czechoslovak statehood abroad, see Andrea Orzoff, *Battle for the Castle:
Nationalist Myth and Propaganda in Czechoslovakia, 1914–1948* (New York: Oxford University Press, forthcoming 2009). Cited with permission of the author.

162. On Czech leaders' presumed influence on Great Britain in particular, see
Anton Czettler, *Pál Graf Teleki und die Außenpolitik Ungarns, 1939–1941* (Munich: Verlag
Ungarisches Institut, 1996), 191. This awe at the Czech propaganda had a variety of
effects. When seeking to jump out of the Axis alliance in November 1943, Romanian
diplomat Raoul Bossy proposed the coordination of Czechoslovak and Romanian
propaganda relating to slights against their respective minorities in neighboring states
on the grounds it would make Romania look better. HIWRP, Dimitri G. Popescu, box
I, folder entitled "Berna," pp. 11–12.

163. Sherman David Spector, *Romania at the Paris Peace Conference: A Study of the Diplomacy of Ioan I. C. Brătianu* (Iași: Center for Romanian Studies and Romanian Cultural
Foundation, 1995), 54; Charles King, "Queen of the Highlanders, Edith Durham in
'the land of the living past,'" *Times Literary Supplement* (August 4, 2000): 13–14, http://
knigite.abv.bg/en/ed/e_durham.html (accessed January 30, 2007). The anti-Hungarian stance of the journal is evident from a number of articles. See, for example, "Magyar
Ideals," in *The New Europe,* vol. 4, August 23, 1917 (London: Constable and Company),
189–91.

164. See R. W. Seton-Watson, *Treaty Revision and the Hungarian Frontiers* (London: Eyre and Spottiswoode Publishers Ltd., 1934); Seton-Watson, *Historian as a Political Force*; R. W. Seton-Watson, review of *The Tragedy of Trianon: Hungary's Appeal to Humanity*, by Sir Robert Donald, *Journal of the Royal Institute of International Affairs* 7, no. 4 (July 1928): 271–75.

165. ANIC, Fond Preşedenţia Consiliului de Miniştri Cabinetul Militar Ion Antonescu, Dosar 194/1940, Factura de subvenţii pentru Seton-Watson, f. 100, 102, 102v. I am indebted to Vladimir Solonari for sharing this document with me.

166. On Macartney's involvement in Hungary, see Miklós Lojkó, "C. A. Macartney and Central Europe," *European Review of History* 6, no. 1 (Spring 1999): 37–57. On Rothermere and the Hungarian Revisionist League, see Miklós Zeidler, "A Magyar Revíziós Liga: Trianontól Rothermere-ig," *Századok*, vol. 131, no. 2 (1997): 303–52. See also Sir Robert Gower, *The Hungarian Minorities in the Succession States* (London: Grant Richards, 1937); Sir Robert Donald, *The Tragedy of Trianon: Hungary's Appeal to Humanity* (London: Thornton Butterworth, 1928); Tibor Frank, *Ethnicity, Propaganda, Myth-Making: Studies on Hungarian Connections to Britain and America, 1848–1945* (Budapest: Akadémiai Kiadó, 1999): 276–95, see esp. 276–79. Other "Magyarophiles" included French politicians Anatole de Monzie, Pierre Cot, and François de Tessan. See HIWRP, Sabin Manuilă, box 11, folder 6, Iuliu Maniu to Benito Mussolini, December 28, 1940, p. 8. For academic and cultural organizations, institutions, and figures suspected of disseminating Hungarian propaganda, see Cornel Grad, *Al doilea arbitraj de la Viena* (Iaşi: Institutul European, 1998), 170–71.

167. To name just a few, for Hungary: The "Publications of the Hungarian Frontier Readjustment League" based in Budapest included several volumes of short works, which included *The Hungarian Minorities in the Succession States*, vol. 1 (Budapest: Victor Hornyánszky Co. Ltd., 1927); *Statistical Data of the Homogeneous Hungarian and German Enclaves in the Succession States*, vol. 2 (Budapest: Victor Hornyánszky Co. Ltd., 1927); *The Letter of Envoy and the Delimitation Commissions*, vol. 3 (Budapest: Victor Hornyánszky Co. Ltd., 1927); Eugene Horváth, *Transylvania and the History of the Roumanians: A Reply to R. W. Seton-Watson*, vol. 9 (Budapest: Sárkány Printing Co. Ltd., 1935). Other publications include Francis Deák, *The Hungarian-Rumanian Land Dispute: A Study of Hungarian Property Rights in Transylvania under the Treaty of Trianon* (New York: Columbia University Press, 1928); *Some Opinions*, vols. 1–2; István Bethlen, *Treaty of Trianon*; Gower, *Hungarian Minorities*; Pál Teleki and Andrew Rónai, *The Different Types of Ethnic Mixture of Population* (Budapest: Athenaeum, 1937); András Rónai, *Population Conditions in Transylvania* (Budapest: Stephaneum, 1939). For Romania: Jonesco, *Policy of National Instinct*; Sylvius Dragomir, *The Ethnical Minorities in Transylvania* (Geneva: Sonor Printing Co., 1927); *Agrarian Reform in Roumania and the Case of the Hungarian Optants in Transylvania before the League of Nations* (Paris: Imprimerie du Palais, 1927); Podea, *Transylvania*; Cornelius I. Codarcea, *Le litige roumano-hongrois* (Bucharest: Editura Universul, 1937), republished in Munich in 1973; Sabin Manuilă, *Étude ethnographique sur la population de la Roumanie/Ethnographical Survey of the Population of Romania* (Bucharest: Imprimeriile Statului, Imprimeriile Naţională, 1938).

168. To name just a few, for Romania: Constantin Sassu, *Romanians and Hungarians, Historical Premises* (Bucharest: "Cugetarea," Georgescu-Delafras, 1940); G. I. Bra-

tianu, *Die Rumänische Frage* (Bucharest: Die Dacia-Bücher/Ediţiile Dacia, 1940), also published in Italian the same year; G. I. Bratianu, *Rumänien und Ungarn: demographische und wirtschaftliche Betrachtungen* (Bucharest: Die Dacia-Bücher, 1940), also published in French and Italian the same year; *Madjarische Ausschreitungen und Greueltaten in dem an Ungarn abgetretenen Gebiet Nordsiebenbürgens* (Bucharest: Die Dacia-Bücher, 1940), also published in French and Italian the same year; Ion Moga, *Siebenbürgen in dem Wirtschafts-organismus des rumänischen Bodens* (Bucharest: Die Dacia-Bücher, 1940), also published in Italian in 1941; Marcu Beza, *Bessarabia and Transylvania: An Explanation* (London: Speedee Press Services, 1940); G. I. Bratianu, *Theorie und Wirklichkeit der ungarischen Geschichte: Bemerkungen zu einigen neueren Arbeiten* (Bucharest: Die Dacia-Bücher, 1940), also published in French and Italian the same year; Tiberiu Morariu, *Entwicklung der Bevölkerungsdichtigkeit Siebenbürgens während der Jahre 1840–1930* (Bucharest: Die Dacia-Bücher, 1940); Sabin Opreanu, *La Transilvania nee'unità naturale della Romania* (Bucharest, 1940); G. I. Bratianu, *Zweite Denkschrift über die rumänische Frage 1940: Aufteilung Rumäniens oder Gebiets- und Bevölkerungsclearing im Südosten Europas* (Bucharest: Die Dacia-Bücher, 1941), also published in French and Italian the same year; Viktor Orendi-Hommenau, *Ihr wahres Gesicht: Ein rot-weiss-grüner Kulturfilm aus Madjarien* (Bucharest: Die Dacia-Bücher, 1941); Zenobius Pâclişanu, *Der Ausrottungskampf Ungarns gegen seine nationalen Minderheiten* (Bucharest: Die Dacia-Bücher, 1941), also published in Italian the same year; Silviu Dragomir, *Die siebenbürgische Frage* (Bucharest: Die Dacia-Bücher, 1941); Zenobius Pâclişanu, *Deutsche und Magyaren: Der Entnationalisierungskampf gegen die Sathmarer Schwaben* (Bucharest: Die Dacia-Bücher, 1941); Laurian Someşan, *Alter und Entwicklung der rumänischen Landwritschaft in Siebenbürgen* (Bucharest: Die Dacia-Bücher, 1941); C. Vâlsan, *Siebenbürgen im einheitlichen Rahmen des rumänischen Staates und Bodens* (Bucharest: Die Dacia-Bücher, 1941), also published in Italian the same year; I. Lupaş, *Siebenbürgen, das Herz des rumänischen Lebensraumes* (Bucharest: Die Dacia-Bücher, 1941), also published in French in 1942; Sabin Manuilă, *Die bevölkerungspolitischen Folgen der Teilung Siebenbürgens* (Bucharest: Die Dacia-Bücher, 1941); G. Vâlsan, *Die Karpathen, Wiege des Rumänentums* (Bucharest: Die Dacia-Bücher, 1941), also published in French in 1942; G. I. Bratianu, *Die geschichtliche Mission Ungarns* (Bucharest: Die Dacia-Bücher, 1941), also published in Italian in 1942; Transylvanus, *Ordeal in Transylvania* (Oxford: D. D. Dimancescu, 1942); Sabin Manuilă, *Antwort an Herrn Tibor Eckhardt* (Bucharest: Die Dacia-Bücher, 1941); Viktor Orendi-Hommenau, *Madjarisches, Allzumadjarisches, 2. Auflage* (Bucharest: Die Dacia-Bücher, 1941); Zenobius Pâclişanu, *Was heißt ungarische Nationalität?* (Bucharest: Die Dacia-Bücher, 1941); Josef Mehedinţi, *Was ist Siebenbürgen?* (Bucharest: Die Dacia-Bücher, 1941), also published in French in 1943; G. I. Bratianu, *Ein Rätsel und ein Wunder der Geschichte: Das rumänische Volk* (Bucharest: Die Dacia-Bücher/Ediţiile Dacia, 1942), originally published in 1937 in French, also published in Italian in 1942; Zenobius Pâclişanu, *Die magyarische Ordnung in Mitteleuropa* (Bucharest: Die Dacia-Bücher, 1942), also published in French the same year; Zenobius Pâclişanu, *L'art et la manière de faire des Hongrois* (Bucharest: Dacia, 1942); Tiberiu Morariu, *Die Maramureş: Ein rumänisches Kerngebiet* (Bucharest: Die Dacia-Bücher, 1942); Pavel Pavel, *Transylvania and Danubian Peace* (London: New Europe Publishing Company, 1943); R. W. Seton-Watson, *Transylvania: A Key Problem* (Oxford: Printed for the author by the Classic Press, 1943); I. Lupaş, *Zur Geschichte der Rumänen: Aufsätze und Vorträge* (Sibiu:

Hauptverlag der Deutschen Volksgruppe in Rumänien, 1943); *La Roumanie: atlas ethnographique/Roumania: Ethnographic Atlas* (Bucharest: Institutul de arte grafice, 194[?]); Victor E. Mitchievici, *Rumänien 1943* (Bucharest: Druckerei "Marvan" S.A.R., [1944?]); Petre Poruțiu, *La Transylvanie et les conséquences économiques de l'acte de Vienne 30 août 1940* (Bucharest: Monitorul Oficial, Imprimerie naționale, 1944). For Hungary: *Siebenbürgen* (Budapest: Ungarische Historische Gesellschaft, 1940); Institute of Political Sciences, *Ethnographical Map of Hungary in the Year 1910* (Budapest: Institute of Political Sciences, 1940); András Rónai, *Hungarians in Transylvania* (Budapest: Royal Hungarian University Press, 1940), also published in German the same year; Andreas Fall, *Ungarns Recht auf Siebenbürgen* (Budapest, 1940); Péter Vida, *How Hungarian Transylvania Became Romanian Transylvania* (Budapest: Royal Hungarian University Press, 1940), published in French the same year; László Makkai, *Transylvanian Towns* (Budapest: Officina Press, 1940), also published in Italian and French the same year; Georg v. Olah, *Sturm gegen den zweiten wiener Schiedsspruch* (Budapest, 1941); László Gáldi, *Zur Frage der rumänischen Kerngebiets in Siebenbürgen* (Budapest: Sárkány-Buchdruckerei, 1942); Jenő Horváth, *Die Geschichte Siebenbürgens* (Budapest: Danubia, 1943); Elemér Mályusz, *Siebenbürgen und seine Völker* (Budapest: Danubia, 1943); Endre Bajcsy Zsilinszky, *Transylvania, Past and Future* (Geneva: Kundig, 1944); *A Companion to Hungarian Studies* (Budapest: Society of the Hungarian Quarterly, 1943); Ernest Flachbart, *Histoire des minorités nationales en Hongrie* (Paris: Clermont-Ferrand, 1944); *Ungarn und die Nachbarvölker* (Budapest: Danubia Verlag, 194[?]).

169. This is evident from their inside covers, which regularly include inscriptions such as "Gift of the Roumanian Legation" or donated by the "Romanian Pavilion" at the World's Fair or by the "Hungarian Library Board" (the Romanian administration counted this as a Hungarian propaganda organization; see Grad, *Al doilea arbitraj de la Viena*, 170.) In the case of both Hungarian and Romanian publications, many were also written by statesmen of those countries (István Bethlen, Pál Teleki, Sabin Manuilă, Nicolae Iorga). Also, in 1942, Mihai Antonescu was explicit about the state's role in creating and distributing international propaganda. He spoke of the role of the Romanian legations abroad in distribution of brochures and other propaganda texts, and also of the role played by the historians of the Romanian institutes of history, who were to concern themselves above all with propaganda. Mihai Antonescu, *Dacă vrei să câștigi războiul*, 23–24, 30–31.

170. In November 1942, a Hungarian diplomat in Bucharest wrote to Pál Balla, council to the foreign minister, about the importance of maps in international propaganda relating to the Transylvanian Question. MOL, K63, 257. csomó., 1940–27. tétel./7./E., Román-magyar viszony—Erdély, iktatlan, II. rész., 449–50. Mihai Antonescu also felt that propaganda brochures should contain plenty of visuals, including maps and diagrams, emphasizing their "powers of evocation." Mihai Antonescu, *Dacă vrei să câștigi războiul*, 24.

171. *Stenogramele*, vol. 1, doc. 3, 70.

172. *La Roumanie: atlas ethnographique*, [1].

173. Ibid., [1], [4].

174. Ádám and Cholnoky, *Trianon*, 117–18.

175. Due to the prominence of the red representing Hungarians, the map became

known as the "carte rouge" in peace conference circles. Anikó Kovács-Bertrand, *Der ungarische Revisionismus nach dem Ersten Weltkrieg: Der publizistische Kampf gegen den Friedensvertrag von Trianon* (Munich: R. Oldenbourg Verlag, 1997), 67.

176. Ádám and Cholnoky, *Trianon,* 118–19.

177. Teleki and Rónai, *Different Types of Ethnic Mixture,* 6–7. See also p. 10 on language frontiers.

178. Manuilă, *Étude ethnographique,* xxxvii.

179. Ibid., xxvi.

180. *Siebenbürgen,* map inset 277. A German reviewer wrote a favorable review of the work in a 1941 periodical, noting the "political necessity" that motivated its publication. Herbert Schönebaum, "Siebenbürgen," in *Ungarische Jahrbücher* 21, nos. 1–3 (November 1941): 239–44, 240. Ion Antonescu expressed the paranoid opinion that "these maps appeared on the streets of Vienna two hours after the arbitration came down, complete with new frontiers and everything, meaning that the arbitration was decided in advance." "Şedinţa consiliului de cabinet din 3 octombrie 1940," in *Stenogramele,* vol. 1, doc. 7, 134–35.

181. Ibid. Antonescu also expressed his indignation about the map to the Slovak ambassador to Romania on November 30, 1940. SNA, MZV, K. 192, 4334/1940.

182. *La Roumanie: atlas ethnographique,* [1], [4]. Despite this accusation of foul play, a similar tactic, complete with red circles—only this time with red representing Romanians, and always positioned at the top of the pie charts—was employed by Romanian demographer Sabin Manuilă in the 1938 *Ethnographical Survey of the Population of Romania.* Manuilă, *Étude ethnographique,* xxxv. The copy of that publication in the Cornell Libraries is inscribed with the words "Gift of the Romanian Pavilion, World's Fair, 10 Dec. 1940."

183. István Bethlen, *Treaty of Trianon,* xix. Bethlen initially represented Hungary at the peace negotiations.

184. Despite the delegation's assertion that demographic considerations should form the basis of the claims of states to territory (essentially an affirmation of national self-determination), they often argued at the same time that the Hungarians were much more cultured than the other peoples living in Hungary and possessed the unique capacity to run the state. Ádám and Cholnoky, *Trianon,* 398.

185. István Bethlen, *Treaty of Trianon,* 127.

186. Ibid., 128.

187. Teleki and Rónai, *Different Types of Ethnic Mixture,* 3–4. Hungarian ethnographer Béla Gunda argued in a 1943 publication that "the Slav and Romanian ethnographic elements are static elements. . . . The Magyar elements are dynamic . . . transforming men and society and culture alike." Béla Gunda, "Ethnography," in *A Companion to Hungarian Studies* (Budapest: Society of the Hungarian Quarterly, 1943), 285–304, 304.

188. "Az Erdélyi értekezlet jegyzőkönyve," MOL, K28, 267. csomó., 45. In this same discussion, Teleki mounted an assault against the notion of a "scattered" (*szórvány*) Hungarian population and complained about how efforts to gather nationality statistics forced people to choose, even when doing so made no sense (ibid., 46).

189. ANIC, Fond Ministerul de Interne, Dosar 438/1941, f. 9v. On October 29, 1942,

Lieutenant Colonel Virgil Bichiceanu, Romanian delegate to the German-Italian Officers' Commission, commented on the need for "a plan" that should include "propaganda and diplomatic activity undertaken with skill and perseverance." ANIC, Fond Delegatul Marelui Stat Major pe lângă Comisie de Ofiţeri Italo-Germană, Dosar 34/1942, f. 55.

190. HDA, 227 (Ministarstvo Vanskih Poslova NDH Zagreb, 1941–1945), kut. 1, Vrlo tajni spisi MVP-a (V.T.), 1941, br. 16–230, V.T. 224/1941.

191. MOL, K63, 257. csomó., 1940–27. tétel./7./E., Román-magyar viszony—Erdély, iktatlan, II. rész., 449–50.

192. Cited in Juhász, *Uralkodó eszmék*, 237. Balogh was the editor of the *Hungarian Quarterly* and *Nouvelle Revue de Hongrie*.

193. SNA, MZV, K. 192, 2563/1940.

194. "Şedinţa consiliului de cabinet," in *Stenogramele*, vol. 1, doc. 8, 160–61.

195. Mihai Antonescu, *Dacă vrei să câştigi războiul*, 6, 35, 40, 50–53. This view had been expressed earlier, in a letter dated November 20, 1940, from Iuliu Maniu to Ion Antonescu, in which Maniu argued that "the losses we have suffered are due in large part to the insistent propaganda of our neighbors and the lack of sufficiently strong reactions on our part." HIWRP, Sabin Manuilă, box 11, folder 6, "20 Novembrie 1940, Domnule General." On the actual international propaganda campaign of Romania during and after World War I, see Spector, *Romania at the Paris Peace Conference*, 51–52.

196. MOL, K28, 55. csomó., 120. tétel. 1941-O-22808, 58v.

197. Stephen D. Kertesz, *Between Russia and the West: Hungary and the Illusions of Peacemaking, 1945–1947* (Hamilton, Ontario: Hunyadi M. Mk., 1992), 75.

198. USHMMA, RG-30.003, Reel 13, Collection of Hungarian political and military records, 1909–45, fr. 1031–7.

199. USHMMA, RG-25.006M, Fiche 37, Selected Records from the Romanian Ministry of Foreign Affairs Archives, Fond SUA, vol. 40, 158, 213.

200. Anton Golopenţia, "Preocupări biopolitice ungureşti," in *Opere Complete*, vol. 2, *Statistică, demografie şi geopolitică* ([Bucharest]: Editura Enciclopedică, 2002), 580. In the spring of 1944, the Romanian government also set up a commission to produce propaganda brochures relating to the ills of Hungarian rule in Northern Transylvania in French, English, and German, "which can be used whenever needed, at the discretion of the government and independently of the brochure itself." HIWRP, box 2, folder titled "Romania-Foreign Relations, 1919–1946."

201. See "Cartierul general unguresc din Montreux," 14 Octombrie 1943, in HIWRP, Dimitri G. Popescu, box 1, folder titled "Benes, Eduard"; Raul V. Bossy, *Recollections of a Romanian Diplomat, 1918–1969: Diaries and Memoirs of Raoul V. Bossy*, vols. 1–2 (Stanford, Calif.: Hoover Institution Press, 2003); György Barcza, *Diplomata emlékeim, 1911–1945*, vol. 2 (Budapest: Európa Kiadó, 1994).

202. *New Europe: Monthly Review of International Affairs* 1 (1941): 1.

203. John Wheeler-Bennett, "Britain and the Future," *New Europe* (October 1941): 278. See also Felix Gross, "Europe's Ideological Crisis," *New Europe* (July 1941): 202.

204. Louis Adamic, *Two-Way Passage* (New York: Harper & Brothers, 1941), 257; second half of quote cited from "Books," *New Europe* (November 1941): 336.

205. SNA, MZV, K. 192, 8.374/1942.

206. J. Noakes and G. Pridham, *Nazism, 1919–1945: Foreign Policy, War and Racial*

Extermination, A Documentary Reader, vol. 3 (Exeter, UK: Exeter University Publications, 1988), doc. 631, 900. Special thanks to Mark Mazower for bringing this source to my attention.

207. SNA, MZV, K. 192, 8.374/1942, 8.632/1942, 8.674/1942. In March 1943, Ribbentrop presented the Führer with a plan for a "European Union of States," but the latter was not interested in clarifying his position on the New European Order. *ADAP,* E, V., doc. 229, 440.

208. Géza Rubletszky, "Magyarország az 'új Európá'-ban," *Magyar Szemle* 41, no. 2 (168) (August 1941): 106–11, 106.

209. Mark Mazower, *Dark Continent: Europe's Twentieth Century* (New York: A. A. Knopf, distributed by Random House, 1999), 182–83.

210. MOL, K28, 213. csomó., 467. tétel. (German-Italian Commission), 1942-O-23890, 55 (289). Béla Bethlen was the lord lieutenant in question.

211. MOL, K63, 253. csomó., 1940–27. tétel./4., 79. MOL, K63, 257. csomó., 1940–27. tétel./7./E., Román-magyar viszony—Erdély, iktatlan, II. rész., 98.

212. MOL, K63, 257. csomó., 1940–27. tétel./7./E., Román-magyar viszony—Erdély, iktatlan, II. rész., 101.

213. See, for example, the booklet of Olah, *Sturm gegen den zweiten wiener Schiedsspruch.* MOL, K63, 257. csomó., 1940–27. tétel./7./E., Román-magyar viszony—Erdély, iktatlan, II. rész., 182.

214. In a communiqué to Mihai Antonescu from December 12, 1942, Romanian diplomat Raoul Bossy lamented that "although the details of the problem are all known," the problem of Transylvania was taken much more lightly than other issues. ANIC, Arhivele Ministerului de Externe, Fond 71/Germania, vol. 90, f. 387.

215. Ádám and Cholnoky, *Trianon,* 116.

216. Pál Teleki, *Válogatott politikai írások és beszédek* (Budapest: Osiris kiadó, 2000), 283.

217. John O. Crane, *The Little Entente* (New York: The Macmillan Company, 1931), 188.

218. In László Ravasz, "Erdély," *Magyar Szemle* 39, kötet 4 (158) szám (October 1940): 225–30, 225.

219. See "Reliefkarte von Ungarn" and "Bild der Pflanzendecke Ungarns," in *Siebenbürgen,* *8, *10. For "natural boundaries" arguments presented at the peace conference in 1920, see Ádám and Cholnoky, *Trianon,* 394. See also Lukács, "Injustices of the Treaty of Trianon," 130; Gyula Prinz, "Geography," in *A Companion to Hungarian Studies,* 271.

220. Sabin Opreanu, *Siebenbürgen: Eine naturgegebene Ergänzung des rumänischen Lebensraumes* (Bucharest, 1940). See also Laurian Somesan, *Die Theissebene: Eine natürliche Grenze zwischen Rumänen und Magyaren, geographische und geopolitische Studie* (Sibiu: Krafft & Drotleff, 1939).

221. Pavel, *Transylvania and Danubian Peace,* 13.

222. Beza, *Bessarabia and Transylvania,* 6.

223. Ibid., 9, 11, 12.

224. László Makkai and András Mócsy, eds., *Erdély története, a kezdetektől 1606-ig.,* vol. 1 (Budapest: Akadémiai Kiadó, 1987), 111–13, 203. See also Domokos Kosáry, "Az oláh bevándorlás," *Magyar Szemle* 39, no. 4 (158) (October 1940): 246–53, 253.

225. See Mehedinţi, *Was ist Siebenbürgen?*; Béla Gunda, "Ethnographisches aus Siebenbürgen," *Ungarische Jahrbücher* 23, nos. 1–3 (October 1943): 322–27.

226. For the nineteenth-century origins and debates of this convergence, see David N. Livingstone, *The Geographical Tradition: Episodes in the History of a Contested Enterprise* (Oxford and Cambridge: Blackwell, 1993), 177–215.

227. In the case of the prefect who wrote to the German-Italian Commission, for example, the author wanted the commission to take the historical role of the Hungarians as buffers into consideration, as doing so would mitigate any reported slights against the Romanian minority in Northern Transylvania. MOL, K28, 213. csomó., 467. tétel. (German-Italian Commission), 1942-O-23890, 55 (289).

228. MOL, K63, 256. csomó., 1940–27. tétel./7.III, 444.

229. *Ellenzék*, August 19, 1941, 1.

230. Ibid.

231. Golopenţia, "Preocupări biopolitice ungureşti," 591.

232. România Mare (radio), 24. iun. 1942, cited from MOL, K63, 257. csomó., 1940–27. tétel./7./E., Román-magyar viszony—Erdély, iktatlan, II. rész, 36. It should be noted that referring to Hungarians as "Asiatic" was hardly a novel practice among Romanian nationalists. In 1870, Romanian poet Mihai Eminescu refered to them as "barbarian" and "asiatic." Eminescu, "Transilvania sub stăpânire dualistă," 94–96. There was a strain of Hungarian right-wing radicalism that celebrated the "Asian/Turkic" origins of the Hungarians, known as "Turanism." Although its founder was a Hungarian Jewish orientalist (Ármin Vámbéry) active mostly during the late nineteenth century, Turanism enjoyed a renaissance in Hungary following Trianon. See Janos, *Politics of Backwardness*, 274; Juhász, *Uralkodó eszmék*, 178–89.

233. *Ţară*, July 18, 1942, cited from MOL, K63, 257. csomó., 1940–27. tétel./7./E., Román-magyar viszony—Erdély, iktatlan, II. rész, 45. The reference to "Asia's discharged magnates" was one the Hungarian foreign ministry read as referring to the Hungarians and took as a propaganda slight on the part of the Romanian press.

234. Cited in Juhász, *Uralkodó eszmék*, 200.

235. MOL, K63, 258. csomó., 1940–27. tétel./7./T.2.d., 205.

236. MOL, K63, 258. csomó., 1940–27. tétel./7./T.2.d., 250–51. During the interwar period, Hungarian propagandists argued that the principle of national self-determination had been imperfectly applied after World War I. "Why was the application of this principle refused to Hungarians alone, when it was applied to the other nationalities?" wrote one Hungarian member of parliament in 1928. Lukács, "Injustices of the Treaty of Trianon," 134.

237. HIWRP, Sabin Manuilă, box 16, folder 5, "România şi revizuirea tratatelor, discursurile D-lor Iuliu Maniu şi C. I. Brătianu în şedinţa adunărei Deputaţilor din 4 Aprilie 1934, Răspunsul d-lui N. Titulescu Ministrul Afacerilor Străine, Monitorul Oficial şi Imprimeriile Statului, Imprimeria Naţională, Bucureşti," p. 5.

238. Mihai Antonescu, *Dacă vrei să câştigi războiul*, 33.

239. MOL, K63, 254. csomó., 27. tétel. 1940–27/7/Ek/I/2/e, 43.

240. Imre Mikó, "Erdély és a nemzetiségi kérdés," in *Erdélyi kérdések—magyar kérdések* (Kolozsvár: Minerva, 1943), 86.

241. MOL, K63, 259. csomó., 1940–27. tétel./7./8., 556.

242. From Olah, *Sturm gegen den zweiten wiener Schiedesspruch*, 1.

243. HIWRP, Sabin Manuilă, box 11, folder 6, Iuliu Maniu to Benito Mussolini, December 28, 1940.

244. România Mare (radio), June 11, 1942, cited from MOL, K63, 257. csomó., 1940–27. tétel./7./E., Román-magyar viszony—Erdély, iktatlan, II. rész., 31.

245. România Mare (radio), July 8, 1942, cited from MOL, K63, 257. csomó., 1940–27. tétel./7./E., Román-magyar viszony—Erdély, iktatlan, II. rész., 41.

246. *Ţară*, July 25, 1942, cited from MOL, K63, 257. csomó., 1940–27. tétel./7./E., Román-magyar viszony—Erdély, iktatlan, II. rész., 48.

247. *Porunca Vremii*, June 20, 1942, cited from MOL, K63, 257. csomó., 1940–27. tétel./7./E., Román-magyar viszony—Erdély, iktatlan, II. rész, 31.

248. On June 9, 1942, Greater Romania Radio cited Marshal Antonescu as having declared that "there will be no peace in this part of Europe until the Romanian people have justice," meaning the reannexation of Transylvania "that the Hungarians unjustly wrenched from Romania." MOL, K63, 257. csomó., 1940–27. tétel./7./E., Román-magyar viszony—Erdély, iktatlan, II. rész, 30.

249. MOL, K63, 257. csomó., 1940–27. tétel./7./E., Román-magyar viszony—Erdély, iktatlan, II. rész, 98.

250. Cited in *Ellenzék*, April 12, 1941, 5.

251. USHMMA, RG-25.013M, Consiliul de Miniştri, Cabinet Militar, reel 1, dosar 29/1940, 103.

252. *Ellenzék*, December 6, 1941, 1–2.

253. Gyula Zathureczky, "A magyarság helyzete Európában," in *Erdélyi kérdések—magyar kérdések* (Kolozsvár: Minerva, 1943), 7–8.

254. *Ellenzék*, January 7, 1942, 1.

255. The emphasis on national particularities was a key attribute of the German-Italian conception of cultural European-ness, one that was to represent a "return" to "true" European values that Western universalist conceptions had threatened to destroy. In fact, Germany and Italy joined forces to become the "the new centers of European culture," rather than centers of a "new" European culture. Bejamin Martin has written an excellent dissertation showing how German and Italian intellectuals championed what they considered an "authentically European culture." Benjamin George Martin, "A New Order for European Culture: The German-Italian Axis and the Reordering of International Cultural Exchange, 1936–1943," (PhD dissertation, Columbia University, 2006).

256. MOL, K63, 259. csomó., 27. tétel.1940–27/7/8, 3. See also Lukács, "Injustices of the Treaty of Trianon," 141.

257. Mihai Antonescu, *Dacă vrei să câştigi războiul*, 20.

258. Alexander Eckhardt, "Das Ungarnbild in Europa," *Ungarische Jahrbücher* 22, nos. 1–3 (October 1942): 153–85, 184.

259. Zsigmond, *DIMK*, 4:577, 743. In a combination *j'accuse* and apologia written in the summer of 1944 while Bethlen was hiding from the Gestapo, Bethlen opened with the rather disingenuous claim—given his position in 1940—that "Germany never stood a chance of winning this war," explaining Hungary's involvement with the Axis as nevertheless the inevitable outgrowth of the fact that only Germany could or would

support Hungary's revisionist aspirations. "Since Trianon, Hungary has had just one goal for the last 25 years and certainly will have [the same goal] far into the future as well: that we should patch together our country which has been chopped to pieces." István Bethlen, *Bethlen István emlékirata, 1944* (Budapest: Zrínyi Katonai Kiadó, 1988), 97, 113.

260. János Makkai, *A természetes béke Európában* (Budapest: Atheneum, 1940), 6–7.

261. C. A. Macartney, *October Fifteenth: A History of Hungary, 1929–1945*, part 2 (New York: Frederick A. Praeger, 1957), 222.

262. Meldungen aus dem Reich (Nr. 248) vom 5. Januar 1942, *In:* Nationalsozialismus, Holocaust, Widerstand und Exil 1933–1945. Online-Datenbank. K. G. Saur Verlag. 18.03.2008. http://db.saur.de/DGO/searchResults.faces?documentId=MAR-0255, Dokument-ID: MAR-0255.

263. *ADAP, 1918–1945*, Serie E: 1941–1945, Band II (Göttingen: VandenHoeck & Ruprecht, 1972), doc. 101, 178.

264. *ADAP, 1918–1945*, series E: 1941–1945, vol. 2 (Göttingen: VandenHoeck & Ruprecht, 197[?]), 101, 178.

265. *Stenogramele*, vol. 1, doc. 3, 70.

266. HIWRP, Sabin Manuilă, box 11, folder 8, "Mult stimate Domnule Manoilă [*sic*]," April 1, 1941.

267. *Roumania at the Peace Conference* (Paris: Imp. Paul Dupont, 1946), Map 2, "Ethnographic map of Roumania within the 1939 boundaries."

268. Mihai Antonescu, *Regimul Agrar Român și Chestiunea Optanților Unguri* (Bucharest, 1928); Mihai Antonescu, *Organizare Păcii și Societatea Națiunilor*, vol. 1 (Bucharest: Tipografia Școlelor Milatare de Geniu, 1929).

269. See the Library of Congress copy of Mihai Antonescu, *Organizare Păcii și Societatea Națiunilor*, vol. 1 (Bucharest: Tipografia Școlelor Milatare de Geniu, 1929).

270. Vladimir Solonari, "'Model Province': Explaining the Holocaust of Bessarabian and Bukovinian Jewry," *Nationalities Papers* 34, no. 4 (2006): 471–500, 473.

271. Zsigmond, *DIMK*, 1:158; *ADAP, 1918–1945*, Serie E: 1941–1945, Band I (Göttingen: VandenHoeck & Ruprecht, 1969), doc. 244, 450.

272. ANIC, Fond Președentia Consiliului de Miniștri Cabinetul Militar Ion Antonescu, Dosar 194/1940, Factura de subvenții pentru Seton-Watson, f. 100. I am indebted to Vladimir Solonari for sharing this document with me.

273. Mihai Antonescu, *Dacă vrei să câștigi războiul*, 51.

274. Golopenția later served in Gusti's cabinet during his tenure as Minister of Education, Culture, and the Arts from 1932 to 1933.

275. Vladimir Trebici, "Anton Golopenția: statisticianul și demograful," in *Opere Complete*, vol. 2, *Statistică, demografie și geopolitică* ([Bucharest]: Editura Enciclopedică, 2002), 21.

276. Ferenc Fodor, "Teleki Pál geopolitikája," *Magyar Szemle* 40, no. 6 (166) szám (June 1941): 337–43, 337.

277. Golopenția later conducted the Romanian census of 1948 but was arrested in 1950 and died in prison eighteen months later. See Trebici, "Anton Golopenția," 9–30.

278. Mihai Antonescu, *Dacă vrei să câștigi războiul*, 53; Valeriu Florin Dobrinescu and Doru Tompea, *România la cele două conferințe de pace de la Paris, 1919–1920, 1946–1947: un studiu comparativ* (Focșani: Editura Neuron, 1996), 176; Marin Radu Mocanu, ed., *România în anticamera conferenței de pace de la Paris, documente* (Bucharest: Arhivele Naționale ale României, 1996), doc. 49, esp. p. 342.

279. Biographical details cited from Vladimir Solonari, "Purifying the Nation: Population Exchange and Ethnic Cleansing in World War II Romania" (unpublished manuscript, cited with permission).

280. István Deák, "Hungary," in *The European Right: A Historical Profile*, ed. Hans Rogger and Eugen Weber (Berkeley and Los Angeles: University of California Press, 1965): 364–407, 364. Deák is well aware of what he calls the "commonly shared irredentism" during the interwar period in Hungary and acknowledges it as the only consistent government policy of the time (ibid., 372). On the primacy of Transylvania as a target of territorial revision, see Pál Teleki cited in A. Simion, *Dictatul de la Viena: Ediția a II-a Revăzută și adăugită* (Bucharest: Editura Albatros, 1996), 49.

281. A personality who embodies these continuities in Hungarian politics is János Vörös, who began his military career in the Habsburg army; in 1919 he served as an officer in the Hungarian Red Army that fought to recover the lost territories. During the interwar period he continued his military training, joining the chief of staff. He was the head of the chiefs of staff starting in 1941 and in that capacity was often explicit about what the goals of military action were, namely the securing of the lost territories. Toward the end of the war, Vörös approached the Soviet military leadership with a proposal for the creation of a Hungarian army made up of prisoners of war to fight alongside the Allies so that Hungarian troops could be seen fighting on the winning side. After the war he became minister of defense to the postwar provisional government and was the head of the chiefs of staff until his retirement in September 1946, in which position he sought to lobby the Soviets to keep the Transylvanian Question open. It is true, however, that his activities were investigated starting in 1945, and he was sentenced to life in prison in 1950. See Peter Kenez, *Hungary from the Nazis to the Soviets: The Establishment of the Communist Regime in Hungary, 1944–1948* (Cambridge: Cambridge University Press, 2006), 33–34; István Ötvös, "A Vörös János elleni vizsgálatok, 1945–1950," in *Katonai perek a kommunista diktatúra időszakában, 1945–1958*, Imre Okváth, ed. (Budapest: Történeti hivatal, 2001), 37–69, 68.

282. Iván Rubido-Zichy to Emil Nagy, January 2, 1928. Pritz, *Iratok a magyar külügyi szolgálat történetéhez*, 244, 371. The letter was part of a longer back-and-forth between the two men, who indeed held sharply different views on the matter.

283. On Teleki and Hungarian eugenics, see Marius Turda, "The First Debates on Eugenics in Hungary, 1910–1918," in *Blood and Homeland: Eugenics and Racial Nationalism in Central and Southeast Europe, 1900–1940*, ed. Marius Turda and Paul Weindling (Budapest: Central European University Press, 2007): 185–221. On Manuilă, see Turda, "The Nation as Object," 424–27.

284. Fodor, "Teleki Pál geopolitikája," 337.

285. Kertesz, *Between Russia and the West*, 81–82. On the group's activities prior to the end of the war, see USHMMA, RG-30.003, Reel 13, Collection of Hungarian political and military records, 1909–1945, fr. 1031–7.

2. Why We Fight

1. Cited in Dániel Csatári, *Forgószélben: magyar-román viszony, 1940–1945* (Budapest: Akadémiai Kiadó, 1968), 85. It is possible this exchange never actually took place. Ciano nevertheless observed in a diary entry dated May 11, 1942, that this "little story" was "going the rounds at Budapest." He observed: "There is a great deal of truth in this series of paradoxes." See also Count Galeazzo Ciano, *The Ciano Diaries, 1939–1943* (Garden City, N.Y.: Doubleday, 1946), 484.

2. Ion Gheorghe, *Rumäniens Weg zu Satellitenstaat* (Heidelberg: Kurt Vorwinckel Verlag, 1952), 250. Gheorghe writes that this response upset the general greatly and that he proposed propaganda measures to inform the troops of the goals of their fight in the East. General Racovița of the Romanian forces reportedly offered to have every third man shot as punishment, but the suggestion was "categorically rejected" by Ruoff (ibid., 250–51).

3. Mihai Antonescu, *Warum wir kämpfen* (Bucharest, 1942), 34, 40.

4. Magda Ádám, Gyula Juhász, and Lajos Kerekes, eds., *Magyarország és a második világháború: titkos diplomáciai okmányok a háború előzményeihez és történetéhez* (Budapest: Kossuth Könyvkiadó, 1959), 153, 396–97.

5. Corporal Balogh's diary cited in Antony Beevor, *Stalingrad* (New York: Viking, 1998), 182. For other Hungarian soldiers' accounts of the offensive, see András Molnár, *Frontnaplók a Don-kanyarból, 1942–1943* (Zalaegerszeg: Zala Megyei Levéltár, 1992).

6. On mass graves, see Krisztián Ungváry, *A magyar honvédség a második világháború-ban* (Budapest: Osiris kiadó, 2005), 195; Miklós Horváth and Péter Szabó, *Pihenj te néma hadsereg* (Budapest: Zrínyi kiadó, 1992). In terms of casualty rates for Romania, Pandea, Pavelescu, and Ardeleanu place the number of "dead, wounded and missing" between 140,000 and 150,000, 100,000 to 110,000 of which were dead or missing between when the Soviet counteroffensive began on November 19, 1942, and when the withdrawal of the last large Romanian units left the front in January 1943. This was out of an estimated total mobilized force in the Stalingrad/Don River Bend/Kalmuk Steppe region of 230,872 for that time period. Adrian Pandea, Ion Pavelescu, and Eftimie Ardeleanu, eds., *Românii la Stalingrad: viziunea românească asupra tragediei din Cotul Donului și Stepa Calmucă* (Bucharest: Editura Militară, 1992), 467–70. The same figures are presented by Vasile-Ozunu and Otu, who also estimate material losses at between 50 and 74 percent for weapons and supplies. Mihail Vasile-Ozunu and Petre Otu, *Înfrânți și uitați: Românii în bătălia de la Stalingrad* (Bucharest: Editura Ion Cristoiu, 1999), 214. For Hungary, Ungváry points out that by October 1, 1942, the total losses of Hungary's Second Army deployed to the Don region was thirty thousand people and almost an entire division's worth of weapons. This was already six times the total losses reported the year before. By April 1943, what had been a fighting force of 204,334 on January 1 had fallen to 108,318, while weapons losses were around 70 percent (close to 100 percent for heavy weaponry). Ungváry, *A magyar honvédség*, 195–96.

7. Manfred Kehrig, *Stalingrad: Analyse und Dokumentation einer Schlacht* (Stuttgart: Deutsche Verlags-Anstalt, 1974), 614.

8. Complaints against the German command for its treatment of Romanian officers and troops were expressed in a letter from Marshal Antonescu to Field Marshal Manstein

on December 9, 1942. Vasile Arimia, Ion Ardeleanu, and Ştefan Lache, eds., *Antonescu-Hitler: Corespondenţă şi întâlniri inedite, 1940–1944*, vol. 1 (Bucharest: Cozia Ed.—Co., 1991), doc. 49, 198–211. See also Kehrig, *Stalingrad*, 457–58; *Stenogramele şedinţelor consiliului de ministri: Guvernarea Ion Antonescu*, vol. 8 (August–December 1942) (Bucharest: Arhivele Naţionale ale României, 2004), 312–13. For German mistreatment of Hungarian officers and soldiers during the retreat from the Don, see Ungváry, *A magyar honvédség*, 194–95.

9. Cited in Charles Messenger, *The Last Prussian: A Biography of Field Marshal Gerd von Rundstedt, 1875–1953* (London: Brassey's, 1991), 149. Erich von Manstein, *Verlorene Siege* (Bonn: Athenäum, 1955), 211.

10. Kehrig, *Stalingrad*, 458.

11. Iuliu Maniu pointed this out in a letter to Ion Antonescu dated September 24, 1942. HIWRP, Sabin Manuilă, box 11, folder 2. See also Peter Gosztony, *Hitlers Fremde Heere: Das Schicksal der nichtdeutschen Armeen im Ostfeldzug* (Vienna, Düsseldorf: Econ Verlag, 1976), 200.

12. SNA, MZV, K. 192, 8.035/1942.

13. Kovács cited in Ungváry, *A magyar honvédség*, 182.

14. Sebastian Balta, *Rumänien und die Grossmächte in der Ära Antonescu, 1940–1944* (Stuttgart: Franz Steiner Verlag, 2005), 314–17.

15. Cited in Balta, *Rumänien und die Grossmächte*, 314.

16. Keith Hitchins, *Rumania, 1866–1947* (Oxford: Clarendon Press, 1994), 440.

17. An agreement was reached on April 4, 1939, according to which Hungary obtained an additional 396 square kilometers of Slovak territory with a population of 41,000. Július Bartl et al., *Slovak History: Chronology and Lexicon* (Wauconda, Ill.: Bolchazy-Carducci Publishers, 2002), 140.

18. László Zsigmond, ed., *DIMK*, vol. 3, *Magyarország külpolitikája, 1938–1939* (Budapest: Akadémiai kiadó, 1970), 453, 474, 475, 494.

19. László Zsigmond, ed., *DIMK*, vol. 2, *A Müncheni egyezmény létrejötte és Magyarország külpolitikája, 1936–1938* (Budapest: Akadémiai kiadó, 1965), 510.

20. Cited in András Bán, *Hungarian-British Diplomacy, 1938–1941: The Attempt to Maintain Relations* (London and Portland, Ore.: Frank Cass, 2004), 141.

21. Cited in Gyula Juhász, *A Teleki-kormány külpolitikája, 1939–1941* (Budapest: Akadémiai kiadó, 1964), 120.

22. Even before France's surrender, Hungarian leaders discussed with the German leadership the possibility of a dual invasion of Romania that spring. Manfred Nebelin, *Deutsche Ungarnpolitik, 1939–1941* (Opladen: Leske und Budrich, 1989), 110–20.

23. Andreas Hillgruber, ed., *Staatsmänner und Diplomaten bei Hitler: Vertrauliche Aufzeichnungen über Unterredungen mit Vertretern des Auslandes, 1939–1941, I. Teil* (Frankfurt am Main: Bernard & Graefe Verlag, 1967), dok.22, 162.

24. *23 August 1944, Documente*, vol. 1 (Bucharest: Editura ştiinţifică şi Enciclopedică, 1984), doc. 10, pp. 11–12.

25. This emerged in a conversation between the Bulgarian ambassador to Romania and the former Minister of Foreign Affairs, Grigore Gafencu, on April 9, 1940. TsDA, MVRI, F176K, op. 7, a.e. 753, 43.

26. Ion Antonescu, *Generalul Antonescu către ţară 6 septemvrie 1940–22 iunie 1941* (Bucharest, 1941), 120.

27. The Romanians had eight divisions in Transylvania and another twenty-two in other parts of the country. Hitchins, *Rumania,* 448.

28. Anton Czettler, *Pál Graf Teleki und die Außenpolitik Ungarns, 1939–1941* (Munich: Verlag Ungarisches Institut, 1996), 111–13; Hitchins, *Rumania,* 448.

29. Ciano, *Diaries,* 287.

30. Valer Pop, *Bătălia pentru Ardeal* ([Romania]: Editura Colosseum, 1990), 173.

31. Czettler, *Pál Graf Teleki und die Außenpolitik Ungarns,* 121–23. Both the size of the territory and the population were contested between Hungarian and Romanian statistical sources, with the critical difference being that both sides claimed to be in the majority. See Ottmar Trașcă, "Relațiile Româno-ungare și problema Transilvaniei, 1940–1944 (I)," *Anuarul Institutului de Istorie "A. D. Xenopol,"* 41 (2004): 311–49, 311–12; Anton Golopenția, "Populația teritoriilor românești desprinse în 1940," in *Opere Complete,* vol. 2, *Statistică, demografie și geopolitică* ([Bucharest]: Editura Enciclopedică, 2002), 549. Statistical battles such as these will be discussed further in Chapter 3.

32. Ciano, *Diaries,* 289; Paul Schmidt, *Hitler's Interpreter* (New York: Macmillan, 1951), 189. Later Manoilescu would be much criticized by the Antonescu regime for his role in accepting the Second Vienna Arbitration. In June 1942, Romanian deputy prime minister Mihai Antonescu declared that he could not consider the person who would sign such an agreement to be a Romanian. Mihai Antonescu, *Dacă vrei să câștigi războiul, trebuie să pregătești pacea* (Cluj-Napoca: Muzeul Etnografic al Transilvaniei, 1991), 27. Despite Ciano's report of Hungarian jubilation, Ribbentrop later declared that nothing could better prove "the justice of the Vienna Arbitration than the fact that, after its announcement, the Romanian foreign minister fainted and the Hungarian foreign minister announced his resignation." Cited in Trașcă, "Relațiile româno-ungare (I)," 311–49, 313.

33. A number of demonstrations that took place during that time (and even before the announcement) were organized by Maniu's National Peasant Party. Ioan Hudiță, *Jurnal politic,* vol. 1 (Iași: Institutul European, 1998), 304.

34. The individual later fled across the border to his estate in Southern Transylvania. In Northern Transylvania, he was tried for slander against the Hungarian nation in absentia. MOL, K28, 58. csomó., 130. tétel. 1942-G-15387.

35. *Universul,* September 3, 1940, cited in *Pe marginea prăpastiei, 21–23 ianuarie 1941,* vol. 1 (Bucharest: Editura Scripta, 1992), 59. Originally published in 1942 in Bucharest.

36. Mihai Fătu and Mircea Mușat, eds., *Horthyist-Fascist Terror in Northwestern Romania* (Bucharest: Meridiane Publishing House, 1986), 29–35. During the course of these demonstrations, the Italian Consulate-General in Cluj/Kolozsvár was trashed by demonstrators. *Keesing's Contemporary Archives,* vol. 4, *1940–1943,* 4227.

37. Pop, *Bătălia pentru Ardeal,* 209.

38. At the time Ion Antonescu became prime minister, his military rank was that of major general. Throughout the coming months, he rose in rank several times, finally reaching the rank of marshal on August 21, 1941, after Romania had recovered the territories of Bessarabia and Northern Bukovina (which it had lost to the Soviet Union in the summer of 1940).

39. János Jászfi, "Napló, Erdély 1940," *Honismeret* 28, no. 1 (2000): 29–34, 30. Jászfi arrived in the city already on the evening of September 9, while the territory was still

technically held by the Romanians. He spent the night in a crowded, closed livestock car. "Singing, talking forbidden. Here and there [you could see] concern on the faces [of the soldiers]."

40. "Horthy Celebrates Growth of Hungary, Hails Recovery of Transylvania at Fete in Old Capital," *New York Times*, September 16, 1940, 5.

41. Indeed, arguably both countries had started to lean in that direction much earlier. In the case of Romania, Hitchins places the turning point at 1935 with the removal of Foreign Minister Nicolae Titulescu. Hitchins, *Rumania*, 437. The Romanian leadership's affinity with Nazi Germany grew as territorial losses mounted during the summer of 1940. When Ciano received the Romanian delegation in late July 1940, he remarked with disgust that "they have become anti-French, anti-English, and anti-League of Nations. They talk with contempt of the *diktat* of Versailles—too honeyed." Ciano, *Diaries*, 297. Hungary had also moved closer to the Axis starting in 1932 under Prime Minister Gyula Gömbös (1932–36), but had—like Romania between 1935 and the summer of 1940—periods of doubt and reversal, somewhat under the government of Kálmán Darányi (1936–38), and thereafter under Prime Minister Pál Teleki, a long-time Francophile who feared Germany's growing power and distrusted its leadership. For more on these doubts and the link between the Second Vienna Arbitration and Hungary joining the Tripartite Pact, see Pál Nadányi, "Damokles kardja," (December 1940), in *Merre, magyarok?* (New York: Amerikai magyar népszava, 1945), 58–60.

42. Ion Antonescu, who would later become Hitler's favorite ally, was military attaché to France and Great Britain between 1922 and 1926, and as of 1936, he was known for his "pro-French" orientation. László Zsigmond, ed., *DIMK*, vol. 1, *A Berlin-Róma tengely kialakulása és Ausztria annexiója, 1936–1938* (Budapest: Akadémiai kiadó, 1962), 158. On the "two options" left to Romania after the Second Vienna Arbitration, see Pandea, Pavelescu, and Ardeleanu, *Românii la Stalingrad*, 25.

43. György Réti, *Hungarian-Italian Relations in the Shadow of Hitler's Germany* (New York: Columbia University Press, 2003), 281.

44. Péter Sipos and István Ravasz, eds., *Magyarország a második világháborúban, lexicon A-Zs* (Budapest: Petit Real Könyvkiadó, 1997), 156–57.

45. Schmidt, *Hitler's Interpreter*, 206.

46. Ion Antonescu, *Către țară*, 246. Speaking of Romania's "rights" in this way may seem a vague formulation, but it was clear to Antonescu's audience what it meant. Following a New Year's speech of the Romanian King in January 1942, for example, the Slovak ambassador to Romania noted that the king's reference to Romania's "rights" was interpreted by everyone as "Romanian rights to all of Transylvania." SNA, MZV, K. 192, 235/1942.

47. This was also true of the military leadership in both states, most notably the formerly Francophile General Ion Antonescu, but also the Hungarian military leadership. Hungarian military historian Sándor Szakály convincingly debunks the notion that the Hungarian army was pro-German because it had been infiltrated by "Swabians." Instead, he cites the disastrous postwar peace treaties and Hungary's revisionist aspirations as among the primary causes of pro-German sentiment among the military elite in Hungary. Sándor Szakály, *A magyar katonai elit, 1938–1945* (Budapest: Magvető könyvkiadó, 1987), 57.

48. Ribbentrop, in *ADAP, 1918–1945*, series D, vol. 5 (Göttingen: VandenHoeck & Ruprecht, 197[?]), 254, 285.

49. *ADAP, 1918–1945*, series E, vol. 2, 95, 167.

50. See Pop, *Bătălia pentru Ardeal*, 169.

51. Ciano, *Diaries*, 288–89.

52. Hungarian chief of staff General Henrik Werth in August 1941, cited in Balta, *Rumänien und die Grossmächte*, 228. Romanians even touted this to the Croat legation on September 1, 1941. HDA, 230 (Poslanstvo NDH u Bukureštu), 6.

53. Raul V. Bossy, *Recollections of a Romanian Diplomat, 1918–1969: Diaries and Memoirs of Raoul V. Bossy*, vol. 2 (Stanford, Calif.: Hoover Institution Press, 2003), 418–19; *ADAP, 1918–1945*, series E: 1941–1945, vol. 1 (Göttingen: VandenHoeck & Ruprecht, 1969), 214, 386–87; USHMMA, RG-25.006M, Fiche 37, Selected Records from the Romanian Ministry of Foreign Affairs Archives, Fond SUA, Volume 40, 158, 207.

54. László Szenczei, *A magyar-román kérdés: történeti és politikai tanulmány* (Budapest: Officina, 1946), 160.

55. The territory acquired by Hungary in April 1941 included the region of Bačka/Bácska, a bit of Baranja/Baranya, and two small bits of Prekmurje/Muravidék and Medjumurje/Muraköz farther west.

56. Ulrich von Hassell, *Vom andern Deutschland: Aus den nachgelassenen Tagebüchern 1938–1944* (Zurich: Atlantis Verlag, 1947), 199.

57. Miklós Horthy, *Horthy Miklós titkos iratai* (Budapest: Kossuth Könyvkiadó, 1962), 297.

58. Miklós Kállay, *Magyarország miniszterelnöke voltam, 1942–1944* (Budapest: Európa História, 1991), 91.

59. Lajos Kerekes, ed., *Allianz Hitler-Horthy-Mussolini: Dokumente zur ungarischen Aussenpolitik, 1933–1944* (Budapest: Akadémia Kiadó, 1966), 118, 344.

60. USHMMA, RG-25.013M, Președinția Consiliului de Miniștrii–Cabinet Militar, 1940–1944, roll 14, dosar 402/1941, f. 60.

61. USHMMA, RG-25.017, Selected Records of the Cluj Branch of the Romanian National Archives, 1934–1952, roll 7, Parchetul General Cluj, 1919–1952, fond 137, nr. inv. 35, dosar 31/1942, f. 50.

62. USHMMA, RG-25.013M, Președinția Consiliului de Miniștrii–Cabinet Militar, 1940–1944, roll 14, dosar 402/1941, f. 113. From the beginning of 1943, "In Ungaria se vorbește ca odata cu primavara se va pornii compania contra Romaniei." See USHMMA, RG-25.017, Selected Records of the Cluj Branch of the Romanian National Archives, 1934–1952, roll 7, Parchetul General Cluj, 1919–1952, fond 137, nr. inv. 35, dosar 34/1943, f. 254. Romanian report on Hungarian plans to move into Southern Transylvania as Romanians are disorganized: USHMMA, RG-25.017, Selected Records of the Cluj Branch of the Romanian National Archives, 1934–1952, roll 7, Parchetul General Cluj, 1919–1952, fond 137, nr. inv. 35, dosar 32/1944, f. 350, 467.

63. USHMMA, RG-25.013M, Președinția Consiliului de Miniștrii–Cabinet Militar, 1940–1944, roll 14, dosar 402/1941, f. 203.

64. HIWRP, Sabin Manuilă, box 11, folder 5, "Copy in Translation of letter to Marshal Antonescu." Maniu and Brătianu repeated these concerns and warnings in subsequent correspondence with Antonescu. HIWRP, Sabin Manuilă, box 11, folder 2,

Iuliu Maniu and C.I.C. Brătianu to Ion Antonescu, September 24, 1942; HIWRP, Sabin Manuilă, box 11, folder 2, Iuliu Maniu and C.I.C. Brătianu to Ion Antonescu, August 12, 1943.

65. In a speech before parliament on November 13, 1941, Endre Bajcsy Zsilinszky, who opposed Hungary's alliance with the Axis, said: "We must take care that the army is as strong and complete as possible, as well-trained and -equipped as possible, as untapped as possible for those historic tasks that still lie before us. . . . We cannot allow ourselves to be surprised the way we were in 1918." BMF, RW 50, Deutsch-italienische Offizierskommision zur Durchführung des Wiener Schiedsspruches vom 30.8.1940, 277, "Kammersitzung vom 13. Nov. 1941."

66. "Feljegyzés Erdmannsdorff budapesti német követ és Bárdossy László miniszterelnök megbeszéléséről," 1941.VI.24, in Zsigmond László, ed., *DIMK, 1936–1945*, vol. 5, *Magyarország külpolitikája a nyugati hadjárattól a szovjetunió megtámadásáig, 1940–1941* (Budapest: Akadémiai kiadó, 1982), 872, 1217. "Erdmannsdorf budapesti követ távirata a külügyminisztériumnak," Budapest, 1941. június 24, in *A Wilhelmstrasse és Magyarország: német diplomáciai iratok Magyarországról, 1933–1944*, ed. György Ránki, Ervin Pamlényi, Loránt Tilkovszky, and Gyula Juhász (Budapest: Kossuth Kiadó, 1968), 415, 596–97. The ultimate decision to join the offensive was German diplomats' touting the fact that Slovakia and Romania already had. See Zsigmond, *DIMK*, 5: 875, 876, 879, 1223–25, 1228; Mario D. Fenyo, *Hitler, Horthy, and Hungary: German-Hungarian Relations, 1941–1944* (New Haven, Conn., and London: Yale University Press, 1972), 20.

67. Ungváry, *A magyar honvédség*, 180, 238. Furthermore, in the period leading up to the 1942 offensive, in a discussion about foodstuff contributions and military support for the Axis, Kállay stressed that Hungary must keep food and supplies in reserve for an unavoidable war with Romania. At a special meeting of the crown cabinet on July 24, 1942, participants resolved to secretly mobilize for war against Romania, using Romania's harsh treatment of the Hungarian minority as justification. *ADAP, 1918–1945*, series E: 1941–1945, vol. 3 (Göttingen: VandenHoeck & Ruprecht, 1974), 102, 225, 180–82, 225.

68. The argument ran that the military action against the predominantly Serb partisans operating in the Délvidék (the territories Hungary had reannexed from Yugoslavia with the invasion of that country in the spring of 1941) posed a significant threat to Hungary and the Axis and that Hungarian troops should be held back from the front to deal with the threat. Loránd Tilkovszky, "The Late Interwar Years and World War II," in *A History of Hungary*, ed. Peter Sugar (Bloomington: Indiana University Press, 1994), 347–48. Horthy's arguments to Hitler on why Hungary could not offer more troops can be found in a letter from January 10, 1942. Horthy mentioned both the instability of the Balkans and the chance of war with Romania as his main reasons, making specific mention of the events in Novi Sad/Újvidék. Horthy, *Titkos iratai*, 314–16.

69. As of fall 1942, there were thirteen Hungarian divisions and twenty-seven Romanian divisions on the Eastern Front. Péter Szabó, "A 2. magyar hadsereg kiszállítása Ukrajnába és előnyomulása a Donhoz, 1942. április-augusztus," in *Hadtörténelmi közlemények* 33, no. 3 (1986): 496–524, 498.

70. Kerekes, *Allianz Hitler-Horthy-Mussolini*, 118, 335. It should be known that a small number of Transylvanian troops were sent to the Eastern Front, but their numbers

were insignificant and a disproportionate number of them consisted of non-magyar nationalities. Péter Illésfalvi, Péter Szabó, and Norbert Számvéber, *Erdély a hadak útján, 1940–1944* (Debrecen: Puedlo Kiadó, 2007), 43–44.

71. The Hungarians' dissatisfaction with the Second Vienna Arbitration solution was clear as well to Janovsky, who noted that both sides had an all-or-nothing stance regarding the fate of Transylvania. HIWRP, Karl Janovsky, "Lagebericht 1942 über die Verhältnisse in Südost," 1942, 10.

72. *Hitler's Table Talk, 1941–1944: His Private Conversations* (London: Phoenix Press, 2000), 516.

73. MOL, K28, 55. csomó., 120. tétel. Alapszám 1943-O-17780.

74. HIWRP, Karl Janovsky, "Lagebericht 1942 über die Verhältnisse in Südost," 1942, 10.

75. von Hassell, *Vom andern Deutschland,* 267.

76. Cited in Nada Kisić Kolanović, *Zagreb—Sofija: prijateljstvo po mjeri ratnog vremena, 1941–1945* (Zagreb: Hrvatski Državni Arhiv, Dom i Svijet, 2003), 163.

77. Beevor, *Stalingrad,* 70. On the ideological motivations for the offensive, see Andreas Hillgruber, *Hitlers Strategie: Politik und Kriegführung, 1940–1941* (Munich: Bernard & Graefe Verlag, 1982), 519–20.

78. Cited in Balta, *Rumänien und die Grossmächte,* 270–71.

79. Cited in Balta, *Rumänien und die Grossmächte,* 273. Hungary had attempted to negotiate a withdrawal of its Mobile Corps in September 1941 in an effort to regroup and prepare for Hungary's "Balkan mission," which was to entail a "showdown with Romania." R. L. DiNardo, *Germany and the Axis Powers from Coalition to Collapse* (Lawrence: University Press of Kansas, 2005), 124.

80. MOL, K28, 55. csomó., 120. tétel. 1941-O-26648. The piece may also have been a song.

81. Gheorghe, *Rumäniens Weg,* 227.

82. *ADAP, 1918–1945,* series E, vol. 2, 64, 108.

83. Cited in Balta, *Rumänien und die Grossmächte,* 228–29.

84. Gheorghe, *Rumäniens Weg,* 227.

85. Andreas Hillgruber, ed., *Staatsmänner und Diplomaten bei Hitler: Vertrauliche Aufzeichnungen über Unterredungen mit Vertretern des Auslandes, 1942–1944, II. Teil* (Frankfurt am Main: Bernard & Graefe Verlag, 1970), 2, 51–53. According to Gheorghe, the problem of Transylvania "preoccupied the marshal's heart and mind like no other. Yes, it was even one of the most important reasons for his resolution to participate so extensively in the east. In this way, he also wanted to make the German leadership aware once more of the contribution Romania was ready to make. This Romanian contribution to victory should move the Reich to settle the Transylvanian question in Romania's favor." Gheorghe, *Rumäniens Weg,* 227.

86. DiNardo, *Germany and the Axis,* 138–39. Meanwhile Germany suspected both countries were keeping oil reserves for an eventual conflict with one another. *ADAP, 1918–1945,* series E, vol. 2, 43, 73.

87. Schmidt, *Hitler's Interpreter,* 244.

88. United States Department of State, *Foreign relations of the United States diplomatic papers, 1942. Europe,* vol. 2 (1942), 841.

89. Jean Ancel, ed., *Documents Concerning the Fate of Romanian Jewry during the Holocaust*, vol. 9 (New York: Beate Klarsfeld Foundation, [1986]), doc. 179, 466.

90. ASFJC, Inspectoratul de Poliție Cluj, Nr. Inv. 399. Dosar Nr. 92/1942(III), f. 64.

91. Ibid., f. 122.

92. MOL, K28, 55. csomó., 120. tétel. 1943-O-17780.

93. BMF, RW 50, 283, "Die Siebenbürgen-Kundgebung vom 19. März 1942 in Bukarest."

94. *ADAP, 1918–1945*, series E, vol. 2, 39, 68–69.

95. Killinger to Bova Scoppa on June 20, 1942; cited in Balta, *Rumänien und die Grossmächte*, 275.

96. Mihai Antonescu, *Dacă vrei să câștigi războiul*, 7.

97. From an article in the Romanian newspaper *Universul* from May 22, 1942. These and other articles were collected and translated to be presented to the Germans in support of their case against Romania. MOL, K63, 257. csomó., 1940–27. tétel./7./E., Román-magyar viszony—Erdély, iktatlan, II. rész., 72.

98. MOL, K63, 257. csomó., 1940–27. tétel./7./E., Román-magyar viszony—Erdély, iktatlan, II. rész., 92.

99. Broadcast from June 7, 1942. MOL, K63, 257. csomó., 1940–27. tétel./7./E., Román-magyar viszony—Erdély, iktatlan, II. rész. 1941–21/28–3736, 30.

100. BMF, RW 50, 148, "Rumänen aus Nordsiebenbürgen die wegen Beleidigung der Nation und des ungarischen Staates verurteilt wurden."

101. ASFJC, Inspectoratul de Poliție Cluj, Nr. Inv. 399. Dosar Nr. 92/1942(III), f. 112. The Cluj inspectorate had been relocated to Turda in the fall of 1940 due to the Second Vienna Arbitration but nevertheless retained its name.

102. MOL, K63, 257. csomó., 1940–27. tétel./7./E., Román-magyar viszony—Erdély, iktatlan, II. rész., 97.

103. From *Pesti Hirlap*, 11.12.1941, cited in BMF, RW 50, 277, Magyarische Sorgen die Armee unberührt zu erhalten für eine mögliche Aufgabe am Schluße des Krieges.

104. BMF, RW 50, 277, "*Pesti Hirlap*, 27.XI.1941." Incidentally, this part of the speech was not included in a collection of parliamentary contributions by Transylvanian representatives for the year 1941. *Erdély a magyar képviselőházban, 1941* (Kolozsvár: Az Erdélyi Párt, 1942), 98–99.

105. From *Keleti Ujság*, May 31, 1942, cited in BMF, RW 50, 286, "Beispiele Revisionistischer Propaganda in der ungarischen Presse."

106. From *Estilap*, May 4, 1942, cited in BMF, RW 50, 286, "Beispiele Revisionistischer Propaganda in der ungarischen Presse."

107. BMF, RW 50, 286, "Beispiele Revisionistischer Propaganda in der ungarischen Presse."

108. Szakály lists 414 high-ranking officers active during the war (up until October 15, 1944), with information on birthplace available for only 385. Of those, 85 were born in what later became Romania, 66 in Czechoslovakia, 50 in Yugoslavia, and 4 in Austria. The percentage of those born in Romania was thus around 22 percent of the total. As a result, he writes, "The elite military leadership, indeed the army itself, were among the main mouthpieces and advocates of revisionism. [They] never renounced the idea of achieving revision through force of arms." Szakály, *A magyar katonai elit*, 64–66.

109. Antal Radnóczy, in Miklós and Szabó, *Pihenj te néma hadsereg*, 5–6.

110. Imre Gróf, in Miklós and Szabó, *Pihenj te néma hadsereg*, 21.

111. János Vörös. cited in Ungváry, *A magyar honvédség*, 203.

112. BMF, RW 50, 146, Rumänische "Sigurantza" Meldungen, "Abschrift aus Berichten der Sigurantza in Bukarest, 8.8.42." Some Hungarians in Southern Transylvania expected the arrival of Hungarian troops there any day. In June 1941, a Lutheran pastor in Southern Transylvania purportedly said he expected the Hungarian army to enter Turda and other cities in Southern Transylvania within ten days. MOL, K63, 258. csomó., 27. tétel. 1940–27/7/T/2/d, 423.

113. HIWRP, Karl Janovsky, "Lagebericht 1942 über die Verhältnisse in Südost," 1942, p. 17.

114. Gheorghe, *Rumäniens Weg*, 228.

115. See, for example, military correspondence relating to the transport of supplies and the possibility of contact between Hungarian and Romanian forces in József Kun, "A német hadvezetés magyarországi politikájához, 1941 március-július," *Századok* 99, no. 6 (1965): 1228–46, 1245.

116. *DGFP*, series D, vol. 13, *The War Years, 1941* (Washington, D.C.: Department of State, 1964), doc. 58, 68; Messenger, *The Last Prussian*, 136; Franz Halder, *War Journal of Generaloberst Franz Halder, Chief of the General Staff of the OKH* (Supreme Command of the German Army), vol. 6, August 14, 1939, through September 24, 1942 (1946?), 260; William Craig, *Enemy at the Gates: The Battle for Stalingrad* (New York: E. P. Dutton, 1973), 14.

117. DiNardo, *Germany and the Axis*, 123–24. A direct conflict was averted.

118. BMF, RW 50, 286, "Ungarische Berichterstattung."

119. In fact, a relative of Henrik Werth, Chief of Staff of the Hungarian Army, served in the Romanian army and fought on the Eastern Front. HDA, F. 1492, Poslanstvo NDH Budimpešta (first folder), 68.

120. In 1939, even before the Second Vienna Arbitration, the Hungarian government compiled testimonies from thirty-one Hungarians who had deserted the Romanian army and who complained of beatings and very harsh treatment of Hungarian minority soldiers on the part of Romanian soldiers and officers. MOL, K63, 251. csomó., 1939–27. tétel./7-I., 648–72. After the Second Vienna Arbitration, there were multiple complaints on both sides regarding the treatment of minority soldiers. MOL, K63, 253. csomó., 27. tétel. 1940–27/3 (outlines harsh treatment of Hungarian soldiers in the Romanian army); USHMMA, RG-25.020*11, Fiche 4, Selected Records from Romanian Diplomatic Missions, 1920–1950, Budapest, Hungary, Fond Budapesta, vol. 5, Politice, 1941–1943, f. 253–54; USHMMA, RG-25.020*11, Fiche 5, Selected Records from Romanian Diplomatic Missions, 1920–1950, Budapest, Hungary, Fond Budapesta, vol. 5, Politice, 1941–1943, f. 327–28; USHMMA, RG-25.020*11, Fiche 6, Selected Records from Romanian Diplomatic Missions, 1920–1950, Budapest, Hungary, Fond Budapesta, Vol. 6, 147 file, f. 5–6, 18–20, 26; ANIC, Fond Delegatul Marelui Stat Major pe lângă Comisie de Ofiţeri Germană, Dosar 15/1944, f. 91–92 (treatment of Romanian soldiers in the military). Another such report named four Romanian soldiers who were beaten and abused by Hungarian officers. USHMMA, RG-54.001M, Selected Records from the National Archives of Moldova, roll 12, F. 680, op. 1, dosar 4475, 87–87v. The report

was based on the testimony of Max Becker, a Jewish man who told Romanian authorities that he "saw many soldiers from the Hungarian army [at an Axis field hospital on the Eastern Front] who were badly beaten and sent to the hospital, all of them ethnic Romanians." After taking his testimony, Romanian authorities sent Becker to the Jewish ghetto beyond the Nistru River, where he likely perished.

121. Cited in Beevor, *Stalingrad*, 181.

122. Numbers are difficult to establish, but a report submitted to the German-Italian Commission by the Hungarian government claims that during the months of September and October 1942 alone, 337 members of the Hungarian minority fled to Hungary from Romania to escape military service, with another 13 fleeing in anticipation of being drafted. BMF, RW 50, 269, Wehrdienst, Fahnenflucht Südsiebenbürgen.

123. Illésfalvi, Szabó, and Számvéber, *Erdély a hadak útján*, 42.

124. Gusztáv Hársasi, in Miklós and Szabó, *Pihenj te néma hadsereg*, 16. For another example, see USHMMA, RG-25.020*11, Fiche 3, Selected Records from Romanian Diplomatic Missions, 1920–1950, Budapest, Hungary, Fond Budapesta, vol. 5, Politice, 1941–1943, f. 189.

125. MOL, K63, 254. csomó., 1940–27. tétel./7.I., 94–95; ASFJC, Inspectoratul de Poliție Cluj, Nr. Inv. 42/1940(I)., 128.

126. Illésfalvi, Szabó, and Számvéber, *Erdély a hadak útján*, 44. The battalion was called "Kolozsvár."

127. Although Hungary and Romania had formally agreed not to call up minority teachers, this agreement was not always adhered to. BMF, RW 50, 123/1942, Wehrdienst der ungarischen bzw. Rumänischen Minderheit in Siebenbürgen und Frage der Reserveoffiziere in Nord- und Südsiebenbürgen, "Abschrift, Bukarest den 21. Juli 1942." The Hungarian army drafted the editor-in-chief of Transylvania's only Romanian-language daily newspaper, for example. When he attempted to desert by crossing into Romania, he was sentenced to eight months in prison. ASFJC, Primăria Mun. Cluj, Inv. 386/1942, Nr. 23694–37140, Alapszám 28545.

128. MOL, K63, 254. csomó., 1940–27/7.I. tétel, 107–8. See also MOL, K63, 260. csomó., 1941–27/1(II). tétel, 85; MOL, K63, 253. csomó., 1940–27/3. tétel, 5–7; USHMMA, RG-25.003, Romanian Ministry of National Defense, Archive of the General Staff concerning the Holocaust in Romania, reel 140, file 2370, 885–86; BMF, RW 50, 123/1942 Wehrdienst der ungarischen bzw. rumänischen Minderheit in Siebenbürgen und Frage der Reserveoffiziere in Nord- und Südsiebenbürgen, "Einberufung der Rumänen aus Nordsiebenbürgen zu Militäreinheiten und Arbeitskompanien"; Mihai Fătu, ed., *Din istoria Transilvaniei: Documente, 1931–1945* (Alexandria: Editura Tipoalex, 1999), doc. 39 and 40, pp. 235–36.

129. A complaint issued by the Hungarian state to the German-Italian Commission charged that members of the Hungarian minority in Romania were being sent, with no training, directly to the front to die. BMF, RW 50, 269, Wehrdienst, Fahnenflucht Südsiebenbürgen, "Ermunterung zur Fahnenflucht von Volksungarn in Rumänien."

130. MOL, K28, 55. csomó., 120. tétel. 1941-O-22808. In the same report, from the police in Kolozsvár, the reporting officer related that within twenty-four hours he had received three appeals from individuals, representing "three distinct social classes," all

calling on the authorities to send Romanian men of military age to the Russian front (ibid., 59v).

131.   Illésfalvi, Szabó, and Számvéber, *Erdély a hadak útján*, 41.

132.   This was much truer of the Romanians than of the Hungarians, as the main losses sustained by the Hungarian forces were over the months starting in January 1943 until April. By the end of January 1943, Gosztony estimates that the Soviets had captured around 180,000 Romanian soldiers and officers. Peter Gosztony, *Stalins Fremde Heere: Das Schicksal der nichtsowjetischen Truppen im Rahmen der Roten Armee, 1941–1945* (Stuttgart: Bernard & Graefe Verlag, 1991), 103. Between the summer of 1941 and December 1943, 8,000 to 10,000 Hungarian soldiers had been captured by the Red Army, and from January to April 1943, an additional 85,000 to 90,000. Sipos and Ravasz, *Magyarország a második világháborúban*, 143.

133.   Mátyás Rákosi, "Ki a felelős? Előadás 1943 szeptember 7-én a 27-es számú hadifogolytáborban," in *A magyar jövőért* (Budapest: Szikra, 1950), http://mek.oszk. hu/04400/04456/04456.htm#54 (accessed December 15, 2007).

134.   Gosztony, *Stalins Fremde Heere*, 102.

135.   Ibid., 106–7.

136.   Ibid., 107.

137.   István Ravasz, *Erdély mint hadszíntér 1944* (Budapest: Petit Real Könyvkiadó, 1997), 52; *23 August 1944*, vol. 3, doc. 959, p. 162; Gosztony, *Stalins Fremde Heere*, 106–7.

138.   Péter Gosztonyi, *Magyarország a második világháborúban*, I. kötet (Munich: Herp Verlag, 1984), 101–3.

139.   Horthy, *Titkos iratai*, 298.

140.   Ibid., 314–15.

141.   HIWRP, Sabin Manuilă, box 11, folder 6, Iuliu Maniu to Benito Mussolini, December 28, 1940.

142.   Bela Vago, "Germany and the Jewish Policy of the Kállay Government," in *Hungarian-Jewish Studies*, vol. 2, ed. Randolph L. Braham (New York: World Federation of Hungarian Jews, 1969), 193.

143.   Mihai Antonescu, *Dacă vrei să câştigi războiul*, 20–21, 37.

144.   von Hassell, *Vom andern Deutschland*, 356.

145.   Broadcast from June 7, 1942. MOL, K63, 257. csomó., 1940–27. tétel./7./E., Román-magyar viszony—Erdély, iktatlan, II. rész. 1941–21/28–3736, 30.

146.   Hungary started putting out feelers in the summer of 1942, Romania likely also in the summer of 1942, most notably with the creation of a commission to prepare materials for an upcoming peace conference (likely initiated at the suggestion of the Italian ambassador to Bucharest, Renato Bova Scoppa). Gyula Juhász, ed., *Magyar-brit titkos tárgyalások 1943-ban* (Budapest: Kossuth Könyvkiadó, 1978), 14–15; Mihai Antonescu, *Dacă vrei să câştigi războiul*; Balta, *Rumänien und die Grossmächte*, 278–83. The Bulgarian legation in Bucharest watched Mihai Antonescu's efforts in this direction with special interest. TsDA, MVRI, F176K, op. 8, a.e. 830, 25, 38.

147.   On April 12–13, 1943, during a visit of Marshal Antonescu to Salzburg, Hitler made it known that he was aware that Mihai Antonescu had put out feelers to the Allies in Turkey, Switzerland, Portugal, and Spain. Hillgruber, *Staatsmänner und Diplomaten*

bei Hitler, 29, 30, pp. 214–33. A few days later, on April 18, 1943, the German foreign ministry sent a memorandum to the Hungarian government containing numerous accusations regarding Hungary's plans to extract itself from the war—and thereby from the Axis—and make contact with the Allies. Among other things, the author of the memorandum gave the details of a contact made between a Hungarian professor and the American ambassador in Turkey. Kerekes, *Allianz Hitler-Horthy-Mussolini,* 119, 346–50. On December 31, 1943, Horthy created an office headed by his son, whose task it was to seek contacts with the Allies so that Hungary could jump out of the war. Horthy, *Titkos iratai,* 411. For more on Romania's attempts to withdraw from the Axis and Mihai Antonescu's role in them, see Balta, *Rumänien und die Grossmächte,* 299–303, 311–12.

148. Horthy, *Titkos iratai,* 371.

149. Ibid., 389.

150. Ibid., 411.

151. Ibid., 410.

152. Antonescu expressed his frustration on this point to Hitler himself in a September 1943 letter. Arimia, Ardeleanu, and Lache, *Antonescu-Hitler,* doc. 63, 106–19.

153. See Ion Calafeteanu, ed., *Iuliu Maniu–Ion Antonescu: opinii și confruntări politice, 1940–1944* (Cluj-Napoca: Editura Dacia, 1994). Maniu's attacks on Antonescu, and the latter's response, will be addressed in more detail in Chapter 3.

154. Cited in Balta, *Rumänien und die Grossmächte,* 284.

155. ANIC, Arhivele Ministerului de Externe, Fond 71/Germania, vol. 92, f. 182. Mihai Antonescu then considered it highly unlikely that Germany would be in a position to determine the outcome of the peace.

156. *23 August 1944,* vol. 1, doc. 224, pp. 300–305, esp. 303. The liberal parties receiving the draft included the National Peasant Party (PNȚ), the Social Democrats (PSD), and the National Liberals (PNL). The attempt to make common cause failed when the non-Communists insisted that the USSR first agree to acknowledge Romania's right to Bessarabia and Northern Bukovina. See Balta, *Rumänien und die Grossmächte,* 288.

157. Hillgruber, *Staatsmänner und Diplomaten bei Hitler,* 31, 32, 33, pp. 233–263; Kerekes, *Allianz Hitler-Horthy-Mussolini,* 119, 346–50. In fact, the Germans had been working on plans for the country's occupation as early as autumn 1943. Tilkovszky, "Late Interwar Years," 351.

158. Kerekes, *Allianz Hitler-Horthy-Mussolini,* 126, 369–70.

159. Ibid., 126, 371.

160. HIWRP, Dimitri G. Popescu, box 1, folder entitled "Berna," pp. 9–10 (letter from Bossy, 5 November 1943).

161. Hillgruber, *Staatsmänner und Diplomaten bei Hitler,* 50, pp. 391–92.

162. Antonescu, in turn, let it drop that the wife of Hungary's ambassador to Stockholm was English. Hillgruber, *Staatsmänner und Diplomaten bei Hitler,* 50, p. 393.

163. In that conversation, Antonescu agreed with Hitler that Hungary was a likely breeding ground for Bolshevism, and he went on to say that, although he was not familiar with the members of the new Hungarian government, "he could nevertheless put no faith in them, or in any Hungarian." Hillgruber, *Staatsmänner und Diplomaten bei Hitler,* 50, p. 394. [This embarrassing truth was also pointed out a year earlier, on April

1, 1943, by Mihai Antonescu, who complained that "the Romanian government and people, together with their army, now find themselves in a situation where they are engaged in a war against those who recognize their [national] rights, and in alliance with those who negate them."] Mihai Antonescu also advocated seeking alternative peace options. ANIC, Arhivele Ministerului de Externe, Fond 71/Germania, volum 92, f. 182.

164. HIWRP, Dimitri G. Popescu, box 1, folder 1 (Events of Aug. 23, 1944—Documents, proclamations, reports, 1942–1946), Reuters London.

165. HIWRP, Dimitri G. Popescu, box 1, folder titled "Antonescu Mihail—Secret Contacts in Bern, 1944."

166. Hitchins, *Romania*, 496–97.

167. HIWRP, Dimitri G. Popescu, box 1, folder titled "Antonescu Mihai—Correspondence relating to events of August 23, 1944."

168. Yehuda Lahav, *Soviet Policy and the Transylvanian Question, 1940–1946* (Jerusalem: Hebrew University of Jerusalem, 1977), 16. The translation in the original has been altered slightly for smoothness. This sentiment was also voiced by the Hungarian ambassador to London at the time, György Barcza, on the occasion of Romania's switch. See György Barcza, *Diplomata emlékeim, 1911–1945*, vol. 2 (Budapest: Európa Kiadó, 1994), 144–45. In its broadcasts to the region, the BBC also made certain to emphasize to listeners that the Allies would soon be in a position to settle the Transylvanian border. See Kálmán Shvoy, *Shvoy Kálmán titkos naplója és emlékirata, 1918–1945* (Budapest: Kssuth Könyvkiadó, 1983), 289.

169. On the inevitability of war between the two states, see *ADAP, 1918–1945*, series E, vol. 2, 234, 400–401; *ADAP, 1918–1945*, series E: 1941–1945, vol. 4 (Göttingen: VandenHoeck & Ruprecht, 1975), 311, 571–72; *ADAP, 1918–1945*, series E, vol. 3, 102, 180–82.

170. Ungváry gives the troop numbers of the two forces as follows: Romanian Fourth Army, 113,759 (with Soviet forces arriving for support starting Septeber 8–10), Hungarian Second Army (plus some support from outside the Second Army), around 180,000. Ungváry, *A magyar honvédség*, 313. See also Ravasz, *Erdély mint hadszintér*, 48, 50.

171. Ungváry, *A magyar honvédség*, 315–17.

172. Ravasz, *Erdély mint hadszintér*, 29–31.

173. Ungváry, *A magyar honvédség*, 309.

174. From September 1944 to May 1945, the Hungarian army sustained losses totalling 715,000, as compared to a total of 224,100 for the period up to September 1944. The Hungarian military suffered its greatest losses in May 1945, when it lost about 490,000 (either dead, wounded, sick, missing, or captured). Many of these losses were in the form of prisoners of war, however. The Don catastrophe took a heavy toll in military deaths (around 50,000, a figure comparable to the number of military deaths between October 31 and December 31, 1944). Starting in late October 1944, Hungarian civilian casualties started to outstrip military ones. Ungváry, *A magyar honvédség*, 478–79.

175. Around forty thousand Romanian soldiers were killed between September 1 and October 25, 1944. Illésfalvi, Szabó, and Számvéber, *Erdély a hadak útján*, 164.

176. Cited in Ungváry, *A magyar honvédség*, 312. First Lieutenant Antal Csernavölgyi made a similar observation, comparing the "will to stay the course, dedication" of the

Hungarian troops to that of the Russian and Serbian partisans. Formerly, he noted, "it was clear that the soldiers only did what they did because they were ordered to do it. Now, however, without the slightest inspiration they make the tasks they are assigned their own" (ibid., 312–13). Ungváry further notes that German situation reports also remarked on the increase in Hungarian troop morale. Even in Joseph Goebbels' diary entry for September 7, 1944, we read how "the Hungarians are attacking the Romanians with great gusto and relish [Lust und Liebe]." Joseph Goebbels, *Die Tagebücher von Joseph Goebbels, Teil II: Diktate 1941–1945*, vol. 13: July–September 1944 (Munich: K. G. Saur, 1995), 425.

177.   Lajos Dálnoki Veress, *Magyarország honvédelme a II. világháború előtt és alatt, 1940– 1945*, vol. 3 (Munich: Danubia Druckerei, 1973), 35–36. See also Gosztony, *Hitlers Fremde Heere*, 427.

178.   *23 August 1944*, vol. 3, doc. 931, p. 113. From a "Sinteză asupra acţiunilor diviziei 11 infanteriei pentru forţarea Mureşului in zona Oarbă de Mureş în intervalul 19–28 septembrie 1944" on September 29, 1944. See also *23 August 1944*, vol. 3, doc. 963, p. 167.

179.   *23 August 1944*, vol. 3, doc. 938, p. 129. From a "Reportaj cu privire la desfăşurarea operaţiilor militare împotriva trupelor hitleriste şi horthyiste," October 9, 1944.

180.   *23 August 1944*, vol. 3, doc. 928, pp. 107–8.

181.   Cited in Ungváry, *A magyar honvédség*, 308–9.

182.   *23 August 1944*, vol. 3, doc. 942, p. 136. And indeed, that bond did prove difficult to dissolve, and Maniu was wary of its consequences. In 1947, his fears were realized when he was arrested and given a life sentence for treason. Mihai Fătu, *Antonescu şi opoziţia, 1940–1944* (Alexandria: Editura Tipoalex, 2000), 507.

183.   *23 August 1944*, vol. 3, docs. 924, 931, 938, 941, 944, 945, 957, 963, pp. 98–99, 111–13, 129–30, 135–36, 138–41, 156–58, 167–68.

184.   Cited in Lahav, *Soviet Policy*, 22.

185.   István Bethlen, *Hungarian Politics During World War Two: Treatise and Indictment*, ed. Ilona Bolza (Munich: Rudolf Tofenik, 1985), 9.

186.   Ibid., 16. (Translation includes minor corrections by the author.)

187.   For Transylvania, see especially Csatári, *Forgószélben*, and Loránt Tilkovszky, *Nemzetiségi politika Magyarországon a 20. században* (Debrecen: Csokonai Kiadó, 1998).

188.   István Rév observes that those who sought to rewind history back to World War II and glorify the country's struggle against Bolshevism believed they had "thus paid their dues for all the years when they had suffered Communist rule without demur." István Rév, *Retroactive Justice: Prehistory of Post-Communism* (Stanford, Calif.: Stanford University Press, 2005), 44.

3. People Between States

1.   MOL, K63, 252. csomó., 1939–27. tétel./7/E, 287.

2.   Géza Laczkó, "Kluj," *Magyar Szemle* 39, kötet 4 (158) szám (October 1940): 254–59, 259.

3.   Ion Negoiţescu, cited in Cornel Grad, *Al doilea arbitraj de la Viena* (Iaşi: Institutul European, 1998), 106n.

4. MOL, K28, 58. csomó., 130. tétel. 1942-G-20015. 5. lap.

5. Ion Negoițescu, cited in Grad, *Al doilea arbitraj de la Viena*, 107n. "Kolozsvár in those days looked like one giant caravan ready to hit the road," one Hungarian publicist observed. Sándor Tóth, *Erdély 22 éves rabsága* (Budapest: Magyar Géniusz Kiadása, 1941), 393.

6. János Jászfi, "Napló, Erdély 1940," *Honismeret* 28, no. 1 (2000): 30.

7. *23 August 1944, Documente*, vol. 1 (Bucharest: Editura Științifică și Enciclopedică, 1985), doc. 70, p. 101.

8. Ion Negoițescu, cited in Grad, *Al doilea arbitraj de la Viena*, 115n.

9. The Romanian government reportedly sent five hundred trucks to Transylvania to assist with the evacuation. "A román polgári hatóságok már elhagyták a kiürítendő városokat," *Népszava*, September 3, 1940, 4. A Hungarian witness commented that "no quantity of trucks, cars, or wagons" could meet the demand of the time. Tóth, *Erdély 22 éves rabsága*, 393. Later, Hungarian officials would complain that far too many documents had been taken and demanded some back. ASFJC, Primăria Mun. Cluj, Inv. 384/1942, Nr. 914–7992, Alapszám 4037.

10. Telegram circulated to provincial administration offices, cited in Grad, *Al doilea arbitraj de la Viena*, 116. Military officers and subofficers were also instructed, in orders given on August 31, 1940, to encourage the civilian population in Northern Transylvania to "remain convinced of its historic mission on the territory it now inhabited." *23 August 1944*, vol. 1, doc. 70, p. 101.

11. "Nagyvárad a várakozás lázában," *Magyarság*, September 4, 1940, 2.

12. "Tüntetések Bukarestben," *Népszava*, September 4, 1940, 6.

13. See Ottmar Trașcă, "Relațiile Româno-ungare și problema Transilvaniei, 1940–1944 (I)," *Anuarul Institutului de Istorie "A. D. Xenopol,"* 41 (2004): 317; C. A. Macartney, *October Fifteenth: A History of Modern Hungary, 1929–1945* (Edinburgh: Edinburgh University Press, 1956), 1:429; Tóth, *Erdély 22 éves rabsága*, 390–407.

14. Aladár Szegedy-Maszák, *Az ember ősszel visszanéz* (Budapest: Európa Kiadó, 1996), 324–25.

15. *Népszava*, September 8, 1940, 9. Special thanks to Gábor Egry for drawing my attention to this article.

16. "Romániában betiltották a tüntetéseket," *Népszava*, September 3, 1940, 4.

17. "A felsőház ünnepélyes ülésén is beszámolóbeszédet mondott Teleki miniszterelnök," *Népszava*, September 5, 1940, 3. It was rumored that in private Teleki was wary that the Second Vienna Arbitration could prove disastrous for Hungary. See Szegedy-Maszák, *Az ember*, 323–25.

18. "Romániában betiltották a tüntetéseket," *Népszava*, September 3, 1940, 4; "Nagyváradon át hömpölyög a kivonuló román hadsereg áradata," *Népszava*, September 4, 1940, 2.

19. For military personnel figures, see Trașcă, "Relațiile româno-ungare (I)," 316.

20. Reference to the city as the "heart of Transylvania" is from Staff Sergeant-Major Ferenc Adonyi. Ferenc Adonyi, *A magyar katona a második világháborúban, 1941–1945* (Klagenfurt, Austria: Ferd. Kleinmayr, 1954), 23.

21. ASFJC, Primăria Mun. Cluj, Inv. 386/1942, Nr. 23694–37140, Alapszám 32562.

22. ASFJC, Primăria Mun. Cluj, Inv. 384/1942, Nr. 8198–15782. Alapszám 15734.

23. *Tolnai Világlapja*, Budapest, September 25, 1940, I, 2–6. See also Ádám Reviczky, *Vesztes háborúk—megnyert csaták: emlékezés Reviczky Imre ezredesre* (Budapest: Magvető Könyvkiadó, 1985), 341.

24. *Irányelvek a megszálló csapatok magatartására* [Guidelines for the Conduct of the Occupying Forces] from August 31, 1940, cited in Trașcă, "Relațiile româno-ungare (I)," 319.

25. Huedin [R].

26. Loránt Tilkovszky, *Revízió és nemzetiségipolitika Magyarországon* (Budapest: Akadémiai Kiadó, 1967), 286.

27. BMF, RW 50, 122/1942, Aufzeichnung über Arbeitslager Fagaras, Fall Todesurteil Schmidt, Volkszählung in Ungarn. "Nr. 36." Seven individuals were tried in Kolozsvár on November 28, 1941, for their involvement in this incident and received sentences of no more than three months in jail. In justifying the mild sentence of the main protagonists, a Hungarian official cited Hungarian suffering during the twenty-two-year Romanian "occupation," claiming the defendants had been "overexcited by national feelings" at the time of the murders.

28. Diosig [R]. Mihai Fătu and Mircea Mușat, eds., *Horthyist-Fascist Terror in Northwestern Romania* (Bucharest: Meridiane Publishing House, 1986), 59.

29. Sălaj [R].

30. Ip [R].

31. Petre Țurlea, *Ip și Trăznea: atrocități maghiare și acțiune diplomatică românească, studiu și documente* (Bucharest: Editura Enciclopedică, 1996), 22–23, 161; Fătu and Mușat, *Horthyist-Fascist Terror*, 75–77, 88, 92; Péter Illésfalvi, Péter Szabó, and Norbert Számvéber, *Erdély a hadak útján, 1940–1944* (Debrecen: Puedlo Kiadó, 2007), 21–24. For a Romanian Uniate priest's account of the killings, see USHMMA, RG-25.026, Reel 1, Selected records from the collections of the Timiș branch of the Romanian National Archive, 1940–1953, Fr. 324–27. For a Hungarian administrator's perspective on the violence, see Béla Bethlen, *Észak-Erdély kormánybiztosa voltam* (Budapest: Zrinyi katonai kiadó, 1989), 27–28.

32. Romanian sources place the total number at 15,893, with the highest numbers in Cluj/Kolozsvár County (6,369). Fătu and Mușat, *Horthyist-Fascist Terror*, 92.

33. "Az Erdélyi értekezlet jegyzőkönyve," MOL, K28, 267. csomó., 10–11.

34. *DGFP*, series D, vol. 11, *The War Years, September 1, 1940–January 31, 1941* (Washington, D.C.: U.S. Government Printing Office, 1960), doc. 365, 636.

35. For examples of Romanian press reports on atrocities committed by Hungarian troops, gendarmes, and civilians, see *Universul*, September 22, 1940; September 23, 1940; October 5, 1940. Hungarian prime minister Pál Teleki mentioned in a speech in parliament on October 3, 1940, that "Romania has declared a press war against us, charging us with massive atrocities," calling such reports "lies." Pál Teleki, *Válogatott politikai írások és beszédek* (Budapest: Osiris kiadó, 2000), 434.

36. Keith Hitchins, *Rumania, 1866–1947* (Oxford: Clarendon Press, 1994), 452. From 1918 to 1920, Maniu served as president of the Council of Directors of Transylvania before the Treaty of Trianon was finalized. Although a Romanian and staunch proponent of the Romanian national cause—which he promoted as president of the

Romanian National Party (1926–1933), as prime minister of Romania (1928–1933) and later as president of the Romanian Peasant Party (1937–1944)—he was fluent in Hungarian and had spent his younger days studying in Budapest and Vienna and indeed was a representative to the Hungarian parliament. As leader of the Romanian National Peasant Party, Maniu headed the interwar government three times between 1928 and 1933. Tiberiu Iancu and et al., *Clujeni ai secolului 20, dicționar esențial* (Cluj-Napoca: Casa Cărții de Știință, 2000), 188.

37. Ioan Hudiță, *Jurnal politic*, vol. 2 (Iași: Institutul European, 2000), 38.

38. HIWRP, Sabin Manuilă, box 11, folder 7, "Chemare către poporul român din Transilvania, Banat, Crișana și Maramureș."

39. HIWRP, Sabin Manuilă, box 11, folder 8, Iuliu Maniu to Traian Leucuția, 1941.

40. Dorel Bancoș, *Social și național în politica guvernului Ion Antonescu* (Bucharest: Editura Eminescu, 2000), 56.

41. Ion Calafeteanu, ed., *Iuliu Maniu–Ion Antonescu: opinii și confruntări politice, 1940– 1944* (Cluj-Napoca: Editura Dacia, 1994), 37.

42. Ibid., 56–57. Antonescu's mention of Yugoslavia here refers to the fate of that country, which was invaded by Germany and Italy on April 6, 1941. The country was divided into many parts, including the Fascist puppet state of Croatia, zones occupied by German or Italian troops, and territories which were the objects of the revisionist ambitions of Italy, Hungary, Bulgaria, and Albania. The invasion came just over a week after Yugoslav military officers had staged a coup to overthrow the pro-Axis government. See Paul Robert Magocsi, *Historical Atlas of East Central Europe* (Seattle and London: University of Washington Press, 1998), 179.

43. Calafeteanu, *Iuliu Maniu–Ion Antonescu*, 57–58.

44. The Hungarian Embassy in Bucharest got wind of these developments and reported on them to the Hungarian foreign minister. MOL, K28, 65. csomó., 134. tétel. 1942-O-17323.

45. See Chapter 2. Maniu made explicit and repeated mention of this lack of a concrete guarantee in his correspondence with Antonescu and others during this time period. See HIWRP, Sabin Manuilă, box 11, folder 5, "Copy in Translation of letter to Marshal Antonescu," December 19, 1941.

46. The documents relating to the "Hungarian Military Administration" [Administrația Militară Maghiară] of Northern Transylvania are listed in the catalog of the ASFJC, but to my knowledge no scholars have been given access to the collection on the grounds that it is being cataloged. My own repeated attempts to view the collection met with no success.

47. László Ravasz, "Erdély," *Magyar Szemle* 39, no. 4 (158.) szám (October 1940): 229.

48. "Az Erdélyi értekezlet jegyzőkönyve," MOL, K28, 267. csomó., 1–190. I would like to thank Béla György for providing me with a copy of the conference proceedings.

49. Zsuzsanna Simon, "Erdély köz- és szakigazgatása a második bécsi döntés után," *Regio* 6, no. 4 (1995): 60–82, 68. Tilkovszky, *Revízió és nemzetiségipolitika*, 297. Among the "parachutists" were some of the refugees of Trianon. Otto Szabolcs,

Munka nélküli diplomások a Horthy-rendszerben, 1919–1944 (Budapest: Kossuth Könyvki-adó, 1964), 138. For Teleki's assertion, see "Az Erdélyi értekezlet jegyzőkönyve," MOL, K28, 267. csomó., 7.

50. Bethlen, *Észak-Erdély kormánybiztosa voltam*, 20–21.

51. As of February 1942, forty-two of the Transylvanian representatives were members of the Transylvanian Party. The parliament as a whole had 373 seats, about 12 percent of which were occupied by representatives from Northern Transylvania. Gábor Egry, "Az erdélyiség színváltozása, az Erdélyi Párt ideológiája: identitáspolitikai elemzési kísérlet," (unpublished manuscript), 6.

52. Macartney, *October Fifteenth*, 1:435, 458. The quotations are from Macartney's paraphrase of the platform. See also "Gróf Teleki Béla bejelenti az Erdélyi Párt ma-galakulását, 1941. jún. 17," in *Erdély a magyar képviselőházban, 1941* (Kolozsvár: Az Erdélyi Párt, 1942), 5–9.

53. Zoltán Tibori Szabó notes that Prime Minister Pál Teleki and the president of the Transylvanian Party, Béla Teleki, were cousins, and he suggests the modus vivendi between the Transylvanian Party and the government was worked out between them. Zoltán Tibori Szabó, *Teleki Béla erdélyisége: Embernek maradni embertelen időkben* (Kolozs-vár: NIS Kiadó, 1993), 12–16, 29–30.

54. On the economic structural and agricultural differences, see Béla Bulla, "Az új országgyarapodás," *Magyar Szemle* 39, no. 4 (158) szám (October 1940): 230–40, 235.

55. Teleki, *Válogatott politikai írások*, 435. The speech was delivered on October 3, 1940.

56. "Albrecht Dezső, képviselő, a képviselőház 1941. június 23-án tartott beszé-dében," in *Erdély a magyar képviselőházban, 1941*, 25, 30–31. Andrew C. Janos points out that "etatism" indeed did indeed enjoy a long history in Hungary, "who likewise justified it in reference to the national interest." Janos, *The Politics of Backwardness in Hungary, 1825–1945* (Princeton, N.J.: Princeton University Press, 1982), 256.

57. Teleki, *Válogatott politikai írások*, 435.

58. "Az Erdélyi értekezlet jegyzőkönyve," MOL, K28, 267. csomó., 36–38, 48, 51, 58.

59. Ibid., 49.

60. Of the differences outlined here, many were supposedly shared by other rean-nexed territories. Even prior to the reannexation of Transylvania, for example, com-mentators were drawing out the uniqueness of the Felvidék (northern territories), formerly part of Czechoslovakia, among which was the social leveling highlighted here for the Transylvanian case. István Weis, "A magyarság úri mivolta," *Magyar Szemle* 38, no. 3 (151) szám (March 1940): 172–76. A radio speech Horthy planned to deliver the day Hungary was occupied by the Germans (March 15, 1944) reveals the defensive stance Horthy had taken on the issue of social inequality in Hungary. Miklós Horthy, *Horthy Miklós titkos iratai* (Budapest: Kossuth Könyvkiadó, 1962), 411. Hitler himself, in March 1944, considered Hungary to be the place most likely to succumb to Bolshe-vism, given how the upper classes and nobility lorded over the peasantry and workers. Andreas Hillgruber, ed., *Staatsmänner und Diplomaten bei Hitler: Vertrauliche Aufzeichnungen über Unterredungen mit Vertretern des Auslandes, 1942–1944, II. Teil* (Frankfurt am Main: Bernard & Graefe Verlag, 1970), 50, 392. On the impact of the work of Romanian

rural sociologists (such as Gusti) on the Hungarian interwar elite, see Zsuzsanna Török, "Planning the National Minority: Strategies of the Journal *Hitel* in Romania, 1935–44," *Nationalism & Ethnic Politics* 7, no. 2 (Summer 2001): 57–74, 64.

61. "Gróf Teleki Béla, az Erdélyi Párt elnöke, a képviselőház 1941. június 17-i ülésén," in *Erdély a magyar képviselőházban, 1941*, 8. Incidentally, this also formed part of the Transylvanian Party platform.

62. ASFJC, Primăria Mun. Cluj, 3/1941, 31848–45797, Alapszám 32003. See also "A munkásságot és a nemzetet nem lehet egymástól elszakítani!" *Keleti Újság*, July 28, 1942, 3.

63. "Gróf Teleki Béla: 'Tudjuk milyen áldozatot jelentett ez a lejövetel a miniszterelnök urnak,'" *Ellenzék*, January 19, 1942, 4. C. A. Macartney also observed that "social antagonism between the Magyars of Transylvania had been partially smoothed out by the years of affliction spent by all classes under Roumanian rule. Moreover, all felt a certain solidarity not against Roumanians alone, but—after the re-annexation—against other Hungarians also." Macartney, *October Fifteenth*, 2:341.

64. "Erdély már számtalanszor példát adott az összmagyarságnak," *Ellenzék*, April 27, 1942, 2.

65. In 1931, for example, Transylvanian voters cast 70.5 percent of the total votes received for Communist Party candidates. Robert R. King, *A History of the Romanian Communist Party* (Stanford, Calif.: Hoover Institution Press, 1980), 33–34.

66. Csatári said of Júlia Szabó, who joined the Romanian Communist Party in 1937, that she "expected socialism to resolve her native land's social and nationality conflicts, not just as a worker, but as a Transylvanian woman." Dániel Csatári, *Forgószélben: magyar-román viszony, 1940–1945* (Budapest: Akadémiai Kiadó, 1968), 161.

67. Police began a roundup of the Communists almost immediately following the reannexation. Another crackdown was to take place in 1942. Edgár Balogh, *Szolgálatban: Emlékirat, 1935–1944* (Bucharest: Kriterion Könyvkiadó, 1978), 168; Egon Balas, *Will to Freedom: A Perilous Journey Through Fascism and Communism* (Syracuse, N.Y.: Syracuse University Press, 2000), 40; Csatári, *Forgószélben*, 142–43, 149, 198–99, 204–5.

68. Csatári, *Forgószélben*, 256; MOL, K617, 1. csomó, 6541/23, 1941, 1–112. On the ban on *Korunk*, see OHA, Bözödi György-interjú. Készítette Békéné Nándor Orsolya 1986-ban. 68. nos. 47–48. o.

69. Csatári, *Forgószélben*, 164. Her collaboration with the DEF resulted in many arrests of the movement's leadership in Transylvania (ibid., 164–85).

70. MOL, K617, 1. csomó, 6541/23, 1941, 1–112.

71. Georgi Dimitrov and Ivo Banac, eds., *The Diary of Georgi Dimitrov, 1933–1949* (New Haven, Conn., & London: Yale University Press, 2003), 249. For other mention of Rákosi and the Transylvanian question, see pp. 282–83. Rákosi would later become the general secretary of the Hungarian Communist Party (after 1948 Hungarian Workers' Party) from 1945 through 1956.

72. Péter Sipos, *Imrédy Béla és a Magyar Megújulás Pártja* (Budapest: Akadémiai Kiadó, 1970), 204.

73. Ibid., 218.

74. In Kolozsvár, for example, the paying membership of the MMP numbered 2,058 as of August 1942, and it had the support of the city's "parachutist" mayor, Tibor

Keledy. Sipos, *Imrédy Béla,* 219–22. For the whole of Kolozsvár County by the end of 1940, Arrow Cross membership numbered 2,503 with 8 party organizations. Margit Szőlősi-Janze, *Die Pfeilkreutzlerbewegung in Ungarn: historischer Kontext, Entwicklung und Herrschaft* (Munich: R. Oldenbourg Verlag, 1989), 130.

75. Sipos, *Imrédy Béla,* 220.

76. Szőlősi-Janze, *Die Pfeilkreutzlerbewegung,* 232–33.

77. Ferenc Szálasi was followed—from one end of Northern Transylvania to the other during his visits—by officials of the secret police and reported on by willing and unwitting witnesses alike. MOL, K28, 65. csomó., 136. tétel. 1942-O-28145; ASFJC, Primăria Mun. Cluj, Inv. 386/1942, Nr. 15785–23352. Alapszám 23141; MOL, Kolozs megye főispáni eln. iratok, 1942, 4062–4063 tekercs, Alapszám 77–1942; MOL, Kolozs megye főispáni eln. iratok, 1942, 4064 tekercs, Alapszám 245. Regent Horthy was very suspicious of the Arrow Cross, saying in a letter dated October 14, 1940, to Prime Minister Teleki that Hungary's Jews "are more loyal to their adoptive homeland than the Arrow Cross." Miklós Nagybányai Horthy, *Horthy Miklós titkos iratai* (Budapest: Kossuth Könyvkiadó, 1972), 261.

78. MOL, K28, 65. csomó., 136. tétel. 1942-O-28145. See also Lóránt Tilkovszky, "A nyilasok törvényjavaslata a nemzetiségi kérdés rendezéséről," *Századok* 99, no. 6 (1965): 1247–58.

79. Sipos, *Imrédy Béla,* 246, 249, 251.

80. "Gróf Teleki Béla, az Erdélyi Párt elnöke, 1941. november 21-án," in *Erdély a magyar képviselőházban, 1941,* 14. Representative Imre Mikó proposed that a land reform be first tried in Transylvania (ibid., 41). Another commentator suggested that the reannexation had reinvigorated plans to overhaul the railroad system in Hungary. Rezső Ruisz, "Vasuti gondok," *Magyar Szemle* 39, no. 5 (159) szám (November 1940): 299–304. Similar claims were put forward about plans for updating industry and trade sectors through education reforms and revamping Hungary's waterways. János Áfra Nagy, "Magyar Iparos- és kereskedőnevelés," *Magyar Szemle* 39, no. 6 (160) szám (December 1940): 376–80; Árpád Trummer, "A magyar viziutak," *Magyar Szemle* 40, no. 4 (164) szám (April 1941): 191–96.

81. Cited in Marta Petreu, *An Infamous Past: E. M. Cioran and the Rise of Fascism in Romania* (Chicago: Ivan R. Dee, 2005), 194–95. Ion Antonescu had similar ambitions for the territories of Bessarabia and Bukovina that were reannexed following the 1941 offensive against the USSR. He planned to make them into a kind of "model province," setting the stage for the social, economic and moral/spiritual overhaul of state, nation, and continent. Vladimir Solonari, " 'Model Province': Explaining the Holocaust of Bessarabian and Bukovinian Jewry," *Nationalities Papers* 34, no. 4 (2006): 471–500. See also Vladimir Solonari, "Purifying the Nation: Population Exchange and Ethnic Cleansing in World War II Romania" (unpublished manuscript, cited with permission).

82. Sebastian Balta, *Rumänien und die Grossmächte in der Ära Antonescu, 1940–1944* (Stuttgart: Franz Steiner Verlag, 2005), 90–91.

83. MOL, K63, 258. csomó., 1940–27. tétel./7./T.3., 53.

84. Nicholas M. Nagy-Talavera, *The Greenshirts and Others: A History of Fascism in Hungary and Romania* (Stanford, Calif.: Hoover Institution Press, 1970), 320. For the

attitude of the Iron Guard with respect to Hungary and Hungarians, see Radu Ioanid, *The Sword of the Archangel: Fascist Ideology in Romania* (New York: Columbia University Press, 1990), 113, 197; Galeazzo Ciano, *Ciano's Diplomatic Papers: being a record of nearly 200 conversations held during the years 1936–42 [t]ogether with important memoranda, letters, telegrams, etc.* (London: Odhams Press Limited, 1948), 37–38.

85. Nagy-Talavera, *Greenshirts and Others*, 321.

86. MOL, K28, 55. csomó., 120. tétel. 1940-O-20215.

87. Nagy-Talavera, *Greenshirts and Others*, 320–26. Antonescu was by no means a philosemite, but he recognized in the Iron Guard a threat to his power.

88. MOL, K63, 260. csomó., 1941–27. tétel./1.II., 320.

89. MOL, K63, 260. csomó., 1941–27. tétel./1.II., 338.

90. Nagy-Talavera, *Greenshirts and Others*, 324–25.

91. Ibid., 331.

92. *Pe marginea prăpastiei, 21–23 ianuarie 1941,* vol. 1 (Bucharest: Editura Scripta, 1992), 66.

93. Interwar estimates give the size of the Romanian Communist Party during the interwar period at between 2,500 at its largest, before it was banned in 1924, to 1,200 by 1931, to a mere 1,000 by the time the Red Army arrived in 1944. Vladimir Tismaneanu, *Stalinism for All Seasons: A Political History of Romanian Communism* (Berkeley: University of California Press, 2003), 57–59. See also Balta, *Rumänien und die Grossmächte,* 287–88.

94. Tismaneanu, *Stalinism for All Seasons,* 69; Florica Dobre, ed., Consiliul Naţional pentru Studierea Arhivelor Securităţii, *Membrii C.C. al P.C.R. 1945–1989, Dicţionar* (Bucharest: Editura Enciclopedică, 2004), 6; Nagy-Talavera, *Greenshirts and Others,* 351.

95. The possibility of the Legionnaires' making common cause with the Communists was almost subzero, given the longtime anti-Communist stance of the Legion. Ioanid, *The Sword of the Archangel,* 98–108. Nevertheless, from the ideological standpoint, there were some similarities. The Legion denounced "capitalist individualism" and called for the destruction of the "liberal economic structure" and its replacement with a centrally planned economy. Talavera notes that there were contacts between guardists and Communists in prison. Nagy-Talavera, *Greenshirts and Others,* 315, 323. Furthermore, there appears to have been at least one meeting between leaders of the two movements during the war. *Pe marginea prăpastiei,* 63–65. For Communists' attempts to make common cause with Maniu and the liberals, see chapter 2, "Jumping Out."

96. Dinu C. Giurescu, *Romania in the Second World War, 1939–1945* (New York: Columbia University Press, 2000), 96–97.

97. In fact, a special rubber stamp was made for official correspondence which read, "Matter relating to liberated territories." MOL, K28, 56. csomó., 128. tétel. 1942-O-17699; MOL, K28, 55. csomó., 121. tétel. 1940-O-20610.

98. MOL, K28, 182. csomó., 372. tétel. 1943-O-18734. See also MOL, Kolozs megye főispáni eln. iratok, 1942, 4064 tekercs, Alapszám 133, 1942. 5. lap; MOL, K28, 64. csomó., 132. tétel. 1942-D-15788.

99. In addition to the two Danubian Principalities of the Regat (Moldavia and Wallachia) plus Northern Dobruja, "Greater Romania" [România Mare] further encompassed the territories of Southern Dobruja (though annexed already in 1913), Bessarabia, and Bukovina, in addition to Transylvania.

100. See, for example, ASFJC, Biroul de cenzură Cluj-Turda, nr. 1/1940–1942, 12. For use of "răpit," see ASFJC, Inspectoratul de Poliție Cluj, Nr. Inv. 399. Dosar Nr. 92/1942(II), 1.

101. Most of the stereotypes discussed in this section were not new, even if they manifested themselves around specifically wartime politics and events. For a refined historical analysis of Romanian and Hungarian stereotypes of one another, see Sorin Mitu, *Transilvania mea: istorii, mentalități, identități* (Iași: Polirom, 2006), 228–45.

102. ASFJC, Biroul de cenzură Cluj-Turda, nr. 1/1940–1942. f. 381.

103. MOL, K28, 55. csomó., 120. tétel. 1943-O-19758. "Noi ți-am ridicat marețe temple/ Te-am facut un centru de cultură,/ Ți-am clădit palate ca-n poveste/ și astazi vin barbarii de le fură!"

104. See, for example, USHMMA, RG-25.013M, Preşedinția Consiliului de Miniştri—Cabinet Militar, 1940–1944, roll 14, dosar 402/1941, f. 29; Grad, *Al doilea arbitraj de la Viena*, 169. Indeed, many Hungarian statesmen were aware of this proclivity of their Romanian counterparts and acted accordingly. MOL, K63, 252. csomó., 1939–27. tétel/7, 69–70.

105. *Stenogramele şedintelor consiliului de ministri: Guvernarea Ion Antonescu*, vol. 6, March 27, 1942 (Bucharest: Arhivele Naționale ale României, 2002), 393.

106. HIWRP, Sabin Manuilă, box 11, folder 6, Iuliu Maniu to Benito Mussolini, December 28, 1940. See also Grigore Ionescu, *Rumänische Bautätigkeit in Siebenbürgen von 1919–1940* (Bucharest, 1943).

107. ASFJC, Biroul de cenzură Cluj-Turda, nr. 1/1940–1942. f. 325. See also "Huni, Vandali," *Tribuna Asociației Refugiaților şi Expulsaților din Ardealul Ocupat*, January 22, 1941, 2.

108. MOL, K28, 55. csomó., 120. tétel. 1944-O-17467.

109. *Erdély a magyar képviselőházban, 1941*, 69.

110. Grad, *Al doilea arbitraj de la Viena*, 198n. Official Romanian propaganda was quick to counter these arguments, suggesting that the reason Hungary looks better is that the Hungarian state does not keep statistics on certain social ills. In a radio program broadcast in early December 1941, it was argued: "We at least have had the courage to count and keep records on syphilitics." Cited in Grad, *Al doilea arbitraj de la Viena*, 199.

111. Ervin Farkasfalvi, "A magyar bűnügyi statisztika anyaga és legújabb eredményei," *Magyar statisztikai szemle* 22, no. 6 (1944): 238–47, 245.

112. Illésfalvi, Szabó, and Számvéber, *Erdély a hadak útján*, 40.

113. ASFJC, Primăria Mun. Cluj, Inv. 384/1942, Nr. 44393–112483/[25086–25104], Alapszám 45406.

114. ASFJC. Fond 170, #55. "Reggel, este, éjjel után vagy délbe, / Egyszer mégis csak bemegyünk Erdélybe. / Mosolyognak a lányok, Mi is vissza reájok. / Nem sírnak ott csak a kényes, zsírtól fényes oláhok." After the Second Vienna Arbitration, the song was printed on postcards complete with a musical score.

115. See Péter Vida, *Magyarország és Románia: két ország Európa színterén* (Budapest: Hornyánszky Viktor Könyvnyomda, 1940), 27–59; György Lukács, "The Injustices of the Treaty of Trianon," in *Justice for Hungary: Review and Criticism of the Effect of the Treaty of Trianon* (London, Bombay, Calcutta, and Madras: Longmans, Green and Co. Ltd, 1928), 152.

116. ASFJC, Biroul de cenzură Cluj-Turda, nr. 1/1940–1942. f. 286. As for official references to Romanians as *oláh*, there was a Romanian army deserter who had fled to Hungary in January 1941. In the file for his case, the official in charge designated him as an *"oláh menekült"* [*oláh* refugee]. ASFJC, Primăria Mun. Cluj, Inv. 386/1942, Nr. 15785–23352. Alapszám 21622.

117. Instead, they were instructed to use the term *román* [Romanian]. *Irányelvek a megszálló csapatok magatartására* [Guidelines for the Conduct of the Occupying Forces] from August 31, 1940, cited in Traşcă, "Relaţiile româno-ungare (I)," 319.

118. Marius Turda, "The Nation as Object: Race, Blood, and Biopolitics in Interwar Romania," *Slavic Review* 66, no. 3 (Fall 2007): 412–41, esp. 416–24.

119. Iordache Făcăoaru, "Socialantropologia ca ştiinţă pragmatistă," *Buletin eugenic şi biopolitic* 9, no. 9–10 (1938): 358, cited in Turda, "Nation as Object," 422.

120. Mihály Malán, "Magyar vér—oláh vér," *Magyar Szemle* 39, no. 3 (157) szám (September 1940): 187–92, 190. In interwar Romania, eugenics experiments of this sort were not uncommon. Two eugenicists in particular tried to prove that the Szeklers were indeed Romanians by examining blood samples. Maria Bucur, *Eugenics and Modernization in Interwar Romania* (Pittsburgh: University of Pittsburgh Press, 2002), 145–46.

121. MOL, K28, 65. csomó., 134. tétel. 1944-L-21883. Lajos Csík and Ernő Kállay, "Vércsoportvizsgálatok kalotaszegi községekben," in *Az Erdélyi Tudományos Intézet évkönyve, 1940–1941* (Kolozsvár: Minerva irodalmi és nyomdai műintézet, 1942), 25–46.

122. "A magyar faji alaptulajdonságokat veszi alapul az inteligencia-vizsgálat," *Keleti Újság*, January 28, 1942, 4.

123. BMF, RW 50, 129. The Nuremberg Laws, adopted in Germany in 1935, defined a Jew as an individual with at least three Jewish grandparents or a person with two Jewish grandparents who was a Jew by religion or had married a Jew. See *Die Nürnberger Gesetze vom 15. September 1935*, http://www.dhm.de/lemo/html/dokumente/nuernbergergesetze/index.html (accessed October 24, 2007).

124. Zsombor Szász, "A Román változás," *Magyar Szemle* 40, kötet 1 (161) szám (January 1941): 9–15, 9.

125. There is perhaps no better evidence of this than the attitude of the Romanian delegation to the German-Italian Officers' Commission, which stressed the importance of playing up some slights against the Romanian minority, while ignoring others. Cases of beatings and executions were to be reported immediately, whereas women looking for their husbands or youth fleeing military service should be left out of reports to the commission. ANIC, Fond Delegatul Marelui Stat Major pe lângă Comisie de Ofiţeri Italo-Germană, Dos. 64/1943, f. 15.

126. Magda Ádám, Gyula Juhász, and Lajos Kerekes, eds., *Magyarország és a második világháború: titkos diplomáciai okmányok a háború előzményeihez és történetéhez* (Budapest: Kossuth Könyvkiadó, 1959), 121, 289–90. See Second Vienna Arbitration, *DGFP*, series D, vol. 10, doc. 413, 581–87.

127. According to a summary report on the situation of the refugees presented to the Hungarian interior minister, Ferenc Keresztes-Fischer, on July 4, 1943, from 1939 to 1941 government aid to refugees was 26.4 million pengős, and from 1942 to 1943, 9.6 million pengős. Cited in Karoly Kapronczay, *Refugees in Hungary: Shelter from the Storm*

during World War II (Toronto-Buffalo: Matthias Corvinus Publishing, 1999), 19. This likely constituted less than 1 percent of the total budget for any given year (given that the budget for 1943 alone was 4.25 billion pengő). *Az 1939. évi június hó 10-ére hirdetett országgyűlés képviselőházának naplója,* vol. 16, 319. ülés, 1942. december 3-án (Budapest: Athenaeum, 1942), 503. Csatári placed the total number of Hungarian refugees fleeing from Romania up to the end of 1942 at around sixty thousand. Csatári, *Forgószélben,* 140–41. Balogh concludes that between September 1940 and February 1941, one hundred thousand Hungarians fled Southern Transylvania, 65 to 70 percent of whom ended up in Northern Transylvania. Béni L. Balogh, *A magyar-román kapcsolatok 1939–1940-ben és a második bécsi döntés* (Csíkszereda: Pro-Print Könyvkiadó, 2002), 311–12. According to the mayor's office of Kolozsvár, as of April 29, 1942, the city had received a total of 6,915 refugees from Romania. ASFJC, Primăria Mun. Cluj, Inv. 386/1942, Nr. 15785–23352, Alapszám 15937.

128.   Ion Antonescu, *Generalul Antonescu către ţară 6 septemvrie 1940–22 iunie 1941* (Bucharest, 1941), 75–76. This amount constituted about 2 percent of the total budget for those months. The figure for expenditure is my own approximation based on Antonescu's year-end report, which offers a combination of figures, estimates, and more nebulous information (like that the "ministries and institutions" of government contributed 2 to 10 million lei apiece). The figure for the total state revenue for that period portends to be precise. In a meeting of Antonescu's Cabinet of Ministers on March 13, 1942, Antonescu said there was a total of 195,000 refugees from Transylvania in Romania. *Stenogramele,* vol. 6, doc. 6, 198. Romanian historian Dorel Bancoş gives much lower figures both for refugees to Northern Transylvania (104,743) and for Romanian refugees from Northern Transylvania (221,697) between 1940 and 1944. Bancoş, cited in Balta, *Rumänien und die Grossmächte,* 93–94. Csatári placed the total number of Romanian refugees from Northern Transylvania as of the end of 1942 at two hundred thousand. Csatári, *Forgószélben,* 140–41. The Romanian delegation to the German-Italian Commission reported in spring 1943 a total of 201,743 Romanian refugees from Northern Transylvania since the Second Vienna Arbitration. ANIC, Fond Delegatul Marelui Stat Major pe lângă Comisie de Ofiţeri Italo-Germană, Dos. 64/1943, f. 12.

129.   Two pengő forty fillér was not a large amount, given that a chicken could sell for eight and a bathing suit for six to twelve pengő. See MOL. K28, 59. csomó., 130. tétel. (in a folder labeled "M.E. K28, 1942"), 418; ASFJC, Curtea de Apel Regală, Fond 740, Inv. 286, 314, Decizii penale şi civile 12/1942, B.I. 47/1942. On the camps, see Andor Csizmadia, *Vázlat Kolozsvár társadalmáról* (Kassa, Hungary Szent Erzsébet Nyomda, r.t., 1942), 9.

130.   ASFJC, Primăria Mun. Cluj, Inv. 384/1941, Nr. 12246–23152, Alapszám 12522; ASFJC, Primăria Mun. Cluj, 3/1941, 24435–31627, Alapszám 25697; ASFJC, Primăria Mun. Cluj, Inv. 384/1941, Nr. 34–12162, Alapszám 7300, 8480; ASFJC, Primăria Mun. Cluj, Inv. 384/1941, Nr. 34–12162, Alapszám 4452.

131.   "Csökkent a munkanélküliek száma Kolozsváron," *Ellenzék,* July 12, 1941, 4. Some of these signed up for work in Germany (nine hundred by July 18, 1941).

132.   This figure represented about 65 percent of the total number of refugees who received government aid, according to Antonescu. Mediating between the government

and the refugees was the Association of Romanians Expelled and Fled from the Territory of Transylvania Lost with the Vienna Verdict [Asociaţia Românilor Expulzaţi şi Refugiaţi din Ardealul Cedat prin Verdictul dela Viena] with its central offices in Bucharest. The association submitted requests on behalf of refugees—mostly professionals—for positions and recommended them for the state's employ on the basis of their refugee status. See ANIC, Fond Ministerul Muncii, Sănătăţii şi Ocrotirilor Sociale, Oficiul Central De Românizare, Dosar 695/1941, "Cereri primite dela Asociaţia Românilor Expulzaţi şi Refugiaţi din Ardealul Cedat prin Verdictul dela Viena," f. 3–77.

133. Ion Antonescu, *Către ţară*, 75.

134. Ibid., 73–85. See also Council of Ministers meeting transcripts from September 18 and 27, October 1, 8, and 17, and November 26, 1940, in *Stenogramele*, vol. 1, doc. 2, 5, 6, 9, 14, 25.

135. Csizmadia, *Vázlat Kolozsvár társadalmáról*, 16. Among the workers at Dermata were several members of the Communist Party, which was illegal in Kolozsvár at the time. Balas, *Will to Freedom*, 43.

136. Ştefan Pascu, ed. *Istoria Clujului* (Cluj: Consiliul Popular al Municipiului Cluj, 1974), 432. Fătu and Muşat, *Horthyist-Fascist Terror*, 166–67.

137. MOL, K63, 259. csomó., 1940–27. tétel/7./8, 703. MOL, K28, 213. csomó., 467. tétel. (German-Italian Commission). Alapszám 1942-O-28380, 2–11, 13.

138. Kapronczay, *Refugees in Hungary*, 19.

139. ASFJC, Primăria Mun. Cluj, Inv. 384/1941, Nr. 34–12162, Alapszám 623; ASFJC, Primăria Mun. Cluj, Inv. 386/1942, Nr. 23694–37140, Alapszám 29589.

140. ASFJC, Primăria Mun. Cluj, 3/1941, 31848–45797. Alapszám 32793.

141. Ibid., Alapszám 44514.

142. *Stenogramele*, vol. 1, doc. 11, 215; Miron Radu Paraschivescu, *Drumuri şi răspîntii, reportaje 1937–1944* (Bucharest: Editura pentru literatură, 1967), 119–29. The Hungarian Consul in Braşov reported that more than one thousand Catholics had left Turda for Hungary proper, a number which did not include Hungarian refugees representing other religions. MOL, K28, 182. csomó., 372. tétel. 1942.O-21252.

143. ASFJC, Inspectoratul de Poliţie Cluj. Its documents are still filed under that name in Romanian archives. It was not only the police headquarters that relocated, but also other county offices and their employees, nor was the city of Kolozsvár/Cluj an exception in this regard. Other county seats were paired with cities across the border in Romania as well. See Traşcă, "Relaţiile româno-ungare (I)," 317n.

144. MOL, K63, 257. csomó., 1940–27. tétel/7/E, Román-magyar viszony—Erdély, iktatlan, II. rész, 593–95; BMF, RW 50, 180, Komitat Cluj-Turda; *Stenogramele*, vol. 8, 575.

145. MOL, K63, 253. csomó., 27. tétel 1940–27/3, 5–7; Ion Antonescu, *Către ţară*, 75.

146. The office in question was the Romanian State Undersecretariat for Romanianization, Colonization and Inventory (SSRCI) and its sub-organ the Directorate of Refugees and Evacuated Populations. See Lya Benjamin, ed., *Evreii din România între anii 1940–1944*, vol. I, *Legislaţia antievreiască* (Bucharest: Editura Hasefer, 1993), doc. 37, 38, pp. 134, 141. See also Vladimir Solonari, *Purifying the Nation: Population Exchange and*

Ethnic Cleansing in World War II Romania (unpublished manuscript, cited with permission).

147. *Stenogramele*, vol. 3, 900, June 17, 1941, 571.

148. Even as early as October 11, 1940, however, Ion Antonescu said that refugees who planned to return to their homes were "very good," while those who planned to return only to transfer their personal property were "less good." "Şedinţa consiliului de cabinet din 1 octombrie 1940," in *Stenogramele*, vol. 1, doc. 11, 217.

149. MOL, K28, 55. csomó., 119. tétel. 1941-O-20341.

150. Alexandru Anca, *Destin ardelenesc* (Cluj: Editura Clusium, 2001), 120.

151. OHA, Bözödi György-interjú. Készítette Békéné Nándor Orsolya 1986-ban. 68. nos. 45–46. o.

152. USHMMA, RG-25.010M, Inspectoratul General al Jandarmeriei, roll 13, dosar 29/1942, f. 214.

153. Paraschivescu, *Drumuri şi răspîntii*, 128–29.

154. *Stenogramele*, vol. 6, 198.

155. This policy did not extend to Hungarians from the Regat. In fact, on November 13, 1940, the Hungarian parliament voted to transfer the Szeklers in Bukovina to Hungary. On that occasion Prime Minister Pál Teleki argued: "We have ensured that all would be done in order to bring back as soon as possible from the Regat of Romania—which is not the homeland of Hungarians—first those Hungarians, who are not tied there by any properties and then those, who have properties but could sell their land." Cited in Tamás Stark, "Migrations during World War II," in *Minorities Research 4*, http://www.hhrf.org/kisebbsegkutatas/mr_04/cikk.php?id=1199 (accessed January 1, 2008).

156. MOL, K28, 56. csomó., 124. tétel. 1941-K-22302.

157. Ibid., 1941-O-17053.

158. Ibid., 1941-K-19410.

159. MOL, K28, 182. csomó., 372. tétel. 1942-O-21252; MOL, K28, 56. csomó., 124. tétel. 1941-K-26471.

160. MOL, K63, 254. csomó., 1940–27. tétel/7.I, 5, 14–16, 73, 94, 107–8.

161. MOL, K28, 56. csomó., 124. tétel. 1941-O-16803. Furthermore, although it is an undocumented phenomenon, I have encountered at least two individuals who managed to enter Northern Transylvania on the pretense of a "visit" and simply stayed on.

162. *Stenogramele*, vol. 1, 216. Sometimes illicit charges for crossing the border were even issued, as in the April 1943 case of some corrupt Hungarian border guards who charged (Hungarian) individuals fleeing to Hungary from Southern Transylvania fifty pengő to cross the border. MOL, K28, 182. csomó., 372. tétel. 1944-O-27948, 231.

163. "Comunicatul Asociaţiei Refugiaţilor şi Expulsaţilor din Ardealul Ocupat," *Tribuna Asociaţiei Refugiaţilor şi Expulsaţilor din Ardealul Ocupat*, December 25, 1940, 5.

164. *Erdély a magyar képviselőházban, 1941*, 13.

165. *Stenogramele*, vol. VI, 318.

166. Mihai Antonescu, *Dacă vrei să câştigi războiul, trebuie să pregăteşti pacea* (Cluj-Napoca: Muzeul Etnografic al Transilvaniei, 1991), 6.

167. Ibid., 8–10.

168. USHMMA, RG-25.010M, Inspectoratul General al Jandarmeriei, roll 13, dosar 29/1942, f. 126.

169. A copy of the form was obtained by the Hungarian authorities and can be found in MOL, K63, 253. csomó., 27. tétel., 1940–27/4, 159. See also ASFJC, Inspectoratul de Poliție Cluj, Nr. Inv. 42/1940(I), 84.

170. MOL, K28, 55. csomó., 121. tétel. 1943-O-15536.

171. Gábor Egry, *Az erdélyiség "színeváltozása": kísérlet az Erdélyi Párt ideológiájának elemzésére, 1940–1944* (Budapest: Napvilág Kiadó, 2008), 82.

172. ANIC, Fond Ministerul de Interne, Dosar 438/1941, f. 9. Document from September 1941. Already in July of that year there were proposals for the creation of an "interministerial commission" to oversee reciprocity in Romania (ibid., f. 19).

173. *Erdély a magyar képviselőházban, 1941*, 13.

174. Loránt Tilkovszky, *Nemzetiségi politika Magyarországon a 20. században* (Debrecen: Csokonai Kiadó, 1998), 93. Although this statement was made in the summer of 1942, I have used it here as it sums up Kállay's official policy (as voiced during his April 1942 Transylvanian visit) quite well. Despite the optimism apparent in the tone of Pataky's remarks, however, a liberal nationalities policy was never truly implemented in Hungary during World War II (ibid., 94).

175. MOL, K63, 258. csomó., 1940–27. tétel./7./T.2.d., 198.

176. *Stenogramele*, vol. 6, 15. He offered a similar evaluation to the Croat ambassador in Bucharest on February 17, 1942. HDA, 230 (Poslanstvo NDH u Bukureštu), 31.

177. *Stenogramele*, vol. 6, 214.

178. MOL, K28, 65. csomó., 134. tétel. 1942-O-24890; MOL, K28, 72. csomó., 149. tétel., 1942-O-15812; MOL, K28, 68. csomó., 144. tétel., 1943-D-22605. See also "Hóman Bálint: 'Nem nézhetjük tétlenül, ha a másik fél nem teljesíti a bécsi döntés kötelezettségeit,'" *Ellenzék*, March 11, 1941, 2; Macartney, *October Fifteenth*, 2: 41. There was even an instance in early 1942 when the Romanian state reciprocated the arrest of a Romanian consular secretary with the arrest of a Hungarian one. *ADAP, 1918–1945*, series E: 1941–1945, vol. 2 (Göttingen: VandenHoeck & Ruprecht, 197[?]), doc. 39, pp. 68–69.

179. Mihai Antonescu, cited in Bancoș, *Social și național*, 239n.

180. MOL, K63, 254. csomó., 1940–27. tétel./7.I. (packet 1), 112–14.

181. MOL, K63, 254. csomó., 1940–27. tétel./7.II. (packet 2), 2653–808, 8.

182. "Román rémuralom a magyarok ellen," *Népszava*, October 8, 1940, 2.

183. Cited in Csatári, *Forgószélben*, 119.

184. From a report of Ferenc Nagy, dean to the deputy bishop of the Transylvanian Calvinist Diocese of Tövis, printed in Balogh, *A magyar-román kapcsolatok*, 395.

185. MOL, K28, 55. csomó., 120. tétel. 1941-O-15382.

186. They found a couple, but it turned out they had translated them incorrectly and they were not nearly as offensive as they first appeared to be. MOL, K28, 55. csomó., 120. tétel. 1941-O-15382.

187. MOL, K28, 55. csomó., 121. tétel. 1941-O-20464.

188. Mihai Eminescu, "Transilvania sub stăpânire dualistă austro-ungară," in *Statul, I. Funcțiile și misiunea sa* (Bucharest: Editura Saeculum I.O., 1999), 95.

189. MOL, K28, 56. csomó., 133. tétel. 1944-O-25780. Because this meeting took place fairly late in the war, it likely reflects a braver tone than would have been expected in the spring of 1942, for example.

190. "Hóman Bálint: 'Nem nézhetjük tétlenül, ha a másik fél nem teljesiti a bécsi döntés kötelezettségeit,'" *Ellenzék*, March 11, 1941, 2.

191. ASFJC, Primăria Mun. Cluj, Inv. 384/1942, Nr. 44393–112483/[25086–25104], Alapszám 56042. Emphasis in the original. The foreign ministry chose not to deliver Gyárfás's response to Mrs. Stanciu. Although no reason was given, it is at least possible that they found his judgment too strict in her case.

192. MOL, K28, 56. csomó., 124. tétel. 1941-K-21641.

193. Pál Péter Tóth, *Szórványban: A magyar és a vegyes (magyar-román, román-magyar) családok helyzete Észak-Erdélyben 1942–1944 között* (Budapest: Püski Kiadó, 1999), 154–57. This information is based on "national reliability" statistics as derived from survey data.

194. No document has yet been found outlining the purpose for the survey. Tóth, *Szórványban*, 5. At the Transylvanian Conference in October 1940, Prime Minister Teleki advised Transylvanian elites to "research" the *szórvány* issue. "Az Erdélyi értekezlet jegyzőkönyve," MOL, K28, 267. csomó., 47. An interest in this kind of information was also expressed in an article on the 1941 census published in December 1940. See Miklós Aldobolyi Nagy, "Népszámlálás," *Magyar Szemle* 39, no. 6 (160) szám (December 1940): 341–45, 344–45.

195. Nevertheless, the data collection remained unfinished and, until recently, the data were unanalyzed. Tóth, *Szórványban,* 211–16.

196. A Hungarian writing in March 1941 argued that the population statistics printed in the "Transylvanian Album" on the eve of the Second Vienna Arbitration "could favorably influence the proceedings." Ilona Pálffy, "Népszámlálás hajdan és ma," *Magyar Szemle* 40, no. 3 (163) szám (March 1941): 137–42, 142.

197. Trașcă, "Relațiile româno-ungare (I)," 311n.

198. Mihai Antonescu, *Dacă vrei să câștigi războiul,* 8.

199. Except for the 1941 Romanian census figures, all figures are from Macartney, *October Fifteenth,* 1:423. Incidentally, this was also true of the First Vienna Award. During the negotiations, tensions arose around the question of which census should be used to determine the national feeling of the population: the Hungarians argued for the 1910 Hungarian census, while the Czechoslovak representatives used their own 1930 census figures. See Holly Case, "Territorial Revision and the Holocaust: The Case of Hungary and Slovakia during WWII," in *Lessons and Legacies: From Generation to Generation* (Chicago: Northwestern University Press, forthcoming); Gergely Sallai, *Az első bécsi döntés* (Budapest: Osiris Kiadó, 2002), 87–90.

200. The 1941 Romanian census, for example, gives the total number of individuals declaring themselves of Hungarian nationality as 407,188, of whom 363,206 lived in Transylvania, Banat, and Crișana. *Recensământul din 1941: Transilvania* (Cluj: Editura Presa Universitară Clujeană, 2002), ix.

201. The case of the Jews is a prime example and will be dealt with in Chapter 5.

202. MOL, K63, 254. csomó., 27. tétel., 1940–27/7/Ek/I/2/e, 69–74. Starting in 1880, Hungary took a census every ten years through 1910 (1890, 1900, 1910, 1930). Romania had censuses in 1859, 1899, and 1930. The Romanian state also made a demographic register in 1920, the figures of which are sometimes cited. See Elemér Illyés, *National Minorities in Romania: Change in Transylvania* (New York: Columbia University Press, 1982), 33.

203. Institutul central de statistică, *Anuarul statistic al României 1937 și 1938,* 58–61, cited in Irina Livezeanu, *Cultural Politics in Greater Romania: Regionalism, Nation Building, and Ethnic Struggle, 1918–1930* (Ithaca, N.Y., and London: Cornell University Press, 1995), 10; MOL, K63, 254. csomó., 27. tétel., 1940–27/7/Ek/I/2/e., 69–70.

204. MOL, K63, 254. csomó., 27. tétel., 1940–27/7/Ek/I/2/e, 70. Similar arguments can be found in the German-language propaganda publication from about the same time. Alajos Kovács, *Das Ungartum in Siebenburgen (Erdély) und die rumänische "Statistik"* (Budapest: Verlag EPOL, 1940).

205. MOL, K63, 254. csomó., 27. tétel., 1940–27/7/Ek/I/2/e, 69. In the case of the Romanian census, individuals were hired for thé purpose of gathering census data, and these individuals included priests, notaries, functionaries, retired state employees. F. Burgdörfer, "Recensământul general al României din 1941, Dare de seamă," *Analele Institutului Statistic al României,* vol. 1 (Bucharest, 1942), 330. Hungarian census officials also often filled out the forms themselves based on verbal responses to the questions. E. Árpád Varga, *Fejezetek a jelenkori Erdély népesedéstörténetéből* (Budapest: Püski Kiadó, 1998), 38.

206. See, for example, ANIC, Fond Delegatul Marelui Stat Major pe lângă Comisie de Ofiţeri Italo-Germană, Dosar 9/1942, f. 50.

207. MOL, K28, 55. csomó., 120. tétel., 1941-O-22808; MOL, K63, 256. csomó., 1940–1942–27. tétel./7.I., 9–10.

208. Questions covered: 1. population statistics by mother tongue for the town/village for 1910, 1930, 1941, 1943; 2. same as question 1 for religion; 3. number of Hungarians who moved to Hungary after August 30, 1940; 4. fate of the property of those from question 3; 5. the cultural and economic situation of Hungarians since August 30, 1940 (schools, clubs closed, etc.); 6. occupation of employed Hungarians; 7. number of schools and Hungarian students and teachers; 8. number of Hungarian clubs and organizations; 9. total number of individuals with a liquor license, number who are Hungarian; 10. names of Hungarian landowners, bureaucrats [*tisztviselők*], teachers, doctors, pharmacists, lawyers, engineers, private clerks [*magántisztviselők*], intellectuals, manufacturers, tradespeople. MOL, K63, 256. csomó., 1940–1942–27. tétel./7.I., 28–29.

209. Anton Golopenţia, "Populaţia teritoriilor româneşti desprinse în 1940," in *Opere Complete,* vol. 2, *Statistică, demografie și geopolitică* ([Bucharest]: Editura Enciclopedică, 2002), 549. These extrapolations were first published in the fall of 1941.

210. MOL, K63, 260. csomó., 1941–27. tétel./1.II., 215.

211. Hungarian historian Gábor Egry has demonstrated how this concern dates back to the late nineteenth century. Gábor Egry, "Egy önlegitimáló politikai és történeti narratíva kérdőjelei, 1861–2003: Nemzetiségi bankok, nemzetiségi mozgalmak a századforduló Erdélyében," *Múltunk* 51, no. 3 (2006): 4–34, 6–12.

212. *Magyarország rendeletek tára, 1941,* vol. 1 (Budapest: Stádium Kiadó, 1942), 221–30.

213. *Erdély a magyar képviselőházban, 1941,* 41.

214. Ibid., 41–42.

215. For figures on how much land and property was transferred in accordance with the decree during the war, see Attila Szavári, "Magyar berendezkedés Észak-Erdélyben (1940. szeptember–1941. április)," *Magyar Kisebbség* 4 (2004): 272–304, 289.

216.   See Dr. Miklós Drágffy és Dr. Pál Villányi, *Az erdélyi ingatlanidegenítések jóvátétele: az 1,440/1041. számú rendelet és azzal kapcsolatos jogszabályok magyarázata, különös tekintettel a bírói gyakorlatra* (Budapest, 1942), 3.

217.   There were a number of executive orders created to this end, among them No. 2,780/1941 M.E., No. 970/1943 M.E., and No. 2,790/1941 M.E. These related to the appointment of custodians for "abandoned property" left behind by Romanians who fled Northern Transylvania, and to the state's annulment of the Romanian land reform's provisions with regard to forests and pastures respectively. Fătu and Mușat, *Horthyist-Fascist Terror,* 164–65. For a more comprehensive list of laws and decrees of this sort, see Fătu and Mușat, *Horthyist-Fascist Terror,* 148–75. See also ANIC, Fond Ministerul de Interne, Dosar 438/1941, 13–16.

218.   For a partial inventory of claims according to amount of compensation requested, as well as the nationality of the plaintiff and defendant, see BMF, RW 50, 160.

219.   ASFJC, Biroul de cenzură Cluj-Turda, nr. 1/1940–1942. f. 311. See also Fătu and Mușat, *Horthyist-Fascist Terror,* 162–63.

220.   See, for example, ASFJC, Biroul de cenzură Cluj-Turda, nr. 1/1940–1942. f. 341. Many of these records were passed on to the German-Italian Commission. BMF, RW 50, 160, "Wirtschaftslage (1,440/1941)."

221.   For a periodization of romanianization initiatives, see Lya Benjamin, ed., *Evreii din România între anii 1940–1944,* vol. 1, *Legislația antievreiască* (Bucharest: Editura Hasefer, 1993), xxxiv–xxxv.

222.   Benjamin, *Evreii din România,* doc. 37, 38, xli–xlii, 133–45.

223.   MOL, K28, 213. csomó., 467. tétel. (German-Italian Commission), 1942-O-28380; MOL, K63, 257. csomó., 1940–27. tétel./7./E., Román-magyar viszony—Erdély, iktatlan, II. rész, 334, 338; ASFJC, Inspectoratul de Poliție Cluj, Nr. Inv. 42/1940(II), f. 141. "A románosítást úgy kell végrehajtani, hogy a zsidók helyére mindenütt románok kerüljenek," *Keleti Újság,* January 23, 1942, 5. MOL, K63, 260. csomó., 1941–27. tétel/1. II, 65. USHMMA, RG-54.001, Moldova National Archives, Chișinău, roll 7, dosar 34/1943, f. 78. Radu Ioanid, *The Holocaust in Romania: The Destruction of the Jews and Gypsies Under the Antonescu Regime, 1940–1944* (Chicago: Ivan R. Dee, 200), 23–26. The issue of "romanianization" will be discussed in more detail in Chapter 5. Incidentally, Bulgarian diplomats also complained that the Bulgarian minority was affected. TsDA, MVRI, F176K, op. 8, a.e. 830, 26–27.

224.   Benjamin, *Evreii din România,* doc. 37, 38, 134, 141.

225.   To give a sense of how close the presumed association between name and national identity was, consider the following: A secret report from the Romanian police in Turda mentions the names of several employees of the Central Bank for Commerce and Industry in Turda suspected of being Hungarian spies. The report, compiled in October 1942, claimed the spies had been delivering information to contacts across the border in Kolozsvár. One of the suspected spies was a "Hungarian" with a "Romanian name" who managed to "deceive many into believing he was of Romanian origin" and in this way was able, in the spring of 1942, to send secret messages to Kolozsvár. ASFJC, Biroul de cenzură Cluj-Turda, nr. 1/1940–1942. f. 423. Another report on suspected Hungarian spies operating in Southern Transylvania can be found in USHMMA,

RG-25.017, Selected Records of the Cluj Branch of the Romanian National Archives, 1934–1952, roll 7, dosar 34/1943, f. 115.

226. "Hóman Bálint: 'Nem nézhetjük tétlenül, ha a másik fél nem teljesiti a bécsi döntés kötelezettségeit,'" *Ellenzék*, March 11, 1941, 2.

227. BMF, RW 50, 129.

228. Viktor Karády and István Kozma, eds., *Név és nemzet: Családnév-változtatás, névpolitika és nemzetiségi erőviszonyok Magyarországon a feudalizmustól a kommunizmusig* (Budapest: Osiris Kiadó, 2002), 257–60. In the separate protocol to the Second Vienna Arbitration, which Hungary signed with Germany, Article 7 expressly stated that "Hungary shall refrain from all measures calculated to accomplish compulsory assimilation, especially through Magyarization of volksdeutsch family names. Members of the ethnic group shall have the right to reassume names formerly borne by their families." See *DGFP*, series D, vol. 10, doc. 413, 581–87.

229. ASFJC, Primăria mun. Cluj, "Reg. de intrare," Inv. 386/1942, Nr. 19275, 19276, 19635, 24578, 29534, 33016, 34157; ASFJC, Primăria Mun. Cluj, Inv. 384/1942, Nr. 1791; ASFJC, Primăria Mun. Cluj, Inv. 384/1942, Nr. 8198–15782, Alapszám 14842, 14843; ASFJC, Primăria Mun. Cluj, Inv. 384/1942, Nr. 37310–44110, Alapszám 39108, 39216, 33769; ASFJC, Primăria Mun. Cluj, Inv. 384/1942, Nr. 44393–112483/[25086–25104], Alapszám 25126, 25139, 44941, 45946, 46867, 48915, 48914, 48916, 57372; ASFJC, Primăria Mun. Cluj, Inv. 384/1941, Nr. 12246–23152, Alapszám 23098; ASFJC, Primăria Mun. Cluj, 3/1941, 24435–31627, Alapszám 29563. Furthermore, all requests for name changes from Hungarian to "foreign" names were denied. ASFJC, Primăria Mun. Cluj, Inv. 384/1942, Nr. 44393–112483/[25086–25104], Alapszám 46574; ASFJC, Primăria Mun. Cluj, Inv. 384/1941, Nr. 34–12162, Alapszám 6853.

230. ASFJC, Primăria Mun. Cluj, Inv. 386/1942, Nr. 23694–37141. Alapszám 24203.

231. Ibid., Alapszám 32924.

232. ASFJC, Primăria Mun. Cluj, Inv. 384/1942, Nr. 8198–15782, Alapszám 13584.

233. "Nemzetállam és statisztika," *Ellenzék*, February 1, 1941, 6. This sentiment is reiterated in a number of newspaper articles from the period. "Az asszimiláció és a magyarság," *Ellenzék*, May 8, 1942, 3; "A szórvány-ügy megoldása érdekében szoros együttműködést kell teremteni," *Ellenzék*, July 18, 1941, 3.

234. János Scheffler, "A szertartásváltoztatás kérdése Erdélyben," *Erdélyi tudósító* (1941): 44. Scheffler noted with regret, however, that "not all of the individuals who converted back [to "Hungarian" religions] were the same ones who abandoned them" under Romanian rule. See also, János Scheffler, "Az erdélyi ritusváltotatások," *Magyar Szemle* 42, 173 szám (January 1942): 7–12. A Romanian Orthodox priest in Nagyvárad/Oradea complained in August 1942 that in his area alone one thousand individuals had converted from Orthodoxy to other confessions since the Second Vienna Arbitration. ANIC, Fond Delegatul Marelui Stat Major pe lângă Comisie de Ofiţeri Italo-Germană, Dosar 9/1942, f. 50.

235. Following a dispute over the symbolism of one of the flags featured on the statue (the flag was recognized as that of Moldavia, a Romanian principality), an additional inscription was added in 1932: "Triumphant in war, beaten only at Baia by his own people [the Romanians] when he tried to defeat the invincible Moldavia." Dániel

Lőwy, V. János Demeter, and Lajos Asztalos, *Kőbe írt Kolozsvár: Emléktáblák, feliratok, címerek* (Kolozsvár: Nis Kiadó, 1996), 207–9.

236. Livezeanu, *Cultural Politics,* 170.

237. See the epigraphs at the beginning of this chapter and also BMF, RW 50, 130, Rechtliche und berufliche Lage der Rumänen in Nordsiebenbürgen. Anschrift SSI, 14.7.1942; Sándor Tóth, "Kolozsvár mint munkaadó, felszabadulása után egy évvel," *Függetlenség,* November 23, 1941, 5; cited in György Gaal, "Kolozsvár kétezer esztendeje dátumokban," in *Kulcsok Kolozsvárhoz, a föl nem adható város,* ed. Lajos Kántor and Gyöngy Kovács Kis (Szeged: Mozaik Kiadó, 2000), 356.

238. *Az 1941. évi népszámlálás demográfiai adatok községek szerint* (Budapest: Stephaneum Nyomda Részvénytársaság, 1947), 90–91, 322–23, 554–55.

239. This is evident from a map of Kolozsvár prepared by the State Hungarian Party of Romania on which the street names appear in Romanian on the map itself, but with their Hungarian variants in the margins. Petru Bortes, "Harta generală a orașului municipal Cluj" (Cluj, 1937). Even today, Hungarian residents of the city refer to streets and squares by their Hungarian names.

240. "Magyar feliratokat!" *Ellenzék,* May 2, 1942, 3.

241. One of the new names, Corvin, was still "foreign" (i.e., Latin), but I suspect as it was part of King Matthias's full name it was likely not considered *truly* foreign. Gaal, "Kolozsvár kétezer esztendeje," 236. In general, movie houses—along with hotels and cafés—were considered especially sensitive terrain as places where people often met. In Southern Transylvania, the Romanian government drew up a list of all individuals of Hungarian nationality who owned or operated businesses of this sort so they could be kept under surveillance. ANIC, Fond Ministerul de Interne, Dosar 438/1941, f. 3–4, 8, 21. During the interwar period, the Romanian government and authorities sought by various means to "romanianize" movie theaters. See Tóth, *Erdély 22 éves rabsága,* 201–2.

242. The part of town was called Monostor in Hungarian (in Romanian, Mănăștur). Marianne Veress, "Kolozsvár szociális képe," *Erdélyi tudósitó* (1941): 32. The advent of the Monostor Romanians' "migration" to the city was looked upon by many Hungarians as a great tragedy. Csizmadia, *Vázlat Kolozsvár társadalmáról,* 5. Following the Second Vienna Arbitration, almost none of the property owners from this area were listed as having fled to Romania leaving their property in the care of an overseer. *Kolozsvári Lak- és Címjegyzék 1943.* comp., based on official data, by Ödön Boga, Aurél Zámbó, Ernő Gál (Kolozsvár: 1943), 160–61. This was in stark contrast to the city's second district, where Romanian government employees and transplanted elites had settled after World War I. On a single street in this district, of the twenty-nine residences on that street in 1942, seventeen were owned by persons who had opted for Romania (ibid., 55).

243. ASFJC, Primăria Mun. Cluj, Inv. 384/1941, Nr. 34–12162. Alapszám 11371.

244. ASFJC, Primăria Mun. Cluj, Inv. 384/1941, Nr. 12246–23152. Alapszám 19156. Prior to World War I, the street was the namesake of the Austrian Emperor/Hungarian King (1848–1916), Franz Joseph (Ferenc József in Hungarian orthography). Bortes, "Harta generală a orașului municipal Cluj." During the period of Romanian rule, its name was King Ferdinand Road, after the King of Romania (1914–27). It was named Horthy Road in honor of Horthy's role in overseeing the reannexation of Northern Transylvania to Hungary.

245. Csizmadia, *Vázlat Kolozsvár társadalmáról*, 6. See also Tóth, *Erdély 22 éves rab-sága*, 315.

246. See Bortes, "Harta generală a orașului municipal Cluj"; and Gusztáv Cseh, "Kolozsvár thj. sz. kir. város átnézeti térképe," (Kolozsvár: László Zsombory, 1941). The policies of the two states vis-à-vis the Jews will be discussed in more detail in Chapter 5. For pointing out the Jewish cemetery on the Romanian map and its absence on the Hungarian one, I am grateful to Charles King.

247. ASFJC, Primăria Mun. Cluj, Inv. 384/1941, Nr. 34–12162, Alapszám 11462. A visitor to the Heroes' Cemetery today will find the new plots added by the World War II Hungarian administration but will quickly discover that although the graves bear Hungarian names, all the stones along the edge of the walkway (i.e., the ones most likely to be noticed by passersby) are inscribed with Romanian names. In this way the Romanian administration has effectively reclaimed the dead of World War I as its own with only minimal effort.

248. MOL, K150 [Belügyminisztérium], 3542. csomó., 30. tétel. File 255.

249. "Székely diszitő elemekkel épitették a hadtestparancsnokság új épületét," *El-lenzék*, January 19, 1942, 3.

250. See MOL, K150 [Belügyminisztérium], 3542. csomó, 30. tétel., 255. It is tempt-ing to view this choice as symbolic, but its symbolism may be less obvious than the mere expression of control or dominance. A little over a year after Northern Transylvania was reannexed, it became illegal to make and print maps of cities and roads, a decision motivated by strategic military concerns. ASFJC, Prefectura Județului Cluj, "Ordine ministeriale și circulare," Inv. Nr. 1, vol. I/1942. Cutia 1145, Nr. 193.557/XII/a./1941. Furthermore, although maps existed with the Hungarian names of the streets, they were either not up to date or not large and detailed enough for use by architects and engineers. Only the Romanian administration of the interwar period had been in a position to keep up-to-date, detailed maps showing property boundaries and numbers, buildings, and so forth. The one map I have found with Hungarian street names was published as an attachment to a guidebook to the city in 1941, itself basically a copy of another map printed during the interwar period. Cseh, "Kolozsvár thj. sz. kir. város átnézeti térképe."

251. "A miniszterelnök az új hadtestparancsnoksági épület felavatásán," *Ellenzék*, January 19, 1942, 2. The rest of the planned square was never completed, due to man-power and material shortages brought on by the war. "Keledy Tibor polgármester beszéde," *Ellenzék*, January 19, 1942, 2.

252. "Székely diszitő elemekkel épitették a hadtestparancsnokság új épületét," *El-lenzék*, January 19, 1942, 3.

253. In the minds of many Hungarian leaders and citizens alike, winning back Northern Transylvania was only the first step on the way to winning back all the ter-ritories Hungary lost to Romania (not to mention Czechoslovakia and Yugoslavia) after World War I. This was true specifically of Bethlen and Horthy. See Macartney, *October Fifteenth*, 2:213, 219. Shortly after the announcement of the Second Vienna Arbitration, Döme Sztójay, the Hungarian ambassador in Berlin, called the exclusion of Arad (in Southern Transylvania) a "sensitive flaw" in the agreement, one that he intended to broach with Hitler. Ádám, Juhász, and Kerekes, *Magyarország és a második világháború*,

304. The diary entry of a Hungarian officer for August 30, 1940, reads: "The decision brought great joy, but also disappointment because Arad and Temesvár were not returned [to Hungary]." Kálmán Shvoy, *Shvoy Kálmán titkos naplója és emlékirata, 1918–1945* (Budapest: Kssuth Könyvkiadó, 1983), 213.

254. "A hadtestparancsnok avató-beszéde," *Ellenzék*, January 19, 1942, 2.

255. There were 65 schools and 650 legally operating taverns. Veress, "Kolozsvár szociális képe," 51. On Kolozsvár as a "city of schools," see Zsombor Szász, "Erdély egyeteme," *Magyar Szemle* 43, kötet 180 szám (August 1942): 62. It was also in the context of the city's educational tradition that Antonescu, in a speech given on October 10, 1940, called Cluj "a holy city in Romanian history." Ion Antonescu, *Către țară*, 182.

256. "Az Erdélyi értekezlet jegyzőkönyve," MOL, K28, 267. csomó., 4, 20–62. See also, MOL, K28, 72. csomó., 149. tétel. "Magyarországon élő románok iskolaügye és iskolánkivüli népmüvelés, II. rész, 1940–1944"; ANIC, Fond Preşedinţia Consiliului de Miniştri, Cabinet Militar, dosar 396/1943, f. 160–200; "Tragedia invăţamântului românesc din Ardealul ocupat," *Tribuna Asociaţiei Refugiaţilor şi Expulsaţilor din Ardealul Ocupat*, January 22, 1941, 3; Fătu and Muşat, *Horthyist-Fascist Terror*, 240–45.

257. "A román polgári hatóságok már elhagyták a kiürítendő városokat," *Népszava*, September 3, 1940, 4.

258. ASFJC, Prefectura Judeţului Cluj, "Ordine ministeriale şi circulare," Inv. Nr. 1, vol. I/1942. Cutia 1145. Alapszám 1225/1942.

259. MOL, K63, 254. csomó., 27. tétel. 1940–27/7/Ek/1, 79–80.

260. Already during the late 1930s, a number of Hungarians were tried for slander of this kind. MOL, K63, 251. csomó., 1939–27. tétel./7-I, 647v; MOL, K63, 254. csomó., 27. tétel, 1940–27/7/Ek/1, 402–408; MOL, K63, 252. csomó., 27. tétel, 1939–27/7/E, 156–57; MOL, K63, 256. csomó., 1940–27. tétel./7.III, 37. Furthermore, in at least one instance, an ethnic German was charged with insulting the nation's honor by singing Hungarian revisionist songs. USHMMA, RG-25.017, Selected Records of the Cluj Branch of the Romanian National Archives, 1934–1952, roll 7, Fond Parchetul General Cluj, 1919–1952, dosar 31/1942, f. 25.

261. The report estimates that, in all three courts, as many as four thousand Hungarians were tried. It is nonetheless true that about a third of the cases were dismissed, suggesting that many of the charges had been trumped up. MOL, K63, 257. csomó., 27. tétel, 1940–27/7/E, 409–10. MOL, K63, 256. csomó., 1940–1942–27. tétel./7.I, 41–42. For specific cases, see USHMMA, RG-25.017, Selected Records of the Cluj Branch of the Romanian National Archives, 1934–1952, roll 6, Inspectoratul de poliţie Cluj, 1916–1948, dosar 410/1944–1945, f. 45; MOL, K63, 254. csomó., 1940–27. tétel./7. I, 76.

262. MOL, K63, 256. csomó., 1940–1942–27. tétel./7.I., 40–41.

263. Although I do not have statistics for the whole of Northern Transylvania, I was able to locate the proceedings of over fifty trials of accused slanderers among municipal and national collections for 1940 to 1942 in the city of Kolozsvár alone. Furthermore, in both Hungary and Romania at the time, it was common for trials of purported slanderers of the nation to be publicized in daily newspapers. Csatári, *Forgószélben*, 199; "Törvényszéki hirek," *Ellenzék*, May 13, 1942, 8; "Törvényszéki hirek," *Ellenzék*, May 19, 1942, 4; "Nemzetgyalázók a törvényszék előtt," *Ellenzék*, July 7, 1942,

4. A number of articles from Romanian newspapers (both Romanian- and Hungarian-language) can be found in MOL, K63, 254. csomó., 27. tétel, 1940–27/7/Ek/1, 402–8. In none of the cases I examined for World War II was the full possible punishment meted out to convicted offenders. Most sentences ranged from two to six months in prison and/or a few hundred pengő in fines. The harshest sentence I encountered was for 2.5 years in jail, but the individual (a journalist) was released after just a few months due to the intervention of the Romanian state through the German-Italian Commission. All of the other sentences ranged from fines (generally fifty to sixty pengő, rather steep for a working-class individual) to one year in jail plus a one- to three-year loss of political rights.

264. See, for example, MOL, K28, 58. csomó., 130. tétel. 1942-G-15017.

265. Of these, only one was a woman. She was indicted while declaredly intoxicated, but the offending statements were made in the courtyard of her own apartment house, not in a tavern. ASFJC, Primăria Mun. Cluj, Inv. 384/1942, Nr. 8198–15782. Alapszám 13738.

266. MOL, K28, 59. csomó., 130. tétel. (in a folder labeled "M.E. K28, 1942"), 238–39.

267. See also MOL, K28, 59. csomó., 130. tétel. (in a folder labeled "M.E. K28, 1942"), 237, 284, 288, 411.

268. Although, when she was initially sentenced, the judge listed Veturia's "crime-less past" among the "mitigating" circumstances speaking for a lighter sentence, she was tried multiple times for slander of the Hungarian nation after 1940. ASFJC, Primăria Mun. Cluj, Inv. 386/1942. Nr. 23694–37140. Alapszám 25664; ASFJC, Primăria Mun. Cluj, Inv. 386/1942, Nr. 23694–37140. Alapszám 25564 (B.I. 148/1942). This was the trial of her appeal, rejected on February 18, 1942, so she must have had to serve her one-month jail term at that point.

269. MOL. K28, 59. csomó., 130. tétel. (in a folder labeled "M.E. K28, 1942"), 288.

270. Ibid., 411.

271. Emphasis mine. It is interesting that although there existed a Hungarian law—created in 1941—outlawing insults to a person's nationality (Hungarian or otherwise), this law was not invoked in these cases. "1941. évi V. törvénycikk a nemzetiségi érzület büntetőjogi védelméről," http://www.1000ev.hu/index.php?a=3&param=8158 (accessed November 26, 2007).

272. MOL, K28, 76. csomó., 151. tétel. 1943–18756.

273. Ibid. Emphasis in the original.

274. MOL, K28, 72. csomó., 149. tétel. 1942-O-15812. The oppression of minorities through restrictions on their religious institutions was common during the interwar period as well. The Romanian government made Hungarian churches and religious schools a primary target starting in the early 1920s. Imre Mikó, *Huszonkét év: az erdélyi magyarság politikai története 1918. december 1-től 1940. augusztus 30*-ig (Budapest: Studium, 1941), 74–78; Vladimir Ortakovski, *Minorities in the Balkans* (Ardsley, N.Y.: Transnational Publishers, 2000), 88–90.

275. ASFJC, Primăria Mun. Cluj, Inv. 384/1941, Nr. 12246–23152, Alapszám 17055. Fătu and Muşat, *Horthyist-Fascist Terror*, 162–63.

276. "Az Erdélyi értekezlet jegyzőkönyve," MOL, K28, 267. csomó., 36.

277. Cited in Balogh and Sipos, eds., *A magyar állam és a nemzetiségek*, 651–652.

278. This was based on an understanding of Hungarianness that was primarily linguistic (if you speak the language, you are a Hungarian). An essay from August 1940 in a Hungarian public affairs journal notes that "since, in the course of the development of modern nationalism, the so-called national principle—according to which the borders of the state have to be drawn according to nationality, ethnographic, or linguistic boundaries—has become dogma, Hungarian public opinion has become convinced that the integrity of the country cannot be preserved if we do not suceed in assimilating the masses of nationalities, absorbing them into the Hungarian-language people." See "A magyar nemzetiségi politika feladatai," *Magyar Szemle* 39, no. 2 (156) szám (August 1940): 57.

279. ASFJC, Primăria Mun. Cluj, Inv. 386/1942, Nr. 23694–37140. Alapszám 23668.

280. "A görög katolikus magyarok kálváriája," *Ellenzék*, July 18, 1942, 5.

281. The combined total of Orthodox and Greek Catholic inhabitants of Northern Transylvania from the census data was 1,194,421 (with 231,035 Orthodox and 963,386 Greek Catholics). The number of individuals who declared Romanian as their mother tongue was 1,069,242, and self-declared Romanians by nationality numbered 1,029,493. On the whole, then, the overlap appears significant, with a maximum of under 15 percent "outliers" (i.e., "non-Romanian" Orthodox and Greek Catholics). *Recensământul din 1941*, 332–34.

282. MOL, K63, 254. csomó., 1940–27. tétel./7.I, 172.

283. See for example, ANIC, Fond Preşedinţia Consiliului de Miniştri, Cabinet Militar, Dosar 396/1943, f. 270–71.

284. György Papp, "A görög katolikus magyarság helyzete Erdélyben," in *Görögsz-ertartású magyarság* (Kolozsvár: Minerva, 1942), 5.

285. Ibid., 14.

286. MOL, K63, 257. csomó., 1940–27. tétel./7./E., Román-magyar viszony—Erdély, iktatlan, II. rész., 761.

287. ANIC, Fond Ministerul de Interne, Dosar 438/1941, 11.

288. MOL, Kolozs megye főispáni eln. iratok, 1942, tekercs 4063, Alapszám 86; MOL, Kolozs megye főispáni eln. iratok, 1942, tekercs 4064, Alapszám 286; ASFJC, Primăria Mun. Cluj, Inv. 386/1942, Nr. 23694–37140, Alapszám 37121; ASFJC, Biroul de cenzură Cluj-Turda, nr. 1/1940–1942, f. 286.

289. ASFJC, Primăria Mun. Cluj, Inv. 384/1942, Nr. 44393–112483/[25086–25104], Alapszám 45042, 47445. As noted above, already by the end of 1940, 774 individuals had converted from Greek Catholicism and Orthodoxy to the Roman Catholic and Protestant faiths. Scheffler, "A szertartásváltoztatás kérdése Erdélyben," 44.

290. USHMMA, RG-25.013, Preşedinţia Consiliului de Miniştrii—Cabinet Militar, 1940–1944, roll 34, dosar 375/1943, 143, 145.

291. Miklós Kállay, *Magyarország miniszterelnöke voltam, 1942–1944* (Budapest: Európa História, 1991), 86.

292. MOL, K28, 55. csomó., 120. tétel. 1941-O-22808.

293. See Sabin Manuilă, *Die bevölkerungspolitischen Folgen der Teilung Siebenbürgens* (Bucharest: Die Dacia- Bücher, 1941); Petre Poruţiu, *La Transylvanie et les conséquences*

économiques de l'acte de Vienne 30 août 1940 (Bucharest: Monitorul Oficial, Imprimerie naţionale, 1944). For comparable Hungarian arguments against Trianon, see, for example, István Bethlen, *The Treaty of Trianon and European Peace* (New York: Longmans, Green and Co., 1934), 90–91.

294. MOL, K63, 260. csomó., 1941–27. tétel./1.II, 314, 316.

295. *Prinz Gyula Magyarország földrajza* (Budapest: Renaissance Könyvkiadó, 1942) cited in HDA, F. 1942, Poslanstvo NDH Budimpešta (first folder), 59.

296. MOL, K63, 256. csomó., 1940–1942–27. tétel./7.I., 84–85.

297. BMF, RW 50, 286.

298. "Az Erdélyi értekezlet jegyzőkönyve," MOL, K28, 267. csomó., 36.

299. In 1943, the number of radio subscriptions in Romania reached three hundred thousand, and nearly six hundred thousand in Hungary in 1941. See Zoltán Kilián, "Rádiófeladatok," *Magyar Szemle* 40, no. 1 (161) szám (January 1941): 53–56; László Ghimessy, "Magyarország rádióvevő-engedélyesei 1942-ben," *Magyar statisztikai szemle* 21, no. 12 (1943), 656; Constantin Antip, *Contribuţii la istoria presei române* (Bucharest: Uniunea ziariştilor din Republica Popular Romín, 1964), 95–96.

300. Kilián, "Rádiófeladatok," 55. See also Tóth, *Erdély 22 éves rabsága*, 309–10.

301. Grad, *Al doilea arbitraj de la Viena*, 171–75. Another clandestine station called "Vlaicu's Fighters" (Luptătorii lui Vlaicu) purportedly inspired Romanians to long for the "conquest of Transylvania." ASFJC, Inspectoratul de Poliţie Cluj, Nr. Inv. 399. Dosar Nr. 92/1942(III), f. 122.

302. MOL, K28, 213. csomó., 467. tétel. (German-Italian Commission). 1942-O-23890; MOL, K63, 257. csomó., 1940–27. tétel./7/E, 2–9. On program length, see Grad, *Al doilea arbitraj de la Viena*, 176.

303. MOL, K28, 68. csomó., 145. tétel. 1943-O-15772. The city approved construction of a new tower in the fall of 1942. ASFJC, Primăria Mun. Cluj, Inv. 384/1942, Nr. 44393–112483/[25086–25104]. Alapszám 50412.

304. MOL, K28, 68. csomó., 145. tétel. 1943-O-15772. The construction of such a station was proposed and approved and supposed to be finished by early 1943.

305. These included the anti-German Kossuth Rádió, and Gábor Áron Rádió. Grad, *Al doilea arbitraj de la Viena*, 181–82. Tibor Frank, *Tanulmányok a Magyar Rádió történetéből, 1925–1945* (Budapest: A Tömegkommunikációs Kutatóközpont, 1975), 172–73. Another source refers to a clandestine, mobile station calling itself Magyar Szabadság Rádió. HDA, F. 1492 Poslanstvo NDH Budimpešta (first folder), 63.

306. MOL, K28, 68. csomó., 145. tétel. 1943-O-15772, 37.

307. "Rádiómánia," *Ellenzék*, April 12, 1941, 8. Author's interview with Ede Laczkó [Lebovits], December 4, 2001, in Budapest. Balas, *Will to Freedom*, 39, 60, 83–84. Balas claims that the Hungarian-language broadcasts of the BBC were jammed by the Hungarian authorities after Hungary joined the war in 1941, but he continued to listen to BBC broadcasts in German.

308. MOL, K63, 256. csomó., 1940–1942–27. tétel./7.I., 54.

309. ASFJC, Inspectoratul de Poliţie Cluj, Nr. Inv. 42/1940(II), f. 104.

310. Paraschivescu, *Drumuri şi răspîntii*, 134–39.

311. MOL, K63, 257. csomó., 1940–27. tétel./7./E., Román-magyar viszony—Erdély, iktatlan, II. rész, 32, 37, 95.

312. BMF, RW 50, 130, Rechtliche und berufliche Lage der Rumänen in Nord-siebenbürgen, Abschrift Bukarest, 24.7.42.

313. HIWRP, Sabin Manuilă, box 11, folder 3, "Declarațiile făcute de d-l Iuliu Maniu la consiliul de Coroană în ziua de 30 August 1940, cu ocazia discuției asupra rezultatului arbitrajului dela Viena," XIII.

314. MOL. K28, 59. csomó., 130. tétel. 262. lap. (In a folder labeled "M.E. K28, 1942").

315. See, for example, MOL. K28, 59. csomó., 130. tétel. (in a folder labeled "M.E. K28, 1942"), 8–9, 284, 389, 467.

316. Lukács, "Injustices of the Treaty of Trianon," 161. Lukács is not to be con-fused with the Marxist literary critic and philosopher of the same name.

317. Mihai Antonescu, *Dacă vrei să câștigi războiul*,15.

318. "Az Erdélyi értekezlet jegyzőkönyve," MOL, K28, 267. csomó., 36; *Stenogra-mele*, vol. 6, 214.

4. A League of Their Own

1. Jean Ancel, ed., *Documents Concerning the Fate of Romanian Jewry during the Holocaust*, vol. 9 (New York: Beate Klarsfeld Foundation, [1986]), doc. 207, 559.

2. "Rajniss Ferenc felszólalása a képviselőházban, 1943. november 26," http://www.geocities.com/nemzszoc/konyvek/rajniss1.htm#r0012 (accessed November 1, 2007).

3. "Levélben sértegette a magyar államot—egy évre itélték," *Ellenzék*, June 23, 1942, 5. According to the article, Irina was married to a local banker who worked at one of the few "Romanian" businesses in town, the Albina bank. Elsewhere one Hungarian official had called the Albina an "expressly chauvinist institution that does not represent Hungarian interests," adding that the bank was in the habit of doing things "against magyardom," such as giving low-interest long-term loans to members of the Romanian nationality in Northern Transylvania. MOL, Kolozs megye főispáni eln. iratok, 1942, tekercs 4063, Alapszám 101/1942, 8–9.

4. "Levélben sértegette a magyar államot—egy évre itélték," *Ellenzék*, June 23, 1942, 5.

5. MOL, K28, 59. csomó., 130. tétel.(In a folder labeled "M.E. K28, 1942"), 187–88. Incidentally, five hundred pengő was quite a lot of money at the time. The daily allow-ance given to refugees from Southern Transylvania in 1940 was two pengő forty fillér. Andor Csizmadia, *Vázlat Kolozsvár társadalmáról* (Kassa: Szent Erzsébet Nyomda, r.t., 1942), 9.

6. BMF, RW 50, 149, B.2654/1942/3. szám, 4.

7. "Levélben sértegette a magyar államot—egy évre itélték," *Ellenzék*, June 23, 1942, 5.

8. BMF, RW 50, 149, Nr. 8.675/P.

9. Ibid.

10. BMF, RW 50, 148, "Rumänen aus Nordsiebenbürgen die wegen Beleidigung der Nation und des ungarischen Staates verurteilt wurden."

11. BMF, RW 50, 122/1942, Aufzeichnung über Arbeitslager Fagaras, Fall Todesur-teil Schmidt, Volkszählung in Ungarn.

12. BMF, RW 50, 123/1942, Wehrdienst der ungarischen bzw. Rumänischen Minderheit in Siebenbürgen und Frage der Reserveoffiziere in Nord- und Südsiebenbürgen, "Heranziehung zum wehr- und öffentliche Dienst."

13. Christoph M. Kimmich, *Germany and the League of Nations* (Chicago and London: University of Chicago Press, 1976), 131–49.

14. Ibid., 150.

15. Cited in K. Schwendemann, *Abrüstung und Sicherheit: Handbuch der Sicherheitsfrage und der Abrüstungskonferenz mit einer Sammlung der wichtigsten Dokumente*, vol. 1 (Berlin: Weidmannsche Buchhandlung, 1936), 498–99.

16. Zsigmond, *DIMK*, 2:227, 413.

17. Ibid.

18. Shortly after the Second Vienna Arbitration, in late September 1940, Germany decided to send a military mission to Romania to secure the oil fields there. *DGFP*, series D, vol. 11, doc. 84. To this end, Hungary allowed the German military passage through Hungary onto Romanian territory (ibid., doc. 131). Also, Germany's lack of support for the Fascist Legionnaire movement in Romania was driven by the desire to "guarantee . . . tranquillity and order in Rumania" (ibid., doc. 269, 446).

19. The right to opt was afforded to all those living in Northern Transylvania and all those "Romanian citizens of Hungarian nationality" living in Romania who were permanent residents of the part of Romania that had been Hungary prior to 1919 (Articles 3 and 4). The window of opportunity for opting was six months from the date of the award. Zsigmond, *DIMK*,5:328, 329. Also see Magda Ádám, Gyula Juhász, and Lajos Kerekes, eds., *Magyarország és a második világháború: titkos diplomáciai okmányok a háború előzményeihez és történetéhez* (Budapest: Kossuth Könyvkiadó, 1959), 121–22, 288–93. See Second Vienna Arbitration in *DGFP*, series D, vol. 10, doc. 413, 581–87.

20. Ministero degli Affari Esteri, *I Documenti Diplomatici Italiani, Nona Serie: 1939–1943*, vol. 5, *11 giugno–28 ottobre 1940* (Rome: Istituto Poligrafico dello Stato, 1965), doc. 560, 561, 567, 568, 553, 558–59.

21. Ibid., doc. 620, 603. This was apparently done at the instigation of Romanian diplomat Raoul Bossy. Raul V. Bossy, *Recollections of a Romanian Diplomat, 1918–1969: Diaries and Memoirs of Raoul V. Bossy*, vol. 2 (Stanford, Calif.: Hoover Institution Press, 2003), 375–79.

22. *DDI*, vol. 5, doc. 682, 661–62. The official request reached the Italian embassy October 9 (ibid., doc. 700, 673–75).

23. Zsigmond, *DIMK*, 5:419.

24. Ibid., 5:419, 660.

25. "Weizsäcker külügyi államtitkár előterjesztése Ribbentrop külügyminiszternek," Berlin, October 11, 1940, in *A Wilhelmstrasse és Magyarország: német diplomáciai iratok Magyarországról, 1933–1944*, ed. György Ránki, Ervin Pamlényi, Loránt Tilkovszky, and Gyula Juhász (Budapest: Kossuth Kiadó, 1968), 360, 540; "Şedinţa consiliului de cabinet din 1 octombrie 1940," in *Stenogramele*, vol. 1, doc. 11, 217.

26. *DGFP*, series D, vol. 11, doc. 179, 303n. On the staff of the commission, see Dorel Bancoş, *Social şi naţional în politica guvernului Ion Antonescu* (Bucharest: Editura Eminescu, 2000), 40.

27. Ibid., 40–41.

28. Ibid., 55n.

29. Ibid., 41; Zsigmond, *DIMK,*5:465.

30. Ciano felt that the events should not be "dramatized," while Hitler promised to head off Romanian protests by reminding Antonescu "that for twenty years the Hungarians had been badly treated by the Romanians and that in the last analysis their present behavior was only a reaction to the wrongs they had had to suffer for many years." Zsigmond, *DIMK,* 5:465, 717; *DGFP,* series D, vol. II, doc. 365, 636.

31. Ibid., doc. 179, 304.

32. Ibid., doc. 365, 636.

33. Vasile Puşcaş, ed., *Transilvania şi aranjamentele europene, 1940–1944* (Cluj-Napoca: Centrul de Studii Transilvane Fundaţia Culturală Română, 1995), 14–16.

34. Zsigmond, *DIMK,* 5:465, 717.

35. Bancoş, *Social şi naţional,* 42.

36. See Puşcaş, *Transilvania şi aranjamentele europene,* 122–26. The head of the commission in Braşov was German (Dehmel), while the head of the Kolozsvár office was Italian (Sircana). MOL, K70 [Külügyminisztérium, Jogi osztály], 351. csomó., 9./b. tétel. (Német-olasz követbizottság Erdélyben, bizottság jelentései), 1942, Tárgyi csoport 9., 32.

37. *DGFP,* series D, vol. II, doc. 179, 304.

38. MOL, K28, 213. csomó., 467. tétel. (German-Italian Commission), 1942-O-23890, 43.

39. Roggeri had served as Italian Ambassador to Latvia (1936–40). Hencke (1895–1984) rose through the military ranks during World War I to the rank of Senior Lieutenant, and began his career with the German foreign ministry in 1922 in the section for Eastern Europe and Scandinavia, and later assumed posts in Moscow, Kiev, and the Protectorate. Altenburg (1894–1984), whose wartime military service saw him to the rank of Lieutenant, began his diplomatic career in 1920. His first assignments abroad were to Rome (1922) and Sofia (1925). Thereafter he served in the foreign office's section on Southern and Southeastern Europe, and later specialized in Austria, Hungary and Czechoslovakia. It is interesting to note that, after serving on the first German-Italian officers' commission, Altenburg assumed the post of Reich plenipotentiary in occupied Greece. Auswärtiges Amt, *Biographisches Handbuch des deutschen Auswärtigen Dienstes, 1871–1945,* vol. 1 (Paderborn, Munich, Vienna, Zurich: Ferdinand Schöningh, 2000), 26–27; Auswärtiges Amt, *Biographisches Handbuch des deutschen Auswärtigen Dienstes, 1871–1945,* vol. 2 (Paderborn, Munich, Vienna, Zurich: Ferdinand Schöningh, 2005), 263–65. On Hencke's friendship with Altenburg, see Andor Hencke, *Augenzeuge einer Tragödie: Diplomatenjahre in Prag, 1936–1939* (Munich: Fides-Verlagsgesellschaft, 1977), p. 19.

40. Hencke later wrote about his experiences in Prague and Kiev. Hencke, *Augenzeuge einer Tragödie;* Andor Hencke, "Erinnerungen als Deutscher Konsul in Kiew in den Jahren 1933–1936," in *Mitteilungen der Arbeits- und Fördergemeinschaft der Ukrainischen Wissenschaften,* no. 14 (1977) and no. 15 (1978).

41. *ADAP,* series E, vol. 3, 51, 85. See also ANIC, Arhivele Ministerului de Externe, Fond 71/Germania, vol. 90, f. 382–84.

42. An example of such a recommendation can be found in MOL, K28, 56. csomó., 133. tétel. 1941-O-22493, 3.

43. The special mission was present and active in Northern and Southern Transylvania from July 15 to September 5, and again from October 20 to November 20, 1942. MOL, K70, 351. csomó., 9./b. tétel. (Német-olasz követbizottság Erdélyben, bizottság jelentései), 1942, Alapszám 141/1942, 20.

44. *ADAP*, series E, vol. 3, 8, 14.

45. Ibid., 12, 18–21.

46. Ibid., 51, 84–6.

47. BMF, RW 50, 87, Bericht der nach Ungarn und Rumänien entsandten deutsch-italienisch Sonderbeauftragten-Kommision; Bancoş, *Social şi naţional*, 55; Sebastian Balta, *Rumänien und die Grossmächte in der Ära Antonescu, 1940–1944* (Stuttgart: Franz Steiner Verlag, 2005), 275–77. For the text of the recommendations in Romanian, see Puşcaş, *Transilvania şi aranjamentele europene*, 84–121.

48. SNA, MZV, K. 192, 8.791/1942.

49. MOL, K28, 213. csomó., 467. tétel. Olasz-Német tisztibizottság ügyei, 1942-O-28962, 13–14.

50. BMF, RW 50, 286/(1940–1941) 1942, Im Geiste des Wiener Schiedsspruches, "Ungarns Einstellung zum W. Schiedsspruch," p. 3. Emphasis in the original expressed with double spaces between letters of stressed words.

51. M. Rakoshi, "Razdory v lagere 'Soyuznikov' Gitlera," *Pravda*, December 7, 1941, 4. The article was written by Hungarian Communist Mátyás Rákosi. Special thanks to Vincent Slatt of the USHMM Library and Kenneth Nyirady of the Library of Congress for helping me to obtain a copy of this article.

52. BMF, RW 50, 286/(1940–1941) 1942, Im Geiste des Wiener Schiedsspruches, "Antideutsche Hetzsender zur Lage an der Wiener Schiedsspruchgrenze."

53. SNA, MZV, K. 192, 8.181/1942. The Hungarian administration blamed the Romanians in general—and Mihai Antonescu in particular—for feeding Allied propaganda with their "lack of discipline." Ibid., 8.310/1942.

54. Ibid.

55. MOL, K28, 213. csomó., 467. tétel. Olasz-Német tisztibizottság ügyei, 1942-O-23890, 23, 55. The lord lieutenant of Szolnok-Doboka at the time was Béla Bethlen.

56. See, for example, the response of Romanian foreign minister Nicolae Titulescu to the proposal of direct League arbitration from 1928 in Francis Deák, *The Hungarian-Rumanian Land Dispute: A Study of Hungarian Property Rights in Transylvania under the Treaty of Trianon* (New York: Columbia University Press, 1928), 150–51.

57. After receiving the Hencke-Roggeri report in June 1942, Mihai Antonescu railed against the commission, both to Marshal Antonescu and to the German ambassador to Romania, Killinger. ANIC, Arhivele Ministerului de Externe, Fond 71/Germania, vol. 88, f. 391. On June 20, Marshal Antonescu asked Killinger to inform the German government that "I am not a vassal . . . if Germany and Italy wish to rewrite all the international mandates in the European community with the belief that the Romanian people is a minor nation that expects tutelage," it is mistaken (ibid., f. 394).

58. Florin Constantiniu, coord., *Antonescu-Hitler: corespondenţă şi întîlniri inedite, 1940–1944*, vol. 2 (Bucharest: Gozia Ed., 1991), 96–97, 103–4. In a conversation with a German diplomat in July 1942, Mihai Antonescu was similarly assertive on this issue: "The Romanian people can be their own master and do not need to appeal to anyone

[for assistance]." ANIC, Arhivele Ministerului de Externe, Fond 71/Germania, vol. 89, f. 51.

59. BMF, RW 50, 124/1942, Flüchtlingsbewegung, Bevölkerungsaustausch und Optionsplan, "Grundtendenzen in der Bevölkerungsfrage," p. 3.

60. "Feljegyzés az 1941 julius 4.-i román jegyzékkel kapcsolatban tehető lépéseket befolyásoló szempontokról," July 29, 1941. MOL, K63, 258. csomó., 27. tétel, 1940–27/7/T/2/d, 198.

61. USHMMA, RG-25.013M, Preşedinţia Consiliului de Miniştrii–Cabinet Militar, 1940–1944, roll 7, dosar 716/1940, f. 811.

62. July 26, 1942. MOL, K28, 213. csomó., 467. tétel. Olasz-Német tisztibizottság ügyei, 1942-O-28380, 19–20.

63. MOL, K63, 256. csomó., 1940–1942–27. tétel./7.I.,165.

64. Ibid., 130.

65. MOL, K28, 56. csomó., 133. tétel. 1941-O-22493.

66. MOL, K70, 351. csomó., 9./b. tétel. (Német-olasz követbizottság Erdélyben, bizottság jelentései), 1942, Alapszám 141/1942, 19–20.

67. Puşcaş, *Transilvania şi aranjamentele europene*, 17–28, esp. p. 26.

68. MOL, K70, 351. csomó., 9./b. tétel. (Német-olasz követbizottság Erdélyben, bizottság jelentései), 1942, Alapszám 141/1942, 21–22.

69. MOL, K63, 256. csomó., 1940–1942–27. tétel./7.I., 94–95, 130, 151.

70. On border disputes, see Balta, *Rumänien und die Grossmächte*, 276. On population movement, see BMF, RW 50, 124/1942, Flüchtlingsbewegung, Bevölkerungsaustausch und Optionsplan, "Grundtendenzen in der Bevölkerungsfrage," p. 3. The commission also estimated that one-sixth of the Romanian population of Northern Transylvania had fled or had been expelled from there since the arbitration. MOL, K63, 256. csomó., 1940–1942–27. tétel./7.I., 111.

71. MOL, K28, 56. csomó., 125. tétel. 1941-O-15607. The author went on to list an example.

72. BMF, RW 50, 196, Glaubwürdigkeit der rum. Minderheit.

73. BMF, RW 50, 124/1942, Flüchtlingsbewegung, Bevölkerungsaustausch und Optionsplan, Mangelnde zuverlässigkeit der Flüchtlings-Protokolle, 26. The head of the Romanian delegation to the commission, Lieutenant Colonel Virgil Bichiceanu, also believed that many Romanian refugees' complaints were "untrue" or "exaggerated," a fact which "decreases the value of the claims we are making." He proposed the testimonies be checked and more strict questioning be introduced to eliminate such testimonies. ANIC, Fond Delegatul Marelui Stat Major pe lângă Comisie de Ofiţeri Italo-Germană, Dos. 64/1943, f. 15.

74. BMF, RW 50, 124/1942, Flüchtlingsbewegung, Bevölkerungsaustausch und Optionsplan, Mangelnde zuverlässigkeit der Flüchtlings-Protokolle, 26. The radicalism of "intellectuals" in particular was often discussed, and not only by the Germans. The Hungarian lord-lieutenant of Szolnok-Doboka complained in August 1942 to the commission that "if a portion of the Romanian intelligentsia would make a conscious decision to distance themselves from the subversive activities of the Romanian bribery world, then there would have been tranquility, order, and peace among the Romanians of the county long ago." MOL, K28, 213. csomó., 467. tétel. Olasz-Német tisztibizottság ügyei, 1942-O-23890, 57.

75. ANIC, Fond Delegatul Marelui Stat Major pe lângă Comisie de Ofițeri Italo-Germană, Dos. 64/1943, f. 15.

76. Ibid., f. 2.

77. "Consiliul in chestiunea refugiaților Ardealului (Retorsiune și represalii) 29 mai 1942 și Conferința cu prefecții de județ cu privire la situația refugiaților 8 iulie 1942," ANIC, Fond Presedenția Consiliului de Miniștri. Cabinetul Militar Ion Antonescu dosar 515/1942, 1–30, 31–49. This document was located by Vladimir Solonari, who was kind enough to inform me of its existence.

78. MOL, K28, 213. csomó., 467. tétel. Olasz-Német tisztibizottság ügyei, 1942-O-23890, 17.

79. ASFJC, Biroul de cenzură Cluj-Turda, nr. 1/1940–1942, f. 381.

80. ANIC, Fond Ministerul de Interne, Dos. 438/1941, f. 9.

81. MOL, K28, 213. csomó., 467. tétel. Olasz-Német tisztibizottság ügyei, 1944-O-15372, 6, 24; MOL, K63, 258. csomó., 27. tétel, 1940–27/7/T/2/d, 294–95.

82. MOL, K28, 213. csomó., 467. tétel. Olasz-Német tisztibizottság ügyei, 1944-O-15372, 6.

83. MOL, Kolozs megye főispáni eln. iratok, 1942, 4063 tekercs, Alapszám 132.

84. The report is from February 17, 1943. MOL, K28, 213. csomó., 467. tétel. Olasz-Német tisztibizottság ügyei, Alapszám 1944-O-15372.

85. From two reports, one from Brașov, USHMMA, RG-25.013M, Președinția Consiliului de Miniștrii–Cabinet Militar, 1940–1944, roll 14, dosar 402/1941, f. 106–7; the other from Aiud, September 12, 1941, Ibid., f. 193–4. See also ANIC, Fond Delegatul Marelui Stat Major pe lângă Comisie de Ofițeri Italo-Germană, Dosar 9/1942, 50–51.

86. BMF, RW 50, 44/1942, Schriftwechsel mit der Offizierskommission in Klausenburg, "Einbürgerung des volksdeutschen Dolmetschers Michael Binder."

87. BMF, RW 50, 2/ 1941–1944, Mietvertrag (Baron Hizdeu).

88. MOL, K28, 213. csomó., 467. tétel. Olasz-Német tisztibizottság ügyei, Alapszám 1943-O-21695.

89. MOL, K28, 213. csomó., 467. tétel. Olasz-Német tisztibizottság ügyei, Alapszám 1943-O-25526.

90. BMF, RW 50, 35, No. 1526/42.

91. MOL, K63, 260. csomó., 1941–27. tétel./4.I.b., 5.

92. MOL, K28, 213. csomó., 467. tétel. (German-Italian Commission). Alapszám 1942-O-25229, 1942-O-28380, 1944-O-15372; MOL, K63, 252. csomó., 1940–27. tétel./1, 133. Ethnic Germans in Hungary also used their identity to claim protection from Hungarian policies and actions against them. ASFJC, Primăria Mun. Cluj, Inv. 384/1941, Nr. 12246–23152, Alapszám 15163.

93. MOL, K28, 213. csomó., 467. tétel. Olasz-Német tisztibizottság ügyei, 1942-O-23890, 57.

94. MOL, K28, 213. csomó., 467. tétel. Olasz-Német tisztibizottság ügyei, 1942-O-25229, 6.

95. MOL, K28, 213. csomó., 467. tétel. Olasz-Német tisztibizottság ügyei, 1942-O-28380, 39–40.

96. The Transylvanian Hungarian Economic Association [Erdélyi Magyar Gazdasági Egyesület] (EMGE) had two branches, one in Northern Transylvania and one in Southern Transylvania. Each had its own president. The president of the Southern

Transylvanian branch, Pál Szász, is cited here. Samu Benkő, "Az Erdélyi Magyar Gazdasági Egyesület nagy korszaka és Szász Pál szervező talentuma," *Magyar Közélet* II.
évfolyam, 12. szám (December 1998–January 1999), http://www.hhrf.org/mk/812mk/
812mk01.htm (accessed November 8, 2007).

97. MOL, K28, 213. csomó., 467. tétel. Olasz-Német tisztibizottság ügyei, 1942-O-
28380, 51.

98. MOL, K28, 213. csomó., 467. tétel. Olasz-Német tisztibizottság ügyei, 1942-O-
28380, 86.

99. Elemér Gyárfás expressed this opinion following a meeting with the commission on June 23, 1941. MOL, K63, 258. csomó., 27. tétel. 1940–27/7/T/2/d, 422–23.
See also the report from the lord lieutenant of Nagyvárad, Endre Hlatky, on the lack
of neutrality on the part of the commission. MOL, K28, 213. csomó., 467. tétel. Olasz-
Német tisztibizottság ügyei, 1942-O-23890, 39.

100. MOL, K28, 213. csomó., 467. tétel. Olasz-Német tisztibizottság ügyei, 1942-O-
28380, 57. The individual in question was Pál Szász, president of EMGE for Southern
Transylvania, who lived in Aiud. The answer he gave to the commissioner is worth
sharing: "I'm not afraid the Hungarians will be massacred. I know the Transylvanian
Romanian people's spirit; we live side by side with them; they wouldn't commit such a
crime without reason unless they were spurred on and provoked into doing so."

101. MOL, K28, 213. csomó., 467. tétel. Olasz-Német tisztibizottság ügyei, 1942-
O-28777, 3.

102. MOL, K70, 351. csomó., 9./b. tétel. (Német-olasz követbizottság Erdélyben,
bizottság jelentései), 1942, Alapszám 141/1942, 17.

103. This is mentioned both in the memo and in the response itself. MOL, K70,
351. csomó., 9./b. tétel. (Német-olasz követbizottság Erdélyben, bizottság jelentései),
1942, Alapszám 141/1942, 17–18, 28.

104. MOL, K70, 351. csomó., 9./b. tétel. (Német-olasz követbizottság Erdélyben,
bizottság jelentései), 1942, Alapszám 141/1942, 17–18.

105. MOL, K70, 351. csomó., 9./b. tétel. (Német-olasz követbizottság Erdélyben,
bizottság jelentései), 1942, Alapszám 141/1942, 22.

106. MOL, K70, 351. csomó., 9./b. tétel. (Német-olasz követbizottság Erdélyben,
bizottság jelentései), 1942, Alapszám 141/1942, 17.

107. MOL, K63, 256. csomó., 1940–1942–27. tétel./7.I., 93–94. See also Horthy's
conversation with the German foreign minister from April 16, 1943, in Andreas Hillgruber, ed., *Staatsmänner und Diplomaten bei Hitler: Vertrauliche Aufzeichnungen über Unterredungen mit Vertretern des Auslandes, 1942–1944, II. Teil* (Frankfurt am Main: Bernard
& Graefe Verlag, 1970), 31, 250.

108. MOL, K28, 213. csomó., 467. tétel. Olasz-Német tisztibizottság ügyei, 1942-
O-29708, 5.

109. MOL, K63, 256. csomó., 1940–1942–27. tétel./7.I., 93–94.

110. In a conversation between Mihai Antonescu, Killinger, and Bova Scoppa,
from July 7, 1942, Antonescu expressed revulsion that Germany and Italy "tolerated
that Hungarians benefit from the advantages of friendship and the [Axis] alliance" even
given "all the injustices and offenses committed against Romania." ANIC, Arhivele
Ministerului de Externe, Fond 71/Germania, vol. 89, f. 38.

III. From a report of late December 1942. ANIC, Fond Delegatul Marelui Stat Major pe lângă Comisie de Ofițeri Italo-Germană, Dosar 9/1942, 41–43.

112. Cited in Balta, *Rumänien und die Grossmächte*, 277. Interestingly, if not surprisingly, the Hungarian leadership found this report to be deeply biased in favor of the Romanians. See MOL, K70, 351. csomó., 9./b. tétel. (Német-olasz követbizottság Erdélyben, bizottság jelentései), 1942, Alapszám 141/1942, 22–23.

113. ASFJC, Inspectoratul de Poliție Cluj, Nr. Inv. 399. Dosar Nr. 92/1942(II), 1. Romanian police reported a similar reaction of the Romanian intellectuals in particular when the commission visited Aiud in September 1941. USHMMA, RG-25.013M, Președinția Consiliului de Miniștrii–Cabinet Militar, 1940–1944, roll 14, dosar 402/1941, f. 193–94.

114. MOL, K28, 213. csomó., 467. tétel. Olasz-Német tisztibizottság ügyei, 1942-O-23890, 17.

115. *ADAP*, series E, vol. 3, 124, 217.

116. MOL, K63, 258. csomó., 27. tétel, 1940–27/7/T/2/d, 294–95.

117. MOL, K28, 213. csomó., 467. tétel. Olasz-Német tisztibizottság ügyei, 1942-O-28962, 3–6. The document concedes that some may have been addressed without the Hungarian consulate's knowledge, however, since the commission reported directly to the Axis powers rather than to the governments of Hungary and Romania.

118. MOL, K70, 351. csomó., 9./b. tétel. (Német-olasz követbizottság Erdélyben, bizottság jelentései), 1942, Alapszám 141/1942, 19.

119. Constantiniu, *Antonescu-Hitler*, 2:96–97, 103–4.

120. ASFJC, Inspectoratul de Poliție Cluj, Nr. Inv. 399. Dosar Nr. 92/1942(II), 1.

121. See ANIC, Fond Președinția Consiliului de Miniștri, Cabinet Militar, Dosar 396/1943, f. 1–285; ANIC, Fond Delegatul Marelui Stat Major pe lângă Comisie de Ofițeri Germană, Dosar 15/1944, f. 89–93; MOL, K28, 213. csomó., 467. tétel. Olasz-Német tisztibizottság ügyei, 1942-O-28380 (Hungarians not permitted to use their language), 1942-O-22511 (internment and firing of Romanians); MOL, K63, 260. csomó., 1941–27. tétel./4.I.b., 3–197 (on slights against Hungarians); *ADAP*, series E, vol. 2, 286, 487 (forceful requisition of Hungarian minority foodstuffs); MOL, K70, 351. csomó., 9./b. tétel. (Német-olasz követbizottság Erdélyben, bizottság jelentései), 1942, Tárgyi csoport 9., 12–16 (murder and mistreatment of Hungarians in Transylvania in August and September 1940).

122. BMF, RW 50, 1, "Aktenvermerk," 18.

123. BMF, RW 50, 1/1944, Organisation, "Aktenvermerk 22." It is unclear whether the picnic basket made it across the border, but the instructions for its evacuation can be found in BMF, RW 50, 1, "Aktenvermerk," 18. Despite the mass destruction of the Kolozsvár office's documentary material, much still remains documenting the activities of the German-Italian Commission in archives in Germany, Hungary, and Romania. The largest such collection is at the Bundesarchiv-Militärarchiv Freiburg, RW 50, and includes 292 packets/volumes of material.

124. Dániel Csatári, *Forgószélben: magyar-román viszony, 1940–1945* (Budapest: Akadémiai Kiadó, 1968), 114, 120–32, 246.

125. Pușcaș, *Transilvania și aranjamentele europene*, lxxv–lxxvi.

126. Mark Mazower, *Dark Continent: Europe's Twentieth Century* (New York: A. A.

Knopf, distributed by Random House, 1999), 149. Germany's concern for the fate of non-German minorities was tied to its own interest. In the words of historian Lóránt Tilkovszky, "the situation of the other nationalities only mattered to them insofar as they could reference them in their efforts to achieve the betterment of the German minority's situation." Tilkovszky, "A nyilasok törvényjavaslata a nemzetiségi kérdés rendezéséről," *Századok* 99, no. 6 (1965): 1249. See also Mark Mazower, *Hitler's Empire: Nazi Rule in Occupied Europe* (London: Allen Lane, 2008), 7. Nevertheless, as far as politicians, statesmen, and diplomats in Hungary and Romania were concerned, it did not so much matter *why* Germany cared about the fates of other minorities, but what their concern meant for the future reordering of Europe.

127.   Petre Otu, ed., *Pacea de mâine: Documentele ale Comisiei constituite în vederea pregătirii conferinței de pace de după cel de-al doilea război mondial, 1942–1944* (Bucharest: Editura Militară, 2006), 81–82.

128.   Árpád Török, "Európa megszervezése," *Magyar Szemle* 38, no. 2 (150) szám (February 1940), 136–42, 142.

5. THE "JEWISH QUESTION" MEETS THE TRANSYLVANIAN QUESTION

1.   Pál Teleki, "A numerus clausus módosításáról," in *Válogatott politikai írások és beszédek* (Budapest: Osiris kiadó, 2000), 199–200.

2.   ANIC, Fond Președentia Consiliului de Miniștri Cabinetul Militar Ion Antonescu, Dosar 194/1940, Factura de subvenții pentru Seton-Watson, f. 100. I am indebted to Vladimir Solonari for sharing this document with me.

3.   T. V. Volokitina, T. M. Islamov, and T. A. Pokivailova, eds., *Transilvanskii vopros. Vengero-rumynskii territorialnyi spor i SSSR. 1940–1946 gg. Dokumenty rossiiskikh arkhivov* (Moscow: Rosspen, 2000), 157.

4.   Historian Nicholas Nagy-Talavera, who was present when the Hungarian troops entered Northern Transylvania, recalls that many Jewish families were among those celebrating the troops' arrival. Nicholas M. Nagy-Talavera, *The Greenshirts and Others: A History of Fascism in Hungary and Romania* (Stanford, Calif.: Hoover Institution Press, 1970), 309. See also Dániel Lőwy, *A Kálváriától a tregédiáig: Kolozsvár zsidó lakosságának története* (Kolozsvár: Koinónia, 2005), 119–22.

5.   BMF, RW 50, 160; *Martiriul evreilor din România, 1940–1944: Documente și mărturii* (Bucharest: Editura Hasefer, 1991), 255–56. See also the Janovics case recounted in this chapter; 4,333 such claims were submitted by the end of 1941 in Northern Transylvania. ASFJC, Biroul de cenzură Cluj-Turda, nr. 1/1940–1942. f. 311.

6.   See Sándor Tóth, *Erdély 22 éves rabsága* (Budapest: Magyar Géniusz Kiadása, 1941), 195–96.

7.   ASFJC, Biroul de cenzură Cluj-Turda, nr. 1/1940–1942. f. 341.

8.   Dániel Lőwy, *A téglagyártól a tehervonatig: Kolozsvár zsidó lakosságának története* (Kolozsvár: Erdélyi Szépmíves Céh, 1999), 176.

9.   Although 153,462 individuals declared themselves Jews by religion on the census, only 45,593 of those declared themselves Jews by nationality. *Recensământul din 1941: Transilvania* (Cluj: Editura Presa Universitară Clujeană, 2002), 332–33. The margin by

which Hungarians were in the majority in Northern Transylvania according to the 1941 Hungarian census was very narrow (with 1,347,012 declaring themselves Hungarian by nationality, and 1,066,353 declaring themselves Romanian by nationality). That margin would have all but disappeared if just over 100,000 Jews had not declared themselves Hungarians and if all adherents of the Greek Catholic and Eastern Orthodox faiths (together totaling 1,194,421) had declared themselves Romanians.

10. Arhivele Județului Cluj, Primăria mun. Cluj, "Reg. de intrare," Inv. 386/1942, Nr. 19276, 19275, 19635, 24578, 29178, 29534, 33016, 34157. Jews in Hungary were denied the right to change their names to Hungarian-sounding ones starting in 1938. Viktor Karády and István Kozma, eds., *Név és nemzet: Családnév-változtatás, névpolitika és nemzetiségi erőviszonyok Magyarországon a feudalizmustól a kommunizmusig* (Budapest: Osiris Kiadó, 2002), 244.

11. On December 3, 1942, Kállay noted that if Hungary got rid of its Jews, there would have to be a higher rate of assimilation of the Germans. *Judenverfolgung in Ungarn, Dokumentensammlung* (Frankfurt am Main: United Restitution Organization, 1959), 121.

12. From a letter to Hungary's minister president Pál Teleki, October 14, 1940. Miklós Nagybányai Horthy, *Horthy Miklós titkos iratai* (Budapest: Kossuth Könyvkiadó, 1972), 261.

13. Tóth, *Erdély 22 éves rabsága*, 225–26. See also Arthur Balogh, "Erdély és a zsidókérdés," *Magyar Nemzet*, January 3, 1941.

14. György Páll, "A zsidókérdés Magyarországon," in *Erdélyi kérdések—magyar kérdések* (Kolozsvár: Minerva, 1943), 38–39.

15. Miklós Nagybányai Horthy, *Titkos iratai* (1972), 221–22.

16. "Kolozsvár főtérréről május elsejétől eltünnek a zsidó kereskedők," *Magyar Nép*, May 9, 1942, 3.

17. George Barany, "'Magyar Jew or Jewish Magyar?': Reflections on the Question of Assimilation," in *Jews and Non-Jews in Eastern Europe, 1918–1945*, ed. B. Vago and G. L. Mosse (John Wiley & Sons: New York, 1974), 56.

18. Ibid., 64.

19. Raphael Patai, *The Jews of Hungary: History, Culture, Psychology* (Detroit: Wayne State University Press, 1996), 279.

20. István Gorove, "Zsidó emancipáció," in *Nemzetiség* (Pest, 1842): 98–109; cited in János Gyurgyák, *A zsidókérdés Magyarországon: politikai eszmetörténet* (Budapest: Osiris, 2001), 272.

21. Ignác Einhorn, "A zsidóügy és a sajtó honunkban," in *Első Magyar Zsidó Naptár és Évkönyv 1848-ik szökőévre* (Pest, 1848), reproduced in *A zsidóság útja* (Budapest: Múlt és Jövő Kiadó, 2000), 27–28.

22. Cited in T. D. Kramer, "From Utility to Catastrophe: Aspects of Hungarian Jewry's Responses to the Holocaust Process with Particular Reference to the 'Jewish Question' in Hungary," draft dissertation submitted to the Department of Semitic Studies, University of Sydney (May 15, 1994), 6; copy located in the USHMM Library.

23. Sz. Ferenc Horváth, "Népcsoportpolitika, szociális kompenzáció és gazdasági jóvátétel: a holokauszt Észak-Erdélyben," *Múltunk*, 3, no. (2006): 102–43, 105–6; Barany, "'Magyar Jew or Jewish Magyar?'" 73–74.

24. See Rolf Fischer, *Entwicklungsstufen des Antisemitismus in Ungarn, 1867–1939*

(Munich: R. Oldenbourg Verlag, 1988), 86. It is also interesting that in places where the dominant minority was German, anti-Semitism was often more intense (ibid., 86–87).

25. István. I. Mócsy, *The Effects of World War I: The Uprooted: Hungarian Refugees and Their Impact on Hungary's Domestic Politics, 1918–1921* (New York: Columbia University Press, 1983), 11–13.

26. Tibor Hajdú and Zsuzsa Nagy, "Revolution, Counterrevolution, Consolidation," in *A History of Hungary*, ed. Peter F. Sugar, Péter Hanák, and Tibor Frank (Bloomington and Indianapolis: Indiana University Press, 1994), 307–9.

27. See especially the contributions to the forum in the Hungarian journal *Huszadik Század* [The Twentieth Century] from 1917; the forum poses three questions to contributors: (1) Is there a Jewish Question in Hungary? (2) What are the causes of the Hungarian Jewish Question? (3) What should be the solution to the Jewish Question? "A zsidókérdés Magyarországon: A Huszadik Század körkérdése," *Huszadik Század*, 2. sz. (1917).

28. Gyurgyák, *A zsidókérdés Magyarországon*, 117–23.

29. Eduard Nižňanský, *Židovská komunita na Slovensku medzi československou parlamentnou demokraciou a slovenským štátom v stredoeurópskom kontexte* (Prešov: Universum, 1999), 242.

30. Pál Teleki's speech before the upper house of the Hungarian parliament, March 13–14, 1928, in Teleki, "A numerus clausus módosításáról," 199–200.

31. Nathaniel Katzburg, "The Jewish Question in Hungary during the Inter-war Period—Jewish Attitudes," in *Jews and Non-Jews in Eastern Europe, 1918–1945*, ed. B. Vago and G. L. Mosse (New York: John Wiley & Sons, 1974), 116. The enforcement of the *numerus clausus* was not rigorous and was tempered by a variety of factors such that the letter of the law was not followed. See Peter Tibor Nagy, "The Numerus Clausus in Interwar Hungary," *East European Jewish Affairs* 35, no. 1 (June 2005): 13–22, 18–20.

32. C. A. Macartney, "Hungarian Foreign Policy during the Inter-war Period, with Special Reference to the Jewish Question," in *Jews and Non-Jews in Eastern Europe, 1918–1945*, ed. B. Vago and G. L. Mosse (John Wiley & Sons: New York, 1974), 125. See also Joseph Rothschild, *East Central Europe between the Two World Wars* (Seattle and London: University of Washington Press, 1988), 157.

33. Cited in Tamás Ungvári, *Ahasvérus és Shylock: A "zsidókérdés" Magyarországon* (Budapest: Akadémiai Kiadó, 1999), 131.

34. Ibid., 130.

35. Bela Vago, "The Attitude toward the Jews as a Criterion of the Left-Right Concept," in *Jews and Non-Jews in Eastern Europe, 1918–1945*, ed. B. Vago and G. L. Mosse (New York: John Wiley & Sons, 1974), 25. The 1924 party statute stipulated that membership in the party was open to anyone who declared the Hungarian language and culture to be their own. Horváth, "Népcsoportpolitika," 109.

36. Nathaniel Katzburg, *Hungary and the Jews: Policy and Legislation, 1920–1943* (Jerusalem: Bar-Ilan University Press, 1981), 48.

37. Fischer notes that "around 60 percent of the people's commissars in the Republic of Soviets were of Jewish origin." Fischer, *Entwicklungsstufen*, 128.

38. Figures vary widely, but Katzburg estimated that about 1,400 people were killed

and 70,000 imprisoned. From August 1919 through May 1920, "bands of officers and units of the Hungarian army staged pogroms and committed mass murders at about fifty localities" across Trianon Hungary. Nathaniel Katzburg, "Hungarian Jewry in Modern Times: Political and Social Aspects," in *Hungarian-Jewish Studies*, vol. 1, ed. Randolph L. Braham (New York: World Federation of Hungarian Jews, 1966): 137–70, 153–55. In Horváth, the figure cited is 5,000 dead, 3,000 of which were Jews. Horváth, "Népcsoportpolitika," 106.

39. Gyurgyák, *A zsidókérdés Magyarországon,* 204–5.

40. Horváth, "Népcsoportpolitika," 108–9.

41. Bela Vago, "The Destruction of the Jews of Transylvania," in *Hungarian-Jewish Studies,* vol. 1, ed. Randolph L. Braham (New York: World Federation of Hungarian Jews, 1966), 171.

42. Ungvári, *Ahasvérus és Shylock,* 131.

43. HIWRP, Sabin Manuilă, box 16, folder 5, "România și revizuirea tratatelor, discursurile D-lor Iuliu Maniu și C. I. Brătianu în ședința adunărei Deputaților din 4 Aprilie 1934, Răspunsul d-lui N. Titulescu Ministrul Afacerilor Străine, Monitorul Oficial și Imprimeriile Statului, Imprimeria Națională, București," p. 9.

44. See Horváth, "Népcsoportpolitika," 112.

45. Nižňanský, *Židovská komunita,* 219. Hungary gained territory from Czechoslovakia in 1938 (S. Slovakia), 1939 (Carpatho-Ukraine), from Romania in 1940 (N. Transylvania), and from Yugoslavia in 1941 (Banat). For how "irredentism also inspired many [in Hungary] to the support the Arrow Cross," see Paul Hanebrink, *In Defense of Christian Hungary: Religion, Nationalism, and Antisemitism, 1890–1944* (Ithaca, N.Y.: Cornell University Press, 2006), 140. See also Randolph L. Braham. *The Politics of Genocide: The Holocaust in Hungary.* Condensed ed. (Detroit: Wayne State University Press, 2000), 24, 41.

46. MOL, K63, 253. csomó., 1940–27/1.II. tétel, 45. The letter was written on November 21 and referred specifically to legislation relating to the confiscation of Jewish property for the benefit of the state, likely including Decree-Laws 3361 of October 4 and 3810 of November 12 on the "transfer of Jewish rural properties to the patrimony of the state." From September 8 to December 4, 1940, the Romanian government enacted a series of twenty-one laws and revisions of earlier laws that limited Jews' right to own property, occupy certain professions, attend certain schools, be active in particular cultural venues, and so on. See Benjamin, *Evreii din România,* doc. 5–25, summarized on pp. 3–4.

47. Randolph L. Braham, ed., *The Destruction of Hungarian Jewry: A Documentary Account,* vol. 1 (New York: Pro Arte, 1963), doc. 74, 152.

48. *Martiriul evreilor din România,* 256; and Vago, "Destruction of the Jews of Transylvania," 178. The early optimism of the Jews of Transylvania regarding their prospects under Hungarian rule tapped into an understanding of Transylvania's historic role as the home of "religious freedom," and indeed freedom more generally. Some felt this "liberal" influence would once again temper the activities of the Hungarian parliament with the return of Northern Transylvania. See Pál Nadányi, "Az Erdélyi szellem," (December 1940), in *Merre, magyarok?* (New York: Amerikai magyar népszava, 1945), 56–57. For more on Transylvania as the home of religious freedom in connection with

the impact of the Second Vienna Arbitration, see Aladár Szegedy-Maszák, *Az ember őssel visszanéz* (Budapest: Európa Kiadó, 1996), 321.

49. USHMMA, RG-25.004M, Romanian Information Service Records, 1936–1966, roll 73, 40027, Ministry of Internal Affairs, vol. 11, f. 14.

50. Páll, "A zsidókérdés Magyarországon," 38–39.

51. See Andrej Angrick, *Besatzungspolitik und Massenmord: Die Einsatzgruppe D in der südlichen Sowjetunion, 1941–1943* (Hamburg: Hamburger Edition HIS Verlagsges., 2003), 116.

52. USHMMA, RG-25.003, Romanian Ministry of National Defense, Archive of the General Staff concerning the Holocaust in Romania, reel 6, file 936, 511. Emphasis in the original.

53. ASFJC, Inspectoratul de Poliție Cluj, 42/1940(I), 197. See also the Council of Ministers' meeting with provincial governments from June 30, 1942. Citation from USHMMA RG-25.013, roll 30, dosar 510/1942, f. 54.

54. ASFJC, Inspectoratul de Poliție Cluj, 42/1940(II), 443.

55. USHMMA, RG-54.001M, Moldova National Archives, Chisinau, roll 9, fond 679, nr. inv. 1, dosar 6293, f. 565. See also ibid., roll 5, fond 696, nr. inv. 1, dosar 84, f. 150.

56. ASFJC, Inspectoratul de Poliție Cluj, 44/1940–1942, 25. See also USHMMA, RG-25.017, Selected Records of the Cluj Branch of the Romanian National Archives, 1934–1952, roll 3, Inspectoratul de Poliție Cluj, 1916–1948, fond 209, nr. inv. 399, dosar 44/1940–1942, f. 25. Categories I and III-a designated by Decree-Law Nr. 2650 from August 8, 1940, affected Jews who came to Romania after December 30, 1918, and the Jews naturalized according to a 1919 decree-law respectively. For specific restrictions, see also ibid., roll 4, dosar 54/1940, f. 75–76; Benjamin, *Evreii din România*, doc. 3, 37–51, esp. pp. 46–47.

57. USHMMA, RG-25.010M, Inspectoratul General al Jandarmeriei, reel 13, dosar 29/1942, 101.

58. Vago, "Destruction of the Jews of Transylvania," 198–99.

59. USHMMA, RG-25.013M, Președinția Consiliului de Miniștrii–Cabinet Militar, 1940–1944, roll 30, dosar 560/1942, f. 12. See also Dennis Deletant, *Hitler's Forgotten Ally: Ion Antonescu and His Regime, Romania, 1940–1944* (New York: Palgrave Macmillan, 2006), 205.

60. The recent report of the International Commission on the Holocaust in Romania concluded that around fifteen thousand Jews were killed in these two pogroms, the overwhelming majority of them in Iași. Tuvia Friling, Radu Ioanid, Mihail E. Ionescu, eds., *International Commission on the Holocaust in Romania: Final Report* (Bucharest: Polirom, 2005), 381–82.

61. For a thorough and incisive overview of Romanian atrocities committed against the Jews in this region, see Vladimir Solonari, "Purifying the Nation: Population Exchange and Ethnic Cleansing in World War II Romania" (unpublished manuscript, cited with permission); Angrick, *Besatzungspolitik und Massenmord*.

62. For claims Jews collaborated with Soviets as part of Romanian propaganda, see USHMMA, RG-25.006M, Fiche 37, Selected Records from the Romanian Ministry of Foreign Affairs Archives, Fond SUA, Volume 40, 213. On the Romanian government's

knowledge of Romanian collaboration with the Soviets, see Vladimir Solonari, "Patterns of Violence: The Local Population and the Mass Murder of Jews in Bessarabia and Northern Bukovina, July–August 1941," *Kritika: Explorations in Russian and Eurasian History* 8, no. 4 (Fall 2007): 749–87, 755; Vladimir Solonari, "'Model Province': Explaining the Holocaust of Bessarabian and Bukovinian Jewry," *Nationalities Papers* 34, no. 4 (2006): 485–87.

63. Friling, Ioanid, and Ionescu, *International Commission,* 381–82. See also Jean Ancel, *Documents Concerning the Fate of Romanian Jewry during the Holocaust,* vol. 9 (New York: Beate Klarsfeld Foundation, [1986]); Jean Ancel, *Transnistria,* vols. 1–3 (Bucharest: Editura Atlas, 1998).

64. Eduard Nižňanský, ed., *Holokaust na Slovensku: Obdobie autonómie, 6.10.1938–14.3.1939, Dokumenty* (Židovská náboženská obec Bratislava: Bratislava, 2001), 328. See also Eduard Nižňanský, *Židovská komunita na Slovensku medzi československou parlamentnou demokraciou a slovenským štátom v stredoeurópskom kontexte* (Prešov: Universum, 1999), 96–97, 100.

65. Braham, *Politics of Genocide,* 41.

66. On the massacre in Vojvodina, see *Magyarország és a második világháború: titkos diplomáciai okmányok a háború előzményeihez és történetéhez,* második kiadás (Budapest: Kossuth könyvkiadó, 1961), doc. 164, 420–21. On the treatment of Jews in the territories annexed from Czechoslovakia, see Eduard Nižňanský, *Holocaust na Slovensku 4.: Dokumenty nemeckej proveniencie, 1939–1945* (Bratislava: Židovská náboženská obec Bratislava, 2003), 299. For an overview of Jewish wartime losses, see Braham, *Politics of Genocide,* 251–53.

67. MOL, K63, 257. csomó., 1940–27/7/E tétel, Román-magyar viszony—Erdély iktatlan, II. resz, 334, 338; ASFJC, Inspectoratul de Poliție Cluj, 42/1940(II), 141; BMF, RW 50, 124/1942, Flüchtlingsbewegung, Bevölkerungsaustausch und Optionsplan, "Grundtendenzen in der Bevölkerungsfrage." On "romanianization" of Hungarian coorporations, see also ANIC, Fond Ministerul de Interne, Dosar 438/1941, 17.

68. MOL, K63, 256. csomó., 1940–1942–27/7.I. tétel, p. 54; MOL, K63, 254. csomó, 1940–27/7.I. tétel, 107–8. See also MOL, K63, 260. csomó., 1941–27/1(II). tétel, 85; MOL, K63, 253. csomó., 1940–27/3. tétel, 5–7; USHMMA, RG-25.003, Romanian Ministry of National Defense, Archive of the General Staff concerning the Holocaust in Romania, reel 140, file 2370, 885–86.

69. BMF, RW 50, 123/1942 Wehrdienst der ungarischen bzw. rumänischen Minderheit in Siebenbürgen und Frage der Reserveoffiziere in Nord- und Südsiebenbürgen, "Einberufung der Rumänen aus Nordsiebenbürgen zu Militäreinheiten und Arbeitskompanien."; Mihai Fătu and Mircea Mușat, eds., *Horthyist-Fascist Terror in Northwestern Romania* (Bucharest: Meridiane Publishing House, 1986), 57–195; Szavári, "Magyar berendezkedés Észak-Erdélyben," 279–80.

70. MOL, K63, 256. csomó., 1940–1942–27/7.I. tétel, 121–22.

71. Miklós Horthy, *Horthy Miklós titkos iratai* (Budapest: Kossuth Könyvkiadó, 1962), 306. Werth was replaced by Ferenc Szombathelyi on Horthy's orders on September 6, 1941. Szombathelyi, Horthy argued, "served the German interest more cautiously, and therefore better," than Werth had (ibid., 307).

72. Krisztián Ungváry, "Kitelepítés, lakosságcsere és a holokauszt egyes összefüg-

gései," in *A holokauszt Magyarországon európai perspektívában*, ed. Judit Molnár (Budapest: Balassi kiadó, 2005): 84–100.

73. See Vladimir Solonari, "An Important New Document on the Romanian Policy of Ethnic Cleansing During WWII," *Holocaust and Genocide Studies* 21, no. 2 (Fall 2007): 268–97, 268. In his recent book on the Einsatzgruppe D in the southern USSR, Angrick asserts that in 1941 the Romanians considered the "liquidation" of Ukrainians in parallel with the solution to the "Jewish Question" in Northern Bukovina. Angrick, *Besatzungspolitik und Massenmord*, 155–58.

74. Cited in Solonari, "An Important New Document," 277.

75. Radu Ioanid, *The Holocaust in Romania: The Destruction of the Jews and Gypsies Under the Antonescu Regime, 1940–1944* (Chicago: Ivan R. Dee, 2000), 262–63.

76. Ibid., 267.

77. In a December 1942 note from Himmler to Ribbentrop, Himmler opined: "It would be extraordinarily gratifying if we could manage to take care of the [Jewish Question] in Hungary, the more so as I believe that in this way Romania, too, will be forced to abandon the hesitant attitude that it has shown with regard to beginning the evacuation of the Jews." *Judenverfolgung in Ungarn*, 120.

78. Bela Vago, "Germany and the Jewish Policy of the Kállay Government," in *Hungarian-Jewish Studies*, vol. 2, ed. Randolph L. Braham (New York: World Federation of Hungarian Jews, 1969), 193.

79. Cited in Deletant, *Hitler's Forgotten Ally*, 207.

80. Ibid., 210.

81. Ibid., 106.

82. *Judenverfolgung in Ungarn*, 127.

83. Ibid., 147.

84. Lajos Kerekes, ed., *Allianz Hitler-Horthy-Mussolini: Dokumente zur ungarischen Aussenpolitik, 1933–1944* (Budapest: Akadémia Kiadó, 1966), 346–50.

85. Ibid., 347–48.

86. ASFJC, Inspectoratul de Poliție Cluj, 42/1940(I), 269.

87. Ibid., 317.

88. ASFJC, Inspectoratul de Poliție Cluj, 93/1942, 86.

89. Margit Balogh, ed., *A szakadék szélén: az MTI bizalmas jelentései 1943. július 22.-1944. március 10.* (Budapest: Napvilág, Magyar Távirati Iroda, 2006), 35.

90. See Jean Ancel, "The Suspension of the Nazi Plan to Deport Romanian Jews to Poland and the Transylvanian Issue," in *The Holocaust in Hungary: A European Perspective*, ed. Judit Molnár (Budapest: Balassi Kiadó, 2005), 327–45. See also László Karsai, "The Fateful Year: 1942 in the Reports of Hungarian Diplomats," in *The Holocaust in Hungary: Sixty Years Later* (New York: Columbia University Press, 2006): 3–16, 12.

91. *Martiriul evreilor din România*, doc. 138, 255.

92. USHMMA, RG-25.017, roll 6, dosar 403/1944–1945, f. 172. See also ibid., dosar 605/1943–1944, f. 13–14.

93. Ibid., roll 5, dosar 605/1943–1944, f. 119.

94. *Martiriul evreilor din România*, doc. 139, 256–60.

95. USHMMA, RG-25.003, Romanian Ministry of National Defense, Archive of

the General Staff concerning the Holocaust in Romania, reel 120, file 1172, 94. Report from May 27, 1944.

96. Ibid., 85. Report from May 20, 1944.

97. Braham, *The Destruction of Hungarian Jewry,* vol. 2 (New York: Pro Arte, 1963), doc. 194, 444.

98. Ibid., doc. 323, 692. See also Nižňanský, *Dokumenty nemeckej proveniencie,* doc. 94, 260.

99. *ADAP,* series E, vol. 8, 54, 103–4.

100. Ibid., 214, 412–13. Romanian statesmen seemed equally aware of the importance of the Jewish issue. In November 1943, a Romanian diplomat in Great Britain lamented the fact that news of anti-Semitic activities in Romania were looked upon with disapproval in Britain. He warned that such activities "could only be extraordinarily disastrous for us." HIWRP, Dimitri G. Popescu, box 1, folder entitled "Berna," (point 2 "In legătură cu nota lui Bossy...").

101. Lya Benjamin, ed., *Evreii din România între anii 1940–1944,* vol. 4, *1943–1944: Bilanțul tragediei–renașterea speranței* (Bucharest: Editura Hasefer, 1998), xx.

102. Jean Ancel, ed., *Documents Concerning the Fate of Romanian Jewry During the Holocaust,* vol. 8 (New York: Beate Klarsfeld Foundation, 1986), 63.

103. Ibid. By May 18, 1944, Romanian officials reported that around three hundred Jews had fled from Hungarian territory. USHMMA, RG-25.017, roll 5, Inspectoratul de Poliție Cluj, 1916–1948, fond 209, nr. inv. 399, dosar 157/1944–1945, f. 19.

104. USHMMA, RG-25.017, roll 5, Inspectoratul de Poliție Cluj, 1916–1948, fond 209, nr. inv. 399, dosar157/1944–1945, f. 21.

105. Ibid., f. 77.

106. Ibid., roll 6, dosar 410/1944–1945, f. 57.

107. Ibid., roll 5, dosar 157/1944–1945, f. 36, 79, 92, 105. The Germans of Romania (Saxons, Swabians, representatives of the G.E.G.) indeed hinted that the occupation of Romania could be imminent, and was, as far as they were concerned, desirable (ibid., dosar 154/1944–1945, f. 172; dosar 157/1944–1945, f. 71–72).

108. USHMMA, RG-25.017, roll 5, Inspectoratul de Poliție Cluj, 1916–1948, fond 209, nr. inv. 399, dosar 157/1944–1945, f. 96.

109. *Martiriul evreilor din România,* doc. 136, 253.

110. Ibid., doc. 141, 262. See also Braham, *Destruction of Hungarian Jewry,* vol. 2, doc. 316, 680. The Germans at this time became aware of the fact that the policy vis-à-vis the Jews in Romania was becoming increasingly typified by "increasing tolerance and significant negligence of originally strong measures" (ibid., doc. 318, 684).

111. *Martiriul evreilor din România,* doc. 142, 262–63.

112. Braham, *Destruction of Hungarian Jewry,* vol. 2, doc. 354, 750–51.

113. Ibid., doc. 355, 752–53.

114. Ibid., 754.

115. Ibid., doc. 406, 828.

116. Toviah Friedmann, ed., *Vor 50 Jahren 1944–1994, Das SS-Sonderkommando Eichmann in Budapest und die Vernichtung der Juden Ungarns-Rumäniens* (Haifa: Institute of Documentation in Israel for the Investigation of Nazi War Crimes, 1994), doc. 677, 3–4. The document was written before July 10, 1944.

117. Ibid., 1–2.

118. Rogers Brubaker, Margit Feischmidt, Jon Fox, and Liana Grancea, *Nationalist Politics and Everyday Ethnicity in a Transylvanian Town* (Princeton, N.J., and Oxford: Princeton University Press, 2006), image 6a.

119. Friling, Ioanid, and Ionescu, *International Commission*, 381–82.

120. Lőwy, *A Kálváriától a tregédiáig*, 68–71.

121. Horváth, "Népcsoportpolitika," 121.

122. Macartney, cited in Nagy-Talavera, *Greenshirts and Others*, 62.

123. Stephen Fischer-Galati, "Fascism, Communism, and the Jewish Question in Romania," in *Jews and Non-Jews in Eastern Europe, 1918–1945*, ed. B. Vago and G. L. Mosse (New York: John Wiley & Sons, 1974), 158.

124. Nicolae Iorga's *History of Romania: Land, People, Civilisation* (London: T. Fisher Unwin Ltd., 1925) thus barely mentions the Jews. R. W. Seton-Watson's 1934 *History of Roumania* also largely ignores them, except for a very short section on Great Power attempts to have Romania adopt provisions for protection of Jews' rights (in which he shows little sympathy for such strivings). R. W. Seton-Watson, *A History of the Roumanians: From Roman Times to the Completion of Unity* ([S.I.]: Archon Books, 1963), 346–53 (first published in 1934). For Hungary, C. A. Macartney's 1937 book *Hungary and Her Successors* mentions Jews almost exclusively in the context of whether or not they count as members of state-enfranchised nationalities or minorities. The only exception is a place where he refers to Romanian anti-Semitism (p. 284). See C. A. Macartney, *Hungary and Her Successors: The Treaty of Trianon and Its Consequences, 1919–1937* (London and New York: Oxford University Press, 1937).

125. The most striking example in this regard is the contrast between the prewar and postwar work of C. A. Macartney. The 1937 *Hungary and Her Successors* glosses over their presence (see note 124). By contrast, after the war, Macartney claimed that the Jewish Question played a part "second to none in all the history, both international and domestic, of Trianon Hungary." C. A. Macartney, *October Fifteenth: A History of Modern Hungary, 1929–1945* (Edinburgh: Edinburgh University Press, 1956), 18.

126. For an overview of some of the drawbacks of undertaking studies of the Holocaust as "national" phenomena, see Holly Case, "The Holocaust and the Transylvanian Question in the 20th Century," in *The Holocaust in Hungary: Sixty Years Later* (New York: Columbia University Press, 2006): 17–40.

127. Mark Mazower, "Violence and the State in the Twentieth Century," *American Historical Review*, October 2002, http://www.historycooperative.org/journals/ahr/107.4/ah0402001158.html (accessed August 6, 2006), 1160.

6. A "New Europe"?

1. Mihai Antonescu, *Dacă vrei să câştigi războiul, trebuie să pregăteşti pacea* (Cluj-Napoca: Muzeul Etnografic al Transilvaniei, 1991), 3.

2. Béla Pomogáts, "Európa közelében: Európai integráció és magyar nemzetpolitika" *Európai utas* 58, no. 1 (2005): 13–15, 13.

3. Othmar Kolar, *Rumänien und seine nationalen Minderheiten, 1918 bis heute* (Vienna, Cologne, Weimar: Böhlau Verlag, 1997), 208.

4. Péter Illésfalvi, Péter Szabó, and Norbert Számvéber, *Erdély a hadak útján, 1940–1944* (Debrecen: Puedlo Kiadó, 2007), 109.

5. Bela Vago, "The Destruction of the Jews of Transylvania," in *Hungarian-Jewish Studies,* vol. 1, ed. Randolph L. Braham (New York: World Federation of Hungarian Jews, 1966), 200–201.

6. Illésfalvi, Szabó, and Számvéber, *Erdély a hadak útján,* 166. The death toll from arbitrary executions perpetrated by the Maniu Guards was likely around twenty-five before the Soviet authorities intervened to stop the violence against civilians. It should not be assumed, however, that the Soviets were categorically benign. Hungarian and German prisoners of war were detained in Soviet POW camps throughout Transylvania, where as many at ten thousand died (ibid., 165).

7. There was apparently more than one Maniu Guard organization: one based in Bucharest, another in Braşov. The latter was reportedly responsible for the killing of forty Hungarians. Marcela Sălăgean, *The Soviet Administration in Northern Transylvania, November 1944–March 1945* (Boulder, Colo.: East European Monographs, 2002), 55–57; Mihály Zoltán Nagy and Gábor Vincze, eds., *Autonómisták és centralisták, Észak-Erdély a két román bevonulás között, 1944. szeptember–1945. március* (Kolozsvár-Csíkszereda: Erdélyi Múzeum Egyesület-Pro-Print Könyvkiadó, 2004): 45–50, 352–67.

8. Cited in Yehuda Lahav, *Soviet Policy and the Transylvanian Question, 1940–1946* (Jerusalem: Hebrew University of Jerusalem, 1977), 18–19. See also Stephen D. Kertesz, *Between Russia and the West: Hungary and the Illusions of Peacemaking, 1945–1947* (Hamilton, Ontario: Hunyadi M. Mk., 1992). Although the guard named itself for Iuliu Maniu, the former statesman denied having any ties to them. HIWRP, Sabin Manuilă, box 11, folder 1, "Discursul Domnului Maniu, Preşedintele Partiduliu Naţional Tărănesc, şedinţa din 4 Iulie 1946," p. 34. See also "Ioan Arhip tábornok, a nagyvezérkar helyettes vezetője átirata Iuliu Maniu államminiszternek a nevét viselő alakulat tetteiről, Bukarest, 1944. október 18," Nagy and Vincze, *Autonómisták és centralisták,* 4, 144.

9. HIWRP, Dimitri G. Popescu, box 1, folder 1 (Events of Aug. 23, 1944—Documents, proclamations, reports, 1942–1946), "Convenţie de Armistiţiu între guvernul Român pe de o parte şi guvernele Uniunii Sovietice, Regatului Unit şi Statelor Unite ale Americei pe de altă parte" (Bucharest, 1944).

10. "Telegrama cifrata, Delegaţia României, Moscova," September 11, 1944, in HIWRP, Dimitri G. Popescu, box 1, folder titled "Events of Aug. 23, 1944—Armistice negotiations in Moscow"; Illésfalvi, Szabó, and Számvéber, *Erdély a hadak útján,* 165–66. It is likely that at least hundreds (some say thousands) of Hungarians, including children, died of disease, starvation, or violence in the camp.

11. *23 August 1944, Documente,* vol. 2 (Bucharest: Editura Ştiinţifică şi Enciclopedică, 1984), doc. 900, p. 833.

12. Ion Gheorghe, *Rumäniens Weg zu Satellitenstaat* (Heidelberg: Kurt Vorwinckel Verlag, 1952), 250–51.

13. *Curierul,* October 20, 1944, cited in Nagy and Vincze, *Autonómisták és centralisták,* 39. It is nevertheless the case that the military administration superseded the power of the governor (ibid).

14. Nagy and Vincze, *Autonómisták és centralisták,* 35–36.

15. Bethlen cited in László Zsigmond, ed., *DIMK, 1936–1945,* vol. 4, *Magyarország*

külpolitikája a II. világháború kitörésének időszakában, 1939–1940 (Budapest: Akadémiai kiadó, 1962), 577, 743.

16. Béni L. Balogh, *A magyar-román kapcsolatok 1939–1940-ben és a második bécsi döntés* (Csíkszereda: Pro-Print Könyvkiadó, 2002), 31–32; Mihály Fülöp and Péter Sipos, *Magyarország külpolitikája a XX. században* (Budapest: Aula Kiadó, 1998), 191–92. These relations were brief and unfruitful, as it quickly became clear that the Soviet Union's primary preoccupation was with Nazi aggression.

17. See T. V. Volokitina, T. M. Islamov, and T. A. Pokivailova, eds., *Transilvanskii vopros. Vengero-rumynskii territorialnyi spor i SSSR. 1940–1946 gg. Dokumenty rossiiskikh arkhivov* (Moscow: Rosspen, 2000).

18. Ervin Liptai, ed., *Magyarország hadtörténete a kiegyezéstől napjainkig*, vol. 2 (Budapest: Zrínyi Katonai Kiadó, 1985), 391; Peter Gosztony, *Hitlers Fremde Heere: Das Schicksal der nichtdeutschen Armeen im Ostfeldzug* (Vienna, Düsseldorf: Econ Verlag, 1976), 427; Josif Constantin Drăgan, ed., *Antonescu Mareșalul României și răsboaiele de reîntregire* (Venice: Fundația Europeană, 1991), 299–315; SNA, MZV, K. 193, 6.536/1943.

19. Due to the awkwardness of the original translation in Sălăgean, I have altered some words in the translation. Sălăgean, *Soviet Administration*, 50.

20. Nagy and Vincze, *Autonómisták és centralisták*, 36; Sălăgean, *Soviet Administration*, 43.

21. Nagy and Vincze, *Autonómisták és centralisták*, 11, 179.

22. Sălăgean, *Soviet Administration*, 40–41.

23. Romanian refugees of the Hungarian army's advance in 1940 faced similar problems on their return to Northern Transylvania after a four-year absence. The legal status of property belonging to ethnic Hungarians who fled—and even many who remained—was a point of tension between the two states well into the 1950s. See Gábor Vincze, ed., *Magyar vagyon román kézen: dokumentomok a romániai magyar vállalatok, pénzintézetek második világháború utáni helyzetéről és a magyar-román vagyonjogi vitáról* (Csíkszereda: Pro-Print Könyvkiadó, 2000), 4, 6, 15, 19–22, 108–10, 115–22, 157–58; Mihály Fülöp and Gábor Vincze, eds., *Revízió vagy autonómia?: iratok a magyar-román kapcsolatok történetéről, 1945–1947* (Budapest: Teleki László Alapítvány, 1998), 3, 40.

24. Sălăgean, *Soviet Administration*, 47, 52, 55.

25. Gábor Vincze, *Történeti kényszerpályák—kisebbségi reálpolitikák II: dokumentumok a romániai magyar kisebbség történetének tanulmányozáshoz, 1944–1989* (Csíkszereda: Pro-Print Könyvkiadó, 2003), 6, 12.

26. Cited in Fülöp and Sipos, *Magyarország külpolitikája*, 305.

27. Nagy and Vincze, *Autonómisták és centralisták*, 50–51; Sălăgean, *Soviet Administration*, 65.

28. Fülöp and Sipos, *Magyarország külpolitikája*, 307, 309–10.

29. Ibid., 312.

30. Nagy and Vincze, *Autonómisták és centralisták*, 48, 352–67.

31. HIWRP, Sabin Manuilă, box 11, folder 8, "Memoriu asupra discuției avute în ședința din 3 Iunie 1946 a Camerei Comunelor în chestiunea Transilvaniei," June 3, 1946.

32. Marin Radu Mocanu, coord., *România în anticamera conferinței de pace de la Paris, documente* (Bucharest: Arhivele Naționale ale României, 1996), doc. 33, 210–23. Cited in Ștefan Lache și Gheorge Țuțui, *România și conferința de pace de la Paris din 1946* (Cluj-Napoca: Editura Dacia, 1978), 263–64.

33. Fülöp and Sipos, *Magyarország külpolitikája*, 313–14.

34. Peter Kenez, *Hungary from the Nazis to the Soviets: The Establishment of the Communist Regime in Hungary, 1944–1948* (Cambridge: Cambridge University Press, 2006), 205–8.

35. HIWRP, Sabin Manuilă, box 11, folder 1, "Discursul Domnului Maniu, Preşedintele Partiduliu Naţional Tărănesc, şedinţa din 4 Iulie 1946," pp. 33, 39.

36. HIWRP, Stephen Kertesz, box 2, bundle IV.2., "Értesitő," Bpest, I. évf., 2–3 sz., 1947. márc.-ápr.

37. The party lobbied hard to win over the minorities and was predictably quite successful. In the city of Cluj, as of January 1946, barely 10 percent of Communist Party members were listed as Romanians. See Virgiliu Ţârău, "Viaţa politică şi problema locuinţelor la Cluj în anii 1945–1946," in *Viaţa privată, mentalităţi colective şi imaginar social în Transilvania*, ed. Sorin Mitu and Florin Gogâltean (Oradea and Cluj: Asociaţia istoricilor din Transilvania şi Banat, Muzeul Ţării Crişurilor, 1995–96), 319; Sălăgean, *Soviet Administration*, 58, 121.

38. Rogers Brubaker, Margit Feischmidt, Jon Fox, and Liana Grancea, *Nationalist Politics and Everyday Ethnicity in a Transylvanian Town* (Princeton, N.J., and Oxford: Princeton University Press, 2006), 108–9.

39. Stefano Bottoni, "The Creation of the Hungarian Autonomous Region in Romania (1952): Premises and Consequences," *Regio* (English issue, 2003): 71–93; Stefano Bottoni, *Transilvania rossa: Il comunismo romeno e la questione nazionale, 1944–1965* (Rome: Carocci editore, 2007), 61–75; Zoltán Szász, "Un 'dar' devaloare îndoielnică. Regiunea Autonomă Maghiară a secuilor," *História* 9–10 (1996): 48–49. The region existed formally until 1968 but was practically dismantled during the course of reforms in 1960.

40. Vladimir Tismaneanu, *Stalinism for All Seasons: A Political History of Romanian Communism* (Berkeley: University of California Press, 2003), 152–57.

41. For an excellent overview of how nationalism permeated Socialist ideology in Romania, see Katherine Verdery, *National Ideology under Socialism: Identity and Cultural Politics in Ceauşescu's Romania* (Berkeley: University of California Press, 1991).

42. On Giurescu as a member of the Historical Section, see Mihai Antonescu, *Dacă vrei să câştigi războiul*, 50. There was a period of several years during high Stalinism when Giurescu was sidelined by the authorities, but he was later rehabilitated and resumed his work. Giurescu's father, who died in 1919, was also called Constantin and was also a historian, as is his son, Dinu (1927–).

43. Constantin C. Giurescu, *Transilvania în istoria poporului român* (Bucharest: Editura Ştiinţifică, 1967), 7.

44. György Földes, *Románia, Magyarország és a nemzetiségi kérdés 1956–1989* (Budapest: Napvilág Kiadó, 2007), 207. Citation from a 1981 essay by Pach in Zsigmond Pál Pach, *Történelem és nemzettudat: cikkek, előadások* (Budapest: Kossuth Könyvkiadó, 1987), 24.

45. Pach, *Történelem*, 69.

46. "A XII. Magyar Találkozó Zárónyilatkozata," in HIWRP, Stephen D. Kertesz, box 2, bundle IV, folder 5/14.

47. "Magyarország biológiai Trianonja," in HIWRP, Stephen D. Kertesz, box 2, bundle IV, folder 5/14, pp. 3–14.

48. Olimpiu Matichescu, *Istoria nu face paşi înapoi* (Cluj-Napoca: Editura Dacia, 1985)

[published in English as *The Logic of History against the Vienna Diktat* (Bucharest: Editura Academiei Republicii Socialiste România, 1988)]; A. Simion, *Dictatul de la Viena* (Cluj: Editura Dacia, 1972); Miron Radu Paraschivescu, *Drumuri și răspîntii, reportaje 1937–1944* (Bucharest: Editura pentru literatură, 1967); Nicolae Corneanu, *The Romanian Church in Northwestern Romania under the Horthy Scourge* (Bucharest: Bible and Mission Institute of the Romanian Orthodox Church, 1986). Most notable in this regard is perhaps the controversy surrounding the three-volume Hungarian *History of Transylvania* that erupted in the late 1980s following its publication. See George Barany, review of *Erdély története, American Historical Review* 94, no. 3. (June 1989): 810–14, 113. On Romanian historiography of the 1970s and 1980s, see also Balogh, *A magyar-román kapcsolatok*, 15–18.

49. Quoted in Brubaker et al., *Nationalist Politics*, 117.

50. Mihai Antonescu, *Dacă vrei să câștigi războiul*, 3.

51. Ibid., 55.

52. Ardeleanu's position is far from unique on the matter of Mihai Antonescu's historical role. In a 1997 article, Romanian historian Petre Dache praised Mihai Antonescu as a "brave defender of [Romanian] national interest and dignity," whose ideas about the ordering of Europe after World War II "are still very important nowadays." Petre Dache, "Mihai Antonescu despre cel de-al doilea război mondial—campania din est—și organizarea Europei postbelice," *Muzeul Național* 9 (1997), http://www.mnir.ro/ro/publicatii/periodice/muzeul-national/rezumate/1997/petre-dache.html (accessed May 30, 2007).

53. The list includes a variety of Hungarian and Romanian publications. Artúr Balogh, *Jogállam és kisebbség* (Bucharest-Kolozsvár: Kriterion Könyvkiadó, 1997); Raul V. Bossy, *Recollections of a Romanian Diplomat, 1918–1969: Diaries and Memoirs of Raoul V. Bossy*, vols. 1–2 (Stanford, Calif.: Hoover Institution Press, 2003); Onisifor Ghibu, *Politica religioasă și minoritară a României* (Bucharest: Editura Albatros, 2003); Emil Ghilezan, *Un martor al istoriei: Emil Ghilezan de vorbă cu Adrian Niculescu* (Bucharest: Editura All, 1998); Ioan Hudiță, *Jurnal politic*, vols. 1 and 2 (Iași: Institutul European, 1998); Vasile Arimia, Ion Ardeleanu, and Ștefan Lache, eds., *Antonescu-Hitler: Corespondență și întîlniri inedite, 1940–1944*, vol. 1 (Bucharest: Cozia Ed.–Co., 1991); A. Simion, *Dictatul de la Viena: Ediția a II-a Revăzută și adăugită* (Bucharest: Editura Albatros, 1996).

54. Such works include, but are not limited to, the following: On the Transylvanian Question, see Corneliu-Mihail Lungu, *Transilvania în raporturile româno-austro-ungare, 1876–1886* (Bucharest: Editura Viitorul Românesc, 1999); Béla Borsi-Kálmán, *Illúziókergetés vagy ismétléskényszer? Román-magyar nemzetpolitikai elgondolások és megegyezési kísérletek a XIX. században* (Budapest: Balassi Kiadó, Kriterion könyvkiadó, 1995); Balázs Trencsényi, Dragoș Petrescu, Cristina Petrescu, Constantin Iordachi, and Zoltán Kántor, eds., *Nation-Building and Contested Identities: Romanian and Hungarian Case Studies* (Budapest and Iași: Regio Books and Editura Polirom, 2001), see especially the selected bibliography of works on the history of Hungarian-Romanian relations published between 1990 and 2000, pp. 307–72. On the Antonescu regime, see Ion Gheorghe, *Un dictator nefericit: Mareșalul Antonescu [și] calea României spre Statul satelit* (Bucharest: Editura Machiavelli, 1996); Teodor Mavrodin, *Mareșalul Antonescu întemnițat la Moscova* (Pitești: Editura Carminis, 1998); Dorel Bancoș, *Social și național în politica guvernului Ion Antonescu*

(Bucharest: Editura Eminescu, 2000); Mihai Fătu, *Antonescu și opoziția, 1940–1944* (Alexandria: Editura Tipoalex, 2000); Gheorghe Buzatu, ed., *Mareșalul Antonescu la judecata istoriei* (Bucharest: Editura Mica Valahie, 2002); on the Second Vienna Arbitration, see Neagu Cosma, *Dictatul de la Viena (30 aug. 1940): consecință a crimei organizate statal de către Ungaria și a colaboraționismului unor unguri din România* ([Romania]: Bravo Press, 1996); Mihai Fătu, ed., *Dictatul de la Viena din 1940 și biserica românească din nordul Transilvaniei (1940–1944), Documente* (Alexandria: Editura Tipoalex, 2001); Cornel Grad, *Al doilea arbitraj de la Viena* (Iași: Institutul European, 1998); Aurel Sergiu Marinescu, *Înainte și după Dictatul de la Viena* (Bucharest: Editura Vremea, 2000); Aurel Socol, *Furtună deasupra Ardealului* (Bucharest: Imprimeria Coresi, 1991); Balogh, *A magyar-román kapcsolatok*. See also Anton Czettler, *Pál Graf Teleki und die Außenpolitik Ungarns, 1939–1941* (Munich: Verlag Ungarisches Institut, 1996); Balázs Ablonczy, *Pál Teleki (1874–1941): The Life of a Controversial Hungarian Politician* (Boulder, Colo.: Social Science Monographs; Wayne, N.J.: Center for Hungarian Studies and Publications, 2006); Benedek Jancsó, *A román irredentista mozgalmak története* (Máriabesnyő-Gödöllő: Attraktor, 2004); Nagy and Vincze, *Autonómisták és centralisták*; Lungu, *Transilvania în raporturile româno-austro-ungare*; Adrian Pandea, Ion Pavelescu, and Eftimie Ardeleanu, eds., *Românii la Stalingrad: viziunea românească asupra tragediei din Cotul Donului și Stepa Calmucă* (Bucharest: Editura Militară, 1992); Nicolae Rădescu, *Un sfert de veac de urmărire: documente din dosarele secrete ale generalului Nicolae Rădescu* (Bucharest: Editura Enciclopedică, 2004); István Ravasz, *Erdély mint hadszíntér 1944* (Budapest: Petit Real Könyvkiadó, 1997); *Recensământul din 1900: Transilvania* (Bucharest: Editura Staff, 1999); *Recensământul din 1910: Transilvania* (Bucharest: Editura Staff, 1999); *Recensământul din 1941: Transilvania* (Cluj: Editura Presa Universitară Clujeană, 2002); Ignác Romsics, ed., *Trianon és a magyar politikai gondolkodás 1920–1953: Tanulmányok* (Budapest: Osiris Kiadó, 1998); Ioan Scurtu, ed., *Documente privind istoria României între anii 1918–1944* (Bucharest: Editura didactică și pedagogică, 1995); Ioan Scurtu, *Iuliu Maniu: activitatea politică* (Bucharest: Editura Enciclopedică, 1995); Pál Teleki, *A földrajzi gondolat története* (Budapest: Kossuth Könyvkiadó, 1996); Pál Teleki, *Válogatott politikai írások és beszédek* (Budapest: Osiris kiadó, 2000); Mihail Vasile-Ozunu and Petre Otu, *Înfrânți și uitați: Românii în bătălia de la Stalingrad* (Bucharest: Editura Ion Cristoiu, 1999). Incisive overviews of the literature relating to Transylvania during World War II can also be found in Ottmar Trașcă, "Relațiile Româno-ungare și problema Transilvaniei, 1940–1944 (I)," *Anuarul Institutului de Istorie "A. D. Xenopol,"* tom XLI 41 (2004): 313–16; Balogh, *A magyar-román kapcsolatok*, 12–32; Gábor Egry, "Az Erdélyi Párt ideológiája és az erdélyiség," *A hét* 48, no. 3 (December 8, 2005), http://regi.ahet.ro/belso.php3?action=cim&name=1987 (accessed Oct 25, 2007).

55. Petre Otu, ed., *Pacea de mâine: Documentele ale Comisiei constituite în vederea pregătirii conferinței de pace de după cel de-al doilea război mondial, 1942–1944* (Bucharest: Editura Militară, 2006), 339–44. See also the homepage for the revived Center for Transylvanian Studies, http://www.hcentruldestudiitransilvane.ro/Detaliu.aspx?t=despre (accessed May 8, 2008).

56. See http://www.centruldestudiitransilvane.ro/Lista.aspx?t=Carti19911995 (accessed May 8, 2008).

57. This is the case both in terms of the venues that publish them and the individuals who write them. For an overview, see Trașcă, "Relațiile româno-ungare (I)," 314–15.

58. Ion Iliescu, *Rumänien in Europa und in der Welt* (n.p.: 1994), 92–94.

59. MOL, K63, 257. csomó., 1940–27. tétel./7./E., Román-magyar viszony—Erdély, iktatlan, II. rész. 1941–21/28–3736, 29.

60. *Magyar Nemzet*, April 22, 2002, cited in Michael Shafir, "The Politics of Public Space and the Legacy of the Holocaust in Postcommunist Hungary," *Zeitgeschichte-online*, http://www.zeitgeschichte-online.de/zol/_rainbow/documents/pdf/asm_oeu/shafir_asm.pdf (accessed October 25, 2007), 29.

61. *Magyar Nemzet*, October 15, 1990, 6.

62. Gábor Albert, "1943—Szárszó—2003," *Hitel* 16 (October 2003): 9.

63. "Orbán Viktor beszéde a Fidesz XVI. kongresszusán," (December 8, 2002), http://www.szajer.hu/esemeny/mnokongr.html (accessed September 24, 2005).

64. Shafir, "Politics of Public Space," 29.

65. "Hungary's Renewed Nation Policy," http://mfa.gov.hu/kum/en/bal/Archivum/Archives/nation_policy_affairs.htm (accessed February 14, 2007; *last modified* November 28, 2005).

66. See "Muddled Amity: Improving the Moldovan-Romanian Relationship," *Romanian Digest* 11, no.9 (September 2006), http://www.hr.ro/digest/200609/digest.htm (accessed March 3, 2007).

67. Constituția României, articles 1–2, http://www.cdep.ro/pls/dic/site.page?den=act2_1&par1=1#t1cos0a1 (accessed Oct. 25, 2007).

68. Cristian Pătrăşconiu, "Monopolul UDMR este atacat cu Băsescu şi discursuri radicale," *Cotidianul*, March 3, 2007, http://www.cotidianul.ro/index.php?id=45&art=10611&cHash=cd23b9f687 (accessed March 3, 2007).

69. Ion Iliescu, *Integration and Globalization: A Romanian View* (Bucharest: Romanian Cultural Foundation, 2003), 67.

70. Béla Pomogáts, *Negyedik Európa: erdélyi kérdések és válaszok* (Budapest: Godolat, 1992), 12.

71. "Németh rendet teremtene Romániában," *Népszabadság*, July 20, 2004. The individual in question, Zsolt Németh, was also a member of parliament at the time, as well as Hungary's former secretary of state to the foreign ministry (1998–2002).

72. *Adevărul Cluj*, July 21, 1995, 1, 4. Similarly, Iliescu in his book *Integration and Globalization* argues that "the confusion created and maintained around the issue of minorities sometimes led to its becoming a source of tension and even of conflict, the generous theme of minority protection being used for political aims or as a support for revisionist tendencies. . . . To remove the unclearness and confusion about this problem area . . . I think I should remind [*sic*] that in the unifying Europe the Community principle has assumed shape that minorities can only be protected by practically guaranteeing the basic rights of persons belonging to those minorities in the frameworks provided by the current state organization, while strictly observing the existing borders." Iliescu, *Integration and Globalization*, 62.

73. In the words of David Adam Landau, "In order for Romania to become a viable candidate, it would have to demonstrate inter alia democratic processes, economic stability, and overall policy liberalization at all levels of government. This includes making all necessary domestic changes to comply with the Copenhagen criterion of respecting and protecting the rights of national minorities." David Adam Landau, "Constitutional Les-

sons from Romania: The Minority Rights Factor," *RFE/RL East European Perspectives: News and Views on Central and Southeastern Europe* 6, no. 20 (October 27, 2004), http://www.rferl.org/reports/aspfiles/printonly.asp?po=y (accessed October 25, 2007).

74. See David Adam Landau and Lisa Vanhala, "Circumventing the State? The Demands of Stateless Nations, National Minorities, and the Proposed European Constitution," paper delivered at the conference "Redefining Europe: Federalism and the Union of European Democracies," Prague, Czech Republic, March 26–30, 2004, http://www.inter-disciplinary.net/AUD/landauvan%20paper.pdf (accessed October 25, 2007), 8; Camera Deputaților, Senatul, "Lege de revizuire a constituției României," http://www.cdep.ro/pdfs/reviz_constitutie.pdf (accessed October 25, 2007).

75. USHMMA, RG-52.003.01, "Randolph Braham, Holocaust in Northern Transylvania, Press clippings, Tribuna Nouă, 1945–1946," *Tribuna Nouă,* "Masacrale dela Trăsnea," October 29, 1945; "Autorii crimelor fasciste din 11 Septembrie 1940 din Cluj, în fața justiției," November 11, 1945.

76. USHMMA, RG-52.003.01, "Randolph Braham, Holocaust in Northern Transylvania, Press clippings, Tribuna Nouă, 1945–1946," *Tribuna Nouă,* "Scrisoarea deschisă către un prieten maghiar din România," January 8, 1946.

77. Ibid., *Tribuna Nouă,* "Întrebări către un psiholog maghiar," January 15, 1945.

78. USHMMA, RG-52.003.02, "Randolph Braham, Holocaust in Northern Transylvania, Press clippings, Világosság, 1946," *Világosság,* "Hibás volna azonosítani a fasizmust a magyar néppel!" February 13, 1946.

79. Ibid., *Világosság,* "Groza Péter miniszterelnök gyujtó beszédben bélyegezte meg a nemzetiségek ellen uszító sovinizmust és méltatta a magyar néppel való teljes megbékélés szükségességét," March 8, 1946.

80. USHMMA, RG-52.003.01, "Randolph Braham, Holocaust in Northern Transylvania, Press clippings, Tribuna Nouă, 1945–1946," *Tribuna Nouă,* "Apărarea și replica în procesul lotului IV de criminali de răsboiu," April 9, 1945.

81. An article from April 30, for example, states: "We Romanians from Northern Transylvania had occasion to become intimately acquainted with the system of banditry of the militaristic state of the Horthy government." USHMMA, RG-52.003.01, "Randolph Braham, Holocaust in Northern Transylvania, Press clippings, Tribuna Nouă, 1945–1946," *Tribuna Nouă,* "Apărarea și replica în procesul lotului IV de criminali de răsboiu," April 9, 1945; "Un nou lot de criminali de răsboiu," April 30, 1946.

82. USHMMA, RG-52.003.01, "Randolph Braham, Holocaust in Northern Transylvania, Press clippings, Tribuna Nouă, 1945–1946," *Tribuna Nouă,* "Apărarea și replica în procesul lotului IV de criminali de răsboiu," April 9, 1945; "Un nou lot de criminali de răsboiu," April 30, 1946; "Fascismul nu cunoaște granițe când e vorba de crimă," May 21, 1946. For other examples of the "denationalization" of criminals and victims in the Romanian press of this period, see USHMMA, RG-52.003.01, "Randolph Braham, Holocaust in Northern Transylvania, Press clippings, Tribuna Nouă, 1945–1946," "Horthy a dat naștere primei dictaturi fasciste din Europa," May 16, 1946; "Fascismul nu e o abstracțiune, ci o conspirație mondială împotriva popoarelor dornice de libertate," June 3, 1946; USHMMA, RG-52.003.02, "Randolph Braham, Holocaust in Northern Transylvania, Press clippings, Világosság, 1946," *Világosság,* "Román, magyar, zsidó, szász háborus bűnösök felett itélkezett a kolozsvári Népbíróság," May 29, 1946; "Nem

lehet könyörület azok számára, akik százok halálát okozták," June 2, 1946; "Hitler mindkét népet befogta a halál szekerébe," April 4, 1946.

83. USHMMA, RG-25.017, Selected Records of the Cluj Branch of the Romanian National Archives, 1934–1952, roll 2, Inspectoratul de jandarmi Cluj, 1920–1949, fond 208, nr. inv. 400, dosar 46/1947, f. 1–2.

84. Andreea Andreescu, Lucian Nastasă, and Andrea Varga, *Minorități etnoculturale, mărturii documentare, evreii din România, 1945–1965* (Cluj: Centrul de resurse pentru diversitate etnoculturală, 2003), doc. 6, 92.

85. Ibid., doc. 99, 297.

86. Andreescu, Nastasă, and Varga, *Minorități etnoculturale*, doc. 76, 243–44.

87. Ibid., doc. 99, 100, 296, 300.

88. Ibid., doc. 140, 360–61.

89. Ibid., doc. 193, 478–79.

90. The mass departure of the Jews from Romania was driven by a variety of forces. One of these was the Zionists, who encouraged Jews to emigrate, sometimes deriding them if they refused to do so. Their attitude was that the Jews had no reason to stay, having lost both their livelihood and respect for the other national groups among which they lived. Another of these forces was the Romanian administration. Rosen argued that "the lower authorities [in Romania] had either forced or encouraged the better part of 123,000 Jews to apply to emigrate." Ibid., 458, 491, 648.

91. Shelomoh Zimroni and Yehuda Schwartz, *Zikhron netsah la-kehilah ha-kedoshah Kolozhvar Kla'uzenburg: asher nehrevah ba-sho-ah* (Tel Aviv: Hug yots'e Kolozsvar be-Yi'sra'el, 1968), 116.

92. Ibid., 117.

93. Stephen Fischer-Galati, "Fascism, Communism, and the Jewish Question in Romania," in *Jews and Non-Jews in Eastern Europe, 1918–1945*, ed. B. Vago and G. L. Mosse (New York: John Wiley & Sons, 1974), 171.

94. Jean Ancel, *Documents Concerning the Fate of Romanian Jewry During the Holocaust*, vol. II (Jerusalem: Beate Klarsfeld Foundation, 1986), 52.

95. Mihai Fătu and Mircea Mușat, eds., *Horthyist-Fascist Terror in Northwestern Romania* (Bucharest: Meridiane Publishing House, 1986).

96. Ion Calafeteanu, Nicolae Dinu, Teodor Gheorghe, eds., *Emigrarea populației evreiești din România în anii 1940–1944: Culegere de documente din arhiva ministerului afacerilor externe al României* (Bucharest: Silex, 1993), 7.

97. Rezső Döndő, "Holocaust és genocídium" [Holocaust and Genocide], *Magyar Nemzet*, October 15, 1990, 6. Incidentally, Csoóri's 1990 assertion was a reiteration of an argument that went back to the debates around the adoption of the *numerus clausus* in 1920. During those debates, the Hungarian minister for religion and education, István Haller, cited at length the work of a Romanian writer and publicist, Octavian Goga, who would himself later usher in anti-Jewish legislation in Romania. In his literary criticism, Goga had claimed that Jews had assimilated Hungarians. See Gyurgyák, *A zsidókérdés Magyarországon*, 119.

98. See also Transylvanian World Federation and the Danubian Research and Information Center, *Genocide in Transylvania: Nation on the Death Row, a Documentary* (Astor, Fla.: Danubian Press, 1985).

99. Shafir, "Politics of Public Space," 7.

100. Cited in Attila Pók, "The Politics of Hatred: Scapegoating in Interwar Hungary," in *Blood and Homeland: Eugenics and Racial Nationalism in Central and Southeast Europe, 1900–1940*, ed. Marius Turda and Paul J. Weindling (Budapest: Central European University Press, 2007), 384–85. Original in *Szent korona* (February 21, 1990), 6–7; cited in László Karsai, ed., *Kirekesztők* (Budapest: Aura, 1992), 150–51.

101. István Rév, *Retroactive Justice: Prehistory of Post-Communism* (Stanford, Calif.: Stanford University Press, 2005), 277–99.

102. Funar, who was mayor of the city for twelve years starting in 1992, was voted out of office in June 2004. The current mayor, Emil Boc, has a much more benign policy vis-à-vis the city's minority population.

103. *Szabadság*, June 23, 1992, 119. szám, 1, cited in Sándor Balázs and Róbert Schwartz, eds., *Funar-korszak Kolozsváron a helyi sajtó tükrében 1992–1996* (Kolozsvár: Erdélyi Híradó Könyv- és Lapkiadó, 1997), 28. At the following year's commemoration, Rosen pointed out that Romania had not apologized for the murder of the Jews, while Hungary and the Hungarian Democratic Party of Romania had. *Tribuna Ardealului*, June 23, 1993, 3, cited in Balázs and Schwartz, *Funar-korszak Kolozsváron*, 106.

104. A Hungarian commentator on the event wondered whether Funar would persecute the Jews—as he had the Hungarians—if they sang the Israeli national anthem. *Adevărul de Cluj*, June 8, 1995, no. 1407, 16, cited in Balázs and Schwartz, *Funar-korszak Kolozsváron*, 283.

105. *Adevărul de Cluj*, July 12, 1995, no. 1431, 4, cited in Balázs and Schwartz, *Funar-korszak Kolozsváron*, 289.

106. *Adevărul de Cluj*, August 30, 1995, no. 1466, 1, cited in Balázs and Schwartz, *Funar-korszak Kolozsváron*, 310.

107. *Adevărul de Cluj*, September 15, 1995, no. 1478, 1, cited in Balázs and Schwartz, *Funar-korszak Kolozsváron*, 319.

108. "Masacrul din Ip," *Wikipedia enciclopedia liberă*, http://ro.wikipedia.org/wiki/Masacrul_din_Ip (accessed November 23, 2007).

109. "Heves vita Antonescu marsallról a parlamentben," March, 27, 2002, http://belpol.transindex.ro/?hir=858 (accessed January 8, 2008).

110. Felicia Wan, "A zsidókérdés és a holocauszt a román tankönyvekben, 1998–2002," *Regio: Kisebbség, Politika, Társadalom* 2 (2003), 160. In 2000, Tudor ran for president and received 28 percent of the popular vote.

111. [H] Szászrégen, [G] (Sächsisch) Regen.

112. [H] Marosvásárhely, [G] Neumarkt am Mieresch.

113. "Wass-szobor megy, Antonescu utca marad?" http://belpol.transindex.ro/?hir=2924, 11:56, 4.4.2003 (accessed January 8, 2008). It is also against the law to name streets after Antonescu in Romania, so the street name was in violation of Romanian law as well.

114. Susan Gal, "Bartok's Funeral: Representations of Europe in Hungarian Political Rhetoric," *American Ethnologist* 18, no. 3 (August 1991): 440–58, 448–49, 451–52.

115. For the Legionnaire movement's Web page, see http://www.miscarea.com/transilvania-romaneasca3.htm (accessed August 22, 2006); for Hungarian revisionism, see http://www.nemnemsoha.hu/kepnagy.php?kep=966.jpg (accessed August 22, 2006).

CONCLUSION

1. Valer Pop, *Bătălia pentru Ardeal* ([Romania]: Editura Colosseum, 1990), 11.

2. A review of the literature on World War II in these two states reveals the extent to which the last months of the war receive the lion's share of historians' attention. For Hungary, this means the period after the German occupation on March 19, 1944, and for Romania, it means the period immediately prior to and following Romania's withdrawal from the Axis on August 23, 1944. Romanian historian Dinu Giurescu, for example, dedicates just under half of his book *Romania in the Second World War, 1939–1945* to the antecedents and results of the events of August 1944. Dinu C. Giurescu, *Romania in the Second World War, 1939–1945* (New York: Columbia University Press, 2000); C. A. Macartney, *October Fifteenth: A History of Modern Hungary, 1929–1945* (Edinburgh: Edinburgh University Press, 1956).

3. See, for example, *Roumania at the Peace Conference* (Paris: Imp. Paul Dupont, 1946), 7–48; Ştefan Lache şi Gheorge Ţuţui, *România şi conferinţa de pace de la Paris din 1946* (Cluj-Napoca: Editura Dacia, 1978), 9–77.

4. Zoltán Szász, ed., *Erdély Története, 1830-tól napjainkig* (Budapest: Akadémiai Kiadó, 1987), 3:1753–59.

5. Gábor Egry, *Az erdélyiség "színeváltozása": kísérlet az Erdélyi Párt ideológiájának elemzésére, 1940–1944* (Budapest: Napvilág Kiadó, 2008), 19.

6. The virtual interwar predecessor of both Hitler's "New European Order" and the European Union, Coudenhove-Kalergi's "Pan-Europe," also stressed that "every nation is a sanctuary—as the hearth and home of culture, as the point of crystallization for morality and progress." Thus, "Pan-Europe" would arise out of the "deepening and broadening of national cultures," rather than their negation. Richard Nicolaus Coudenhove-Kalergi, *Pan-Europe* (New York: A. A. Knopf, 1926), 161. Similarly, the notion of an "Europe d'états," propounded by Charles de Gaulle, placed the national interest first, as an element that contributed to the strengthening of Europe as a whole. In a speech on May 31, 1960, De Gaulle declared that France desired to "contribute to building Western Europe into a political, economic, cultural and human group, organized for action, progress and defense," but that "the nations which are becoming associated must not cease to be themselves, and the path to be followed must be that of organized cooperation between States, while waiting to achieve, perhaps, an imposing confederation." Charles de Gaulle and French Embassy, Press and Information Division, *Major Addresses, Statements and Press Conferences of General Charles De Gaulle* (New York: French Embassy, 1965), 78. This notion is echoed by Jürgen Habermas and Jacques Derrida in their now (in)famous "Core Europe" piece, wherein they suggest: "The population must so to speak 'build up' their national identities, and add to them a European dimension." Jürgen Habermas and Jacques Derrida, "February 15, or, What Binds Europeans Together: Plea for a Common Foreign Policy, Beginning in Core Europe," in *Old Europe, New Europe, Core Europe: Transatlantic Relations After the Iraq War*, ed. Daniel Levy, Max Pensky, and John Torpey (London; New York: Verso, 2005), 6. Alan Milward has also argued convincingly that "the European Community only evolved [post-1945] as an aspect of . . . national reassertion and without it the reassertion might well have proved impossible. To supersede the nation-state would

be to destroy the Community." Alan Milward, *The European Rescue of the Nation-state* (Berkeley: University of California Press, 1992), 2–3. See also Mark Mazower, *Hitler's Empire: Nazi Rule in Occupied Europe* (London: Allen Lane, 2008), 570.

7. "A Magyar Lobbi Heti Akciólevele, 2007 január 6.-án—Sólyom László Újévi Beszéde," *Magyar Online Forrás,* http://hungaria.org/articles.php?id=1428 (accessed October 25, 2007).

8. Cited in Ottmar Traşcă, "Relaţiile Româno-ungare şi problema Transilvaniei, 1940–1944 (I)," *Anuarul Institutului de Istorie* "A. D. Xenopol," 41 (2004): 319.

9. Romanian literary theorist and historian Adrian Marino thus spoke of "the Europe that watches us." Adrian Marino, *Pentru Europa, integrarea României: aspecte ideologice şi culturale* (Iaşi: Polirom, 1995).

10. Lucian Boia, *Romania: Borderland of Europe* (London: Reaktion, 2001); Tony Judt, "Romania: Bottom of the Heap," *New York Review of Books* 48, no. 17 (November 1, 2001); Susan Gal, "Bartok's Funeral: Representations of Europe in Hungarian Political Rhetoric," *American Ethnologist* 18, no. 3 (August 1991), 442–47; Balázs Sipos and Pál Pritz, eds., *Magyarország helye a 20. századi Európában: Tanulmányok* (Budapest: Magyar Történelmi Társulat, 2002).

11. See, for example, Ion Ardeleanu in the preface to Mihai Antonescu, *Dacă vrei să câştigi războiul, trebuie să pregăteşti pacea* (Cluj-Napoca: Muzeul Etnografic al Transilvaniei, 1991). See also László Diószegi, "The Western Powers and the Danube Basin in the 1930s," in *Twentieth-Century Hungary and the Great Powers,* ed. Ignác Romsics (Boulder, Colo., and Highland Lakes, N.J.: Columbia University Press, 1995): 119–36, 136.

12. Tibor Tamás, "Ösztön és politika, Makkai János és a magyar reformjobboldal a két háború között," *Népszabadság,* April 3, 2003,http://www.nsz.prim.hu/cikk/104621/ (accessed January 8, 2008).

13. Douglas R. Holmes, "Experimental Identities," draft chapter for *The Politics of European Identity Construction* (Working title), ed. Jeffrey Checkel and Peter Katzenstein (Cambridge: Cambridge University Press, forthcoming 2008 or 2009), cited with permission. See also "Budapest brune—Le Pen invité par l'extrême droite hongroise," *Réflexes* (November 19, 2003), http://reflexes.samizdat.net/spip.php?article180 (accessed October 25, 2007).

14. Mihai Antonescu, *Warum wir kämpfen* (Bucharest, 1942), 25.

15. On the philosophy behind the charter, see Djura Ninčić, *The Problem of Sovereignty in the Charter and in the Practice of the United Nations* (The Hague, Netherlands: Martinus Nijhoff, 1970), 32.

16. On perception of Great Power approval of territorial claims, see G. P. Genov, *Rukhna poslednata postroĭka na vesaĭlskata sistema* (Sofia, Bulgaria: Vsebŭlgarski sŭiuz, Otets Paisiĭ, 1941), 12–13.

17. Genov, *Rukhna poslednata,* 7–8.

18. The Fascist notion of "Lebensraum" or "spazio vitale," for example, goes "beyond national unification," which was the primary goal of East-Central European states allied with the Axis. See Aristotle A. Kallis, *Fascist Ideology: Territory and Expansionism in Italy and Germany, 1922–1945* (London and New York: Routledge, 2000), 27–60.

19. Mihai Eminescu, "Transilvania sub stăpânire dualistă austro-ungară," in *Statul, I. Funcţiile şi misiunea sa* (Bucharest: Editura Saeculum I.O., 1999), 94.

Index

tives of, 100. *See also* Calvinists; Eastern
Church; Greek Catholics; Lutherans;
Orthodoxy (Eastern); Roman Catholics
Ciano, Galeazzo, 71, 75, 153, 155, 257n1,
259n32, 260n41, 296n30
Cioran, Emil, 109
Cipariu, Timotei, 19
citizenship, 11–12, 36, 154; Hungarian, 28;
of Jews in Romania, 33
city planning, 132
civilization(s): conflict between, 233n11; of
Europe, 150; interests of, 47, 53, 55, 58;
levels of, 57, 112; Western, 20, 53, 57–58
clergy, 122, 125, 141. *See also* Calvinists; Eastern Church; Greek Catholics; Luther-
ans; Orthodoxy (Eastern); Roman
Catholics
Cleveland, 206
Cluj (*also known as* Kolozsvár, Cluj-Napoca): Arrow Cross in, 84; atrocities in,
272n27; battalion named after, 266n126;
books/newspapers in, 143, 150, 206;
and border with Romania, 138, 146–47,
177, 190, 281n143, 286n225; as a "city
of schools," 137, 290n255; Communists
and leftists in, 107, 205, 281n135, 313n37;
courts/trials in, 139, 150, 290n263; demonstrations in, 25, 72, 147, 259n36; entry
of Hungarian Army into, 72, 99, 100–
101; expulsion of Romanian intellectuals
and professionals from, 102; factories
in, 116; German-Italian Officers' Commission in, 156, 167–68, 173, 296n36,
301n123; Gheorghe Funar as mayor of,
13; ghettoization and deportation of
Jews from, 190–91, 195, 211; Hungarian Party of Renewal membership in,
275n74; Hungarian theater in, 175, 195;
and the legacy of the Holocaust, 212–14,
216–17; Italian consulate in, 259n36;
maps of, 134, 288n239, 289n250; nationalization of, 97, 99, 132–36; nomen-
clature of, xvii, 72, 132; police in, 82,
117, 266n130; population of, 30; public
registry in, 130; refugees in/from, 112,
138, 271n5, 280n127, 288n242; return of
Romanian state control over, 93, 193,

202; Rogers Brubaker's (et al.) study of,
194–95; Romanian claims on, 77, 79, 81;
Romanian consul(ate) in, 118, 165, 190;
Romanian Office of Military Statistics
in, 183; situation/events in, 50, 79, 83,
113, 150, 212; slums in, 117; taverns/pubs
in, 137; Transylvanian Party in, 117, 183;
university in, 114. *See also* Plugarul; Transylvanian Conference; Turda
Codreanu, Corneliu Zelea, 109–10. *See also*
Iron Guard; Legionnaires
Cold War, 3, 226
collective rights, 19, 21
colonization, 242n106. *See also* State Undersecretariat for Romanianization, Colonization, and Inventory
Communism, 107, 196, 205, 220, 222; collapse of, 95, 201, 215, 218, 223. *See also*
anti-Communism
Communist historiography, 6, 94–95, 173
Communist movement, in Transylvania,
107
Communist Party of Hungary [Kommu-
nisták Magyarországi Pártja, KMP], 106;
illegal, 281n135; after the Second World
War, 275n71
Communist Party of Romania [Partidul
Comunist din România, PCR], 85, 88,
106–7, 111, 202, 205, 275n65, 275n66,
277n93, 313n37. *See also* National
Democratic Bloc; United National
Front
Communist publications/propaganda, 9,
85, 93. *See also* Korunk; Scînteia
Communist regime(s), 94, 207, 212, 220,
270n188; in Hungary in 1919, 180. *See
also* Hungarian Republic of Soviets
Communists, 4, 85–86, 90, 93, 95, 109,
203; imprisonment/persecution of, 107,
110–11, 275n67; Jews as, 180, 216; leaders,
25, 107, 205, 275n71; and Legionnaires,
277n95. *See also* Dimitrov, Georgi; Kun,
Béla; Rákosi, Mátyás
Conducător. *See* Ion Antonescu
confederation, 108, 320n6. *See also* Danube
Federation; federation
confiscation: of church property, 141; of

Hungarism, 108. *See also* Arrow Cross
Huns, 150; Hungarians as, 112
Huntington, Samuel, 233n11
Huszadik Század, 304n28

Iaşi, 184
ideology, 86, 95, 107, 108, 153, 221, 222, 313n41
Iliescu, Ion, 207, 210, 218, 316n72
illiteracy, 113
Imrédy, Béla, 66, 88, 108
Imrédyists, 108
independence, 2, 10, 18, 20–22, 33–34, 70, 85, 89, 178, 204, 220, 223, 227, 239n66
individual rights, 18, 19, 29
intellectuals, 27, 39, 65, 120, 146, 165, 193, 207, 254n255, 298n74; Romanian, 62, 102, 149, 187, 206, 301n113
interior minister, 63, 118, 279n127. *See also* Hungarian interior minister; interior ministry
interior ministry, 48, 98, 115, 117–18. *See also* Hungarian interior ministry; Romanian interior ministry
interior ministry's Ninth Social Work Division (Hungary), 115
international law, 12, 28, 64, 188, 225
interwar period, xvii, 27–31; anti-Semitism, 6; Communism, 106, 111, 277n93; German diplomacy of, 156; eugenics, 279n120; governments, 5; historiography relating to, 196–97, 238n64; Hungarian revisionism/irredentism, 79, 180, 207, 256n280; Hungarian and Romanian propaganda of, 2, 30, 39–40, 44, 52, 56, 64, 196, 205–6, 236n37, 240n84, 253n236; Hungarians in Transylvania during, 17, 27, 53, 181, 275n60; Hungary in, 5, 31, 36, 87, 180, 196; ideas of Europe, 210, 218, 220, 223, 225, 320n6; and individual versus collective rights, 29; Jews during, 135, 176, 181, 183; and the Legion of the Archangel Michael, 109; literature of, 16; Jews during, 180, 184; maps, 43–44, 82, 134–36, 289n250; minorities/minority rights, 28, 33, 37–39, 53, 115, 129, 160–61, 174, 176, 180, 207, 237n43, 238n64,

291n274; minority treaties, 161; population statistics, 128; and the reordering of Europe with the "Versailles System," 6, 58–61, 153, 208, 218, 225; Romania in, 5, 88, 129, 132, 273n36; romanianization, 125, 132, 135, 245n155, 288n241; state- and nation-building, 16; and the Transylvanian Question, 205. *See also* League of Nations; Trianon Hungary; Versailles System
invasion, 18, 64, 76, 80, 85, 88, 258n22, 262n68, 273n42
Iorga, Nicolae, 109, 236n37, 249n169
Ip (*also known as* Ipp), 102, 200, 213, 217
Iron Guard, 109, 110, 276n84, 277n87. *See also* guardists; Legion of the Archangel Michael
irredentism, 256n280, 305n45
Israel. *See* Palestine, emigration of Jews to
Italy: as an Axis power, 1, 5, 164, 225, 254n255; capitulation to the Allies, 89, 156; diplomacy of, 70, 151–53, 164, 297n57, 300n110; and historiography of Europe, 3, 232n1; military activity of, 98, 273n42; and minorities, 152–55, 172; and the Triple Alliance, 22. *See also* Ciano, Galeazzo; German-Italian Officers' Commission; Mussolini, Benito; Roggeri, Delfino

Janos, Andrew C., 236n31, 274n56
Janovics, Jenő, 175, 176, 195, 198
Janovsky, Karl, 78, 84, 263n71
Jeszenszky, Géza, 215
Jewish Laws, Hungarian, 182, 185–86
Jewish National League, 182
Jewish policy, 185, 187, 188–90, 192, 196
Jewish Question, 6, 11, 174, 175–97, 211, 303n22, 304n27, 308n73, 310n123
Jews, 152, 174–97, 307n66; Communism and, 107, 111, 205; expropriation of, 116, 129, 150, 211; historiography relating to, 310n124; in Hungary, 6, 78, 130, 211, 276n77, 303n11, 305n48, 309n103, 318n97; and labor service, 85; and name changes, 130, 303n10; persecution of, 34, 78, 110, 116–17, 129, 211, 305n38, 306n60,

Toshev, Dimitar, 175
trade, 144, 276n80
trade permits, 186; denial/revocation of,
    143, 172
tradespeople, 285n208
Transnistria: expulsion/deportation of
    Jews to, 187; Romanian occupation of,
    76, 184–85
transportation, infrastructure, 104, 113, 132
Transylvania: autonomy/independence
    of, 10, 201, 203, 207, 210; integration
    into the Kingdom of Hungary, 179; as
    "litmus test" for European order, 12,
    160; military administration of, 104,
    311n13; people of and their importance
    to territorial claims, 115, 149; unique-
    ness of, 10, 105. *See also* Association of
    Refugees and Expellees from Occupied
    Transylvania; diversity; Jews; Northern
    Transylvania; statistics; Southern Tran-
    sylvania; Transylvanian Conference;
    Transylvanian Hungarian Economic
    Association; Transylvanian Hungarians;
    Transylvanian Question; Transylva-
    nian Party; Transylvanian Romanians;
    Transylvanian Saxons; Transylvanian
    Scientific Institute; Transylvanian World
    Federation
Transylvanian Conference, 104–5, 138, 141,
    145, 149, 234n12, 284n194. *See also* Teleki,
    Pál
Transylvanian Hungarian Economic Asso-
    ciation [EMGE], 178, 299n96, 300n100
Transylvanian Hungarians, 11, 84, 105–6,
    141, 182, 194, 205, 238n65, 301n121. *See
    also* Transylvanian Hungarian Economic
    Association; Transylvanian Party
Transylvanian Party [Erdélyi Párt]: estab-
    lishment of, 105, 108; members/repre-
    sentatives of, 61, 113, 128, 177, 183, 208,
    274n51; president(s) of, 106, 117, 119,
    274n53; program/platform of, 121, 128,
    176, 275n61. *See also* Teleki, Béla; Teleki,
    Pál
Transylvanian Question, 23, 27; Axis ar-
    bitration and, 162; Communists/Com-

munist regimes and, 205–6, 275n71;
    and conceptions of Europe, 6, 11, 13,
    222–23, 226; culture and, 16; defini-
    tion, 1, 13, 210, 221–22; as a European
    problem, 2, 9, 12, 39, 48, 53, 62, 218,
    239n73; the Hungarian right and, 108;
    and the "Jewish Question," 192, 195–97,
    216; propaganda relating to, 40, 43, 49,
    53–54, 59, 62, 115, 158, 207, 218, 249n170,
    256n281; proposed solutions to, 10–12,
    19, 37, 59, 66, 76–79, 109, 201, 203, 208,
    220, 263n85; Romanian statesmen and,
    81, 89, 103, 109; uniqueness of, 224. *See
    also* Transylvania
Transylvanian Refugees Association. *See*
    Association of Refugees and Expellees
    from Occupied Transylvania
Transylvanian Romanians, 11, 23, 112, 169,
    238n61. *See also* National Convention of
    Transylvanian Romanians
Transylvanian Saxons, 36, 38. *See also*
    Saxons
Transylvanian Scientific Institute, 114
Transylvanian World Federation, 318n98
Trăznea, 200, 213
Treaty of Eternal Friendship (between
    Hungary and Yugoslavia), 76
Treaty of Paris, 161
The Treaty of Trianon and European Peace, 45,
    47. *See also* Bethlen, István
trials: postwar, 211–12; for slander against
    the nation, 15, 150, 290n263, 291n268. *See
    also* justice; tribunals
Trianon, Treaty of, xvii, xix, 2, 25, 28, 43,
    49, 70, 72, 87–88, 94, 126, 144, 163,
    179–80, 190, 199, 204, 206, 216, 253n232,
    272n36, 293n293; castle in France, 37;
    clauses of, 243n120; revision/reversal
    of, 10, 27, 30, 105, 149, 162, 182, 191,
    225n259; and Romanian territorial gains,
    59, 70, 148. *See also* peace settlement;
    The Treaty of Trianon and European Peace;
    Trianon Hungary; Versailles
Trianon Hungary, 30, 106, 118, 145,
    225n259, 305n38, 310n125; compared
    with Transylvania, 105, 108, 113; Ger-

Made in the USA
Monee, IL
12 May 2020